Praise for PURE INVENTION

"A masterful exploration of a history, a people and a culture that have shaped our use of technology, our conception of storytelling, and our fascination with Kitties named 'Hello.'" —*The Irish Times*

"From karaoke to manga, emoji to Pokémon, the creations of modern Japanese style have transformed that country and daily life around the world. *Pure Invention* is a delightful and highly informed view of the people, ideas, and insights behind this pop-cultural revolution." —James Fallows, author of *China Airborne*

"A kinetic canter through the social history of globalized Japanese culture." —Peter Guest, *Mekong Review*

"*Pure Invention* is part careful ethnography, part insightful cultural history of the creative men and women who reimagined Japan in the postwar period. Matt Alt tells their backstories and illuminates the impact of their creations, from toy army jeeps stamped out of tin cans in the rubble of World War II to a torrent of anime streamed on Netflix. It's difficult to imagine a more instructive or entertaining account of a fascinating place, people, and period." —Stephen Snyder, professor of Japanese studies at Middlebury College and translator of Yoko Ogawa's *The Memory Police*

"A brilliant cultural survey . . . Alt's careful history is a reminder of [Japan's] spirited creativity." —*Booklist* (starred review)

Japandemonium Illustrated: The Yokai Encyclopedias of Toriyama Sekien

Yokai Attack!: The Japanese Monster Survival Guide

Ninja Attack!: True Tales of Assassins, Samurai, and Outlaws

Yurei Attack!: The Japanese Ghost Survival Guide

Hello Please!: Very Helpful Super Kawaii Characters from Japan

Pure INVENTION

HOW
JAPAN
MADE
THE
MODERN
WORLD

MATT ALT

CROWN
NEW YORK

For Jean Morden,
who taught me the fundamentals of Japanese

In fact the whole of Japan is a pure invention.
There is no such country, there are no such people . . .
The Japanese people are, as I have said, simply a
mode of style, an exquisite fancy of art.

—OSCAR WILDE, "The Decay of Lying," 1891

CONTENTS

PURE INVENTION

INTRODUCTION

A WOMAN'S FACE emerges from darkness. She kneels before a machine whose output bathes her angular features in an eerie green light. She rises and walks away, footfalls echoing on the pavement. A basket of flowers sways from the crook of one elbow, the only sign of organic life in this dark, mechanized place. As she moves from shadow into the light of a streetlamp, a strange-looking car roars by, momentarily obscuring our view. The camera pulls back to reveal our heroine standing before a shuttered storefront, pedestrians hurrying past. Who is she waiting for? We barely have time to wonder as the camera pans up to reveal enormous neon signs and billboards, cryptic brand names looming over the cityscape. This is a consumer metropolis, from the looks of it—but where? Is this Times Square? Downtown Tokyo? The camera pulls farther back, revealing more of a mysterious urban landscape that, it becomes obvious, is nowhere we have ever seen—nowhere that has ever existed. We soar over rooftops, turrets, and machinery, all encircled by high walls marked with a mix of Arabic numerals and Asian calligraphy. A tense drumbeat swells as smokestacks belch into the midnight sky. This is less a city than a fortress; a literal military-industrial complex.

The screen flares, and a title appears: *FINAL FANTASY VII*. The rising strains of a synthesizer—haunting, melancholic—hint at wonders to come.

Final Fantasy VII was a video game, and when it debuted in 1997, the world had never seen anything like it. It was the latest installment in a popular (and increasingly misnamed) series, but previous *Final Fantasy* titles had been delivered in the standard, two-dimensional, squashed and flattened perspective of traditional video games. *Final Fantasy VII* was a different beast altogether. Though blocky and primitive by modern standards, it was fully rendered in three dimensions—a major technological feat for the era. Even more groundbreaking, it dared to presume something new: that a video game could have the dramatic pull of a Hollywood blockbuster.

Rather than the usual twitch-reflex fisticuffs and gun battles, *Final Fantasy VII* plunged players into the midst of a drama. Their role was one of a ragtag band of ecoterrorists determined to stop a faceless corporation from sucking their planet dry of its lone energy source. We learn that the waiting woman is Aeris, a flower peddler who turns rebel in the course of her quiet romance with the player-character, a former soldier with the disarming name of Cloud. *Final Fantasy VII* presented gamers with a cast as well developed as those from television shows or movies, and it followed them through an unpredictable, at times deeply moving narrative. The game's dramatic peak—Aeris's shocking, too-soon death—affected young players so profoundly that one modern critic has called it "the moment when gaming culture stood still."

Of course, the brave new world of *Final Fantasy VII* wasn't actually out of Hollywood at all. It was a Tokyo blockbuster, and it would inject a megadose of Japanese sensibilities into the American mainstream: big-eyed, bushy-haired anime characters and their manga-style melodrama; androgynous heroes; the very idea that video games could be meditative explorations as well as thrill rides.

Sony's marketing team poured $30 million, unprecedented for a video game, into an all-out media blitz modeled on the campaigns for tentpole American films. They targeted young audiences with ads in Marvel and DC comic books, adults with spots in *Rolling Stone*, *Playboy*, and *Spin*, and everyone with slick commercials that aired in movie theaters, during football games, on MTV, even during *Saturday Night Live*. "They said it couldn't be done in a major motion picture," teased one ad, taking aim at the establishment. "They were right!" Each commercial ended with a close-up of the PlayStation logo, with a young female voice robotically intoning the word as pronounced in Japanese: "purei-sutayshon!"

The previous bestselling PlayStation title, the British-made *Tomb Raider,* sold a very respectable one hundred fifty thousand copies in the first quarter of 1997. *Final Fantasy VII* sold a million copies in the quarter after its September release. Players didn't seem to mind the game's rushed translation, with occasionally misspelled character names and meme-worthy moments like Aeris declaring of another character, "This guy are sick!!" If anything, the garbled language only added to the game's exotic cachet, reinforcing the idea that it had emerged from a real-life technopolis almost as alluring as the fictional setting of the game itself. Sales would eventually reach thirteen million copies worldwide.

IN THE LATE 1800s, right at the cusp of the twentieth century, a new craze swept the Western world: "Japonisme." Japan had reopened its ports only a few decades earlier. Tastemakers in England, France, and America pounced on its art and literature, projecting upon the nation values they believed their own societies had abandoned in the drive for industrial advancement. Japan was "a great and glorious country whose people are brave beyond all measure, wise beyond all telling, amiable to excess, and extraordinarily considerate," in the opening lines of a picture book based on the smash-hit 1885 Gilbert and Sullivan play, *The Mikado.* This was the enthusiastically condescending mindset Oscar Wilde invoked and subverted when he referred to Japan as "pure invention": Japan as Western fantasy. The "antique land," as the Victorians called it, would prove a compelling vision for many years. It would take World War II to derail it.

After Japan's inglorious defeat in 1945, the nation's makers did their best to obscure the origins of the products they sold to the world. A decade later, notoriously gruff secretary of state John Foster Dulles blithely informed Prime Minister Shigeru Yoshida that Japan should never expect to find a big market for its products in America, because "Japanese don't produce the things that we want." He was even more condescending in private, telling a confidant that "suicide is not an illogical step for anyone concerned about Japan's economic future."

Indeed, the first Japanese products that trickled into the global marketplace after World War II did inspire derision, not admiration. "Made in Japan" became a punchline, a synonym for cheapo crap from a defeated joke of a nation: one-dollar blouses, tin toys made out of recycled cans, the flimsy paper umbrella in your tiki drink. *Breakfast at Tiffany's* laid the postwar relationship bare, with Mickey Rooney yellowfacing as the bumbling, bucktoothed, kimono-clad Yunioshi, positioned as the pathetic antithesis to Audrey Hepburn's sexy all-American social striver, Holly Golightly.

Yet things were already changing. In the winter of 1957, just three years after Dulles's pronouncement, a certain pocket-sized transistor radio steamrollered the competition to become the nation's must-have Christmas item. The colorful TR-63 was the first product to bear the logo of Sony, a name chosen for its culturally ambiguous sound. The TR-63 seemed just another holiday fad—but the way it upended American expectations of what Japanese products could do was merely a taste of things to come.

The steady drip of sixties novelties turned into a flood of high-quality consumer electronics and cars in the late seventies and early eighties. Suddenly the joke seemed to be on the Americans. As interlopers like Toyota and Honda toppled Ford, Chevy, and other cherished American brands, condescension turned into fury. My own childhood was punctuated by images of aggrieved Americans smashing Japanese products in publicity stunts on the nightly news, such as when a trio of Republican congresspeople took a sledgehammer to a Toshiba boom box on Capitol Hill. On this topic, at least, both sides of the aisle agreed: "If we don't get cracking, get serious, and get leadership . . . our kids will be cheated," declared Democratic senator Walter Mondale during his unsuccessful 1984 presidential bid. "Their jobs will consist of sweeping up around Japanese computers!"

But it was difficult for us kids to square the rage of the grown-ups with the Japan we were coming to know. Because alongside politically fraught imports of cars, appliances, and consumer electronics—essential things that our boomer parents often only reluctantly bought—had come an influx of must-have inessentials. Many corresponded to nothing we knew from American culture: irresistible gadgets like the Walkman and the karaoke machine. A cute kitty whose name seemed to be "Hello" and who appeared on an endless array of products tailored for the schoolgirl set. Cleverly engineered toys, imported to fill a need for merchandising for Saturday morning cartoons. Video games, anime, and manga, catering to niches and demographics we'd never even imagined.

Anyone born after about the mid-seventies had the same experience. We grew up reenacting *Power Rangers* on the playground. Revealing the "robots in disguise" of the *Transformers* toys. Impatiently waiting for five lions to form into *Voltron*. Doodling hearts on Sanrio stationery, organizing *Pokémon* and *Yu-Gi-Oh!* cards while flipping between the latest Mario game and episodes of *Sailor Moon* on the basement TV. How many hours of our youths—and adulthoods—were spent plugged in to various iterations of karaoke machines, Walkmans, and Game Boys? These things were more than the fads of a global consumer society. They had a strange ability to nourish our dreams as they entertained, to deliver and cultivate new fantasies in us.

I was obsessed with Japanese culture from my earliest encounters with its toys. As I stared at the exotic Japanese script adorning the stomach of the giant Shogun Warrior robot my grandmother gave me for my fifth birthday, I was filled with a sense of wonder. Somewhere far, far away from suburban Maryland dwelled a nation of people who thought giant monsters and robots were just as cool as I thought they were. I was very fortunate in that my local high school just so happened to offer the only Japanese language class taught at a public school in America at the time. It was run by an American woman, a talented polyglot who had studied Japanese as a naval intelligence officer during World War II. Hers was a different Japan, and while she supported anything that excited us about our studies, it was obvious that my interest in toys, anime, and Godzilla movies utterly mystified her. I went on to college; I became a Japanese translator; I eventually moved to Japan.

I have now spent close to twenty years as what is known as a "localizer," embedded in Japan's pop-cultural complex, translating games, comic books, and toy-related content into English for foreign consumption. In the early years, this often involved more than simple translation, as I helped creators redraft names and entire concepts to better appeal to audiences unfamiliar with certain aspects of Japanese culture. But as the years went on, I began noticing something new: Foreign fans increasingly wanted their Japanese fantasies to be as Japanese as possible, hewing as close to the original as possible, and released in translation as quickly as possible. The release of *FFVII* was a mainstream tipping point for this phenomenon, I would later realize: Sony, the same company that had chosen its name in part to obscure its Japanese origins, had produced a commercial that openly celebrated the Japanese pronunciation of "pureisutayshon."

Was it simply a consequence of the massive quantities of Japanese entertainment exported abroad over the decades? Was this new-wave Japonisme? It would take me quite some time to figure out that I was asking the wrong questions. It wasn't that foreign consumers wanted things more Japanese. It was that they were increasingly resembling the Japanese themselves. By the late aughts it was apparent that East and West were synchronizing. Milestones Japan had hit decades earlier—a great financial crash, political chaos, the exodus of a generation of youth into increasingly elaborate virtual escapes— all of it was now happening abroad, too. The things Japan produced weren't simply products. They were tools for navigating a strange new landscape, by turns more connected and more isolating than ever before. Japanese creators and consumers weren't just trendsetters. They were harbingers for all the weirdness of our late-stage capitalist lives.

THE STORY OF Japan's rise from postwar ashes into economic tiger is well-explored territory. So too the stock-market crash that brought the nation to its knees in the nineties. But big-picture narratives of politics and markets and finance can frustrate, for they fail to capture the way most of us really interact with Japan: through its products, on an individual and a societal level. That's why *Pure Invention* takes a different tack. It uses the economic picture as the backdrop for a much larger story: how Japanese creators redefined what it means to be human in the modern era. This is no hyperbole; the inventions in these pages transformed how we interact with the world, how we communicate with each other, how we spend time alone with ourselves, how we shape our very identities. To understand that seismic shift, one needs to understand the makers of the things that moved us so, their triumphs and struggles. But so too must one understand how countless users, empowered by these creations, unexpectedly emerged as agents of change. As such, this book is broadly split into two halves.

In the first, set in the sixties, seventies, and early eighties, Japan rises improbably from a war-shattered nation into a pioneering Tomorrowland. Its fuel-efficient cars and miniaturized gadgets redefine the way we envision the future, and transform Japan from a joke into a new kind of threat to Western hegemony. But Japan's "bubble," as it was known at the soaring heights of economic power, pops in December of 1990. The Nikkei stock index plunges and the real estate market crashes. A surging yen undercuts the competitiveness of Japanese exports abroad, giving China and Korea their longed-for chance to leapfrog the market. Debt mounts and gloom sets in. Dreams of global dominance evaporate. In 1989, headlines screeched of a "Japan Different, Unprecedented, and Dangerous"; just five years later, pundits were declaring *The End of Japan Inc.*, as the title of a 1994 book had it.

Japanese call the years after the burst of the bubble the Lost Decades. The name is no exaggeration. During the 1990s and the first decade of the twenty-first century, college grads who trusted that they, like their parents before them, would enjoy lifetime employment at top companies suddenly couldn't land jobs of any kind. A lexicon of new terms erupted to describe previously unthinkable new social ills: *hikikomori*, hermits who refused to leave their homes for school or work; "freeters" forced to flit among part-time gigs the entirety of their careers; "parasite singles" unable or unwilling to leave the nest. Grown-up society was faring little better. Politicians flailed helplessly; fourteen prime ministers came and went. Many thousands came under the sway of religious cults, most infamously the Aum Supreme Truth fanatics who engineered a nerve-gas attack on the Tokyo subway system in 1995. When an earthquake leveled huge sections of Kobe that same year, killing six thousand people and displacing many more, the government bungled its response so thoroughly that the Yamaguchi-gumi—a yakuza gang—took charge of dispensing relief supplies to stricken residents. By 2011, the birth rate had plunged so low and the population grown so aged that adult diapers began outselling baby diapers.

Yet, amid the gloom and doom, something interesting started happening. The Lost Decades are also when Japanese video game companies rose to dominate the mindshare of the world's youth, when the sales of Japanese comic books so outstripped American fare that *The New York Times* was compelled to spin off an independent manga bestseller list; when hyper-niche fashion brands like A Bathing Ape and Evisu Jeans started outfitting the world's celebrities; when fashion visionaries like Rei Kawakubo and Yohji Yamamoto transitioned from local stars into global luminaries; when mega-retailers like Uniqlo and Muji found their stride. It's when the novelist Haruki Murakami began acquiring foreign readers in huge numbers, and when director Hayao Miyazaki won an Academy Award for an animated film, and an incredibly Japanese one at that (*Spirited Away*, 2003). Thanks in large part to the peculiar tastes of a generation of young Japanese consumers, precisely as their nation's economic might waned, its cultural clout soared. Japan made itself rich after World War II by selling us the things we *needed*—all those automobiles, appliances, and portable electronics. But it made itself loved by selling us things we *wanted*.

This is the history of a nation's dramatic rebirth, told through the tales of truly transcendental products with literally planet-sized cultural gravity. Gloriously weird yet strangely necessary, things like the Walkman, the Game Boy, or Hello Kitty represent more than hit products. They transformed our tastes, our dreams, and eventually our realities as we incorporated them into our lives, from Tokyo to Toledo.

I call these enchanting products "fantasy-delivery devices," and each chapter in the tale that follows is anchored by one of their stories. But why consider the karaoke machine, to name just one example to come, a fantasy-delivery device and not a Honda Civic? Why the Nintendo Entertainment System and not a VCR? Wasn't the video deck a machine designed to serve up fantasies? In order to be considered a true fantasy-delivery device, a product had to satisfy what I call "the three *ins*": inessential, inescapable, influential. Cars are inescapable, but hardly inessential; our Hondas represented a calculus of cost and features, not an embrace of Japanese tastes. The VCR was certainly inessential and inescapable, but it would be hard to argue that it changed anyone's mind about Japan. The world's youth seized on the Japanese pedigree of video games as a badge of authenticity and quality; VCRs, on the other hand, were merely vehicles for consuming one's own country's fantasies in the form of Hollywood movies or recorded television shows.

Interestingly, these fantasy-delivery devices weren't even made with the Western consumer in mind. They emerged through fierce competition for the mindshare of young Japanese with a voracious hunger for novelty and escape. The incandescent, irrepressible sense of play that fueled their creation made them equally compelling to legions of foreign fans. In fact, from the earliest days of contact, the effort Japanese devoted to devising toys and games shocked Western observers. One of the first was the British diplomat Rutherford Alcock, who in 1863 dubbed Japan "a paradise of babies." They were even more shocked by how many of these babies grew into adults who unabashedly continued to enjoy the pleasures of childhood. "We frequently see full-grown men and able-bodied natives indulging in amusements which the men of the West lay aside with their pinafores," gasped the American educator William Elliot Griffis in 1876. He referred to traditional forms of play such as spinning tops and flying kites, but the "amusements" grew more sophisticated as time went on, with Japanese creatives distilling fantasies old and new into ever more potent concoctions. As new technologies like transistors trickled from labs into the consumer marketplace and modern life grew stranger, fantasy-delivery devices ceased being simple products of their times; they began transforming the very times in which they emerged. Amusements became tools—tools whose utility appealed far beyond the local demographic for which they were designed. That's why when Japan collapsed in on itself economically in the 1990s, it exploded outward culturally, scattering its hopes and dreams across the globe: a societal supernova, fueled by play and fantasy. From our adoption of Japanese fantasies emerged new ideas of cool, of cosmopolitanism, of femininity and masculinity.

The stories of their creators have rarely been told in either English or Japanese. The survivor of a fallen city who transformed literal trash into globally coveted playthings. A medical student, very nearly expelled from school for cartooning during lectures, who elevated comics from kid stuff into a shorthand for adolescent rebellion around the world. A talented college co-ed shut out by the male-dominated business world who turned a simple sketch of a kitty into the single most recognized icon of feminine power. And the secretive, and until now largely anonymous, *otaku* who channeled a generation's ennui and rage online, nourishing the growth of fringe political movements across the planet.

In these interlinking stories is a drama of world-changing successes, soul-searching screw-ups, and infectious fever dreams. It's the often surprising, sometimes dismaying, unvarnished truth of a group of total weirdos who remixed our realities without any of us quite realizing it. So much of our modern lives originated in Japan. The roots of social media and the rise of anonymous online political extremism, with its often frightening manifestations in the real world. The gamification of human interactions through virtual rewards such as points, trophies, and likes. The blurring of the lines between creator and consumer, amateur and pro, auteur and superfan. The way in which people of all ages spend their days in virtual spaces, defining themselves through the fantasies they consume— and not simply for purposes of entertainment but as desperately needed escapes. The COVID-19 pandemic further accelerated all of these phenomena. Now they are such a part of the fabric of daily life that it's easy to take them for granted. That makes the stories that follow more than a chapter in the history of globalization or pop culture. They're essential for understanding ourselves.

Part I

FALL 1945

PEACE! IT'S OVER. . . . . . Forty-three and a half square miles in four of Japan's largest cities—Tokyo, Nagoya, Osaka, and Kobe—were destroyed. . . . . . *JAPAN A HOLLOW SHELL.* . . . . . . *Amazement at Japan's state of exhaustion was the first reaction of American correspondents.* . . . . . . Work harder, longer with *Philopon*™ amphetamine tablets! Sold in convenient twenty, fifty, one hundred, and five hundred count packages. . . . *HEY, KIDS! ACORNS CAN BE TURNED INTO CRACKERS AND CANDY AND BREAD TO FILL UP YOUR TUMMIES! GET COLLECTING SO YOU CAN EAT UP!* . . . . . . **WASHINGTON—** The return of toys and games to the shelves of toy departments appeared closer at hand today as the War Production Board revoked Limitation Order L-81. . . . . . **Ueno station reports having to dispose of up to six bodies of starvation victims every day.** . . . . . . "Japan has fallen to a fourth-rate nation," General MacArthur told *The Chicago Tribune.* "It will not be possible for her to emerge again as a strong nation in the world."

1

TIN MEN

In the toy-shops of Japan one may see the microcosm of Japanese life.
—WILLIAM ELLIOT GRIFFIS, 1876

Toys are not really as innocent as they look. Toys and games are the prelude
to serious ideas.
—CHARLES EAMES, 1961

RIDING CHARIOTS BUILT in Detroit, American conquerors surveyed
the nation they had brought to its knees. The devastation wrought
by months of firebombing was almost beyond imagination. Prior to
the outbreak of war in the Pacific in 1941, Tokyo was the planet's
third-largest city, home to nearly seven million people. Through military conscription, civilian casualties, and mass evacuations, by the
fall of 1945 fewer than half remained. The same could be said of the
city itself. "Skeletons of railway cars and locomotives remained un-
touched on the tracks," wrote the war correspondent Mark Gayn of
his first drive into the fallen metropolis. "Streetcars stood where the
flames had caught up with them, twisting the metal, snapping the
wires overhead, and bending the supporting iron poles as if they
were made of wax. Gutted buses and automobiles lay abandoned by
the roadside. This was all a man-made desert, ugly and desolate and
hazy in the dust that rose from the crushed brick and mortar."
Charred bodies still lay beneath the rubble, filling silent streets with
their stench. The only sound of industrial civilization in this grim
landscape was the rumble of the American jeep.

The "U.S. Army Truck, ¼-ton, 4×4, Command Reconnaissance,"
as it was officially designated, was designed for hauling things around

American jeeps rolled into every corner of Japan, including holy ground
like this Shinto shrine.

and nothing else. Mass-produced to military specifications by the automakers Willys–Overland and Ford, the jeep offered little in the way of amenities save the promise of near indestructibility. It was boxy, open to the elements, and painful to ride in for any length of time. The drab yet dependable vehicle was somehow down-to-earth and larger-than-life; even the Americans knew it. General Eisenhower went so far as to credit the jeep as one of the four things that won the war for the Allies, right alongside the Douglas C-47 transport plane, the bazooka, and the atomic bomb.

Japan spent the rest of the decade occupied by a foreign military power, literally picking up the pieces of its major cities. Jeeps zipped freely through the streets all the while. For Japanese adults, the jeep stirred complicated feelings of loss and longing—an unavoidable symbol of capitulation and powerlessness. To children, they represented thrillingly loud and fast candy dispensers, dishing out tastes of American culture in the form of Hershey's bars, Bazooka gum, and Lucky Strike cigarettes. And they did radiate a sort of charm; bug-eyed headlights and a seven-slotted grill evoking a toothy grin, as though the jeep were a cartoon of a car. The iconic nickname, in fact, likely came from a Popeye comic book. The sailorman's sidekick Eugene the Jeep first appeared in 1936. He emerged as the Pikachu of his era, a fuzzy yellow fantasy creature whose utterances were limited to the monosyllable "jeep"—which sounded a lot like "GP," as in General Purpose, another designation for the vehicle.

Officially, the occupation lasted until 1952, when much of Japan regained independence under a new constitution authored by American framers. (Okinawa would remain under American control for another two decades.) Even still the jeeps remained, for sovereignty hinged on the adoption of the Treaty of Mutual Cooperation and Security Between the United States and Japan, better known as Anpo—an abbreviation of its Japanese name. Grossly inequitable and hugely unpopular among a war-weary citizenry from its very inception, the treaty obligated Japan to host a series of American military bases along its entire length, operating independently and beyond the reach of Japanese law: permanent islands of occupation.

Police were required to salute as the American soldiers roared past, whether they were on official business or driving around with their newfound local girlfriends. The first English words most Japanese kids would master in those postwar years were "hello," "goodbye," "give me chocolate," and "jeep."

THE TOTAL DESTRUCTION of the industrial sector in 1945 obliterated Japan's manufacturing capabilities—a crippling blow for any nation, but doubly so in one as singularly obsessed with material *things* as Japan. From the earliest days of contact with the West in 1854, Japan relied on manufactured products to build bridges with the outside world.

The unexpected appearance of an American naval fleet in Japanese waters in the mid-nineteenth century compelled the shogunate to end more than two centuries of self-imposed isolation. The Americans undoubtedly presumed they would find a backward nation with a low standard of living, ripe for exploitation. What they discovered was a vibrant consumer economy that not only met its citizens' daily needs but delivered books, artwork, furniture, decorations, and fashion accessories to an eager populace. Even in these preindustrial times, Japanese citizens sought out and cherished little luxuries.

Boxes both metaphoric and literal define Japan's material culture. Artfully arranged bento boxes showcase ingredients and stimulate appetites. The challenging limitations of haiku, just three lines of five, seven, and five syllables, channel creativity into the art of what might be called single-serving verse. So too in the art of wrapping, putting as much effort into the aesthetics of presentation as the object itself, whether it be the careful plating of kaiseki haute cuisine or the presentation of gifts in envelopes or boxes so elaborate that they can rival or even exceed the value of the actual contents.

These packaged pleasures are the products of a hereditary caste system that sorted citizens into boxes of their own: samurai at the top of the social pecking order, followed in turn by farmers, artisans, and merchants at the very bottom. Yet a passion for packaging extends throughout all levels of society, whether in the functional *furoshiki* cloth wrappings used for daily purchases on the street or in the meticulous packaging seen at luxurious *hyakkaten*.

Written with the characters for "hundreds of products," hyakkaten were the traditional analogue of what we now call department stores and the Japanese call *depaato*. It is no coincidence that Japan is home to two of the world's very first and longest-running such establishments: Matsuzakaya, founded in 1611, and Mitsukoshi, whose roots extend back to 1673. With a million residents, Edo, as Tokyo was known prior to 1868, ranked as the world's most populous city for most of the eighteenth century. For many generations, department stores like Mitsukoshi and its many rivals prided themselves on carrying the choicest wares for discriminating urban customers. Fine kimonos; beautifully wrought housewares, jewelry, and accessories; decadent delights of all kinds, from sweets to toys, all of it wrapped just so and presented with a deep bow from the clerk to the customer—the flourish of the presentation just as important as the contents inside. Packaging was always about something more than protection from the elements; it was an art form in and of itself, a show of respect to object and consumer both.

And what might lurk inside those exquisite boxes? In the late nineteenth century, sophisticated books created from woodblock prints, ceramic ware, fashion accessories, brocades, and other pleasures intended for savvy Japanese consumers so charmed Western artists that they began to question long-held assumptions about aesthetics and design. Impressionists and those inspired by them, such as Degas, Whistler, van Gogh, and Toulouse-Lautrec, immersed themselves in the playful artwork of Kuniyoshi and Hokusai to free themselves from the strictures of ossified European style. Before long, things Japanese began to transform what it meant to be cultured. Charles Tiffany harnessed Japanese flourishes to elevate a humble stationery emporium into America's top purveyor of urban sophistication. To familiar luxuries such as combs, servingware, silver, and stained glass, he added exotic motifs inspired by or even copied directly from the work of Hokusai and others: fish, turtles, flowers, butterflies, and insects. Such was the impact of the Western world's first encounter with the handiwork of the *shokunin:* Japanese artisans who poured heart and soul into their craft, because their craft was their lot in life, all but ordained by the social order of their era. Taking a cue from the often brutal apprenticeships of the martial arts, *shokunin* tradition places innovation secondary to the mastering of a chosen medium's form, finish, and presentation. Only after long years of rote practice might one aspire to making something new. You might call it thinking inside the box.

Ironically, given this hyperfocus on detail, form, and etiquette, it was the sense of playfulness that most struck early observers of this exotic land. The American educator William Elliot Griffis noted in 1876:

> We do not know of any country in the world in which there are so many toy-shops, or so many fairs for the sale of things which delight children. Not only are the streets of every city abundantly supplied with shops, filled as full as a Christmas stocking with gaudy toys, but in small towns and villages one or more children's bazaars may be found.

While Western tastemakers voraciously consumed prints, glassware, textiles, and other grown-up delights, it was in fact toys that formed the backbone of Japan's burgeoning export industry in the late nineteenth century. By this time the medieval caste system was out; modernization and catching up with the West were the orders of the day. One of the ways in which the nation strove to catch up was with exports. Toy making was big business, then as now. Germany, the United Kingdom, and France jostled for the lead in supplying the children of the world with dolls, rocking horses, and cast-iron soldiers; Japan watched with envy. The chaos of World War I provided the opportunity for which it had long waited.

At the 1915 Panama–Pacific International Exposition in San Francisco, an opulent display brimmed with roly-poly papier-mâché *daruma* dolls, miniature paper umbrellas, celluloid figures, and exquisite porcelain dolls from toy makers in Tokyo, Nagoya, Kyoto, and Osaka. The Japanese government heralded its ambitions there and at other world's fairs; soon enough, these purveyors of playthings leapfrogged Western makers with a variety of new products that were far lower in price, thanks to a far cheaper labor force. A skilled Japanese craftsman might earn in a day what an American would demand to be paid per hour. Toy makers from the land of the rising sun proved so adept at their task that, in 1934, U.S. toy companies petitioned the government for tariffs to help stem the "invasion of the American market by Japanese toys."

The outbreak of war in the Pacific put an end to Japan's designs on the global toy industry, seemingly forever. Yet, in fact, the very first manufactured item to emerge from the fires of war was a toy. This humble product—fashioned by a master craftsman who hadn't made a toy in many years—represented Japan's first step back onto the world map, winning hearts among Japan's adults, children, and conquerors alike.

MATSUZO KOSUGE WAS born in 1899 on Japan's farthest frontier: Etorofu, a frigid island in the Sea of Okhotsk northeast of Hokkaido. Ringed by soaring white cliffs and long inhabited by the indigenous Ainu peoples, Etorofu first appeared on local maps in the late seventeenth century, beginning a long tug-of-war among Ainu, Japanese, and Russians for control of the territory. Remote it may have been, but it was also strategically located—and surrounded by deep and fertile waters, to boot. (It was from Etorofu's port that an imperial carrier fleet would make final preparations in November of 1941 before setting steam for Pearl Harbor.) After prolonged negotiations, the Russians officially ceded the island to Japan in 1855, opening it for development.

Life on Etorofu was hard. The sea was too cold for swimming, even at the height of summer. There was no school available beyond the elementary level, and a young man had but two choices for work: a fishing boat or the local cannery. But the ambitious and eternally curious Kosuge had bigger ideas, and at the age of seventeen he struck out for Tokyo. There he took an apprenticeship with Tashichi Inoue, the owner of a company that specialized in making toys out of tin. The same low cost, workability, and durability that made tin the material of choice for cans also made it the ideal material for crafting durable toys. And Kosuge was arriving at a thrilling moment for the Japanese toy industry. The global toy trade had long been dominated by German companies, but the outbreak of World War I compelled them to turn from manufacturing playthings to making things of war. In leapt Japanese toy makers, eager to take over the lucrative market the Germans had abandoned. Exports of playthings from Japan to the United States alone quadrupled in just five years, between 1912 and 1917, with no end to the potential growth in sight.

Over years of tutelage from elder craftsmen, Kosuge mastered the largely unglamorous elements of the trade: blueprints and planning, fitting and soldering, painting and printing the colorful designs onto the tinplate stock, and above all else, the molds—anvil-like chunks of cold steel, carefully hand-tooled to form sheets of tin into the series of shapes peculiar to each product. Mounted on giant clanking press machines, the molds were the beating hearts of any tin-toy workshop.

In 1922, Kosuge launched the Kosuge Toy Manufacturing Company. He was only twenty-three years old. We don't know exactly how he managed to acquire the resources to go independent; back then, apprenticeship was akin to indentured servitude, and Kosuge had to work for a full year without a salary before his master let him venture off on his own. In spite of the name, Kosuge's company was more of a studio than a factory. It was a think tank for toys, with all the expertise and equipment needed to create playthings from nothing more than imagination and raw material. Some they built to the specifications of wholesalers; many others they created themselves after a great deal of experimentation, shopping the prototypes around to bigger firms in hopes of landing an order.

About the only thing Kosuge's firm didn't do was sell toys to actual children. That was the business of the wholesalers, who fronted the money for Kosuge's production runs, then packaged the result under their own brand names. This was the way of the toy industry, as with all Japanese industry: boxed in, regimented, hierarchical. Neighborhood toy stores ordered products from wholesalers, who in turn bought their stock from cottage workshops like Kosuge's, which toiled in obscurity. But these tiny "neighborhood factories," as the Japanese called them, were where the vast majority of playthings were actually made—produced and assembled entirely by hand. Some factories specialized in simpler products like tin horns, watering cans, or rattles for the domestic marketplace. Elaborate mechanized contraptions such as spring-powered cars, Kosuge's specialty, were mainly intended for foreign buyers, though more than a few found their way into local shops as well.

Most of his competitors were content simply to copy the creations of foreign toy makers like Germany's Schuco, whose intricate windups set the prewar standard for clockwork toys. Kosuge deeply respected these rivals, but he had a real antipathy toward imitation. "We're in business to make our own designs," he told his employees. He took a personal hand in every project, thinking up new designs and drafting the blueprints himself.

Kosuge dreamed up all sorts of toy contraptions. Some were inspired by daily life, like a crawling clockwork baby made of cloth and celluloid; others were more fanciful, like circus seals or dancing animals. Sometime in the thirties he created the world's first mass-produced toy robot, a boxy tin man named Lilliput. But he loved automobiles most of all. His intricate windup portrayal of Graham-Paige's sleek 1933 Blue Streak sedan was an early success. In the early thirties, there were only 1,600 private cars registered in all of Tokyo, and rickshaws still plied the street. Toy versions of futuristic foreign vehicles like the Blue Streak and a later Packard Eight gave young Japanese a tantalizing glimpse of the modern world abroad. Before long, everyone in the toy industry called him "Kosuge the Car Man." By 1935, his little workshop wasn't so little anymore. He employed some two hundred workers, among them many of the city's top tinsmiths. Their efforts contributed to making Japan the world's second-largest producer of toys, the majority of which were exported to eager customers in the United States and Great Britain.

Japan was poised to overtake Germany as the leader of the global toy trade. But three years later, in 1938, the Japanese economy ground to a halt. International protests over Japan's invasion of China led to crippling economic sanctions. As the prime minister declared ambitions to build a new order in East Asia, parliament passed a frightening National Mobilization Law giving him the unilateral ability to set prices, institute rationing, and even conscript citizens into forced labor, effectively ending democratic rule in Japan. The entire nation

Kosuge's Graham-Paige Blue Streak

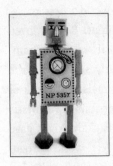

A modern reproduction of the Lilliput, the first known robot toy. In a sign of the times, the original was manufactured in the imperial Japanese puppet state of Manchukuo, China.

went on war footing—even its children. "From now on, Japanese boys will have to settle for toys made of cardboard and wood," reported the *Yomiuri Shimbun* newspaper in August of 1938. "The manufacture of metal toys has been prohibited, following new restrictions on the use of metal materials. . . . This represents a delightful opportunity for mothers to explain to their children the importance of Japan's battle to establish a new order in East Asia." The authorities ordered Kosuge to stop making toys and retool his presses to stamp out the casings for bomb fuses instead. *Shikata ga nai*—it couldn't be helped. When the streets were plastered with signs reading LUXURY IS THE ENEMY and housewives were being publicly shamed for getting perms, how could anyone make toys? Down came the KOSUGE TOY MANUFACTURING sign; up went a decidedly less playful-sounding one reading PRECISION FABRICATION.

Sanctions led to a 1941 U.S. embargo on metal and petroleum exports, a freeze on Japanese assets in U.S. banks, and then after the attack on Pearl Harbor, all-out war. Desperate for raw materials, in the summer of 1942 the government began collecting and melting down priceless bronze statues and prayer bells from Buddhist temples. A few months later, authorities went door-to-door confiscating pots and pans, forcing families to exchange metal currency for paper IOUs. They even stripped school classrooms of their cast-iron stoves, forcing children to shiver through the winter months. In 1943, the government finally came calling for Kosuge and his fellow toy makers. They were compelled to hand over their most precious assets: the steel molds they had been quietly storing in hopes of restarting business once the war ended. If it ended.

By early 1945, as the Japanese military lost control of the skies over its cities, the American forces readied a series of firebombing attacks designed to crush military production and public morale. For the first trial of this new strategy, code-named Operation Meetinghouse, planners targeted Kosuge—not by name, but *shokunin* like him were in the crosshairs. "It made a lot of sense to kill skilled workers by burning whole areas," explained General Ira Eaker, former deputy commander of the U.S. Army Air Force, in a 1962 interview. The Asakusa neighborhood of Tokyo, where Kosuge's company was located, wasn't simply the heart of the toy industry. It was a bustling commercial-residential district filled with small workshops and factories of all kinds that had been converted from civilian to wartime production. It was also one of the most densely populated places on the planet. It also happened to be constructed, as was nearly all of Tokyo at the time, entirely out of wood and paper.

The raid, which began in the predawn hours of March 10, sent close to three hundred B-29 Superfortresses into the skies over Tokyo. Their incendiary payloads of phosphorous and napalm were carefully concocted to trigger a firestorm in the city streets below. The results were apocalyptic. One hundred thousand Japanese died that night, most of them civilians. The stench of charred flesh grew so thick that bomber crews reported smelling it more than a mile overhead. More than 250,000 buildings burned to the ground, leaving millions homeless. It was the single most destructive conventional bombing attack in human history, a grotesque record that stands to this day.

Kosuge left no memoirs. We can only guess at the horrors he must have seen that terrible day, the devastating sense of loss he must have felt at losing both his lifework and so many friends and acquaintances. What is known is that the military ordered him to gather any equipment that survived the bombing and move to a distant city. Did he resist? It didn't matter. He wasn't a toy maker anymore, just another cog in his nation's war machine. He was sent to Otsu, a picturesque hamlet on the shores of Lake Biwa, outside Kyoto. There Kosuge spent the remainder of the war churning out military camera housings and other components for a fight he must have suspected, as did so many of his countrymen, that there was no hope of winning.

When Japan surrendered in August, Kosuge stayed put. There wasn't much of a Tokyo left to go back to. He couldn't even return home. The Soviets had taken the opportunity of Japan's defeat to reclaim Etorofu, and rumor had it the citizens would be taken prisoner.

Shikata ga nai. There were worse places to wait things out than Otsu. Long a vacation spot for the aristocracy, it was where Murasaki Shikibu penned the first chapters of *The Tale of Genji* a thousand years earlier. The lakeside neighborhood where Kosuge lived and worked was famed for its scenery. The charming pine tree–lined boulevards and soaring mountain peaks had captivated the ukiyo-e printmaker Hiroshige, who included them in his *Eight Views of Omi.*

That Kyoto happened to be Japan's only metropolitan center still standing gave Kosuge an idea. Only months after the war's end, he set up Kosuge Toy Works in the first suitably sized space he found available for rent: a former cattle shed. It had been shuttered for many years, the cows long since slaughtered to feed hungry residents. The structure was rustic, to put it generously. Sunlight—and cold breezes—filtered through gaps in the boards. Signs of its former life abounded: the musky scent still hanging in the air, the clumps of straw littering the floor, the dried flecks of dung clinging to the support posts. But it had plenty of space for Kosuge's equipment and men. It would do.

Freed from military service, Kosuge could make any kind of toy he wanted. The only question was what to make. It's easy to imagine him thinking: *What on earth can I offer kids who've spent their entire lives trying to survive a war?*

As it happened, the answer came to him. The occupation forces had requisitioned nearby Biwako Hotel as a temporary barracks, making GIs a familiar sight on Otsu's once-quiet streets. "American jeeps were everywhere back then," wrote the toy historian Osamu Kato in 1960. "The envy of kids and adults alike. There was something about them that made you wish you could take a ride." As Kosuge made his way home from the public bathhouse one evening in the fall of 1945, he spotted a jeep parked on the street—and nobody was in it. Given the hour, the occupants were likely off scouting for female companionship in the nearby red-light district. The unoccupied vehicle gave Kosuge the Car Man his first chance to inspect a jeep up close.

Normally, toy makers referred to the catalogs and promotional materials released by auto manufacturers to design their toys. This obviously wasn't an option for a piece of military equipment. So Kosuge used the only tool he had on him to take measurements: his bath towel. Stretching it out to capture the rough dimensions of the jeep's chassis, he hurried back home to draw a blueprint. He repeated the process with the towel over subsequent evenings to refine the design. Before long, the plans were complete. The Car Man was back in business. Neither he nor anyone else could have realized what a pivotal moment this was: a first step toward putting Japan back on the cultural map for something other than military conquest and mayhem.

There was just one problem. He had no molds—they'd long since been handed over to the government. There was no raw material, no metal to work with at all. Yet Kosuge was determined. In the heaps of American trash rapidly growing behind the Hotel Biwako, Matsuzo Kosuge saw treasure. He negotiated with the army to let him haul away the empty food tins and beer cans. Back at the workshop, he and his staff cleaned the castoffs with a caustic soda, cut them open, ran them through a roller press to flatten them, pounded the resulting sheets into shape over improvised wooden molds, then assembled the parts by hand. After a quick coat of paint, they were done. Off the makeshift assembly line rolled a tiny convoy of ten-centimeter-long windup replicas of the U.S. military's ubiquitous daily conveyance.

It wasn't exactly up to the standards of the toys Kosuge had produced before the war. A lack of the metal springs needed for windup

Along with the Americans came copious quantities of garbage, which locals mined for reusable materials.

mechanisms forced him to resort to a simple rubber band to power the tiny vehicle. But, in spite of his having measured the original with nothing more than a damp towel, each miniature copy featured a surprising amount of detail, even down to the distinctive white stars on the sides and hood. They weren't exactly precise, but they captured the aura of the jeeps; they *felt* right. Kosuge must have smiled as he looked over his handiwork. After all these years, he had a new toy.

The philosopher Walter Benjamin famously wrote of the "aura" that an original work of art or nature possesses, which is inevitably missing from a mechanical copy. But in Japan, a nation where the 1,300-year-old Ise Grand Shrine is demolished and expertly rebuilt every twenty years, the line between original and replica has long been blurred. In Japan, "copy" lacks the pejorative meaning that it often carries in Western societies. Abroad, a copy implies the end of a process; in Japan, where the process of creation begins with imitation, copying signals the beginning of something new.

Now he just needed a place to sell his replicas. The long-dormant instincts of a veteran toy maker kicked in. He took a sample to Kyoto and struck a deal with the city's largest department store, Marubutsu. For Kosuge, Marubutsu was an easy enough choice: It was the only major retailer open in the city. The department store, for its part, must have been happy to carry the toy. It had been five years since a 1940 government edict formally prohibited the sale of jewels, precious metals, and fancy clothing, forcing department stores to focus on simple tableware, humble *mompei* work clothes, and the most basic of confectioneries. Even the latter weren't intended for customers, but rather purchased as care packages for soldiers abroad. Kosuge's jeep was the first true luxury to appear on the market in many years—even if it happened to be hammered out of old tin cans.

Kosuge and his employees toiled throughout the fall in anticipation of the January 1946 New Year holiday season, the nation's first under peace in close to a decade. The first batch of jeeps went on sale in December of 1945, just four months after the end of the war. They were priced at ten yen apiece, the cost of a quick meal in a black-market food stall, making them affordable to impoverished customers. They didn't even have boxes—at any other time than this, an unforgivable sin for something sold at a department store. But paper, too, was in critically short supply.

Kosuge's entire first run of jeeps, several hundred pieces, sold out in an hour.

He immediately scaled up his operation, renting more cattle sheds for added work space and hiring dozens of local laborers, even enlisting housewives to assemble parts in their homes. Together, the citizens of Otsu churned out thousands more jeeps for the department store. Being handmade, with none of the precision tools that had been available before the war, no two lots were the same. Little improvements creeped in over the course of time: replacing the rubber band with a windup mechanism here, adding a trailer-wagon accessory there. Eventually Kosuge even managed to procure rudimentary boxes from a Tokyo supplier: unbleached brown cardboard, rubber-stamped in English: JEEP!

A specimen of Kosuge's jeep from the collection of the Otsu City Museum of History

Every time a new batch arrived, customers queued in lines around the block, seemingly oblivious to the December chill. In a land where children had been stripped of their heroes and everything else, Kosuge made the occupying army his brand. Every Allied jeep that whizzed by on the streets unwittingly promoted the product. By the end of the month, Marubutsu sold one hundred thousand of what came to be called "Kosuge's jeep"—an astounding number given Japan's situation. Transforming the conqueror's chariot into a palm-sized plaything had clearly tapped into something profound.

THE TOY JEEP might seem like just a blip on the proto-pop-cultural radar at a strange time in history. But Japan had quickly learned what happened when a generation of children grew up deprived of toys. Even children fortunate enough to still have families and homes at war's end played at roles that sadly evoked the era: "pretend black market," "pretend gambling," "pretend protest demonstrations," and, most disturbingly, "pretend *pan-pan*"—imitating the strolling pairs of

GIs and young women so ubiquitous on Japanese streets of the era. Many other children were left orphaned, homeless, or both. Some turned to crime, raiding warehouses for whatever stockpiled wartime matériel that they could liberate and trade for food to black-market scalpers. In a plea to readers of the *Mainichi Shimbun* newspaper, the head of a Tokyo orphanage lamented: "We can keep them fed, but what they really need, even more than clothes or books, are things to play with."

Word of Kosuge's triumph in Kyoto was music to the ears of the few remaining toy makers still in the capital. "Everyone in the industry said to each other, 'Who on earth made this?'" recalled the historian Osamu Kato. "'How could anyone manage to make such an excellent toy at a time like this?'" Inspired by Kosuge's success, a Tokyo firm called Takamine began producing its own take on the jeep. Although less detailed than Kosuge's, it proved equally popular among the children of the capital. By May of 1946, the factory was turning out more than one hundred a day, with plans to expand that to five hundred.

To kids, the jeeps were desperately needed playthings; to adults they represented the stirrings of a working economy, of a normal society. It wasn't long before the American forces took notice. Young soldiers scooped up the tin replicas of their cars and aircraft as souvenirs, while occupation economic planners, keenly aware of the prewar success of Japan's toy industry, watched intently. The toys became a symbol—and a tool—of bridges built between enemies turned uneasy allies. In a 1946 pictorial in the Pacific edition of *Stars and Stripes*, a Japanese boy and a young GI are seen racing tin jeeps atop the hood of a real one.

Key to the jeep's success was the ambiguity of its message. "Japanese grown-ups hated toys of military vehicles, because they're why we lost the war," recalled Eiichiro Tomiyama, founder in 1924 of the toy company Tomiyama, now known as Tomy. "To Americans, it's different; they're shining examples of military success. I knew they would sell abroad." So it was that in August of 1947,

General MacArthur's economic team directed that "all efforts be made to ramp up production of toys for export, as collateral material for the critically needed food rations being imported for Japanese citizens." The only other products so recognized were silks. Thanks to toys, Japan could finally begin rebuilding its export trade. The only condition was that the products clearly be marked MADE IN OCCUPIED JAPAN.

The timing was fortuitous. Christmas of 1947 was fast approaching, and America was experiencing a toy shortage of its own, one of the many lingering effects Stateside of wartime labor and material shortages. Even Lionel, the famed maker of toy trains, had been reduced to manufacturing its products out of cardboard during the war years. Japan's toy makers were more than happy to fill the gap with their effigies of popular American passenger cars and military vehicles. Tomiyama's intricate tin replica of a B-29 bomber, the very same type that had only a few years previously rained incendiary death on the actual neighborhood now producing the toy, became a major hit abroad. When the toy's distributor, Yonezawa Shokai, displayed it at a 1951 toy fair in New York, buyers placed orders for hundreds of thousands of the planes. Yonezawa eventually sold close to a million of them in the United States alone. Products like the B-29 propelled the tin-toy industry from eight million yen a year in 1947 to eight *billion* yen a year by 1955. The vast majority went to eager children in the United States and Great Britain.

The ambivalence with which average Japanese had long regarded these symbols of war finally bubbled to the surface in 1951, when an organization of teachers and women's groups launched a nationwide campaign against the manufacture of military-themed toys. Toy makers fired back that their products merely reflected the world in which children lived. Children saw jeeps, tanks, and military planes on a daily basis. They were, for better and worse, part of the fabric of daily life. What purpose would be served by hiding toy versions of the same things?

As it turned out, the question would soon be moot, for the end of the occupation in 1952 signaled a great pop-cultural pivot for Japanese children. Like the rest of the postwar world, Japan idolized American culture: so strong, so powerful, so sexy and stylish. A young toy executive from a tiny Japanese firm would soon exploit this understanding, to great success. He would do it by harnessing an expression of the American dream even more potent than that of the jeep. It went by the name "Cadillac."

FEW BUILDINGS WERE available for rent in war-ravaged Asakusa, still recovering from the carpet-bombings years earlier. In 1947, Haruyasu Ishida, together with his younger brother, Minoru, and a third partner, founded the toy company Marusan Co. Ltd. He ran it out of his home, which also served as warehouse, dormitory, and kitchen for its ten employees—a common arrangement in the early days after the war. Rather than making new things, the brothers specialized in brokering deals between countryside toy factories and the Tokyo wholesalers who serviced the region's retail stores. Marusan's specialty was "optical toys"—a fancy-sounding name for cheap plastic binoculars and telescopes. They sold well enough to earn a steady return. But Minoru, youngest of the company's three founders, wanted to be more than just a purveyor of novelties.

Passionate and creative, Minoru quickly emerged as Marusan's idea man. Haruyasu, a consummate businessman, served as a counterweight, arguing from a position of markets and numbers. By 1952, one thing both agreed on was that their rivals were making small fortunes exporting tin toys abroad. They resolved to design one of their own.

The idea of making miniature cars deeply appealed to Minoru. He was obsessed with the real thing. As a teen in Singapore he'd sped around the city in a Citroën 11 CV; right after launching Marusan, he procured a used Studebaker from an American soldier, ostensibly as a company car, then added a fire engine–red MG T-type open-seater to the fleet. "We really turned heads making deliveries in that MG," chuckled former employee Saburo Ishizuki as he recounted the scene to me. "There wasn't anything like it on Tokyo's streets at the time."

Minoru wanted something that would turn heads on toy store shelves, too. A toy car like no other manufacturer was making—scaled like the real thing, large, and filled with features that would really wow foreign buyers. Only an uncompromising veteran craftsman could pull off such a feat. Minoru knew just who to call.

Matsuzo Kosuge returned to Tokyo in 1947. There he launched a design studio and tin factory called Tokyo Zosaku Kogeisha (Tokyo Creative Arts). It was located in the Sumida ward, just a stone's throw from where his old factory had been before the war. Kosuge wasted no time in releasing the firm's first product, a windup car that could "sense" the edge of a table and turn around before falling off; he sold ten thousand of them. As the orders poured in and his reputation grew, he changed the name to what everyone had taken to calling the company anyway: Kosuge Toys.

After batting around ideas with Kosuge, Minoru settled on the model: a 1950 Cadillac sedan. It was the obvious choice. As U.S. soldiers and their jeeps became less of a presence on the streets of a newly independent Japan, children thrilled to new fantasies of technology and prosperity: the absurdly oversized, gloriously chromed, and thrillingly aerodynamic passenger cars produced by American automakers. And the Cadillac was America's number one car.

Kosuge the Car Man had cannily hit two birds with one stone in choosing the jeep. It was a symbol of both American military might and automotive prowess, wrapped in a compact olive-drab package. He and his fellow Japanese toy makers were keenly aware of the sway that American passenger cars held over the midcentury imagination, not only in Japan but in their country of origin. Postwar America was obsessed with cars. In 1950, there were just twenty-five million registered automobiles on American roads; by 1958, that number had more than doubled. Everyone wanted a Cadillac, even if it was only a toy.

This time, there would be no need for compromise. After the outbreak of the Korean War in 1950, the American government funneled nearly $3 billion in orders to Japan for the production and transport of war matériel to the Korean peninsula—things like rope, wire, clothing, foodstuffs, ammunition, and even copies of American jeeps, built on license by Mitsubishi and Toyota. Blood money this may have been, but it was an undeniable boon for a nation in dire financial straits. As Japanese firms constructed factories and transport infrastructure to fill the American military procurement orders, Japan became "one huge supply depot, without which the Korean War could not have been fought," as Ambassador Robert Murphy put it in 1952. Watching Japan's economy grow by double digits thanks to the investment, the president of the Bank of Japan called it "aid from the heavens."

Now that foundries had been restarted and were once again producing high-quality domestic steel, there was no need to comb through filthy trash heaps for discarded tin. Thanks to the reappearance of machine shops capable of turning out gears, springs, and other precision components, craftsmen were able to upgrade their toys with new clockwork mechanisms that put even the prewar best to shame. Under Minoru's direction, Kosuge's team toiled for a year refining the sculpting, the molds, and all the tiny details.

The end result was exquisite. At thirteen inches long, the Cadillac was perfect from its shiny ebony roof down to its white-walled tires. The glossy sheen came from numerous painstakingly applied coats of lacquer paint; the bumpers and grille were finished in gleaming chrome, with glistening jewels of translucent plastic for headlights. The hoods sported miniature Cadillac crests, each painted by hand. Inside, state-of-the-art lithographic printing technology replicated the finest details, from the pattern on the tin "upholstery" down to the numbers on the speedometer. It looked real enough to drive, as though some mad scientist had fired a shrink ray at the actual car. At some point along the way, everyone involved had almost given up caring if it would sell or not. It was about the craftsmanship—the *shokunin* spirit.

Every package featured KOSUGE FACTORY in small letters underneath the Marusan logo. It was an unprecedented accolade for a craftsman who, like so many before him, had quietly toiled in the shadows of name-brand retail toy companies. Aficionados affectionately refer to it as "Kosuge's Cadillac" today.

The no-compromise approach forced Marusan to sell the product for 1,500 yen in Japan—a small fortune at the time, far beyond the means of any child. The only shops Minoru could convince to carry it were department stores, the hope being that well-heeled grownups would purchase them for their kids—or, equally likely, for themselves.

In fact, the price was so high that the government deemed it a luxury item rather than a plaything, forcing Marusan to file extra paperwork and pay additional taxes on the sales. They didn't sell particularly well in Japan, but this was to be expected given the price tag. Minoru calmed Haruyasu down by assuring him that the real customers lay abroad. And he was right. Virtually from the moment foreign buyers first saw the Cadillacs at the International Toy Fair in New York, Marusan could barely keep up with the demand. It represented a little piece of the American dream, re-envisioned by toy

Kosuge's Cadillac

makers who had been fighting the Americans only a few years earlier.

Just as he had with the jeep, Kosuge quickly adapted to the new hunger for his handiwork. With few professionals available, he scaled up production the same way he had in Otsu: by hiring local housewives. Lined up at long tables, they assembled parts and applied finishing touches. At its peak this manufacturing line turned out 270 finished cars a day, in a range of colors and specifications including friction-powered, battery-powered, and eventually even remote-controlled versions. Nobody knows how many were produced in total, but another product hints at how successful it must have been with foreign buyers. In 1954, Marusan released a kit of a tin Buick Roadmaster, the most regal of the automaker's sedans. The packaging, entirely in English, reads: "Sister car of our famous 'Cadillac,' favored by our young friends . . . A toy, but more than a toy. Another hit item for this year produced by MARUSAN." The package for the Japanese edition of the Roadmaster boasted that it "is currently being exported to department stores throughout North and South America and Australia, where it outsells similar products from Germany and Britain."

Almost as soon as they arrived on the shelves of American toy stores, highly detailed and reasonably priced Japanese cars began crowding out domestically produced models. By the end of the fifties, Japan emerged as the world's single largest exporter of toys, producing a full three-quarters of the playthings consumed around the globe. (Even that all-American idol Barbie was actually made in a Japanese factory, her clothing hand-sewn by Japanese seamstresses on production lines similar to Kosuge's.) Global toy makers found it impossible to compete with this crack labor force of highly skilled workers, who carried out their tasks at wages that were shockingly low by Western standards. In 1959, furious British toy companies responded by banning Japanese companies from local toy fairs. Little did they know that toy cars were merely a taste of trade wars to come.

Kosuge's operation, like many neighborhood factories, relied heavily on the efforts of local housewives.

• • •

IN THE MEANTIME, the situation at home was better described as turmoil. A 1958 proposal to revise the controversial Anpo, the United States–Japan security treaty, provided a rallying point for citizens' groups, student protesters, and labor unions who had long opposed the agreement. They joined forces to organize mass protests against the administration of Prime Minister Nobusuke Kishi, grandfather of Japan's long-serving prime minister, Shinzo Abe.

Kishi was an unlikely United States ally. In fact, he managed to almost single-handedly embody everything foreigners and locals alike despised about imperial Japan. He had been the economic administrator of Japan's puppet state of Manchukuo, a co-signer of the declaration of war against the United States, the architect of Japan's wartime forced labor program, and an unrepentant ultranationalist who dedicated his later years to arguing the innocence of Class-A war criminals. Yet all his flaws were trumped in the eyes of American strategists by the singular attribute of rabid anti-Communism. It earned him a quiet pardon from the war crimes tribunal in 1948, and secret financial backing from the CIA to fuel his political comeback. Within a decade Kishi would be prime minister. When he visited Washington, D.C., in January of 1960 to sign the documents renewing the treaty, President Eisenhower lavished him with all the pomp and circumstance official diplomacy could muster, while the media fêted him with cover stories showcasing the "Friendly, Savvy Salesman from Japan"—as though Japan were being re-boxed into its prewar role of trinket seller to the world.

In reality, things weren't nearly so cheery back home. Society was coming apart at the seams. Fifteen months of political deadlock and demonstrations drew some thirty million Japanese—a third of the nation's population—into the protest movement. The moment of truth arrived on May 19, 1960. That was the official deadline for parliament to ratify the treaty Kishi had signed, which instituted a series of sovereign U.S. military bases stretching the length of Japan's territory, from Aomori at the northern tip of Honshu to the tropics of Okinawa, which would be untouchable by Japanese law. Fully aware of Kishi's wartime history and wary of being dragged into more American military conflicts abroad, furious citizens rallied by the hundreds of thousands outside the parliament building in anticipation of the vote. A mix of blue-collar laborers, students, and intellectuals, the group churning outside the gates represented a broad spectrum of Japanese society. Inside parliament, fistfights broke out as members of the opposition party desperately formed a human wall around the podium. After several hours of this, Kishi ordered the politicians removed by force. Five hundred police officers arrived to drag minority party members from the room. The elderly speaker of the parliament was physically wrestled through the scrum and into his chair like a ragdoll, whereupon he gaveled the Anpo through without a floor vote.

"Not exactly an advertisement for democracy," dryly noted a British Pathé newsreel of the spectacle. The imperious behavior enraged protesters and the general public alike, drawing more and more demonstrators into Tokyo and paralyzing the city for weeks on end. Eventually a massive group of radicals from Japan's elite universities calling themselves Zengakuren (a portmanteau formed from a longer name meaning "The All-Japan League of Student Governments") succeeded in smashing down the gates of the National Diet Building. As waves of Japan's best and brightest went head to head with heavily armed riot police, hundreds were injured, and a young female college student was trampled to death in the pandemonium.

Broadcast widely in Japan and abroad, footage of the 1960 protests offered many television viewers their first sight of public demonstrations on such an epic scale. The spectacle transformed the Japanese rebels into a source of inspiration for later protest movements. Of particular interest was the distinctive way in which they linked arms and quick-marched in looping patterns that police found difficult to disperse. In what must be the first example of a Japanese subcultural trend finding its niche abroad, the "Japanese snake dance," as it came to be called in English, would be deployed by American protest groups during the anti-war rallies of the late sixties.

Another incident that occurred several months later, in October of 1960, would have an even more profound effect on Japanese, and much later, American audiences. It involved a politician named Inejiro Asanuma, the sixty-one-year-old chairman of Japan's Socialist Party. On the afternoon of October 12, Asanuma took the stage for a debate among the heads of the nation's top three political parties, railing against Prime Minister Kishi and the Anpo treaty to an audience of three thousand. In the midst of his speech, a man burst forth from the wings and drove a foot-long traditional sword into Asanuma's chest, mortally wounding the politician as television cameras rolled. The culprit, Otoya Yamaguchi, was a seventeen-year-old so fanatically right-wing that he found Japan's ultraright Great Japan Patriotic Party too politically neutral for his tastes. After being subdued, he declared that he had saved Japan from Communism; a month later he would hang himself in his jail cell, leaving behind an imperial slogan of support for the emperor smeared on the wall in toothpaste. In the meantime, domestic and later foreign media outlets rebroadcast footage of the horrific scene over and over. The American magazine *Life* even ran a frame-by-frame analysis of what it called "the most thoroughly witnessed murder in history." In a breathless photo spread, the magazine compared the assassination to the famed *Tale of the 47 Ronin*, right under a reproduction of a nineteenth-century ukiyo-e woodblock print of the climax of the story. The murder had shocked and scandalized Japan; Yamaguchi's attack wasn't part of a political conspiracy but rather the work on the part of a mentally unstable young man, and few if any saw samurai drama in the tragedy there. The American media's mingling of reality and fantasy represented another narrative of Japanese exoticism, one that would resonate throughout the decades with some surprising consequences.

IN SPITE OF it all, Japan's global export industry only continued to grow. The ingenious little vehicles of Kosuge and his fellow craftsmen played a huge part in jump-starting their nation's shattered economy. But the Soviet Union's launch of the *Sputnik* satellite in 1957 instantly transformed the world's fantasies and nightmares, forcing toy makers to adapt. As news of the "space race" between the planet's nuclear superpowers filled headlines and airwaves, kids rapidly lost interest in cars, tanks, and planes. By the time Kosuge passed away in 1971, his jeeps were long forgotten; it wasn't until the early twenty-first century, in fact, that a curator at the Otsu City Museum of History managed to reconfirm what the original looked like by surveying elderly locals. By the early sixties, the reality of a nation finally at peace no longer stimulated the imagination. Instead, children craved flights of fancy from the future, symbols of a bright new era of science and technology: rockets, ray guns, and robots.

2

THE REVOLUTION WILL BE TELEVISED

Anime
1963

It seems almost inevitable that the world's greatest animator should be
Japanese.
—*THE NEW YORKER*, 2005

IT IS THE year 2003. A young man pilots his hover-car over space-age
highways that thread through an inviting future cityscape of soaring
glass-walled skyscrapers. He races beneath bridges, through tun-
nels, and around city corners—until a cargo truck pulls out in front
of him. The young man is killed instantly in the collision. His griev-
ing father is a scientist, and he devises a mechanical substitute for
his lost son: a little robot boy. The mechanical lad is sent to school,
where he solves mathematical equations faster than his teachers can
write; at home, he is provided with piles of toys and doted on by his
inventor-father. Many years go by. The little robot, naturally, doesn't
grow like a flesh-and-blood child would. This torments his creator,
serving as a constant reminder of all he has lost. Though blameless,
the little robot is disowned and banished to the circus, forced to
entertain humans in bouts of gladiatorial combat and dangerous
stunts with other lonely castoffs. When a trick goes wrong and blows
up the circus tent, the mechanical boy doesn't take the opportunity
to escape; he uses his super-strength and rocket feet to free the audience and spirit the circus ringleader to safety. Nevertheless, the ringleader refuses to release the boy and his friends from servitude.
Supported by a kindly scientist who later becomes the robot child's
surrogate father, the mechanical menagerie launches a global revolu-

By 1966, anime was a full-blown fad, enchanting children everywhere from the Imperial Palace all the way down to these scalawags on the streets.

tion, hoisting signs reading LONG LIVE ROBOT RIGHTS and ROBOTS ARE NOT YOUR SLAVES!

As the first episode of *Mighty Atom* concludes, humanity grants the robots of the world citizenship, and Atom, the spiky-haired, rocket-booted mechanical boy with a heart of gold, becomes a new hero. This was the very first cartoon ever produced for television in Japan. After it aired on New Year's Day 1963, things would never be the same.

Mighty Atom was a bootstrap affair, produced on a shoestring budget with only a third the number of frames used in a standard animated production. The resulting imagery was so stilted that industry pros derided it as "moving paper cutouts." Kids didn't care. They had seen cartoons on television before in the form of imports such as *Popeye* and *The Flintstones*, but *Mighty Atom* was the first show made just for them, based on a popular comic book that they knew and loved. The show's success was due in large part to its novelty and charm, but it was also due to excellent timing. Tokyo, poised to exceed ten million residents in early 1963, became the largest city on the planet later that year. In fact, it was beginning to look a lot like the metropolis in the first episode of *Mighty Atom*. Scaffolding for new skyscrapers, highways, subways, and high-speed train lines snaked across city and countryside at a breakneck pace in preparation for a special event that would signal a defeated nation's re-acceptance into global society: the 1964 Tokyo Olympics. With the space race in full swing, the idea that hover-cars and intelligent ro-bots might soon be zipping along the elevated highways threading between Tokyo's steel-and-glass towers didn't seem far-fetched. (Nor, thanks to the widely broadcast Anpo protests, did the idea that protests might be happening on those same streets.)

Mighty Atom perfectly captured youngsters' excitement about the future. Born in a postwar baby boom, they were too young to re-member wartime deprivations, and grew up amid an economy grow-ing by leaps and bounds. At the show's peak more than 40 percent of Japanese households tuned in, a figure rivaling the viewership of the Olympic broadcasts. In getting to the airwaves first, the cartoon established both the business model and the artistic conventions that fuel Japan's animation industry even today, more than a half century later: giant-sized eyes, wild hairstyles, theatrical poses, lin-gering static shots. It also introduced the world to a new word: *anime*, proudly coined by the show's creator to distinguish his creation from theatrical and imported *animeshon*, as the animated medium was pronounced in Japanese.

This wasn't idle vanity. The show really didn't easily slot into the pattern of any other nation's cartoons. *Silly Symphony* or *Looney Tunes* this wasn't, nor even a sitcom-y *The Jetsons*. Named after the fear-some power that ended the war, yet cushioned by cartoonish curves, *Mighty Atom* helped contextualize a future unfolding so quickly that even grown-ups were struggling to keep up. Whiplashing from zany sight gags to serious social commentary and back provided the tem-plate for anime both as a new form of entertainment and as a power-ful new pop-cultural tool: Disney with a biting edge. From the very first episode of this very first televised anime production, young viewers were presented with the fundamental conundrums of advanced technological societies. The same fearsome energies that obliterated Hiroshima and Nagasaki might be harnessed for peace. Technology can be thrilling, but so too can it be dangerous and alienating. Progress often came with winners and losers. Authority figures don't always know best. Changing things might necessitate taking to the streets. In distilling these complexities into a simple dramatic conflict between good guys and bad guys, *Mighty Atom* promised children that no matter how weird things got, a kind heart had the power to change them—even if that heart was a miniaturized atomic reactor instead of flesh and blood.

Thematically and visually, *Mighty Atom* provided the road map for every broadcast anime to come. Refined by generations of successors, manga comics and televised anime would evolve from simple methods for keeping children entertained into vibrant mediums of expression. They would stoke the dreams of the young, provide surprising nourishment for social movements, and later emerge as a cherished counterpoint to Western fantasies. The peculiar universality of anime's appeal made it both entertainment and something more: a method for transmitting cultural values. In 2003, the world still wouldn't have hover-cars or flying robots. Yet that year would mark a moment that would have seemed equally far-fetched to the audiences of 1963. In a measure of anime's sophistication and growing global influence, America's Academy of Motion Picture Arts and Sciences awarded the Oscar for Best Animated Feature Film to an anime called *Spirited Away*. But that moment of glory for the animators of Japan lay many years in the future.

IN THE ANIME, Atom's father was a mad scientist named Dr. Tenma. In reality, he was the brainchild of a comic-book artist named Osamu Tezuka, who was born into a prominent Osaka family in 1928. Tezuka's wealth gave him the freedom to indulge in his twin passions growing up: going to see the Takarazuka Revue, a popular all-

Mighty Atom gave technology a face anyone could love.

female troupe famed for its florid gender-bending musical productions, and watching the animated films of Walt Disney. From the Revue he would learn of melodrama and the power of feminine heroes; from Uncle Walt, he would adopt stylistic conventions like rounded forms, oversized eyes, and the use of anthropomorphic woodland creatures as protagonists. His fascination bordered on obsession: Catching up to five showings a day, Tezuka later watched *Snow White and the Seven Dwarfs* 50 times and *Bambi* more than 130 times during their theatrical runs in Japan. That he immersed himself in these foreign fantasies was a testament to how few domestically produced animated cartoons existed in the Japan of the day. (In 1941, the imperial military screened a copy of *Fantasia,* discovered aboard a captured American transport ship, for propaganda filmmakers. The idea was that they might better know the enemy. It seems to have worked. One of the men in attendance was so moved by its craftsmanship that he burst into tears at the finale.)

As World War II drew to a close in the summer of 1945, Tezuka slogged through the medical program at Osaka Imperial University. In spite of failing out of high school—he'd spent all day, every day, drawing—he still managed to pass the grueling entrance exams. The fact that he, like every able-bodied young man in the nation, was sure to be drafted if he didn't make it into college undoubtedly provided powerful motivation. Whip-smart but an indifferent student, Tezuka redoubled his drawing efforts in the halls of higher education. Years later he would parody this time in autobiographical manga. In one, a med student named "Osamu" gets caught drawing pornography on campus; in another, a professor begs him to quit medicine for cartoons, lest he kill a future patient.

Tezuka was ideally positioned to take advantage of the advice. With Tokyo's publishing industry thrown into total disarray by the firebombing of the city, dozens of tiny publishers from Tokyo's eternal rival, Osaka, rushed in to fill the gap. Osaka, Japan's second-largest city, was the nation's capital in the seventh and eighth centuries; its earthy, pragmatic merchant culture served and continues to serve as a foil to Tokyo's polish and glamour. (The Osaka dialect, considered rougher around the edges than cosmopolitan Tokyo-ese, is the de facto idiom of choice for Japanese comedians today.)

Osaka, too, had seen its share of incendiaries. One of them had in fact very narrowly avoided killing Tezuka, who had been assigned to fire-watching duty with a high school spotter brigade. (How differently would postwar Japanese pop culture have turned out had the bomb found its mark?) In spite of it all, Osaka was first to restart the presses. Perhaps sensing the same pent-up demand for play that energized Matsuzo Kosuge to release his tin toy jeep only months after the war's end, these early postwar publishers focused not on literature but on a form of manga called *kashi-hon*: pulpy comic books for children, loaned out for a fee through neighborhood pay libraries, something akin to the video rentals of their day.

These were not very sophisticated operations. "They would barely even read the work, and it would go straight to publishing, which meant that in terms of content, you could make and create whatever you wanted," recalled the artist Yoshihiro Tatsumi, Tezuka's contemporary and rival. Newspapers of the day railed against vulgar comics filled with ninja and samurai gangs, with op-eds gravely warning of content that "will make your hair stand on end." Predictably, none of this grown-up hand-wringing stanched a young public's ravenous hunger for escapist content, making cheap manga a perfect platform for artists both established and aspiring.

Tezuka made his long-form debut at the age of eighteen in January of 1947 with a fast-paced, two-hundred-page adventure called *Shin Takarajima* (*New Treasure Island*). It was based on a script by a veteran cartoonist and animator named Shichima Sakai, who'd taken

In comparison to its predecessors, *Shin Takarajima* looked almost like the storyboard to a film.

the promising young Tezuka under his wing. Guided by his mentor, Tezuka teased out the action over many panels, making the manga read more like a movie than like the funny papers. In an era when publishing a thousand copies was considered a big deal, it would go on to sell a stunning four hundred thousand with absolutely no marketing save word of mouth. Tezuka received nothing beyond the three thousand yen he'd been paid to draw the pages. That was par for the course. But Sakai had quietly retouched many of the faces before handing the pages off to the publisher, a slight Tezuka would never forgive.

Shin Takarajima represented a revolutionary moment for Japanese comics. In the twenties, artists inspired by American political cartoons and Sunday funnies began producing their own strips for monthly magazines. During the war years, however, censoring authorities reduced manga to harmless family fare or funny-paper propaganda with "plotlines" like "increasing production in the name of our fallen hero, Admiral Yamamoto!"

Now artists could express themselves once again. Tezuka and Sakai's creation pioneered what came to be called story-driven manga, unlocking new doors for illustrated entertainment through the intensity and seriousness of its execution. Through its unexpected popularity, thrilling new ideas rippled across the comics industry: that comics could be more than silly diversions; that actions didn't need to fit into a single panel, or even a single page; and that you could tease stories out over hundreds of pages, like a novel. It made manga feel a lot less like pulp and more like a worthy alternative to literature and film.

Because they were printed on cheap paper and kept in circulation until they fell apart, few copies of this seminal work in comics history have survived into the modern era; for a seventies reissue, Tezuka redrew the entire thing from scratch, and left Sakai's name off the cover for good measure. A true replica of the original would only be reprinted in 2008, many years after Tezuka's death.

As the locus of the manga publishing industry shifted to a rapidly rebuilding Tokyo, Tezuka followed in 1952. Somewhat incredibly, he'd managed to pass his medical program's final exams and complete a yearlong hospital residency—all while juggling deadlines for three different boys' magazines. Though wealthy both by birth and from his increasingly popular manga work, Tezuka chose to live in a no-frills flophouse called the Tokiwa-so. In this grubby crash pad for the city's up-and-coming comic illustrators, Tezuka basked in adulation and collaborations with fellow artists. He shared freely of his artistic and business knowledge and paid starving colleagues to assist him in meeting his crushing deadlines. More than a few of those Tezuka took under his wing would later become stars of the manga world. Their work reached more children than ever before, thanks to the emerging new medium of weekly comics anthologies, including *Weekly Shonen Magazine* and *Shonen Sunday*—both of which launched in 1959 and quickly replaced rental libraries as the medium of choice for comics artists and readers throughout Japan.

Absurdly prolific, Tezuka maintained numerous series, in a mind-bending array of genres. In addition to his mainstay, the science fiction of *Mighty Atom*, he added Disneyesque animal dramas like *Jungle Emperor* (later released abroad as *Kimba the White Lion*) and romantic adventures for young girls like *Princess Knight*, the tale of a beautiful princess who masquerades as a prince to fight for her kingdom. His ever-present work came to dominate the comics magazines.

However, even as his style reached peak influence, a new generation of artists began chafing against the pervasiveness of Tezuka's cartoonish melodramas set in imaginary neverlands. They dreamed of using the medium to explore themes more suited to their own tastes and experiences. To differentiate their darker, moodier work from manga intended for little boys and girls, these new creators dubbed it *gekiga*—literally "dramatic pictures," but more colloquially "graphic novels." Its appearance would quite literally shift the direction of Japanese comics, dramatically expanding the potential of the medium.

The term was dreamed up by an ambitious twenty-four-year-old artist named Yoshihiro Tatsumi, who in 1957 began placing it on the title pages of the comics he penned, to accentuate his preferred hard-boiled themes. Six years younger than Tezuka, Tatsumi came of age during the occupation in a neighborhood not far from Tezuka's home. He revered *Shin Takarajima* as a sacred text and had even visited the older artist for advice. But Tatsumi and his friends felt that a certain spark had faded from Tezuka's work after he moved to the big city and abandoned long-form storytelling for serials. In 1959, Tatsumi convinced six other artists to join him in a collective he called the Gekiga Workshop. Their first act was to mail out a postcard manifesto announcing their existence to publishers, newspapers, editors, and fellow artists—including Tezuka himself. Its concluding lines read:

The supersonic growth of film, radio, and television in recent years has spawned a new form of story-driven manga that we call gekiga. There is a demand for entertainment intended for adolescents, one unfulfilled because there has never been a forum for such content. These readers are gekiga's target audience.

The Gekiga Workshop's first project, a monthly comics anthology called *Matenrow* (*Skyscraper*), found an eager market in the rapidly fading rental libraries. Gone was Tezuka's theatrically whimsical style, with all its cartoonish characters and their pratfalls and sight gags. In its place was a new, grittier form of illustrated storytelling filled with shadowy contrasts, sharp linework, and seething adolescent energy. *Matenrow* looked like nothing that had come before. The covers were lurid: full-color close-ups of hands gripping chains, lonely railway crossings, automatic pistols. So too the content, with contributions including titles such as "Murder Incorporated," "The Night's First Customer," and "Blow It Up with Dynamite." Stories involving hit men, dirty cops, and duplicitous dames predominated. Some of the art was so rough-hewn it resembled sketchwork, as though the artists were hastily penning the panels beneath their desks while the violence unfolded around them.

Matenrow's simple but evocative title reflected a dramatic shift in the way many Japanese were living their lives. At the end of World War II, the vast majority of the population dwelled in rural areas, many of them refugees from the firebombings of major cities. By 1970, nearly three-quarters of Japanese citizens would live in industrial centers such as Tokyo, Osaka, Kobe, and Nagoya. America had once experienced a similar process of urbanization, but it had played out over the course of a century. In postwar Japan, the de-

Matenrow set a new standard for illustrated cool.

mands of rapid industrialization compressed the mass migration into just a quarter of the time.

Tatsumi and his comrades weren't the only ones making a splash among savvier readers. So too was the work of Sanpei Shirato, creator of the 1959 rental-library manga *Ninja Bugeicho* (*Arts of the Ninja*) and 1964's gekiga *Kamui-den* (*The Legend of Kamui*). Shirato had grown up during the war years watching his father, an avant-garde painter, repeatedly harassed by the police for his liberal beliefs. Deeply mistrustful of authority figures, Shirato penned stories so steeped in leftist social commentary that later activists would recommend them as a substitute for reading Marx. Set in samurai times, both *Ninja Bugeicho* and *Kamui-den* flipped the usual script by portraying Japan's legendary warriors as brutal oppressors of a long-suffering peasant class, with antihero ninja playing both sides off each other for their own ends. The battles were often literal bloodbaths, Shirato splattering his pages by blowing through an ink-soaked brush held over the paper. His moody linework, meticulously choreographed martial arts scenes, ferocious violence, and defiantly anticapitalist worldview deeply resonated with a new generation of young city dwellers disillusioned by the promises of Japan's economic miracle.

The vast majority of these newcomers were young men, recruited in the countryside and brought into big cities via the system of chartered "employment trains," which ran every year from 1954 to 1975. As the trains appeared each graduation season, rural station platforms filled with families bidding tearful farewells to their teenaged children. Many were compelled by economic necessity to enter the workforce directly out of middle school. Gekiga's portrayals of antiheroes and alienation, punctuated by copious amounts of sex and violence, deeply resonated with this rapidly swelling demographic of adolescent blue-collar workers. Living in unfamiliar urban surroundings far from their families, they hungered for stimulation, entertainment, and simple human connection. Working long shifts in construction, factories, or the service industry left little time for building social lives. Gekiga offered a cheap and convenient escape.

The Gekiga Workshop lasted but three years before disagreements over direction drove its members their separate ways in 1960, but the die was cast: Japanese adolescents were jumping ship to gekiga-inspired content in droves. Contrast this to America, where concerns over juvenile delinquency led to the establishment of the draconian Comics Code of 1954. It reads like a mirror-world doppelgänger of Tatsumi's declaration, demanding the elimination of "lurid, unsavory, gruesome illustrations," insisting that "crime is depicted as a sordid and unpleasant activity," declaring "sex perversion" and even the concept of "seduction" as off-limits, and stipulating that "in every instance good shall triumph over evil." The Comics Code relegated a generation of American comic-book talent to the role of babysitters.

Not so in Japan, where artists had free rein so long as their work sold, allowing them to wholeheartedly embrace this dark new alternative to the mainstream.

TEZUKA PACED AROUND his office, reading dozens of gekiga borrowed from the pay libraries by his assistants for study. Insecure by nature, he viewed the proliferation of these gritty works as an existential threat to his hard-won hegemony over the comics world. After receiving the Gekiga Workshop's manifesto, he published a furious missive entitled "To New Children's Manga Artists," chastising the newcomers for abdicating their supposed duty in entertaining kids. "Besides," he couldn't resist adding, "your drawings aren't good enough to withstand adult scrutiny anyway." *So there!* Still, the existence of rivals chewed at Tezuka. He grew more and more agitated as he paced, absorbed in stories so unlike his own—until he tumbled down a flight of stairs.

He emerged physically unscathed, but the writing was on the wall. Hate mail from readers poured in, and his own assistants were reading gekiga for pleasure in their spare time! Tezuka plunged into an uncharacteristic funk. It proved so deep that he consulted a therapist, a practice virtually unheard of in the Japan of the day. The doctor told him the only cure was a three-year vacation. When this triggered a panic attack, the doctor coolly advised him to get married, too. Back at his studio, fuming over the impossibility of his situation, Tezuka worked himself into such a lather that he tripped down the same flight of steps again.

Ironically, this personal low point coincided with a breakthrough moment, when Tezuka's work began attracting the attention of Japan's fledgling postwar animation industry. In 1958, Toei Doga, the nation's biggest studio, approached Tezuka to collaborate on an animated feature based on his manga *Boku no Son Goku* (*My Sun Wukong*). Serialized from 1952 to 1959 in a popular comics magazine, it was loosely based on a sixteenth-century Chinese classic called *Journey to the West*. The action-packed folk story showcased the adventures of the Monkey King, a superpowered simian who can walk, talk, and fight better than any man. (Three decades later, the artist Akira Toriyama would mine the same myth to create the manga and anime series *Dragon Ball*.) Tezuka's popular adaptation recast the legendary hero with Disneyesque flair, with huge Mickey ears framing oversized eyes and a ball nose. Toei, aiming to appeal to children both in Japan and around the world, seized on the character as the perfect protagonist for its newest feature-length animated film.

Founded three years prior with the explicit aim of becoming the Disney of the Far East, Toei Doga was Japan's largest and most successful animation company. For Tezuka, their offer would, at first glance, seem a dream job. He had toyed with becoming an animator as early as his university days; a rejection by a Tokyo animation studio in 1946 had channeled his energies into comics instead. Now Toei was essentially offering him another chance. He would be charged with what was (and remains) the most important aspect in creating a cartoon in Japan or anywhere else: drafting the storyboards. A series of sequential drawings that articulate the flow of the production scene by scene, the storyboards are the heart and soul of any animated production—and a cherished chance for artists to leave their unique creative fingerprints on a project.

But Tezuka was no longer a wide-eyed student desperate for recognition. In spite of his hand-wringing over competition from gekiga rivals, he remained Japan's top-earning comics artist by a wide margin. With a packed schedule and long used to operating on his own timetables, by his own admission he "didn't take the deadlines very seriously." After delivering the critical storyboards months late, he found many of his original ideas second-guessed by staff who had been forced to make creative decisions without him.

Tezuka's pride may have been wounded, but the result was a hit. Released in 1960, *Journey to the West* opened to raves among Japanese kids. One of its fans was a seven-year-old named Shigeru Miyamoto who, as a video game designer decades later, would use an ox that appears in the film as the inspiration for Bowser, the final boss of *Super Mario Bros.* An Americanized edition of the movie fared far less well. Heavily rewritten and sanitized of virtually all its Asian references, *Alakazam the Great* flopped so terrifically among Western audiences that it earned an entry in a 1978 bestseller called *The Fifty Worst Films of All Time (And How They Got That Way).*

Journey to the West's success belied troubles brewing within Toei Doga's eternally overworked and underpaid ranks. To make the film, each of the animators had been obligated to put in more than ninety hours a month of unpaid overtime to meet schedules. Now that the film was finished, they formed a union to petition the management for better working conditions. Meeting in secret at a nearby noodle shop, the animators prepared a thirty-one-point list of demands, ranging from higher salaries and more reasonable work schedules to the provision of food during mandatory overtime periods. The studio offered to discuss the suggestions, but after a year of tortuous negotiations, the only concession the union managed to extract was a single officially sanctioned fifteen-minute break every afternoon. In early December of 1961, the frustrated animators launched a series of two-hour work stoppages to press their points.

The standoff was a first for animators, but there was ample precedent for labor disputes in Japan. Unions had a long and storied history in the prewar years; crushed by the authorities during wartime, they were quickly revived and promoted by the U.S. occupation forces, who initially saw organized labor as a democratizing force. The honeymoon didn't last long, as the military grew alarmed by how enthusiastically workers were striking for better pay and working conditions. There were more than a hundred such actions in 1946 alone. On the eve of a national multi-industry strike organized for early 1947, General MacArthur suddenly reversed course and banned general strikes altogether. A working class struggling amid hunger and runaway inflation took this whiplash decision as a hypocritical slap in the face: the first crack in the façade of the benevolent liberating conqueror. "What kind of democracy is this?" demanded labor organizer Yashiro Ii of the occupation authorities. "Japanese workers are not American slaves!"

Those who toiled in the entertainment world were no exception. In early 1948, after a long series of failed negotiations, the union of

"They sent in everything but the battleships," recalled an actress involved with the 1948 strike at the Toho movie studios.

stagehands at Toei's rival, Toho, had locked themselves inside the company lot's soundstage. As they pressed for higher wages and more input into deciding production schedules, they transformed the tools of moviemaking into makeshift weapons. Special-effects technicians prepared paint bombs. Electricians modified rain machines into water cannons and rigged industrial fans to spew cayenne pepper powder at would-be strikebreakers. Among those who manned the barricades was a young Akira Kurosawa. It took two thousand riot police and the assistance of the U.S. Army's First Cavalry to oust the occupiers.

Even thirteen years later, in 1961, memories of the bitter, costly siege were fresh in the minds of industry insiders. Toei's animation corps were hardly agitating for violence; during the work stoppage, they gathered at the nearest train station to hand out leaflets accusing the studio of infringing on their human rights. But even such a gentle public airing of dirty laundry infuriated the president of Toei. At nine A.M. on December 5, he took the extraordinary step of locking the animation staff out of the studio.

The shutdown lasted only a few days before the management and the union reached an agreement, but the damage was done. Disenchanted with both the studio and their own union's compromises, veteran animators began to quit. Part of this was due to the fact that few believed anything would really change. But most of it was due to rumors of a new studio in town: Osamu Tezuka Productions, Animation Division, a spin-off of Tezuka's booming manga studio. Within a year it would be renamed Mushi Productions, *mushi* written with the kanji character for "bug," the same with which Tezuka spelled his given name of Osamu. It was a fitting name for a studio poised to become the gadfly of the cartoon establishment. But could Tezuka translate his skill with pen, ink, and paper to the silver screen? That remained an open question.

TEZUKA'S EXPERIENCE AT Toei had humbled him. He had learned that "human relationships far outweighed the art itself," as he later wrote. "Animation is a cooperative endeavor, the product of many specialists working in concert like clockwork. There is no room for lone wolves."

With this in mind, Tezuka did everything he could to build the most talented wolf pack he could find. At his new studio, launched from a room over his home office's garage in June of 1961, he paid two to three times Toei's average salaries, finally bringing top animators' incomes in line with those of other white-collar workers. He also offered much-appreciated perks like free lunches and afternoon snacks. This was a dream come true for long-suffering artists, who jumped ship from Toei in droves. There was one nagging issue: For many months after its inception, the studio didn't have any projects. There was nothing to work on save the promise of things to come. Even still, word of Japan's top comics artist launching an animation studio drew a great deal of public interest. In numerous interviews with the press, Tezuka ostentatiously parried comparisons to Disney. "What they're doing, basically, is children's literature," he told the magazine *Shukan Koron*. "Disney's fine for a starting point, but I'm confident I can take things to the next level"—an ironic turn of phrase for the man who had so railed against the mature themes of gekiga.

Tezuka funded everything out of his own pocket using the royalties from his comics, which he continued to draw at an undiminished pace. Mushi Production's first project, a forty-minute experimental film called *Tales of a Street Corner*, portrayed a bustling metropolis whose posters and signs come alive, only to be ravaged by jackbooted soldiers. Tezuka envisioned it both as a calling card to the industry and as a test bed for a new American technique called limited animation, which used the barest minimum of moving images to save cost and time. The end result was undeniably stylish. But an excruciatingly slow pace and heavy-handed moralizing made it unsuitable for mainstream audiences—or, it seems, professional ones. Sitting in the theater at the premiere was a new Toei employee by the name of Hayao Miyazaki. He was one of the replacements hired after the big defection of veteran animators to Mushi. The film's syrupy sentimentality so disgusted him, he later wrote, that chills ran down his spine.

"Drawing a salary from a company that wasn't making any money felt awful," recalled the animator Yusaku Sakamoto. "All of us in the animation division would go out drinking and try to come up with something that would turn a profit." Television commercials? Lucrative but boring. Movies? Most of the animators were refugees from Toei, and knew full well the grind of turning out full-length feature films. Eventually they settled on the idea of making "a manga for television"—in other words, an animated TV series. It wasn't such a crazy idea. The country was now the world's second-largest consumer of televisions behind the United States. And there was a precedent: *Popeye*. The television station TBS started broadcasting translations of the American animated shorts in 1959. It was huge, the sort of thing that compelled schoolkids to drop everything and dash for home right before it aired.

The more Sakamoto thought about it, the more sense it made. All they needed was a story. The obvious choice was *Mighty Atom*. Every kid knew it—it was Tezuka's most popular manga. Still running strong more than a decade after its debut, it had more than enough plotlines to keep an animated series going. And the best part was, they were practically already storyboarded out, right there on the pages of the comics. Yes, *Mighty Atom* was perfect. When Sakamoto and the staff presented the idea to Tezuka, he enthusiastically approved the project.

But scaling up to make a thirty-minute cartoon every week would require far more money than even a bestselling comic-book artist had in his coffers. Tezuka estimated that production costs would run in excess of a million yen an episode. Even with limited animation techniques, there was no getting around the fact that creating cartoons was incredibly time- and labor-intensive. This was, in fact, precisely why nobody in Japan had ever tried producing an animated series for television before, not even big studios like Toei. Potential investors balked at the costs involved.

What he needed was a sponsor. In a booming consumer economy like Japan's, there were plenty of companies interested in seeing their names featured prominently in the credits of popular television series. Everyone knew how popular Tezuka was. Making a cartoon based on a comic book as popular as *Mighty Atom* seemed like a no-brainer. The problem was that corporate sponsors were used to live-action shows, which could be made for far less than 500,000 yen an episode. "There's no way they'll invest three or even two times that amount in an untested show," lamented Tezuka.

After weeks of trying, only one sponsor showed a flicker of interest: A candy company called Meiji Seika. Desperate, Tezuka pledged to deliver each episode for just 550,000 yen, promising to make up any difference out of pocket. The company accepted, and Fuji Television green-lit the show. But echoing his experience on *Journey to the West*, the victory would prove bittersweet for Tezuka. "By modern standards—no, even by standards of the day—it was a stupidly low number," sighed Tezuka in his autobiography. He called it the biggest mistake of his career.

Mighty Atom was a success, proving the viability of domestically produced televised animation, but it also placed an arbitrarily low cap on budgets for decades to come, to the detriment of studios across Japan, his own included. The beloved hallmarks of Japanese animated fare—the striking of theatrical poses, the lingering freeze-frames, the limited ranges of motion—evolved from desperate cost-saving workarounds into the key factors that distinguish anime from content produced in other lands. But they are more than stylistic flourishes. They are the direct result of that fateful choice Tezuka made so many decades ago.

An English-dubbed version of *Mighty Atom*, retitled *Astro Boy*, debuted on America's NBC network in 1963. What intrigued NBC about *Mighty Atom* wasn't that it was groundbreaking. What they liked most was that it was cheap. Anything smacking of violence, mature themes, or Japanese content was carefully scrubbed out of the productions. If a buyer hears that the show is of Japanese origin, went the thinking of the day, he's going to think it must be chintzy. So it was that little Atom became Astro Boy, setting the pattern for later imports. Leo, the feline protagonist of Tezuka's *Jungle Emperor,* was rechristened as Kimba the White Lion. The hotshot driver Go Mifune turned into Speed Racer. And so on and so on. There wasn't any grand plan here. NBC had in fact stumbled across *Mighty Atom* entirely by accident, when one of its employees caught an episode in his hotel room during a trip to Tokyo. The question wasn't whether Japanese cartoons would revolutionize American tastes but rather if they could compete with *The Flintstones* for a fraction of the cost. Thus *Astro Boy* was less a flagship than a trial balloon. NBC didn't even run it on its home channel; it relegated it to smaller regional stations instead. *If we bomb with this,* execs thought, *at least we'll have kept our losses to a minimum.*

It didn't bomb. *Astro Boy* was a ratings hit, at least for the local stations that carried it. But this success did nothing to dissuade the industry powers that be that Japanese animation was anything more than a cheap alternative to superior American-made productions. This status quo would persist for many years. In concert with stilted, hastily dubbed English versions of monster movies like *Godzilla* and its even lower-budget brother *Gamera,* anime slotted neatly into a widespread postwar perception of things "made in Japan" as occasionally amusing and inevitably inferior.

In a personal triumph for Tezuka, *Astro Boy*'s ratings during the fall of its initial release handily beat those of *The Mickey Mouse Club.* Among its fans was the director Stanley Kubrick, who mailed a letter inviting Tezuka to collaborate on creating visual concepts for a new science fiction movie set in the first year of the twenty-first century. Overscheduled as always, Tezuka sent his regrets, but it is tempting to wonder how *2001: A Space Odyssey* might have turned out with a little of Tezuka's visual and comedic sensibilities injected into the mix.

• • •

"THE GOD OF COMICS." That's what fans and critics alike were calling Tezuka now, after an appellation bestowed upon him in a glowing 1964 profile written by the novelist Takeshi Kaiko. Through sheer drive and ambition, the artist was rapidly evolving from a creator into an institution. Mirroring the peripatetic energy of its founder, at its peak in 1966 Mushi Productions juggled the production of three animated series simultaneously for Japanese television: *Mighty Atom*, *The Wonder 3*, and *Jungle Emperor*, plus a *New Treasure Island* special and plans for *Princess Knight*.

Behind the scenes, however, Mushi Productions was in serious trouble. The problem was that Tezuka had always been more of an idea man than a businessman. In an industry ruled by precedent, the artificially low budget that he'd proposed to get *Mighty Atom* on the air solidified into conventional wisdom. If 550,000 yen an episode was good enough for a "god," how could mere mortals ask for more? Even more concerning for Tezuka was the undeniable fact that tastes were changing. While young children continued to consume traditional manga at an undiminished clip, adolescents overwhelmingly preferred

Empress Michiko and young Crown Prince Naruhito interacting with puppets of Mighty Atom and Professor Ochanomizu on a visit to the Tokyo Tower in 1965.

gekiga. By the late sixties, that darker, edgier form of illustrated storytelling had so thoroughly saturated the weekly comics magazines that it had started affecting children's fare, too. Bright and shiny heroes like Atom were looking increasingly outmoded. Forced to ratchet back its slate of programs, Mushi Productions ended the *Mighty Atom* show on New Year's Eve, 1966. Tezuka brought the manga series to a close in 1968.

To his credit, Tezuka made a concerted effort to evolve with the times. But as he attempted to channel the bolder, more grown-up themes of gekiga through his unique style of manga, his cartoonish-looking protagonists increasingly found themselves in situations that would have made his hero Walt Disney blush. "Those cute characters are dying! They're having sex!" wrote the child psychologist Tamaki Saito. "It makes you want to say, 'Sir, isn't this going a little too far?'" But the refined and the vulgar have long existed side by side in Japan; the revered nineteenth-century woodblock print artist Hokusai produced both the iconic *Great Wave off Kanagawa* and the delirious *Dream of the Fisherman's Wife,* in which a woman is portrayed in erotic congress with a giant octopus. Still, fans' acceptance of Tezuka's explorations did not translate into influence. Adolescent and young adult readers weren't interested in his melodramatically cartoonish characters, no matter how naughty the situations into which they were being thrown. What they craved was the gritty stimulation of the gekiga world.

One of their favorites was a 1968 gekiga entitled *Ashita no Jo* (*Tomorrow's Joe*). Written by Ikki Kajiwara and illustrated by Tetsuya Chiba, it portrayed a juvenile delinquent's rise from the Tokyo slums to become the nation's greatest boxer. The series occupies roughly the same spot in the Japanese collective imagination that Sylvester Stallone's *Rocky* does in the American; it grew so popular that when Joe's archrival, Riki-ishi, died in the ring, more than seven hundred fans gathered for a faux funeral held in the offices of *Shonen Magazine.* American sailors introduced the sport to Japan with a series of public exhibitions held in 1854, and while it never replaced sumo wrestling in the hearts of the Japanese, it quietly flourished on the edges of the mainstream, making it the perfect canvas for an outsider hero. On the surface, *Tomorrow's Joe* was simply a gripping sports story. But those so inclined could read into it a metaphor for Japan's postwar struggles—or a parable for the working man, fighting his way through a social system stacked against him. Drawn using stylishly rough-hewn art to portray the sweaty, bloody brutality of training and matches, *Tomorrow's Joe*'s cast were the polar op-

In the trials of boxer Jo Yabuki, a generation of young Japanese saw their own struggle.

posite of Tezuka's polished and cute characters.

That increasing numbers of young adults embraced illustrated entertainment as a form of leisure was fueled in part by the depth and quality of the work. Unfettered by anything like the American Comics Code, Japanese artists pushed the limits again and again to establish manga and gekiga as the planet's most vibrant illustrated art form. But its popularity was also due to the fact that there wasn't a lot for cash-strapped laborers or students to do in the Tokyo of the era. The city's entertainment options were far more limited than they are today; cheap diversions such as convenience stores, video game arcades, and karaoke rooms lay decades in the future. While the mass media enthused about the widespread adoption of "the three c's"—color televisions, coolers (air conditioners), and cars—this holy trinity of the modern lifestyle remained far beyond the means of poor students or young laborers who'd arrived on one of those employment trains with little save the clothes on their backs. A 1968 survey asking young men how they spent their free time within the last three months was topped by "reading," followed by "drinking at home." A large proportion of that reading took the form of comic books, and gekiga in particular. Stuck on the outside of a rapidly growing consumer society, many of these same young men began adding another pastime to their leisure lives: rioting in the streets.

The passage of the Anpo in 1960 dealt a serious blow to the movement that had so fiercely opposed it. Wracked by doubt and recrimination, Zengakuren—the league of student governments

that had smashed down the gates of the Diet during those protests—
shattered into warring factions known as sects. These smaller
groups, lacking the unified sense of purpose that had driven the original protest movement, shed members over the first half of the 1960s.
A 1964 protest of a U.S. nuclear submarine docking at the Port of
Yokosuka attracted only a handful of student activists. In a 1965 poll
of what students enjoyed most about college life, the majority answered, "Clubs and personal hobbies." Only 1 percent replied, "Par-
ticipating in the student movements."

Yet there was a growing sense of frustration among students of
the era. Groomed since childhood by parents and teachers for academic excellence, they had spent many a sleepless night cramming
to pass the entrance exams for the best schools. But their expectations were betrayed as a baby boom–fueled surge in student enroll-
ment pushed university services beyond the breaking point. Students
complained of being forced to attend "mass-produced lectures," sitting shoulder to shoulder in jam-packed halls listening to cookie-
cutter lessons delivered via impersonal amplification systems. When
they graduated, they found it all but impossible to land white-collar
jobs. "We all had high hopes when we entered university, but the
product we received was extremely shoddy," one activist wrote. "The
overwhelming increase in students has greatly diminished the status
of university graduates, and graduating from university no longer
guarantees employment at a large company." What was the point of
it all?

Amid the growing dissatisfaction, a new youth movement began
to coalesce.

THE LITERAL AND metaphorical spark came in August of 1967. It was
a dramatic accident in which a tanker train laden with American
military jet fuel exploded just outside of Tokyo's Shinjuku Station. In
those flames, activists saw their nation's complicity with America's
war in Southeast Asia. Two months later a Zengakuren sect launched
an assault on Haneda Airport in an attempt to prevent Prime Minis-

ter Eisaku Sato from visiting Saigon. A force of students some two thousand strong, clad in construction helmets and armed with two-by-fours, battled armored riot police to a standstill on the streets leading to the airport. Three hundred were arrested, seven hundred injured, and one protester killed as the authorities wrested control of the situation.

Images of the violence, broadcast on the nightly news in vivid color, energized a new generation of young people to participate in political rallies. As the sects saw a surge in membership, previously warring factions made alliances and reunited once again. In the summer of 1968, students at the University of Tokyo and Nihon University merged into a new organization calling itself Zenkyoto (The All-Campus Joint Struggle Councils). On October 21 of that same year, a coalition of ten thousand workers and radical students marched on Shinjuku Station, occupying the building and halting all traffic for three hours. Invoking a long-dormant and soon to be hugely controversial public order law, the authorities dispatched three thousand riot police to sweep them from the area. As onlookers spontaneously joined the growing fray, the mob grew to twenty thousand in size. They smashed windows, ripped benches from their moorings, hurled bricks at police, and set vehicles afire. More than seven hundred protesters were hauled off to jail. Today the incident is known as the Shinjuku Riot.

These disillusioned young elites proved fertile ground for sects recruiting new members. In the West, folk songs and protest rock provided the soundscape for young activists. Not so in Japan. Even for those who could afford guitars or record players, cramped quarters—urban housing of the sixties was often denigrated as "rabbit hutches"—generally precluded them from playing or listening to music in personal spaces. Many activists turned instead to left-wing folk anthems such as "The Internationale" that were sung in unison at rallies and *utagoe-kissa* (sing-along coffee shops, a precursor of karaoke clubs). But for the average Japanese youth, the heartbeat of

Train platforms transformed into battlegrounds during the Shinjuku Riot.

their generation wasn't measured in musical beats. It was metered out in the panels of comic books.

This did not go unnoticed by society at large. "The youth of Zengakuren developed their revolutionary movement from the gekiga of Shirato Sanpei," observed the novelist Yukio Mishima. A slogan published in the Waseda University student newspaper put it even more succinctly: *Migite ni Janaru, hidarite ni Magajin* ("[left-leaning] *Asahi Journal* in our right hands, *Shonen Magazine* in our left"). When Zenkyoto-led student groups seized control of buildings at the University of Tokyo and Nihon University in 1968, erecting barricades to keep officials and the police out, illustrated entertainment helped ease the tedium of weeks and months spent stuck inside makeshift fortresses. "Because the widely held notion was that manga were for children, reports of students reading manga behind the barricades were initially met with surprise," writes the sociologist Eiji Oguma. "Manga characters were even used as mascots for the student uprisings, appearing on placards and flyers or even painted on activists' helmets to identify their sect affiliation." Taking direct inspiration from the animated and live-action television heroes of their child-hood, participants cast themselves in the role of the good guys in an epic battle against the forces of evil.

The occupation began after a demonstration by medical students to protest the working conditions of interns. It quickly snowballed into a broader movement that welcomed anyone with an axe to grind against the establishment. Continuing over the remainder of the year, and getting a great deal of media coverage in the process, the occupation inspired similar actions at hundreds of universities and high schools across Japan. Although the sight of passionate young students sticking it to the Man initially elicited sympathy from a press and public still smarting over the Anpo debacle, the mood quickly soured as the activists failed to articulate anything in the way of actionable demands. "We only worried about justifications after we had taken over the campus," admitted one Zenkyoto member. The animation director Mamoru Oshii, who was a high school activist at the time, put things even more bluntly. "We didn't care about Marxist philosophy," he said in 2016. "We just wanted to wreck everything."

This couldn't last, and it didn't. In January of 1969, more than eight thousand riot police marched on the University of Tokyo barricades under a rain of Molotov cocktails, acid-filled bottles, and chunks of concrete that students had ripped from the structures they occupied. Police responded with fire hoses and tear gas. The siege lasted ten hours; by the end of it, 370 students had been taken into custody and much of the university's infrastructure left in ruins. Before the riots, law enforcement traditionally treaded very lightly on campuses, wary of backlash from citizens and government. Now lawmakers hastily passed euphemistically named "university management laws" giving police more leeway to suppress disturbances on campuses. The failures of the campus uprisings drove the most fervent believers in the politics of the movement to increasingly desperate behavior. In September of 1969, a radical group calling itself the *Sekigun-ha* (Red Army Faction) declared war on Japan.

• • •

EARLY ONE MORNING in March of 1970, a group of eight young men and one woman boarded a Japan Airlines flight at Haneda Airport bound for the city of Fukuoka. After takeoff, the nine rose from their seats. Unsheathing concealed katana and pipe bombs they had smuggled aboard, they took control of the aircraft, tying passengers into their seats with rope for good measure. Leader Takamaro Tamiya was twenty-seven; the youngest member just seventeen. After landing at Fukuoka, the hijackers released a handful of the 129 passengers. Then they forced the pilot to set a course for Pyongyang, North Korea. After an unintended stop in Seoul, where the hostages were released, they finally arrived at their destination. The idea was to fly from there to Cuba for training to launch a Communist revolution in Japan.

Ironically, the plot's mastermind, Takaya Shiomi, never made it aboard the flight. Arrested in a police sweep two weeks before the hijacking was to take place, Shiomi's capture forced Tamiya to lead the attack in his place. Just before boarding the flight with the other eight attackers, Tamiya mailed a letter to a newspaper taking credit for the hijacking. It ended with the cryptic declaration "Never forget: We are *Tomorrow's Joe*." In a memoir published after spending eighteen years in a Japanese prison, Shiomi reminisced openly about the group's influences. "We certainly read a lot of manga. We loved *Shonen Magazine, Manga Sunday; Tomorrow's Joe* and Shirato Sanpei's *Ninja Bugeicho* were perennial favorites. . . . I suppose you could say we students were the beginning of the gekiga generation."

Shiomi served eighteen years in prison for his role in the hijacking. Arguably, he was the lucky one. In their haste, the hijackers hadn't planned any further than taking the plane. Neither North Korea nor Cuba was aware of their intentions. North Korean authorities allowed the nine in, listened to their plan, and promptly forbade them from leaving. One died in an escape attempt; two managed to find a way out but were sentenced to lengthy prison terms upon their return to Japan; and the remainder lived out their lives as permanent guests of the impoverished and hermetic nation.

The month after the hijacking, Mushi Productions released its newest project, the very first one on its slate not based on an Osamu Tezuka manga. It was an animated television series based on *Tomorrow's Joe.*

Already many months in the making before the incident, the project had been devised by a group of young upstarts in the office eager to modernize Mushi's slate of productions. Many other animation studios had entered the marketplace after the surprise success of *Mighty Atom,* and Mushi struggled mightily to land sales in an increasingly competitive marketplace. Casting about for less crowded markets, the studio turned to erotica, producing 1969's *A Thousand and One Nights* and 1970's *Cleopatra: Queen of Sex,* which later vied with *Fritz the Cat* for the title of first X-rated cartoon to be released in the States. Both proved costly failures, plunging the studio deep into the red.

One might think Tezuka would see the acquisition of *Tomorrow's Joe,* a rival artist's biggest hit, as something of a personal coup. Ever competitive, he all but ignored the team as they went about making what turned into a very successful show. During its run, Tezuka stepped down as company president to focus full time on his comics work; shortly after the final episode aired in 1972, key members of the production staff defected to launch their own firm, Madhouse. The success wasn't enough to dig Mushi out of debt, and the studio declared bankruptcy in 1973. When NBC attempted to return the negatives of *Astro Boy* after its run in the United States, the executor of Mushi's affairs couldn't scrape together enough to pay the shipping. The film was destroyed instead.

WHEN TEZUKA DIED at the age of sixty in 1989 from stomach cancer, the entire nation mourned the passing of the God of Comics. The only voice of dissent arose from Hayao Miyazaki, who was at the time still basking in the mainstream success of his animated film *My*

Neighbor Totoro. In a scathing obituary, Miyazaki declared that "in terms of animation, everything that Mr. Tezuka talked about or emphasized was wrong." He was referring partly to the artistic compromises, such as "limited animation" techniques, that Tezuka embraced to speed along the production process, but mainly to the precedent of absurdly low budgets that Tezuka had established. The aftereffects of that momentous decision continue to reverberate through the anime industry today. Established veterans who illustrate the "key frames" of an animated production are able to command high sums for their talents. But in a legacy of those earliest days, the average animator working in the trenches—the "in-betweeners" in industry parlance, so named for their task of producing the many still frames of art needed to fill in the action between the key images—are paid just a few hundred yen per frame. According to a 2019 study, animators in their early twenties earn paychecks averaging just 128,800 yen (roughly $1,100) a month—literal poverty wages.

In spite of all the public accolades, there was no question that the average popular manga or anime production owed more to gekiga-inspired fare than to Tezuka's pioneering style of illustrated storytelling. Yet through it all he never once gave up, never stopped evolving. In a testament to his incredible skill and flexibility as an artist, Tezuka incorporated gekiga art styles and storytelling conventions to powerful effect in later successes: the 1973 hit *Black Jack,* a gritty, decade-long manga series focusing on an underground surgeon-for-hire, and the time-tripping Buddhist epic *Phoenix* (1967–1988), which Tezuka considered his greatest artistic achievement. And while fans may have found his traditional characters old-fashioned (a 1980 television reboot of *Mighty Atom* in full color failed to match the ratings of the original), in a big-picture sense one might say that they paved the way for another emerging business: a burgeoning market for children's products featuring cute kitty cats and other characters. But that is a story for another chapter.

It is impossible to imagine anime or manga existing in the form it does today without Tezuka, Japan's first international content creator. The appearance of so many rivals over the years is a testament both to the sheer power of his creative force and to the role illustrated entertainment played in nourishing the rise of an entirely new creative class in Japan. In choosing to express themselves through manga and anime, young adults established these art forms as something more than entertainment: a new type of identity for young outsiders and rebels. As we will see, the ways in which Japan's youth rebelled would change over the decades to come, but the use of illustrated storytelling as the medium of choice for those outside the system would remain a constant, both at home and abroad.

In the meantime, one might wonder: What were the grown-ups doing while all this was going on? The answer is simple: They were singing.

3

EVERYBODY IS A STAR

The Karaoke Machine
1971

Hell is full of musical amateurs.
—GEORGE BERNARD SHAW

ON A SWELTERING summer evening in 1971, a group of musicians gather in a public hall in the red-light district of the city of Kobe. They aren't here for practice or performance. They're here because they are very, very angry. This is an emergency meeting of the Sannomiya chapter of the Kobe Musical Artists Association. Sannomiya is the epicenter of the port city's nightlife, home to some four thousand drinking establishments crammed into a cluster of streets and alleys just a kilometer in radius, ranging from opulent cabarets to hole-in-the-wall dives.

The meeting has been convened by a group of musicians called *hiki-katari*. The word means something like "player-singers." They are freelance musicians who specialize in sing-alongs, retuning their performances on the fly to match the singing abilities and sobriety levels of paying customers. This isn't unique to Kobe; other places have their sing-along specialists, too. In many cities, itinerant artists called *nagashi* (drifters) ply the sing-along trade. The Kobe twist is that its *hiki-katari* tend to play in bands that stay put, contracting with a bar to play for an evening, a week, or a month to draw clientele.

Tonight's atmosphere is tense. The *hiki-katari* believe there is a traitor in their midst, and they want justice. The target of their fury is a man named Daisuke Inoue, or more precisely, a device he invented. It's called the 8 Juke. It is a cube-shaped vending machine, sized just right for a bar's countertop. But the product it dispenses isn't food or drink. It is song: instrumental numbers at the drop of a coin, the accompaniment for customers who croon into an attached microphone. For the last few months, Inoue has been placing 8 Jukes in snack bars and pubs throughout Sannomiya. Patrons love them. They can't get enough of the unprecedented novelty of hearing their own voices come through speakers, right along with their favorite tunes.

Inoue isn't an engineer or a tinkerer. He'd very nearly flunked out of his vocational high school. He had an electrician friend build the gadgets to his specifications. But he knows his *hiki-katari* adversaries well, because he is one of them. In fact, he is one of the best. Local customers call him "Dr. Sing-along" for his almost magical ability to keep up with their drunken warbling. He'd created the machine for a purely pragmatic reason: He was in such demand that he was having to turn down requests for private gigs. This didn't just eat into his income; it upset his most loyal and deep-pocketed customers. To Inoue, the 8 Juke was a service, an electronic doppelgänger, on call whenever someone felt the urge to sing and he couldn't be around. His fellow *hiki-katari* saw it differently. To them, Inoue's machine was a monster, proliferating through Sannomiya's dives like the enchanted brooms in *Fantasia*'s "The Sorcerer's Apprentice." As far as they were concerned, every yen that customers put into the things was a yen stolen out of their goddamn pockets.

"You tryin' to put us out of business, you bastard?" yells one from the audience. Inoue, like most who worked late nights in the red-light district, was a veteran of dealing with rough customers. He'd played everywhere, from ritzy cabarets to stripteases. Once, he even helped fend off a backstage assault from a pair of junior yakuza who'd been kicked out for manhandling a stripper, watching in awe as a bandmate brought a heavy *shogi* chessboard crashing down on an attacker's head. They'd all wound up in jail that night. What was a bunch of angry musicians compared to that? Quietly absorbing the abuse, he waited patiently for an opening.

Entirely self-taught, Inoue is no one's idea of a musical prodigy. At thirty-one, he still plays the keyboard with just two fingers and the thumbs of each hand. Yet he is also a hard worker who unflinchingly embraces his own shortcomings. He loves performing and has never known another job, never wanted one. He's worked the Kobe night scene for the entirety of his career, first as a backup drummer while still in high school, then later teaching himself the vibes and the Electone—one of the first electronic organs. Unable to read musical notation, he instead memorized by brute force a huge repertoire of hundreds of songs. Lacking any formal musical training, he compensates with affability and dependability. Unlike many other performers in Sannomiya, he doesn't drink—well, not too much, anyway, usually—nor does he touch drugs, and perhaps most important, he wholeheartedly embraces the business side of it all. He knows that music is money.

All this has helped Inoue grasp a key fact about the *hiki-katari*. Their craft was only partly about musicianship. Their real purpose was making the amateurs doing the singing feel good. If one simply stared down at their score and dutifully played the song as a trained musician, it would force the singer to try to keep up with their expertise. Inoue's illiteracy with sheet music freed his eyes to "sight-read" the singers and help them along. Picking up on cues from the way they sway, often unsteadily, or the shapes of their lips, Inoue lets the customers lead instead of the other way around. He knows they want to feel like pros themselves.

Suddenly, Inoue leaps from his chair.

"We're musicians!" he shouts. "We can change our playing to match every customer. Order-made! You gonna roll over and die 'cause of a stupid machine that plays the same way every time?"

There was a long silence. Suddenly one of the musicians broke it: "Yeah. Forget the machine."

The others nod in agreement. Karaoke would live to see another day, it seemed.

• • •

KARAOKE MACHINES WERE independently invented no less than five times in Japan between the years of 1967 and 1972, each version cobbled together by creators apparently unaware of the others' work.

The concept of singing along to recorded music was not unique to Japan. The Fleischer brothers' popular *Screen Songs,* sing-along cartoons featuring a bouncing ball over the lyrics, debuted in American theaters in 1929. A New York record company called Music Minus One sold instrumental albums for students of music in the fifties, and from 1961 to 1964 NBC aired a popular show called *Sing Along with Mitch* that invited audiences to join in at home. And the 8-track tapedeck, the mechanical "guts" of the first karaoke machines, was American technology, not Japanese.

The karaoke machine wasn't even the earliest mechanical rival for the services of human sing-along artists like the *nagashi* and *hiki-katari*. That would be the coin-operated jukebox—and this, too, was an import. First introduced to Japan by the American forces, by the sixties a juke was de rigueur at any cabaret, club, bar, or coffee shop, stocked by their owners with records for a clientele with an increasing taste for global music culture: French *chanson;* American jazz, folk, and soul; British rock and roll. These were more than just songs: Sony's chairman Akio Morita described the music brought over by servicemen as nothing less than "ideas of freedom and democracy, planted on very fertile soil after so many years of thought control and military dictatorship." A few high-end jukeboxes even included built-in microphones, though they seem to have been intended for emcees rather than singers. Whatever the case, jukeboxes were expensive and intricate gadgets requiring constant maintenance, spawning a cottage industry of local rental-and-repair firms. Several would evolve into the nation's biggest makers of arcade games: Industry titans such as Sega, Taito, and Konami all got their start dealing and servicing these monstrous mechanical musical servers.

Given this history, by all rights it seems America should have created the first sing-along device. Yet it was Japan that did so first—profoundly changing the way the nation, and later the world, sang.

Why were so many Japanese people so focused on creating an automated sing-along machine? An anthropologist might wax poetic about the integral role singing played in traditional life. The nation's very creation myth involves the sun goddess Amaterasu being lured out of hiding with a raucous song-and-dance number. A cultural historian might point to the prevalence of public singing in Japan; the first postwar singing contest, convened by the public broadcaster NHK just months after war's end in January of 1946, attracted more than nine hundred eager participants in a sort of *Japanese Idol*. Japan, then and now, is a nation of shared song: summer festival marches and *minyo* folk ditties, school songs and corporate anthems, and *Kohaku*—a year-end televised "song battle" among pop stars first broadcast in 1953, to which it seems the entire population of Japan tunes in every New Year's Eve.

But the real reason karaoke was invented in Japan instead of somewhere else—and five times over, at that—can be summed up in a single word: "salaryman."

A portmanteau of borrowed English, a salaryman is what the Japanese call a salaried office worker. The term was first bandied about by the intellectual elite in the years before World War I. Seeds of modernization planted in the nineteenth century bore fruit in the form of Asia's first society to experience industrialization. In those prewar years, office workers represented but a tiny fraction of the Japanese workforce. In a country largely powered by farmwork, service industries, and blue-collar labor, theirs was an aspirational image. A few decades later, when the sun set on the empire of Japan at the close of World War II, the duty of building a democratic new "Japan, Inc." fell squarely atop the shoulders of the salarymen.

One of the earliest and most famed chroniclers of the salaryman was the celebrated filmmaker Yasujiro Ozu. In his 1956 drama *Early Spring*, Ozu deftly captured the ennui of this strange new middle-class lifestyle: countless identically besuited men, packed shoulder to shoulder on train platforms, en route to unrelentingly drab office grinds—alleviated only by nights of drunken song. As for the women, they were expected to abandon their own careers in their mid-twenties to raise families. Their grind was in the home, rising long before their husbands to prepare breakfast and staying up late to welcome their men home with bowls of *chazuke*, warm tea over rice, a classic Japanese comfort food. All-but-mandatory after-hours socializing with co-workers led salarymen to *izakaya* restaurants where they would dine and drink away their troubles, joining voices and clapping hands to the rhythms of old military marches and festival chants as the night grew long. This was song as a form of group bonding.

Even amid the protests wracking Japanese society in the late fifties, the salaryman remained an object of respect. Japan's counterculture was not America's counterculture. Certainly there was a shared anti-war component to the protests: pushback against the Korean conflict of the fifties, and Vietnam a decade later. But even at the peak of the unrest in the late sixties and early seventies, an equal or perhaps greater number of the student radicals who manned the barricades at Japanese universities didn't want to topple the system because they hated it, but rather because they felt excluded from it. Tellingly, on surveys throughout the sixties and seventies asking schoolboys what they wanted to be when they grew up, "salaryman" consistently ranked among the top three choices. One issue was the postwar baby boom: There were simply too many boys to go around. A glut of qualified talent emerging from universities starting in the mid-sixties made it increasingly difficult for graduates to land coveted positions at top companies. And landing one represented a real prize, for the salaryman was virtually guaranteed a well-compensated job through retirement. Raises were predictable, based on simple seniority; layoffs were all but unknown. Late-sixties university kids jumped through all the right hoops, suffered through all the right "examination hells," and landed in all the right schools to earn their tickets to the Japanese dream, but were crushed to learn the train had already left the station.

Just as the American counterculture differed from the Japanese, so too did American businessmen differ from the salarymen. Of course, American companies valued loyalty in their employees, and there was no shortage of bonding with colleagues over libations. But so too was there a greater measure of independence, which began from the very moment an American left his house. No crammed subways for the average American; he drove his own car in to work, perhaps in one of the gloriously chromed real-life inspirations for Kosuge's tin Cadillac. And when he arrived at his office, he might very well arrive in *his* office—as in a room of his very own, assuming he'd worked his way through enough three-martini lunches to climb the corporate ladder. For American execs of the day, drinking was something you did *on* the clock.

Japanese salarymen inevitably worked in open floor plans, their motions visible to all, cogs in a bigger machine. While Japanese companies valued aptitude in their employees, they valued the ability to follow the rules even more, as befit a system designed around seniority rather than personal triumphs. Individual initiative paled in the

face of team effort. That's why so many companies put their employees through group calisthenics every morning—followed, perhaps,
by a rousing stanza or two of the corporate anthem. (Yes, any company worth its salt had a theme song. Though, to be fair, so did more
than a few foreign firms of the era. Next time you boot up your PC,
point your browser in the direction of IBM's "Ever Onward.")

A 1969 newsreel for Japanese audiences portrays the scene of the
era. "Behold the symbol of what these men have wrought," gravely
intones a narrator over footage of Tokyo's gleaming canyons of
concrete-and-glass skyscrapers. "Industrious as bees! Obedient as
sheep! This is their accomplishment." The reel was intended to
champion the collective effort of the nation's office workers, but
from a modern perspective, there doesn't seem much cause for celebration. Hordes of commuters, forcibly crammed into jam-packed
Tokyo subway cars by uniformed pushers, are disgorged into downtown office districts. At an electronics firm, late arrivals are tallied
for shaming in the monthly corporate newsletter. At a cosmetics
company, new young hires chant corporate slogans and swab down
toilets—in dress shirts and ties!—before launching out the door on
sales runs, like paratroopers leaving a plane. At an automobile manufacturer, salesmen are assigned cutting-edge "pocket bells," Japanese for the newfangled pocket pagers that had been invented in
America, which linked them to their offices by an "unbreakable cord
of radio waves." At the end, all trudge home to their *danchi*, dreary
mass apartment complexes hastily constructed in far-flung suburbs
to ease a desperate housing crunch in the city.

Notwithstanding the talk of bumblebees and sheep, the life of a
salaryman in the sixties and seventies was a Spartan one, his worth
determined in large part by how much suffering he could take—
whether in terms of hours worked, time spent without sleep, number of beers downed with colleagues after work, or songs drunkenly
belted out late in the evening. For a salaryman's work never ended
with the workday.

Unwinding after hours with co-workers or clients was considered

Salarymen giving a cheer as their pocket pagers charge

part of the job, both for business purposes and simply as a safety valve for blowing off steam. What happened in these sessions stayed in these sessions, whether it be venting about a superior or client (an absolute no-no inside the office) or naughtily sneaking off to a euphemistically named "Turkish bath"—a brothel. They came to call it *nomyunication*, a tongue-in-cheek fusion of *nomu*, the Japanese word for "drinking," and the English word "communication." As the ranks of the salarymen grew over the fifties and sixties, an entire ecosystem of entertainment businesses arose to support them.

Ubiquitous *izakaya* and bars left customers to their own devices, but a host of new hangouts emerged to help businessmen connect with colleagues and clients through the use of music. The most elaborate were cabarets that offered choreographed stage shows with an orchestral backing—perfect for impressing a client in town for a deal. Hostess clubs were more intimate environments, expensive and quiet, promising one-on-one interaction with young beauties trained to keep the mood going with small talk should the conversation flag. And for those drinking on their own dime, there were the ubiquitous "snacks," so named for the barest minimum of foods they kept on hand to circumvent laws compelling bars to close at midnight. In these cheap taverns, patrons bantered over the counter with the lady who ran the joint, often a retired hostess, launching into the occasional sing-along when a *nagashi* musician happened to come around. Then back home to start the cycle all over again.

Perhaps the real question isn't why the karaoke machine was invented in Japan first—it's whether it could have been invented anywhere else.

DAISUKE INOUE IS the most celebrated inventor of karaoke, but he isn't the first. I find myself sitting in the kitchen of the man who is, on one sunny autumn Tokyo day. His name is Shigeichi Negishi, and I tracked him down through the All-Japan Karaoke Industrialist Association. That such a thing exists shouldn't have surprised me, but it did. I was half expecting to interrupt a karaoke party when I opened the door to their offices, but alas, inside was like any other office in Japan: open floor plan, overflowing bookshelves, men and women in business attire quietly working the phones from their desks. Only the posters for karaoke equipment suppliers and industry trade events hanging on the walls gave it away. After I'd exchanged business cards with the right people and explained my mission, phone calls were made. Introductions were arranged, addresses written down. That's how I came to be here, sipping green tea with the first man to come up with the concept of the karaoke machine.

"Industrialist" conjures up images of mustachioed robber barons of old. Visually, anyway, Negishi fits the bill. A very young-seeming ninety-five, he sports a Wilford Brimley physique and mustache, accentuated by a dapper gray suit and a yellow cravat he's worn for the occasion, even though we're only meeting in his kitchen in a Tokyo suburb. Quick with a smile and a joke, his hardness of hearing is the only thing that truly gives his age away. A hazard of the trade, perhaps.

In 1967, forty-four-year-old Negishi ran a small factory right next door to where his home stands today, in Itabashi City. A sleepy mixed residential-industrial quarter on the northwestern outskirts of Tokyo, this far-flung section of town with little in the way of nightlife would at first glance seem an unlikely spot for innovations in entertainment. Today, when efficient train and subway lines network the city, Itabashi doesn't feel particularly isolated. But things were different in times of old; in the nineteenth century, Itabashi was practically the countryside. This physical remove from the urban center led the area to be chosen as the site of Japan's first modern gunpowder factory. In the decades after, it quietly flourished as a center of military manufacturing. In 1945, the American magazine *War Week* described the destruction of the "Itabashi arsenal" by B-29s as responsible for eradicating "quite possibly the greatest item in the Japanese war machine behind the front lines."

After the surrender, many of the craftsmen, chemists, and engineers who had served here remained in the area. Some launched new ventures of their own. Over the course of the fifties and sixties, their combined expertise transformed Itabashi from a producer of wartime matériel into a miniature Silicon (or more accurately, transistor) Valley. Itabashi was where the grunt work of building the consumer electronics branded by bigger firms fell to countless smaller contractors. A product might say Panasonic or Sony on the front, but chances are it was actually put together here. One such company was Negishi's Nichiden Kogyo, which employed around eighty technicians and engineers. At the time he thought up the Sparko Box in '67, Nichiden Kogyo was engaged in assembling 8-track car stereos for a major audio company.

The 8-track tapedeck, created by a consortium including the Ford Motor Company, RCA, Lear Jet, and Motorola, represented the state of the art in mobile audio when it debuted in 1964. Until that moment, the only way to listen to recordings in moving vehicles was on specialized mobile record players—a dicey prospect at high speeds, let alone over rough roads or in turbulent skies. The 8-track's quarter-inch magnetic tape, spooled inside a sturdy plastic case, rendered it impervious to thumps and bumps. Though boxy by modern standards—a paperback-book-sized four by five inches—the new medium transformed how people listened to music. In addition to offering stability, the tapes accommodated eighty minutes of music with their eight recording tracks—double that of a standard LP record. Another bonus: With the tape wound in an endless loop, there was no need to flip sides. Instant background music.

Negishi was an inveterate tinkerer. He held patents on everything from factory-line conveyor belts to foldable speakers to improvements on "marking rounds"—designed to be hurled at robbers to stain them with dye. He had even, at one point, dabbled in manga-character merchandising. In the mid-sixties, he'd visited Mushi Productions to obtain the rights to produce pocket-sized transistor radios emblazoned with Mighty Atom's likeness. Given a look around the studio during his negotiations with the head of licensing, he watched in amazement as Tezuka, ensconced in an open loft on the building's top floor, used a rope-and-pulley contraption to lower manga pages down to his assistants below for finishing. Seeing the way in which Tezuka industrialized his art form left a deep impression on Negishi.

Negishi's preferred art form—for relaxation, anyway—was singing. He began every morning with a long-running radio sing-along show called, straightforwardly enough, *Pop Songs without Lyrics*—a sort of nationwide precursor of karaoke served up over the airwaves. One morning, Nichiden Kogyo's head engineer caught Negishi crooning as he walked to the office. This led to some gentle ribbing, and that, Negishi says, was what gave him the idea for the machine.

"I asked the engineer," he remembers, "'Can we hook a microphone up to one of these tapedecks so I can hear myself singing over a recording of *Pop Songs without Lyrics*?' 'Piece of cake, boss,' he told me."

Negishi's request arrived at his desk three days later. The engineer had wired a microphone amp and a mixing circuit to a surplus

8-track deck; the string of naked components looked like something off a mad scientist's laboratory bench. Negishi turned it on and slotted in an instrumental tape of "Mujo no Yume" ("The Heartless Dream"), an old favorite from the thirties. His voice came through the speakers along with the music—the first karaoke song ever sung. *"It works!* That's all I was thinking. Most of all, it was fun. I knew right away I'd discovered something new." He told his engineer to build a case for it, wiring in a coin timer they had lying around for good measure. He instantly grasped that this was something he could potentially sell.

He called his baby the Sparko Box. As eventually finished, it was a cube about a foot and a half per side, edged with chrome and finished with a beige Formica-like material of the sort one might see on the counter of a sixties luncheonette. There was a rectangular opening for a tape on top, surrounded by knobs for controlling volume, balance, and tone, flanked by a microphone jack and a hundred-yen coin slot. The machine took its name from another Negishi innovation: Its front panel was a sheet of corrugated translucent plastic hiding a constellation of multicolored lights that strobed in time with the music.

But, for now, all he had was his mad-scientist prototype. He carried the components home that evening as a surprise for his wife and three children. One by one, they took turns singing over the tape. His daughter, who dropped in during my discussion with her father, was in middle school at the time; she recalled the shock and thrill of hearing her voice coming through a speaker together with music. This was a true moment: Negishi had convened the world's first karaoke party in his kitchen. It was primitive by modern standards,

Negishi and the Sparko Box, in all its sparkly glory

just a singer and a tape, with none of the voice-changing effects, or pitch-bending, or video subtitles, or any of the helping hands we take for granted in karaoke systems today. Soon, Negishi would print up songbooks with lyrics for singers to read along with as they sang. For now, it was just a tapedeck, an amplifier, a speaker, and a microphone. Yet something had changed, even if only in this one kitchen for the moment. Adding your own vocal track to a musical backing was no longer something reserved for professional performers.

Negishi ran a factory. His customers were big corporate concerns. He didn't have the experience or infrastructure to market and sell products to consumers himself. As he had with his other inventions, he sought out a distributor. In the meantime he approached a friend who worked as an engineer at the national television channel, NHK. He might know where to find more instrumentals of the sort they used for *Pop Songs without Lyrics*. He'd need as many as he could lay his hands on to make the venture worthwhile.

"He said, 'Karaoke. You want karaoke tapes.' That was the first time I'd heard the word. It was an industry term, you see. Whenever a singer would perform out in the countryside, they'd use instrumental tapes, because it was a real pain to get a full orchestra out there with them. So they'd perform with a taped backing track instead—with the orchestra pit 'empty.' That's what karaoke means."

Negishi found a distributor. "But he wouldn't let me call it a karaoke machine! Said karaoke sounded too much like *kan'oke*," the word for a coffin. And so the Sparko Box went out into the world under a variety of other brand names: The Music Box, Night Stereo, and Mini Jukebox, among others. Negishi also knew he couldn't rely on NHK to supply music for an actual product, so he turned to yet another friend, who ran a tape-dubbing business. "Instrumental recordings were actually easy to find back then," recalls Negishi. They were sold for use in dance halls, where a hired performer would sing over them, or purchased by those who simply really enjoyed singing. Negishi picked a few dozen of the top songs for his friend to record onto custom 8-tracks.

There wasn't any attempt to contact the rights holders, nor would there be any demands from them for compensation; Negishi's serving up of instrumentals via his new contraption fell into a legal twilight zone. Before the Sparko Box, there wasn't any karaoke. "Back then, if you wanted to sing, the only way to do it was with *nagashi*"—those wandering guitarists who plied their trade from bar to bar, charging patrons for performances—"and those guys were expensive!"

The Sparko Box promised to bring sing-alongs to the masses, offering up performances for just a hundred yen a pop rather than the minimum thousand yen *nagashi* or *hiki-katari* charged for a few songs. And therein lay a problem. As Negishi and the distributor demonstrated the singing machines at bars, the owners would grow excited at the prospect of selling songs to their customers—then call back sheepishly the next day asking the men to retrieve the devices, and quickly. "They'd tell us that their patrons couldn't get enough, and that we should never come back," Negishi said with a sigh. "It was the *nagashi*! They were complaining. Everywhere we put the box, they'd force the owners to take it away." With *nagashi* still a great draw for customers in this pre-karaoke era, threats to withhold their services carried real weight with barkeepers. "They were like yakuza, the way the *nagashi* pushed me around. We were archenemies. From Akita up north all the way down to Osaka, it was always the same."

Some of Negishi's most enthusiastic customers turned out to be the owners of euphemistically named "love hotels." The hotels emerged less out of lasciviousness than necessity in Japan, where multiple generations of a family often slept under one roof, separated by little more than paper screens. What attracted the hotels' clientele wasn't the singing, though. It was those groovy flashing lights, which perfectly suited the gaudy interiors of the sort only by-the-hour accommodations could get away with. Love-hotel sales turned Negishi a reliable if limited profit. But was this really as far as karaoke would go? Negishi himself seems to have had doubts about its viability. After discussing the idea of patenting the Sparko

Box, he and his partner decided the cost and headache weren't worth it; it was, at the time, extremely expensive and time-consuming to obtain a patent. And besides, it wasn't like they had any competition. None that they knew about, anyway.

IN SPITE OF neither man having any awareness of the other's existence, let alone the other's invention, Daisuke Inoue's 8 Juke looked quite a bit like Negishi's Sparko Box. Created three years after the Sparko Box, the 8 Juke was a wooden cube housing an 8-track car stereo, modified to Inoue's specifications by a friend who ran a musical-instrument repair shop. It lacked the sparkly light show, but it had something else: a form of rudimentary audio processing. Inoue had his friend wire in a reverb box, a device that ran the microphone's output through a metal spring to add twang to the vocals. Dr. Sing-along was intimately acquainted with an undeniable fact of the human condition: Most of us are horrible singers. The reverb effect greatly helped mask an amateur's vocal deficiencies.

Inoue had another trick up his sleeve. He might not be able to read music, but he had firsthand knowledge of his audience's favorite songs, and of how much difficulty a given song gave the average singer. He was also a bandleader, which gave him the ability to organize musicians. All of Inoue's predecessors, Negishi included, relied on commercially available instrumentals—essentially the same ones professionals sang along to. But Inoue knew these weren't really what customers wanted, even if they thought they did. He was so sure of it that, even after finishing the first 8 Juke in early 1970, he kept it under wraps for a full year. This gave him time to record a library of covers of popular songs with a local band, retuned into lower pitches and slower tempos that were easier for average singers to match.

Inoue didn't have the connections or money to use a professional recording studio, but he had a side gig playing music at a local wedding hall. The Japanese use the Western calendar today, but aspects of traditional beliefs involving auspicious and inauspicious days remain. A repeating six-day cycle calculated from ancient Chinese calendars means that several times every month falls *butsumetsu*— a day traditionally associated with bad luck. Back then, even modern-thinking sorts tended to avoid it for big festivities like marriages, and the hall was inevitably closed on those days. Inoue used the opportunities to record songs for the 8 Juke. There was no professional gear, no production save Inoue's arrangement, no overdubbing, no multitrack recording, no editing—just a microphone and an 8-track recorder, with each song laid down in a single take. In the beginning, Inoue and his musicians struggled to finish just a few songs in a session; as they got into the groove, they could lay down as many as ten tracks in a day. They weren't instrumentals so much as "virtuals": authentic enough to recognize, yet subtly simplified for the uninitiated.

In the meantime, Inoue had placed orders with local electricians and woodworkers for the components to build nine 8 Jukes in addition to the prototype. By the end of 1970, he'd constructed his initial army of ten machines, plus a library of several hundred songs custom-recorded to make amateurs feel like stars.

The moment of truth came in January of 1971. Inoue convinced ten snack bars to host that first batch of 8 Jukes. Their presence was met with absolute silence. It was obvious, really: Customers didn't know what the machines were, or how to use them. Ever resourceful, Inoue paid several of his hostess friends to visit the bars, relying on the power of a cute girl in a revealing outfit to draw interest. The girls made a big show of singing on the 8 Jukes, pulling customers in for impromptu duets.

It paid off. By March, he had more requests for machines than he and his friend running the repair shop could handle. He contracted with a factory in Yokohama, driving five hundred kilometers to pick up the machines, stacking them in the bed of a rented light truck, then driving five hundred kilometers back. In a testament to how unsteady the whole scheme was at first, he continued working as a *hiki-katari* performer for quite some time after the 8 Jukes' debut.

Occasionally, during a gig, Inoue would get a message that one or another of his machines had jammed. He'd excuse himself on the pretense of needing a bathroom break and make a mad dash to the 8 Juke that needed fixing. Invariably, it had stopped working because its coin box was jammed full. This was great news for Inoue, whose business model was loaning the machines to the bars for free and then splitting any monthly earnings above twenty thousand yen. Given that many customers would spend a thousand yen in a session, it was easy money. Suddenly, he found himself besieged with orders for more 8 Jukes—more than he could possibly handle himself. It was right around this time that his fellow *hiki-katari* must have noticed their own revenues dropping off and called the emergency meeting of the Kobe Musical Artists Association.

Inoue's brother-in-law suggested he patent the 8 Juke. It might seem like a no-brainer today, but Inoue simply lacked the where-withal to make it happen. He had his hands full performing and running his new company—Crescent, he called it—and was pouring most of the profits back into making more machines. And so it was that the karaoke machine failed to be patented for the second time. "I didn't build the thing from scratch," explained Inoue in an interview years later, when pressed on the question of why he hadn't asserted his rights over the design. "I had the idea for the business model. The amp, the microphone, the 8-track player—even the hundred-yen [coin] box machine—all had patents on them. Today I could take out a patent on the business model, have someone else make it, and get the royalties from the original idea. But at the time, getting a patent for a business model just didn't seem possible." And while the 8 Jukes were booming in Kobe's red-light district for the moment, it was far from clear whether sing-along machines were anything more than a local flash-in-the-pan fad.

AS IT HAPPENED, neither Negishi nor Inoue nor any other individual would ever control karaoke's destiny. It wasn't long before electronics manufacturers learned of the existence of the singing machine—

undoubtedly through their own salarymen employees encountering the device in the course of their own nights out on the town. It took even less time for them to realize that the concept was essentially public domain. The first to get its own machine to market was the consumer-electronics titan Japan Victor Company (JVC), which released its BW-1 in 1972. Rivals including Toshiba and Pioneer would quickly follow with competing devices. As these big players fought for market share in the years to come, karaoke machines inspired by the 8 Juke's basic model spread inexorably—from Kobe to nearby Osaka and, over the course of the seventies, all throughout Japan. This is precisely what allowed it to flourish as it did. Owned by nobody, karaoke became everybody's.

In a measure of karaoke's growing impact on society, police found themselves overwhelmed by noise complaints as the machines' reach expanded from salaryman hangouts into nearly any sort of watering hole at all, transforming previously quiet neighborhoods into stages for amateur performances. As less savory elements of society took up the microphone, violence occasionally ensued. In the early hours of December 26, 1977, as the employees of a Kawasaki brothel unwound over drinks and music in a local supper club, a dispute over who sang next erupted into an eighteen-customer melee. Four wound up in the hospital with contusions from beer bottles and fists—history's first recorded victims of what might be called karaoke rage. The medium's mix of alcohol, enthusiasm, and implied competition has fueled similar incidents both domestically and abroad in the years since; in the Philippines, for example, no less than half a dozen singers have been murdered over renditions of Frank Sinatra's "My Way," forcing many karaoke purveyors there to scrub the popular song from their lists altogether.

Other effects were subtler and, to critics, more insidious. "We're losing the art of bar conversation," complained the sci-fi writer Ryo Hanmura to the *Asahi Shimbun* in 1978. "Now everyone just sits there with their brains turned off, waiting their turn to sing." A 1979 Japanese newspaper op-ed derided the "false bravado" of karaoke aficionados and their obsession with being the center of attention. And in 1984 the music critic Tadashi Fujita bemoaned a "karaoke boom that has swept up amateur and pro alike, where everyone is happy to sing the same rhythms, tempos, lyrics, and melodies as everyone else," a "Harrison Bergeron"–esque world where standout voices were suppressed by the limited skills of amateur singers. (Lest you think him some fuddy-duddy, Fujita cited American hip-hop culture as a counterexample of how one might create new forms of expression from commercial songs.)

For the first decade plus of its existence, karaoke's library of songs *was* stagnant and repetitive, almost entirely composed of *enka*, a schmaltzy genre of sentimental ballads sung in a distinctively wavering vibrato. *Enka* lyrics offer up a healthy dose of rose-tinted romance, filled with longing for hometowns, mothers, and young lovers left behind: a sonic version of those employment trains that carried so many wide-eyed country boys and girls into the big cities. The word *enka* literally means "speech-song," and its roots date back to the late nineteenth century, when democracy activists put their slogans into verse to skirt government sedition laws. As it evolved over the decades, *enka* shed its political roots but retained a certain defiant, go-it-alone, "My Way"–esque spirit. After World War II, as the thrillingly bombastic big band music (and jazz, and later rock) of the occupation forces swept Japan, *enka*'s tearfully wistful ballads re-emerged as a counterpoint for an older generation less interested in assimilating the newfangled tunes of the conquerors. *Enka*'s romanticization of stoicism and personal sacrifice deeply appealed to the machismo of middle-aged working-class blokes and salarymen both, long before they ever picked up the microphones of those earliest karaoke machines. And for many years after, *enka* remained so indelibly associated with the devices that the word "karaoke" struck terror into the hearts of young employees, for it meant yet another evening of listening to their over-the-hill bosses crooning tunes from a bygone era. "The youth have their guitars," explained a newspaper article from 1977. "The middle-aged men have their *enka* and military marches on karaoke."

It took until the mid-eighties for all that to change—and when it did, it changed quickly, thanks to another Boss: Bruce Springsteen. Seas of local fans singing along to his 1985 Japan tour inspired his Japanese label to produce karaoke versions of Springsteen songs. In December of that year, *Born in the U.S.A.* became the very first rock album "translated" into karaoke in its entirety. "That exact feeling of singing with the Boss, if not making you feel like him inside and out!" declared the packaging in gloriously broken English.

They'd made it as a lark. Two million records, tapes, and CDs of the karaoke version of *Born in the U.S.A.* flew off the shelves. The surprise success shone a spotlight on an emerging home-karaoke phenomenon in Japan, as manufacturers incorporated karaoke functions into home stereos and laserdisc players. The unexpected success of rock and roll karaoke also established a pair of beachheads that would forever change the medium: the idea that teens and young adults might want to sing every bit as much as their parents did, and the concept of singing privately rather than on the open stages of pubs and bars—a trend accelerated by the appearance, in 1985, of a new type of establishment partitioned into soundproof rooms for small groups or solo singers. These "karaoke boxes" and "karaoke capsules," as they were variously called, quickly proliferated throughout the cities and countryside of Japan, ushering in new demographics of singers—kids, women, the elderly—who wouldn't normally set foot in a cabaret or hostess club. It was the final nail in the coffin of the *nagashi* and *hiki-katari* artists. Their fears of karaoke making them obsolete had been entirely well founded. At the peak of their influence in the early sixties, it is said that more than a hundred *nagashi* serviced Tokyo's downtown watering holes every night. Automated out of their livelihoods by karaoke, today only a few elderly stalwarts ply the trade: defiant anachronisms, performing for nostalgia's sake instead of any real demand.

• • •

THE KARAOKE MACHINE wasn't just about singing. Its democratiza-
tion of talent would have profound effects on the fantasy lives of
Japanese and Westerners both. It was the first device in any sphere
of life that let rank amateur performers feel like total pros; those
simple assists of retuning and echo effects were the forerunners of
all of the high-tech helping hands we take for granted in our modern
lives: image-stabilization technologies and Instagram filters that
bring snapshots closer to the work of pro photographers; the
computer-assisted rhythm guides of concert simulators like *Rock
Band;* the enhanced video game physics that help fumble-fingered
Fortnite players feel like Navy SEALs in combat. In giving everyone
the chance to be a star, if only for the duration of a song, karaoke
paved the way for even more immersive and transformative technologies to come. Karaoke is the original user-generated content,
the first network of populist remixers unfettered by gatekeepers—
save for the companies happily supplying the machines and recordings to all of us waiting, with our brains switched off, for our turn to
sing.

At the peak of the phenomenon, in the mid-nineties, there were
some 170,000 rooms available for singing karaoke in Japan. An industry survey estimated that close to sixty million people—nearly
half of the nation's entire population—indulged in karaoke at least
once a year. Even after the turn of the millennium, facing stiff competition from newer forms of mobile and interactive entertainment,
the number hovered around fifty million. All this amateur singing
had a profound effect on the Japanese music industry as a whole,
particularly in the early nineties. That's when the advent of digital-
streaming technologies allowed Japanese record companies to see
what people were singing in real time.

In the West, things played out a little differently. The very first
karaoke machines imported to the United States appeared in Japanese restaurants. "After a long day at the office, many Japanese like
to unwind in snack bars over Scotch or saké and sing a kind of nos-

talgic ballad known as enka," wrote *The New York Times* in its first-ever mention of the phenomenon in May of 1983. "The practice has helped fuel what's known as the karaoke boom, and some Japanese manufacturers now are hoping that something similar will happen in America." It was a curiosity largely confined to bars, restaurants, and private dining rooms intended for entertaining Japanese businessmen, then arriving in the States in record numbers and hungry for ways to unwind after a hard day of driving up the U.S.-Japan trade deficit (as American politicians would have it).

American entrepreneurs began launching karaoke businesses aimed at English-singing customers in the mid- to late-eighties. New York City and Los Angeles were early hotbeds for karaoke lounges. Almost in the blink of an eye, the concept of the singing machine truly seized hold of the American imagination. By 1992, the word had entrenched itself enough in the lexicon for President George H. W. Bush to declare during his campaign, "We're running against the karaoke kids, and they'll sing any tune they think will get them elected."

While Japanese consumers embraced private rooms that eliminated the stress of public performances and enhanced the intimacy of singing with friends, in the West (and America in particular) karaoke thrived as an exhibition sport in malls, bars, and restaurants. The young people who flocked to these places tended to approach the mic in one of two ways: amusing the crowd with cheesy or rowdy party songs, or peacocking their vocal skills in battles against similarly talented patrons. And for its most devoted practitioners, karaoke wasn't about unwinding at all. It was "a gritty, real-life road to fame," as *Indianapolis Monthly* put it in a 2005 profile of local *American Idol* aspirants who were "hanging by a fingernail on the hope that somewhere in the shadows, someone important is sitting in a corner booth smoking a fat cigar and waiting to discover you." (Tantalizingly, the dream sometimes really did become reality: The singer Mary J. Blige launched her career with a tape she recorded in a shopping-mall karaoke booth.) The seductive idea that we're all stars waiting to be discovered manifested most prominently in the long popularity of reality singing shows like *American Idol*.

And what of Negishi and Inoue? Negishi managed, in spite of all the resistance, to place some eight thousand Sparko Boxes in venues throughout Japan. It was a modest success, even if it seemed that more used them as portable jukeboxes than singing machines. But when his partner got out of the distribution business in 1973, Negishi called it quits, too. He'd had enough of pushback from professional musicians, and he had plenty of other projects to keep him busy. He owned his own successful company to start with, after all. He focused on that instead, and he and the Sparko Box faded from karaoke history.

Inoue, on the other hand, made out like a bandit. While the 8 Juke was eclipsed by the slicker offerings of the large electronics companies, he shifted gears to focus on the music side by arranging recordings and, more important, rights. By the mid-seventies he had established himself as a sort of go-between for record labels and the karaoke companies who desperately needed hit songs for their libraries. While he never saw a dime in royalties for the karaoke machine itself, at his peak he was doing the equivalent of $100 million a year in sales as an agent, producing karaoke recordings and selling machines made by other companies.

For his efforts Inoue is widely hailed as the official inventor of karaoke. In 1998, a Singaporean karaoke channel launched a search to identify the creator of the singing machine. Their inquiries prompted the All-Japan Karaoke Industrialist Association to hurriedly suggest Inoue as the progenitor of the karaoke boom. The reason the karaoke cognoscenti picked his creation over Negishi's was simple. Negishi had invented a device. But Inoue invented the total package of hardware and custom software that allowed karaoke to grow from a local fad into an enormous global business. As Inoue became karaoke's face, word quickly spread from Singapore to local Asian news bureaus: That crazy Japanese singing machine has a creator!

In 1999, *Time* magazine cheekily included Inoue on their list of the twentieth century's most influential Asians, profiling him alongside the likes of Mao Zedong, Gandhi, and Sony's Akio Morita. Much was made of the fact that an "Eastern Walter Mitty," as the writer Pico Iyer somewhat misleadingly described the vivacious Inoue, had invented a machine that united the world in song. Five years later, in 2004, the Ig Nobel committee sealed his reputation by awarding him the annual Peace Prize "for inventing karaoke, thereby providing an entirely new way for people to learn to tolerate each other." At the awards ceremony, Inoue led the crowd in a round of the seventies Coca-Cola commercial song "I'd Like to Teach the World to Sing (In Perfect Harmony)."

BACK IN NEGISHI'S kitchen, the Sparko Box sits on the table between us. Its diner counter–esque linoleum finish has faded somewhat over the years, but the chrome buttons and dials still gleam. So does the coin slot, which tantalizingly promises "roughly ten minutes" for a hundred yen. I ask if we can give it a spin.

The old inventor obligingly drops a coin and slots in a chunky 8-track cartridge, which slides home with a satisfyingly resonant click. The instrumental of pop singer Teresa Teng's 1984 ballad "Tsugunai" ("Atonement") whirs up to speed, like an old windup toy creaking to life. The front of the machine sparkles and pulses in time with the music. "That's how I came up with the name," Negishi says, laughing, as we take in the light show. It's the sort of thing that would look right at home sitting atop a deep-shag rug, next to a lava lamp.

Once upon a time, he sold thousands of the devices to bars and hotels across Japan. You could say he laid down the basic template for every karaoke machine to follow, even if none of his successors remembered it. Fifty-one years later, this is the very last Sparko Box left in the entire world, a forgotten keepsake. *It belongs in a museum*, I think, like Indiana Jones stumbling across some ancient cultural relic.

Miraculously, this half-century-old machine still works. Negishi holds out the microphone, gold mesh still gleaming even after long years in storage. I take it gamely, but the song is a curiosity from a foreign land, long before my time here. I don't know the melody, nor even a word of the lyrics. Unlike modern machines, the Sparko Box offers no helping hands to singers. No echo effects, no video screen, no wacky generic video, no words changing color in time with the music. Only the sparkle of the disco lights and a paper pamphlet of song lyrics—and Negishi seems to have misplaced the latter.

It doesn't matter. This is the very spot where karaoke was born, so many years ago, and it seems fitting to give the little machine a moment of its own. We laugh as the music plays on.

4

CULT OF CUTE

Hello Kitty
1975

All things small,
No matter what they are,
All things small are adorable.

—SEI SHONAGON, *THE PILLOW BOOK*, CA. 1002

Small gift, big smile.

—SANRIO SLOGAN

IN MARCH OF 1975, an innocuous product called the Petit Purse debuted to absolutely zero fanfare. A tiny translucent vinyl pouch with a metal clasp, intended for little girls to carry their pocket change, it retailed for just 220 yen, less than a dollar at the time. Sanrio, the company that made it, hedged its bets by producing several varieties. But as the weeks went by and Sanrio's staff tallied up sales, they noticed something odd. Only one of the Petit Purse patterns was selling, and it was selling in huge numbers: the stylized kitty cat dressed in overalls, sitting in profile beneath a single English word: HELLO!

Before there was Kitty, there was just Hello: the seminal Petit Purse.

Although she superficially resembled them, the kitten was a character unlike those in popular comic books or cartoons. At this point in time she had no personality, no story line, not even a name. She betrayed no emotional expression. And her medium wasn't even media. It was stuff—the stuff of everyday life for Japanese elementary-schoolers. The purse was quickly followed by things like cups, plates, sandals, pencils and pens, notebooks for school, and stationery for passing notes to girlfriends.

It certainly doesn't seem like the kind of thing empires are built on. Yet more than forty years later, the design we now instantly recognize as Hello Kitty is more than a decoration. She's one of the world's largest licensed properties. She's as iconic as Snoopy or Mickey, a standard unit, the yardstick against which all other adorable mascots are judged. She is the cornerstone of a massive multimedia franchise, regularly earning half a billion dollars a year or more in global revenues, making Sanrio the eighth-largest licensor in the world, ahead of bruisers like the National Football League (number 12), the omnipresent Pokémon company (number 30), and, in an apparent triumph of cuddling over sensuality, Playboy Enterprises (number 45). She has worked her way into the fabric of modern life around the globe; Hello Kitty flies above us, adorning jumbo jets and bobbing down Fifth Avenue during the Macy's Thanksgiving Day parade. Her ubiquity means she shows up in some truly incongruous places. When Islamic Front commander Zahran Alloush addressed his troops in Syria in 2014, he did so armed with a semiautomatic pistol slung in a shoulder holster and a Hello Kitty notepad on his podium. Hello, indeed.

How on earth did Hello Kitty get, well, everywhere on earth? The secret to her success is something that the Japanese call *kawaii*. Pronounced similarly to "Hawaii" as "kah-*wah*-eee" (and feel absolutely free to make that a scream-y little "eee!" on the end), the word overlaps to a degree with the Western concept of cuteness. But only to a degree. The word "cute" derives from "acute," making it by turns both unthreatening and a little suspect. The *Oxford English Dictonary* lists the earliest known usage of "cute" from the 1700s as a synonym for "shrewd," a clever and conniving image that survives in phrases like "Don't get cute." The Japanese kawaii is absent this linguistic baggage. Puppies are kawaii. Kittens are kawaii. Babies are kawaii. In fact, until just about a hundred years ago, kawaii was nothing more than a patronizing descriptor, deployed in the sense of "Oh, isn't that just *adorable*?"

The first known modern use of kawaii dates to 1914. That's when an enterprising woman by the name of Tamaki Kishi, ex-wife and business partner of the celebrated pop artist Yumeji Takehisa, used the word on a flyer advertising the Tokyo boutique that they launched together. It was called Minato-ya (the Harbor Store), and its logo of a clipper ship on the waves hinted at dreamy imports from exotic lands. In fact, the shop's wares were entirely domestic, clever blends of Japanese and foreign flair. Yumeji's illustrations of willowy young Japanese beauties in kimonos, set against Western backdrops such as Parisian-style cafés, redefined feminine chic in the prewar era: You could be both traditionally Japanese and cosmopolitan all at once. His art proved so popular in Japan's roaring twenties that his name itself became an idiom for a fashionable woman: *Yumeji-shiki*—"Yumeji-esque." Tamaki's was the first recorded usage of kawaii to describe a taste or fashion, applied to the sorts of things young women might previously have called *kirei* (attractive). Thanks in part to this new branding, the boutique's stock of pretty pictures and postcards, illustrated books of poetry, brightly patterned fabrics, and fashion accessories flew off the shelves.

Later, in the sixties, kawaii became intertwined with manga design: the soft and rounded shapes of Tezuka's characters and the glittering promise of feminine sophistication in romantic *shojo manga* comic books for young girls. By the end of the millennium it had evolved into a hyperbolic, all-purpose superlative for the young and young at heart, for all ages and genders and orientations: a Platonic ideal of the concepts of innocence and positivity—"the most widely used, widely loved, habitual word in modern living Japanese," according to a 1992 survey in one women's magazine.

Yet trying to define kawaii is an exercise in folly. Tellingly, in

Japanese the antonym for kawaii isn't ugly or unlovable; it's *kawaiku-nai*—literally, un-kawaii. This isn't an adjective. It's a state of mind. What is love? You know it when you feel it. So too kawaii. For a great many, Hello Kitty represented their first exposure to this intoxicating new emotion. Kitty's birth in 1975 represented the first time it was successfully bottled for mass production. Tezuka's manga were certainly cute, but he was a dealer in stories; Sanrio dealt in cuteness itself.

How did Hello Kitty metamorphose from the decoration on a cheap coin purse into the cornerstone of an empire? The easy answer is: canny merchandising and marketing on the part of the company that created her. But so too did Kitty create Sanrio, almost single-handedly transforming what was originally a local distributor of trinkets into a sprawling multinational behemoth.

Few realized it at the time, but the moment of Hello Kitty's creation represented a confluence of social, cultural, and economic streams running through Japanese society. Thanks to postwar reconstruction, citizens were healthier and wealthier than ever before. A baby boom produced legions of children whom families doted upon with all sorts of toys and presents. And as those boys and girls grew into adulthood in a land of plenty, they yearned to break out of the constant cycle of study, homemaking, and work that had defined their parents' lives in the early postwar era. Hello Kitty was the lightning strike, a miracle of a doodle that coalesced and channeled these social threads into the aesthetic of a generation—and one of the nation's most recognizable symbols everywhere else.

That was the power of kawaii.

BEHIND SANRIO, BEHIND all the flowers and frills and kitties and bunnies, behind the global bottling of kawaii, is a man. He was a poet, chemist, and onetime bootlegger by the name of Shintaro Tsuji.

Long before Kitty and Sanrio, Tsuji had been just another restless eighteen-year-old high school graduate wrestling with the problem of his generation: how to avoid getting killed in World War II. It was but the latest struggle in an altogether grim adolescence. Tsuji barely knew his father. He was raised by his single mother, a business-woman whose family owned a successful chain of inns in Yamanashi Prefecture, eighty miles west of Tokyo. This afforded her the luxury of sending her son to an exclusive Christian kindergarten for expatriates. The foreign religion didn't stick, but one of the foreign traditions did. "The birthday parties," recalled Tsuji dreamily in a 2008 interview. "Nobody back then knew the birthdays of their children. Japanese didn't have a custom of celebrating birthdays or holding birthday parties. I was deeply moved."

After losing his mother to leukemia in 1940, when he was just thirteen, Tsuji was sent to live with a foster family in the countryside. Though they were better off than most Japanese citizens, food was in increasingly short supply as Japan's war machine crumbled, and his new guardians made no effort to hide their annoyance at having another child in their care. There would be no more parties for young Tsuji. "They rode me constantly. 'You eat too much.' 'You shit too much.' 'Now go scrub out the toilets,'" he wrote in his 2000 memoir, *These Are Sanrio's Secrets*. A romantic at heart, he was drawn to the worlds of Greek mythology, poetry, and literature. Once, he was even suspended from school for penning a love story—something very much frowned upon in an era of total martial law, and particularly so for a boy, who was expected to be stoic, resolute, and ready to lay down his life for his country. (One of the final issues of the popular boy's comic monthly *Shonen Club,* published just before war's end in 1945, replaced the comics with patriotic essays and, chillingly, concluded with detailed instructions on how to arm and detonate a hand grenade.) Much as he yearned to write, Tsuji knew that Sophocles wouldn't keep him off a battlefield. When the new school year started in April of 1945, Tsuji enrolled in the local technical college, declaring a major in the decidedly unromantic field of organic chemistry. A desperate shortage of doctors and engineers meant studying medicine or the sciences was the best way to stay out of combat.

On August 15, 1945, the head professor, a lieutenant commander in the Imperial Navy, sent the young men to an assembly, where they gathered to hear an unprecedented national radio address by Emperor Hirohito. The declaration of surrender that followed was delivered in such exquisitely formal speech that few citizens could even parse the words, but everyone knew what it meant. The war was over, and Japan had lost. As Tsuji and his classmates glumly filed back into their classroom, they were met with another shock: The lieutenant commander had shot himself to death at his desk.

Anthropologist Ruth Benedict quotes a typical Japanese reaction to the end of the war in her 1946 bestseller, *The Chrysanthemum and the Sword*. "The relief is wonderful. But we are not fighting anymore and know no purpose. Everyone is in a daze, not caring how he does things. I am like that, my wife is like that, and the people in the hospital." The listlessness proved so pervasive that the Japanese press soon gave it a name: *kyodatsu jotai*—a persistent state of lethargy. But if anything the collapse of society seemed to energize Tsuji. He snuck into the school's lab to secretly synthesize desperately needed staples such as soap, saccharine sweetener, and something even more in demand: hard liquor. Like Betty Crocker turned *Breaking Bad*, Tsuji found eager customers for these illicit products among the yakuza who ran the local black market.

Only a sudden bout of tuberculosis put an end to his bootlegging days. On the other hand, it was perfect timing. The men he associated with appalled his upper-crust family, and the authorities were starting to crack down on the black markets anyway. Tsuji returned to school, graduated in 1949, and used connections to secure a coveted job with the Yamanashi regional government. He spent the next decade cycling through a series of well-paying but mindless postings. Most of his countrymen would have given a kidney for the plum positions; in spite of the political protests and strikes wracking postwar society, the public still held career bureaucrats in high esteem. Tsuji called it "the second adversity, after my boyhood." Buried in bureaucracy, he couldn't see the fruits of his labors or measure his progress. This was work for work's sake. It was enough to make him yearn for the black markets.

Eventually, enough was enough, and he resolved to quit. Colleagues told him he was crazy. But, as would happen many times over, he proved the naysayers wrong and then some. Rather than quietly submitting his resignation, he strode right over to the nearby local chamber of commerce, talked his way into the office of the governor of Yamanshi Prefecture, and declared a vague desire to go into business for himself. Tsuji emerged from the meeting with a million yen in venture capital from the city in his pocket. He struck out for Tokyo, where he used the investment to found a company called the Yamanashi Silk Center.

It distributed regional products like wine, fruit, vegetables, and of course silk. Tsuji assembled a small army of traveling salesmen, who offered these wares wholesale to shops in the capital and directly to customers via open-air markets in resort areas. Profits grew quickly; it was a resounding success by any normal definition. But not Tsuji's. He dreamed of being something more than a glorified greengrocer. That's when the memory of his kindergarten parties came back to him.

"Back then, around 1960, my son was attending an elementary school in Tokyo's Meguro ward, so I asked his classmates how many of them had received any gifts on their birthdays, and only three out of thirty-five said they had," recalled Tsuji. "Nobody had ever experienced having birthday parties. And the three students who had received birthday gifts all said the gifts came from their mothers. So I thought I wanted to do a business related to birthdays and gift giving."

Idiosyncratic as it seems, Tsuji's fascination with fancily wrapped presents tapped into a deep vein of Japanese social customs. Grownups called it *giri*. What takes one word to express in Japanese takes many in English: the unspoken obligation of reciprocating a favor someone has done for you. Few cultures have codified the giving of gifts like the Japanese. There's *Ochugen,* the summer gift, and *Oseibo,* the winter gift, presented to those who supported you in some way during the year: perhaps a client, or your boss, or a teacher, or a landlord. It was (and is) considered common sense to bring a present of some sort when visiting someone's home in Japan, or when incurring any sort of obligation at all, really. It isn't about the value of the product; *Ochugen* and *Oseibo* often take the form of consumables like beer or fruit or other daily necessities—even something as seemingly humble as soap or soy sauce or cooking oil makes a perfectly acceptable offering. But the trick is that they're never, ever presented as is. Dropping a bottle of canola oil on your boss's doorstep? As weird in Japan as it would be in the States. In the West, the thought might count, but in Japan, it's about the effort put into the presentation. This is why Japanese have enthusiastically embraced gift-centric imported holidays like Valentine's Day and Christmas, in spite of the fact that less than 1 percent of the population identifies as Christian: more opportunities to give elaborately wrapped gifts!

Tsuji's genius was recasting this grown-up social exchange for children. "Small gift, big smile"—in the years to come, that would be his company's motto. In the meantime, what to sell?

The answer came to him through one of the Yamanashi Silk Center's contractors. She arrived for a meeting carrying an accessory decorated with a stylized strawberry. The look was in that season, thanks to the work of a girl's fashion illustrator named Rune Naito. In the fifties, Naito's fashion spreads featuring drawings of slim beauties with impossibly long necks and enormous eyes—bigger even than those of Osamu Tezuka's characters—injected a sense of glittering, aspirational, foreign sophistication into the lives of little girls throughout Japan. In 1961, Naito branched out into product

Naito's doe-eyed beauties brought foreign styles to a generation of postwar girls.

design, launching a series of ceramic mugs and kitchenware featuring cartoon fruit and vegetable motifs. His sensibilities appealed to the young women of postwar Japan in much the way Yumeji's sensibilities had appealed to the young women of the roaring twenties. So too, apparently, to Tsuji. The strawberry-festooned accessory fascinated him. "Oh, it's so *cute*," he murmured, as though he were a little girl himself rather than a middle-aged man.

In 1962, Tsuji debuted the Yamanashi Silk Center's take on the concept: a pair of rubber sandals sized for children, adorned with a strawberry motif. He quickly sold through the lot. Sensing potential, Tsuji quickly followed up with handkerchiefs, small pouches, drinking cups, and juice glasses featuring the same juicy-looking berry. These strawberry products sold like wildfire—far better than anything the Silk Center had ever released before.

This was it! Tsuji knew that, by their very nature, fanciful gifts had to be more than just products: They had to be special. Through the strawberries he learned just how simple that extra adornment could be. Less than a generation earlier, citizens lacked food and roofs over their heads. Now that they had achieved a modicum of comfort, as the sixties rolled on, people wanted something extra, not only for themselves but for their children—little luxuries. Not least among these essential inessentials were the manga and anime that laid the groundwork for generations of boys and girls with surprisingly sophisticated tastes in illustrated design. Underlying it all was a long-standing fascination with "fancy goods"—an old-timey term of the trade borrowed from American English.

In the Western world of the nineteenth and early twentieth centuries, "fancy" actually meant "Japanese": exotic silks, ceramics, silver, and art imported from the Far East. Tiffany's, that bastion of sophistication, began life in 1837 as a "stationery and fancy goods emporium" before rebranding itself as a fine jeweler twenty years later. In a successful effort to transform his little shop into the nation's gatekeeper for luxury and style, co-founder Charles Tiffany boasted of his dedication to making wares "even more Japanese than the Japanese themselves," debuting items such as sterling silver tableware with motifs swiped from prints by Hokusai: a luxury product further elevated by its association with the exotic Orient.

A Japanese fancy good, on the other hand, is almost precisely the opposite. It is humble, inevitably soft, round, adorable, frilly, or fluffy. Even more important it must radiate a dreamy, aspirational foreign style—American or European in particular. This latter requirement can be traced back to Tamaki and Yumeji, way back in 1914. The wartime years smothered the nation's fascination with foreign things, but interest rekindled almost the very moment those first American jeeps rolled into Japanese cities after the war's end.

Tsuji had dipped a toe into a powerful new current emerging in Japanese popular culture: a hunger for more than the necessary—indeed for the complete *opposite* of necessary; for the small and frivolous and dreamy. Not just any design would work, though. Kawaii was a fickle mistress. He would learn that the hard way.

THE CHERRIES WERE an abject failure.

Emboldened by the success of his line of strawberry-themed gifts in 1962, Tsuji quickly launched a sequel that same year, re-releasing identical products with cherries instead. He figured the little bunches of brightly colored fruits would prove even more popular with the girls who had bought out his strawberry line. He thought wrong. "I wasn't disappointed, exactly, more like shocked," recalled Tsuji. "I mean, cherries and strawberries are red fruits, right? Why were strawberries good and cherries bad?"

He knew he needed help, and he needed it quickly. Tsuji was self-aware enough to understand that his skills lay in business, not design. He needed artists. The first one he approached was a twenty-three-year-old woman by the name of Ado Mizumori. Of their first meeting she recalled, "He was almost like a little girl: 'It's kawaii; your art's so kawaii!' He felt it personally." Tsuji might not have been able to conjure cuteness out of thin air, but he certainly knew it when he saw it.

In her prime, Mizumori was the living embodiment of Japan's kawaii culture.

Today, Mizumori is better known by her stage name of Ado-chan. Her presence looms large in Japanese entertainment, a multi-hyphenate illustrator-vocalist-actress-performance-artist Renaissance woman. She would go on to great fame as the host of a popular children's program, illustrating stories on a translucent acrylic sheet suspended between her and the audience, drawing with both hands—backward, from her perspective. But before all of that came to pass, she would rise to fame as the creator of a character that would move more products than Tsuji's strawberries ever had. It was, prophetically, a little cat. Its popularity helped Ado shatter the glass ceiling for the vanguard of a new wave of young female creators.

In picking a talented young woman like her, Tsuji was ahead of the curve. The choice might seem like a no-brainer for a company whose raison d'être was making stuff for schoolgirls. But in the fifties and early sixties, the majority of work aimed at girls, whether in the form of illustrations for fashion magazines or the nascent industry for *shojo manga* (girls' comics), was drawn by men. Rune Naito was one such illustrator. Another was manga artist Osamu Tezuka, who in 1953 published *Ribon no Kishi* (*Princess Knight*), the tale of a young princess who dresses—and fights—as a boy. In the wake of his success, publishers debuted numerous magazines dedicated to this unexpected new audience of young women. But the manga industry of the day was, like the rest of Japan, a man's world. Women were recognized as consumers, not as creators. In their hunger for content, editors even pressed gekiga artists like *Ashita no Jo*'s Tetsuya Chiba into service penning girls' comics.

It was Mizumori's girls that first propelled her to fame and caught Tsuji's eye. Mizumori wasn't a manga artist, but her cartoony illustrations—which Tsuji had seen other companies use to decorate items such as handkerchiefs, or as design elements for magazine articles or books—tapped into much the same vibe. Her work stood out for a certain foreign-feeling hippie beach-bum charm, the influence of a gap year she spent in a Hawaiian high school after failing to get into art college. Ado's girls were bright, happy, occasionally undressed (but always artfully obscured), usually spotted planting an innocent kiss on the cheek of a would-be boyfriend. It was a balance of gentle suggestiveness and childhood naïveté, a sort of striptease minus the naughtiness.

Among Mizumori's influences were actual stripteases, in particular those she'd seen at Tokyo's legendary Nichigeki Music Hall. Final stop of countless salarymen's nights on the town, the Nichigeki featured jazz and sequins, legs a-kicking and nipple tassels a-spinning, all of it packaged under the highbrow mission statement, articulated in the program for a 1952 show called *Summer Scandals,* of dedication to "the art of nudity, with a burning ambition of elevating it to a higher level."

Mizumori's bohemian father took her to one of the club's earliest shows when she was still in her early teens. The scene made such an impression that she sneaked out of her seat to explore the venue. "Backstage, the dancers were totally nude, their bottoms as pretty as peaches," she wrote in her memoir. "Later, when I went to see revues in America and France, all I did was stare at their bottoms. It was all about their bottoms. I didn't want to see their souls. I didn't want reality destroying the dream. I wanted them to be like angels, forever kawaii."

But she didn't design a girl for Tsuji. She delivered to him a cute kitten, a spiritual precursor to Hello Kitty called "Ado's Cat, Mii-tan." Ubercute baby talk, the name meant something like "meowy-meow." A ceramic figurine of Mii-tan, released in 1965, sold in huge numbers. In the years to come Tsuji released more than fifty products featuring Mizumori's work, making Mii-tan one of the iconic characters of the sixties.

He tried collaborating with other artists as well, some of whom became icons in their own rights. Among them were Toshiko Muto, who later helped design the Japan pavilion for Walt Disney World's Epcot Center, and Takashi Yanase, a manga artist who achieved great fame with *Anpanman,* Japan's most popular cartoon character for kindergartners. But in spite of Tsuji's eye for talent, none of these artists' work performed anywhere nearly as well as Mizumori's had. He was hemorrhaging money on the licensing fees he was paying to artists for products that simply weren't selling. Ever resourceful, Tsuji experimented with other ventures. He acquired the rights to distribute Mattel's Barbie dolls in Japan, but the imported toys couldn't compete with cheaper domestically produced versions. He signed on as Hallmark's Japanese distributor, but despite Japan's long tradition of giving gifts, the concept of sending illustrated greeting cards failed to catch on among the public.

Mizumori's use of the English alphabet gave her creations a gentle touch of the exotic. (*Yochi* is the equivalent of "good boy" for a pet.)

He was losing a fortune. He needed to figure out what made his successes— what made kawaii—tick.

. . .

IT WASN'T UNTIL the mid-twentieth century that someone set out to quantify what makes humans go "Aww." And he wasn't Japanese.

His name was Konrad Lorenz, and he was a Nazi. After graduating from medical school, he obtained a second doctorate in zoology and gained renown for his studies of animal behavior. Drafted in 1941, he served in a psychological division of the German military, providing research and commentary to support the regime's bilious obsession with eugenics and racial purity. In 1943, Lorenz turned his attention to the concept of human attachment, proposing a set of bodily and facial features that, when encountered, trigger a person's hardwired neural desire to nurture something. These features included a relatively large head in comparison to the body, large and low-lying eyes, bulging cheeks, stubby extremities, a "springy, elastic consistency," and wobbly movements. He referred to them as "innate releasing mechanisms," and collectively as the "baby schema." (After a four-year stint in a Soviet prison camp, Lorenz renounced his Nazi beliefs and went on to share a Nobel Prize for his contributions to the science of animal behavior.)

Despite its unseemly origin, the "schema" made some intuitive sense. Babies are exhausting—loud, messy, demanding constant attention—yet we love them nonetheless. There are obvious biological reasons for cherishing our own infants, but why do we dote on other children? And why do we lavish similar adoration on animals—the smaller and more seemingly helpless the better? Lorenz offered a very literal answer.

Years later, the evolutionary biologist Stephen Jay Gould applied Lorenz's schema to an unlikely subject: Mickey Mouse. In his earliest appearances, "the original Mickey was a rambunctious, even sadistic fellow," Gould noted in his 1979 essay, "A Biological Homage to Mickey Mouse." But as Mickey's personality softened, so too did his appearance begin to change. With a pair of calipers, Gould measured portrayals of the iconic character from the thirties, the forties, and the seventies. Citing the "power juvenile features hold over us,"

Gould quantified how Disney's artists—consciously or not—had applied the baby schema to tame their star rodent, making it more appealing to audiences.

Peanuts provides another example. When it debuted in October of 1950, it was utterly unlike anything Americans had seen in the funny pages. The very first strip's punch line involved an adorable tyke declaring his hatred for Charlie Brown. *Li'l Abner* creator Al Capp described the cast of elementary-schoolers as "good mean little bastards eager to hurt each other." In the introduction to a 2015 collection of *Peanuts* strips, *The Simpsons* creator Matt Groening recalled being "excited by the casual cruelty and offhand humiliations at the heart of the strip." To Garry Trudeau of *Doonsbury,* it "vibrated with fifties alienation."

It's hard to square this adulation with the *Peanuts* of later years, by which time the motley crew of "little bastards" had been boiled down into cute and lovable archetypes. And Snoopy the four-legged beagle had morphed into a bipedal, anthropomorphic creature with an enormous head in comparison to his body, stubby extremities, a springy, elastic consistency, and clumsy movements. Well, maybe not that last bit. He could dance, that Snoopy.

It was this later, gentler, cuter incarnation of *Peanuts,* and Snoopy in particular, that bewitched Sanrio's Tsuji. In an exploration of the history of the character, *The Atlantic* dated the infantilization to 1966, when the animated *It's the Great Pumpkin, Charlie Brown* devoted roughly a quarter of its screen time to Snoopy's imaginary adventures. Tsuji acquired the license two years after that, in 1968. It's entirely possible he never even knew of Snoopy's earlier four-legged incarnation.

He might not have figured out what his strawberry had in common with Mizumori's cartoons, but he had found another hit. In the space of a year, Snoopy products single-handedly revived the Yamanashi Silk Center's flagging fortunes.

Tsuji knew it was only a matter of time before rivals flooded the marketplace with similar products of their own. Why compete with them? As he later put it, Japan was "a world in which 'making money' meant 'making things.' I desperately wanted to leapfrog the 'things'—the 'hardware'—and make a business out of the intellectual property—the 'software.' I suspect everyone around me thought I was nuts."

In 1971, Tsuji launched an in-house design department and staffed it with young people, the majority of them women straight out of art school. In the wake of *Peanuts'* ongoing success, Tsuji gave the team a simple directive: "Draw cats and bears. If a dog hit this big, one of those two is sure to follow." He needed these designers because he planned to launch the first of a series of specialty boutiques in downtown Tokyo that same year, and it would require a steady stream of new products to stay well stocked.

Tsuji called it a Gift Gate. Telegraphing his ambitions, he ostentatiously chose a gloriously expensive spot in the heart of Tokyo's Shinjuku ward—in the shadow of Japan's luxe retail chains Mitsukoshi and Isetan. He took the basic formula from the Hallmark stores he had visited on trips to the United States. But the execution was pure Tsuji, and stepping inside the Gift Gate was like stepping inside his mind. The walls were made to look like a gingerbread house. A glossy white piano of the sort Liberace might play sat in the center of the room. And, of course, all around it were shelves packed with cards, notebooks, pens, stationery, storybooks, and every other kawaii product his company had to offer. In another innovation borrowed from Hallmark, Tsuji used the controlled environment of the shops to test new products and track sales, down to the individual unit—helping him pick the winning products for the next season.

Two years later, in 1973, he took the audacious step of renaming his firm. Inspired in part by Sony's example, Tsuji dreamed of taking his own products to the global marketplace, and he knew that a local-sounding mouthful like "Yamanashi Silk Center" wouldn't cut it anymore.

"'Sanrio' is a contraction of the Spanish *san rio,* which in English means 'sacred river,'" he explained. "The world's great civilizations flourished along rivers: the Tigris, the Euphrates, the Nile, the Yellow. That's what I was thinking when I named us, to promote our creation of a brand new culture." Such was the official line, anyway. But as it happens, the characters for "Yamanashi" can also be read "sanri," and "o" sounds variously like "man" or "king." Thus Sanrio sounds suspiciously like a homonym for "the lord of Yamanashi." Tsuji has never confirmed or denied this. "Companies need their inside jokes" was as much as he'd admit when pressed on the topic in a late-seventies interview. "You lose that, you're done."

. . .

Ultimate beauty. Life eternal. Fathomless horror. Unsolvable riddles . . . A deluge of blood and cold fingertips and melancholy smiles . . . Blood! The source of life! I get chills just imagining it!

THIS SURE DIDN'T sound like a comic for little girls—a *shojo manga*, as the genre was known in Japanese—but that's exactly where the scene was from. It was called *The Poe Clan*. Gekiga was about blood and sweat. The currency of *shojo manga* was tears, served up in dinner saucer–sized eyes hugely inspired by Naito's design work, quivering with anger, happiness, sadness, shame, or whatever emotional quandary the protagonist found herself in at the moment. Little lost waifs searching for amnesiac mothers or the other way around. Kind ballerinas triumphing over mean girls. Hearts torn asunder, then reunited. The stuff male editors expected girls to like. In their defense, it sold well enough. But fans of the genre ached for something more. *The Poe Clan*, first serialized in 1972, delivered it.

In a manga industry dominated by male talent, *The Poe Clan* was the first roar of a female artist named Moto Hagio. Hagio devoured sci-fi and fantasy growing up, both domestic and foreign. As an artist she was entirely self-taught, having strict parents who believed manga to be a detriment to a child's healthy development. She furtively studied Tezuka's *Cartoon College*, a tutorial he published detailing all the techniques professionals used, from sketchwork and framing down to specific types of papers, pens, and inks. But even after going pro, she kept her cartooning career a secret from her parents. (For many years, they thought she was an art teacher.)

Superficially *The Poe Clan* resembled the average girl's comic. Cleanly drafted lines and elaborately detailed backdrops, visual montages overlaid with poetic verse, overwrought declarations of eternal love. But *The Poe Clan*'s protagonists were not little girls. Edgar and Alan were a pair of young "vampirnellas," immortal and eternally beautiful, whiling away the decades sipping tea in rose gardens under the light of the moon, occasionally entwining hands. Through an idealized Victorian European landscape, they quested for blood and companionship years before *Interview with the Vampire* and *Twilight* introduced homoerotic vampires into the young-adult fiction of the West. *The Poe Clan* wasn't kawaii—it was too dark and suggestive for that—but it hit much the same sweet spot for teens as Sanrio's products did for the elementary school crowd, and in much the same way: intermingling an idealized sense of beauty with Western fantasy.

To their credit, the male gatekeepers of the *shojo manga* world indulged Hagio's fantasies, no matter how much they were confused by them. Upon seeing the first pages of *The Heart of Thomas*, a story of forbidden love between two high school boys, her editor begged her to "end it quickly." (He quickly relented after the first printing of a collection of *The Poe Clan* sold its entire initial print run of thirty thousand copies in a day.)

Who was buying it? The answer to that question was made clear in a Tokyo community center on a chilly winter day in December of 1975. It was the debut of Comic Market, Japan's first convention dedicated to self-published illustrated fanzines—what Japanese fans called *dojinshi*. Homages and parodies of popular manga and gekiga comics, they were created, sold, and traded by fan circles of amateur artists in a legal-copyright twilight zone. Comic Market promised to give them their first moment in the sun—or what passed for it—in an old conference room in the Fireman's Hall in Tokyo. In an inauspicious start, the organizers arrived late to their own event, leaving the grumbling participants locked out in the cold for a full half hour as they rushed to help the vendors set up.

Comic Market was dreamed up by a group of young men, most of them students at Tokyo's Meiji University, where they ran a manga fan club called *Meikyu* (The Labyrinth). They saw themselves as refugees from what was then Japan's biggest mainstream fan event, the Japan Manga Convention, an organization that venerated professionals and viewed fan fiction as an affront to established creators. Comic Market's organizers dreamed of shattering this imaginary wall. They assumed their event might attract a few dozen like-minded fans—even big events like the Japan Manga Convention and the annual Japan Science Fiction Convention, where the industry handed out its version of America's Nebula Award, pulled in a few hundred visitors at most.

They were shocked when their event was besieged by more than seven hundred visitors—and even more surprised by the demographic. They expected participants who looked like themselves. But 90 percent were teenage girls, trafficking in fan fiction based on neither the mainstream of boys' manga nor men's gekiga, but *shojo manga*. And a huge percentage of it was downright steamy. In parody after parody, fan-artists explored in thrillingly explicit ways the relationships Hagio had left implicit: lovingly detailing secret rendezvous between male characters that had only been hinted at in the originals. In time, female fans would christen this fetishistic genre *yaoi*, an acronym of the Japanese words "No climax, no closure, no meaning." It wasn't about storytelling; it was only about, in the words of aficionados, "the yummy parts"—the moments of beautifully androgynous boys aching to hook up with each other. Their work would dominate Comic Market for many years to come.

Hagio's success paved the way for female artists to flip the script and take over the girls' manga scene in the seventies, weaving often explicit themes borrowed from fan cultures like Comic Market into increasingly complex and powerful mainstream works. No longer would a wall stand between pro and fan; from this point on it would be a dialogue.

For the rest of the seventies, these superfans would remain a small but growing subculture. Meanwhile, an even younger female audience began to assert themselves as powerful consumers in their own right, using their pocket money to vote for the aesthetics that spoke to them. And Sanrio's Shintaro Tsuji, always a little ahead of the curve, was perfectly poised to oblige.

AS IT TURNED out, the first original hit of the Sanrio era wasn't a cat or a bear. It was a little girl, a tiny blonde in braids, created by a twenty-year-old designer working under the pen name Roko Maeda. Working for Sanrio was Maeda's first job out of art school, and she'd already enjoyed some success with a series of motifs featuring apples—a sort of throwback to Sanrio's earliest strawberry products. She created the character as the decoration for a canvas tote bag in 1974. The front of the bag featured the girl, and below her the phrase "Love is," while the reverse showed her from behind above the words "a little wish." It looked fresh and cute, with the English lettering giving it a little foreign-seeming flair, and customers snapped it up. The character, with her bulbous head, low-slung eyes, baggy cheeks, and vestigial-looking arms, resembled a toddler hippie—Ado Mizumori's frolicking cherubs as filtered through a Charles Schulz sensibility. It proved a pivotal moment for the company: Even if you've never seen her before, the little blonde with no mouth is instantly recognizable as classic "Sanrio style."

Tsuji hated it. "Honestly, I told everyone I thought it was no good," he says. "I was totally convinced it wouldn't sell at all." He didn't like that it was a little girl; he didn't like cluttering up the design with English lettering. If this ruffled Maeda, she didn't show it. No sooner had the tote bag hit the shelves than she introduced a boyfriend for her little creation, together with the beginnings of a background story. The girl's name was Patty; the boy was Jimmy.

They hailed from Kansas City (which one was never specified). She loved sports; he was the bookworm. Whether by design or simple cultural osmosis, Sanrio's first pair of stars followed the pattern set down decades earlier by Yumeji and the original pioneers of kawaii: Japanese sensibilities seasoned with just a teasing hint of foreignness. The duo would reign among the company's top sellers throughout the seventies; tellingly, a 1977 article in the *Asahi Shimbun* introduced Sanrio not as the Hello Kitty company but rather "Sanrio of 'Patty & Jimmy' fame," explaining to grown-up readers that "virtually every schoolgirl knows them," portraying the duo as a ray of sunshine in a dreary daily grind of school exams.

Maeda wasn't the only one designing characters at Sanrio, of course. At roughly the same time Patty & Jimmy leapt into existence on Maeda's desktop, one of her co-workers was quietly at work on a new creation of her own. Her name was Yuko Shimizu, and she was yet another twentysomething Sanrio had drafted straight out of art school. Because Shimizu loved cats, her work hewed closer to Tsuji's original request for animal mascots. "What I was thinking was, *Wouldn't it be really fun if one of these cats could talk like a person, lick ice cream like a person, go shopping like a person?*" she explained in an essay for Sanrio's in-house organ, *Strawberry News*, years later. "The very first drawing I did was of a kitten drinking milk from a straw. I did two types, a front view and a side view. I'd only just started on at the company, and when I showed the drawings to my assistant, she pointed to the one sitting sideways and screamed, 'This is it! This one is totally kawaii!'" Even among the experts in the trenches, it seemed, kawaii was something you couldn't define—you simply knew it when you saw it.

Tsuji didn't like this one, either. "I only thought it was okay," he often confesses in interviews, smiling and shaking his head. For the moment, it was nothing but another idea for a potential character. She wouldn't actually debut until the following year, in 1975, when the as-yet-unnamed cat turned out to be the hottest-selling variation on a certain vinyl coin purse.

The success came as a surprise to everyone, not least its creator. "It was selling way more than expected," recalled Shimizu. "Even I was shocked." Following the template established by Patty & Jimmy's success, Shimizu scrambled to create a backstory for the cat. She dubbed her Kitty, after the name of the protagonist's pet cat from her favorite book, *Alice's Adventures in Wonderland*.

What pop-cultural historians now call, in the manner of epidemiologists pinpointing an outbreak, "the first Kitty boom" occurred in 1977. A new series of Kitty products released for the start of the school year turned into that season's must-have items for the elementary-school-girl crowd. Sanrio products, and those of copycat competitors, quickly pushed generic products off the shelves in stationery shops—and drove new customers to Gift Gates in search of even more supercute stuff. Sanrio's "image as a purveyor of dreams and happiness seems to resonate with children immersed in tests and cram schools," noted the *Asahi Shimbun* in a profile published later that year, marveling at the firm's revenues doubling annually amid an economy soured by galloping inflation. A minor backlash ensued when the spokeswoman for a nationwide federation of housewives decried the craze by branding character-festooned school products unnecessary and expensive.

Ironically, Shimizu wasn't there to see it, or at least not from the inside; she'd left Sanrio the year before, after getting married and starting a family. As shocking as it might sound for the creator of such an iconic design to lay down her pen so early in her career, it was common sense in Japanese society: Women were expected to drop everything and focus on family matters after becoming pregnant. (Thus the existence of a "nationwide federation of housewives.") For all his progressiveness in empowering female employees, this was one cultural trend Tsuji didn't buck. To his thinking, it ensured a regular turnover, keeping the talent fresh and young—far closer in age to Sanrio's customer base than he was. Japan had nothing in the way of an Equal Employment Opportunity Act at the time, and this sort of marginalization of female talent was endemic in workplaces of the day.

Shimizu's former assistant, Setsuko Yonekubo—the same one who had declared Shimizu's initial illustration so very kawaii—oversaw Kitty during the boom years. She introduced incremental innovations like the first portrayal of Hello Kitty in a standing pose, but otherwise made a point of hewing closely to her predecessor's linework, down to using a photocopied template of Kitty's face to ensure uniformity. Whether because of this conservative approach or because of the ever-changing whims of young children, the first Kitty fad ran out of steam around 1979. Yonekubo took the opportunity to announce her own retirement, for she wanted to start a family of her own. In a testament to how little even Kitty's own creators understood the character's magic, Sanrio made no particular effort to replace her designer, and Yonekubo's departure left Kitty in a sort of kawaii limbo. In the face of steadily declining sales of Kitty products, the design team unsentimentally shifted focus to a promising new pair of up-and-comers called Little Twin Stars, a pair of angelic children in the Patty & Jimmy mode. Goodbye, Kitty.

Artists like Maeda and Shimizu had obviously tapped into something with their work, but it was equally clear from the hits and misses, the booms and busts, that nobody really understood why any particular doodle might resonate with Sanrio's customers. Not even Sanrio's own employees, nor even its owner. All they knew was that what worked was kawaii.

While Sanrio's artists couldn't have known it at the time, it turns out that kawaii design was proving a boon to their counterparts in a completely different field. Its successful application there provided the first hints that kawaii might be something more than girls' stuff, or even kid stuff. It proved so successful, in fact, that many people around the world would get their first taste of kawaii design sensibilities from it rather than through Sanrio's products. It was the field of video games.

. . .

SHIGERU MIYAMOTO WAS naked when the idea hit him. This was only natural, because he was sitting in a bathtub. It was in fact a traditional communal bath of the sort commonly found throughout Japan, the type where you soaped up and showered off before climbing in with everyone else for a long soak. Only, Miyamoto was alone; he had the whole tub to himself. This particular bath sat in the corner of a factory used to make traditional Japanese playing cards. That process required steam, and some of the hot water from the boilers was diverted into the baths as a perk for the laborers who worked there. The bath was empty because there weren't many laborers working there anymore; it was 1981, and Miyamoto's employer, Nintendo, was pivoting from cards into video games.

The pivot wasn't going so well. Nintendo's arcade games were derivative copies of better-selling titles. None were attracting players. Meanwhile, rivals were making a fortune. Out of desperation, the president of the company tasked the shaggy-haired twenty-nine-year-old with creating a hit.

Miyamoto didn't have a lick of programming experience. He was in fact a graphic designer. But this would prove to be a surprise asset. Video games of the era didn't look much like the ones we know today. There were no photorealistic 3-D graphics or thumping EDM soundtracks. They were bare-bones experiences, in which players were obligated to imagine that the crude squares and rectangles on-screen represented real-life objects like racquets and balls, or cars, or spaceships. By the time Miyamoto joined the industry, the technology had improved to the point where one could draw recognizable characters. Barely.

Miyamoto faced much the same problem as Sanrio's designers. For all its whimsy, Sanrio was in fact a purveyor of humdrum commodities like pencils or stationery or tableware. Its genius was in harnessing the power of cute characters to make these otherwise innocuous daily necessities stand out in a crowded marketplace. Miyamoto knew he needed a character to make his game stand out, too. But while Sanrio's designers were only limited by their imaginations, Miyamoto's ambitions were tightly constrained by the very real technical limitations of the computers and televisions of the era.

For example, his game's hero would need to fit inside a grid just sixteen pixels to a side. In the art world, conventional wisdom held that the average human body was equivalent to eight heads high. But a sixteen-by-sixteen matrix left little room for capturing realistic proportions. The number of dots was so small that if Miyamoto followed anatomical design principles, his hero's face would have ended up an unrecognizable two pixels high.

After struggling with this conundrum for weeks, he finally had his eureka moment: He didn't have to capture realistic proportions! He could go for something stylized, something squashed—something kawaii.

Once Miyamoto made that decision, everything else fell into place, letting him strip his hero down to the essentials. By giving the character a mustache, it wouldn't need a mouth; by giving it a cap, it wouldn't need a hairstyle; by putting it in red overalls, he could hint at the shape of arms without needing to draw them. Like Kitty, the resulting character used the barest minimum of elements and let users fill in the rest with their imaginations. "He was the first to bring that kawaii perspective to game characters," Masayuki Uemura, the designer of the Nintendo Entertainment System, told me. So it was that Mario was born—though, in this first incarnation as the player-character of 1981's *Donkey Kong*, he would be known simply as Jumpman.

That he debuted at the tail end of the Hello Kitty boom was no coincidence. They were cut from the same cultural cloth, one whose strands were now extending around the globe.

Donkey Kong thrived abroad because it was a well-crafted game, but also because its distinctively kawaii designs contrasted so strongly with the military-themed fare being produced by American makers, like *Missile Command* and *Battlezone*. The differences were more than skin deep. *Donkey Kong* didn't just look kawaii, it practically embodied it. No lasers, no spaceships, no explosions—just a little bobblehead running, jumping, and climbing. He had no enemies, really, save for the existential threats of careening oil barrels and simple gravity. And the antagonist Donkey Kong himself, of course, proving that kawaii design had the power to make even a ferocious escaped gorilla look cute.

Gamers in the West dubbed *Donkey Kong* and other kawaii-style fare from Japanese companies "cute games." At first, industry insiders were skeptical of these Japanese invaders that looked and sounded so different from American productions. "Their games don't cut it here," Tim Skelly, creator of American hits such as *Armor Attack* and *Star Castle,* told a journalist in 1982. "I foresee them losing a lot of business in the States." Things didn't play out that way. Cuties like *Pac-Man, Dig Dug,* and *Frogger* soon began outearning their macho rivals by a huge margin—one of Japan's earliest international pop-cultural triumphs on American soil. In fact, within a few short years it would be game over for the entire American industry. But that's a story for a later chapter.

YUKO YAMAGUCHI JOINED Sanrio in the midst of the Kitty boom in 1978, at the age of twenty-two. At the time, nobody—least of all her—realized just what a cultural force the little cat was destined to become.

As an art student, Yamaguchi didn't have any particular love for Sanrio's products; she dreamed of working in Japan's burgeoning advertising industry. But she was keenly aware of the hurdles young women faced in Japanese offices. She knew the men who ran ad firms would never let a woman direct ad campaigns. "I joined Sanrio not because I wanted to do character design but because I wanted to explore my potential," Yamaguchi explained years later.

Tsuji hadn't been particularly enthusiastic about Kitty when she debuted, but the president had warmed to her charms in the years since. (Undoubtedly, buckets of cash from the boom year helped.) When Tsuji learned that the team planned to abandon her, recalled

Yamaguchi, he flew into an uncharacteristic rage. "She's a symbol of friendship," she remembered him shouting. "You are *not* giving up on her!" He ordered the design department to stop what they were doing and hold an in-house competition for new Kitty concepts.

Everyone submitted ideas, but in the end it was Yamaguchi's that won: a whimsical illustration of Hello Kitty sitting at a piano surrounded by adoring family—a charming visual of a deeper backstory that had previously only been hinted at by Yamaguchi's predecessors. She was awarded the post of Hello Kitty's chief designer in 1980. To her, it was a bittersweet victory. "I feared that once you were appointed as the person to draw Hello Kitty, you wouldn't be able to draw other stuff," she explained in a 2002 interview. In her memoir, she is even more blunt. "Even after they told me, 'Kitty's yours now,' I didn't feel any particular love for her. Her head's huge, she's totally unbalanced, and nothing you make her wear looks good. She's got no expression. And if you ask me, those ears look like a pair of demon horns. . . . I just looked at her and thought, 'How the hell am I going to make her glow again?' I had no idea. I really didn't."

Yamaguchi took charge at a profoundly transformative moment for women in Japanese society. The early eighties marked the rise of what the Japanese mass media dubbed the *gyaru*, from the English word "gal." The word entered the lexicon in 1979, with the title of a hit Kenji Sawada song called "Oh! Gal," whose refrain declared "every woman is a superstar." Like English, the Japanese language brims with a wide variety of ways of referring to women, from the matter-of-fact *onna* (woman) or *josei* (female) to more nuanced terms such as *onna-no-ko* (little girl), *musume* (daughter), *ojosan* (young lady), *shojo* (young woman), and *obasan* (middle-aged lady). That Japanese felt the need for a new term was due to the latest crop of college girls and recent graduates. Defying societal expectations, they were less interested in settling down than in having a good time.

Grown-up Japanese of the era saw this newfound self-centeredness as utterly scandalous. The journalist Kazuma Yamane framed things in provocatively predatory terms. "If a 'gal' were an animal, she'd be a cat," he wrote in his 1991 book *Gyaru no Kozo* (*The Structure of the Gal*). "Not a *tanuki* [Japan's folkloric equivalent of the weasel], not a fox. Cats hide their claws behind cute faces and purrs, but possess the instincts to feed themselves."

Having been born in the early sixties, these young women had once been some of Sanrio's earliest customers. Now, as young adults, their ongoing obsession with things fancy proved a perfect fit for the glitzy excesses of "The Bubble Era," that peak of Japan's economic prowess in the second half of the eighties. Publishers rushed out new magazines with titles like *Gal's Life*, *Carrot Gals*, and *Popteen*, chock-full of juicy stories about young women cutting loose and loving it. The eighties were when slickly produced, hypercute idol superstars like Seiko Matsuda and Noriko Sakai first flooded the airwaves—the fuel for the emerging karaoke phenomenon and the forerunners of mass-market idol collectives like AKB48 that dominate Japanese entertainment today. It's when Haruki Murakami's self-described "100-percent love story" novel *Norwegian Wood* lofted him to superstardom, and when a twenty-four-year-old woman with the perky pen name of Banana Yoshimoto rocked the male-dominated literary world with *Kitchen*, her surprise 1988 bestseller about a college coed's ennui.

As gals' kawaii tastes saturated the mainstream, they spawned baby-talk fads among both genders, meta-slang like *burikko* (posers, trying too hard to look cute) and *bodikon* (body-conscious, skintight fashions). Spending their days shopping for Louis Vuitton and their nights out clubbing with cute boys, "gals embodied everything a proper young lady did not," wrote the sociologist Koji Namba: "frivolous, playful, easy, sexy, and ready for action." But the exploits of gals in the late eighties were just a taste of what was to come.

In the nineties, a generation of young women, inspired by the gals' example, emerged as a new breed of tastemakers in a culture long dominated by the tastes of men. Defiantly adopting the little-girlish and infantile as symbols of independence and power, teens used Sanrio's stuff as a sort of unspoken code to connect with one another, launch scandalous sexy-cute fashion trends, and decorate the latest new gadgets from pagers to early digital photography to cellphones and texting. Unabashedly embracing their inner children while maniacally adopting any gadget that expanded their social spheres, Japanese teens and young women unwittingly transformed themselves into global trailblazers. Yamaguchi would surf this societal wave to reorient Hello Kitty from a quaint Japanese phenomenon for kids into a global icon for everyone, internationalizing kawaii culture in the process. But that's a story to be continued in the pages to come.

In the meantime, what of that little plastic Hello Kitty purse that started it all? Somewhat incredibly, Sanrio neglected to keep a sample of this seminal product for itself. In the early nineties, employees made a concerted effort to find one in the storerooms of Sanrio's many offices and Gift Gates without success, and the Petit Purse was presumed lost forever. Then, a miracle: a woman who had received one as a little girl heard of the search and donated her sample to the company. It remains the only 1975-vintage Petit Purse known to exist anywhere in the world, and currently resides in a locked safe in Sanrio's headquarters in Tokyo. (A replica, produced as a limited-edition product in 1998, has become something of a collectors' item itself.)

For his part, Tsuji took a mostly hands-off role in the creation process, ceding most of the decisions to the largely female design team. The Japan of the seventies and early eighties was still very much a man's world, but Tsuji was still bucking the trend. By 1979, 70 percent of Sanrio's new hires were female. While the upper management remained entirely composed of men, simply giving young women as much freedom to propose, create, and manage their own design lines as Sanrio did was utterly unprecedented in the Japanese business world of the day.

Perhaps Tsuji's progressiveness in this regard can be traced back to the "little girl" those such as Mizumori noticed within him. Sanrio's second-in-command, Terry Ogisu, once spoke of visiting Tsuji's Tokyo home in the late seventies. Catching a glimpse inside his boss's open bedroom door, he was astounded to see a bed covered with Hello Kitty quilts, decked out with a pair of Little Twin Stars pillows with a teddy bear between them and a baby's mobile hanging from the ceiling. It looked more like a nursery than the bedroom of a married CEO pushing fifty. The lonely little orphan from Yamanashi had grown into a man who lived every day like it was his birthday. His personal tastes might have been a little peculiar, but in wanting to escape into his own private world, he was far from alone.

5

PLUGGING IN AND DROPPING OUT

The Walkman
1979

The Sony Walkman has done more to change human perception than any
virtual reality gadget.

—WILLIAM GIBSON

STEVE JOBS WAS on his worst behavior as he toured the factories of
Japan in 1983. He desperately needed a supplier of 3.5-inch floppy-
disk drives for his newest creation, a revolutionary personal computer system he called the Macintosh. Yet he wore jeans and sneakers
to meetings with formally dressed CEOs and their salaryman under-
lings. He showed no appreciation for the meticulously wrapped gifts
they presented him, often committing the unthinkable faux pas of
forgetting them on the table after a meeting. And he snapped at the
engineers bearing what were, to them, the jewels of their company.
"This is a piece of crap! Anybody could build a better drive than
this!"

There was one exception, and that was Sony. When the Silicon
Valley wunderkind met Sony co-founder and chairman of the board
Akio Morita, Morita was a young-looking sixty-two and Jobs a practically teenage-looking twenty-eight. Jobs was, to put it mildly, a
Sony fanboy. Apple had shared a building with Sony in Cupertino for
several years after its founding, and Jobs made a point of visiting
their offices regularly for the latest product catalogs. He even collected samples of their corporate letterhead, so fascinated was he
with the company's typefaces and layouts. Some thought his fascination bordered on the fetishistic. The younger Jobs peppered the

The TPS-L2 Walkman

elder Morita with questions about the products, the factories, even the uniforms Sony employees wore. Like an indulgent uncle, Morita patiently answered each in turn. At the end of their meeting he bestowed upon Jobs a gift of his own. It was called the Walkman. A personal stereo system, Morita explained. So that you could listen to music anytime, anywhere.

For once, Jobs didn't leave his gift behind. He was a lifelong music aficionado who worshipped Bob Dylan, briefly dated Joan Baez, meticulously assembled a top-of-the-line home stereo from the best available gear, and insisted that the Macintosh design offices were outfitted with a high-fidelity music system at all times. But concerts and stereos were public listening experiences, something you shared with those around you. The Walkman wasn't a great hi-fi; it couldn't be, at its size, with the technology of the era. But it marked the advent of something we take for granted today: individualized, personal listening, whenever and wherever you want it. Few could have predicted how game-changing this innovation would prove to be. Jobs was one of them.

Even after getting home, Jobs didn't listen to his Walkman. He took it apart piece by piece. No component, no matter how tiny, escaped his gaze, how all the little pieces fit together in the sleek plastic-and-metal housing. Jobs didn't need to put on the Walkman's headphones to know that it was more than the sum of its parts. In its array of tiny levers, gears, capstans, and miniaturized motors was written an entirely new narrative of cool. This company from Japan, with its genial silver-haired chairman, had cracked the code of making the high-tech fashionable.

"He didn't want to be IBM. He didn't want to be Microsoft. He wanted to be Sony," recalled John Sculley, whom Jobs had just lured away from PepsiCo to become CEO of Apple. At the time, very few American businessmen saw Sony in the way Jobs did. For a long while, none at all had. But the hints had long been there, if you knew where to look for them.

THE HEADLINE IN the January 24, 1958, issue of *The New York Times* read, "4,000 Tiny Radios Stolen in Queens." It was obviously a professional job. The crew approached the Delmonico International warehouse on Orchard Street from the neighboring rail yard at dusk, climbing atop a freight car and then leaping onto the roof of a garage to gain access to a second-story window.

After jimmying it open, they entered and began meticulously picking through towers of boxes for their quarry, the must-have item of the previous holiday season: tiny, colorful Sony TR-63 transistor radios. They loaded four hundred cartons onto wooden pallets, then broke through the locks of four rooms lying between them and the freight elevator to the ground-level loading platform, where a truck was already waiting. Hiding in plain sight, the thieves loaded the boxes in full view of a busy freight yard and local businesses, then drove off into the night. With them disappeared $160,000 worth of transistor radios, the single largest heist of its kind in American history. The police questioned more than fifty witnesses. Nobody saw, or admitted to seeing, anything. The perpetrators were never caught or even identified.

You'd naturally expect the victims to be outraged, but in fact they were quietly overjoyed. A series of newspaper articles and radio reports over the next few days repeatedly emphasized the fact that only one company's radios had been stolen, and that company was Sony. The *Times* coverage practically read like a press release: "The Delmonico Corporation says it is the sole importer and distributor of Sony Radio, built in Japan. Each of the $40 radios is 1¼ inches thick, 2¾ inches wide, and 4½ inches high. The police said twenty cases of [other brands'] radios were left behind, in addition to thousands of dollars of other electronic equipment." You couldn't buy publicity like this! For a few days, at least, Sony was on every New Yorker's lips as the story of the daring break-in and the discriminating thieves' focus on high-tech pocket-sized radios made the rounds. For weeks afterward, businessmen ribbed Sony's representative in New York City for tips on how they might be robbed so successfully themselves. All he could reply was that Sony hadn't planned it this way, and that they were at wit's end trying to ramp up production to replace the four thousand units. Their "pocketable" transistor radios, the world's smallest, were selling—and in this one case, getting stolen—faster than Sony could keep up.

When Morita had made the rounds of New York retailers three years earlier, he was just thirty-four. The buyers for the department stores practically laughed in his face. "Everybody in America wants big radios! We have big houses, plenty of room. Who needs these tiny things?" To which Morita would calmly reply, again and again: "Yes, your houses are big—big enough for every family member to have their own room, where they might turn on this tiny radio and listen to whatever pleases them." The warehouse theft was a crime, of course, but it was also a sort of vindication. Only a decade and change out from a devastating war between the United States and Japan, and now Americans wanted Japanese radios badly enough to steal them.

The story of how that came to be begins during World War II. That is when Morita met Masaru Ibuka, the man who would found Sony. At the time both were assigned to a special naval engineering group. Morita, the scion of a prosperous saké brewer and miso maker, had been raised in the lap of luxury in Nagoya. He studied physics before he was drafted into the navy's research division. Ibuka, thirteen years Morita's senior, ran a company that produced precision-measuring instruments. A brilliant electrical engineer, Ibuka served as the research group's leader. Their mission was devising, among other things, heat-seeking missiles. This was fantastically cutting-edge stuff; the first viable weapons of this sort wouldn't debut for decades after war's end. It was a fool's errand, given the shortages of materials and manpower facing Japan at the time, but the nation was losing the war, and the military was desperate.

They worked in a deliberately nondescript facility located far from any big cities, in the rugged hills of the Miura Peninsula, near the mouth of Tokyo Bay. Even still, it was hard to focus on their work. Air-raid sirens interrupted them constantly as B-29s passed overhead, returning from unleashing their deadly payloads on the capital or neighboring Yokohama. More than once Morita and Ibuka would catch sight of an American bomber, fatally wounded by anti-aircraft batteries, arcing on a last fiery plunge into the sea.

After war's end, the pair parted ways. Morita returned home, while Ibuka moved to Tokyo to open his own laboratory, which he soon incorporated under the name Tokyo Tsushin Kogyo (Tokyo Telecommunications Engineering), or Totsuko for short. It wasn't easy recruiting employees; the city was a shambles, and food was scarce. Like Kosuge with his jeep of salvaged tin, Ibuka and his first seven hires picked through dumps and black markets for the parts to make first an automatic rice cooker, then a bread maker—neither of which worked well enough to commercialize. Finally, Ibuka came up with the firm's first hit: a gadget for converting normal FM radios into shortwave receivers, letting listeners pick up international broadcasts. With little in the way of commercial components available, the devices were assembled from vacuum tubes scavenged from the black markets, housed in cases made from scrap wood. Even still, they proved popular among citizens hungry for news from abroad, and earned Ibuka a profile in the national *Asahi Shimbun* newspaper. Seeing the article, Morita leapt on a train to rejoin his old mentor. Shortly thereafter, Morita convinced his father to invest 190,000 yen in the company. This was an unthinkable sum for the average Japanese in those drab postwar years, far more than the annual salary of a well-paid white-collar worker.

Even with the shot in the arm, Totsuko's early years were hand-to-mouth, as the company focused on producing the shortwave adapters and replacement parts for keeping phonograph players running. These products found an eager audience both in homes and in the restaurants and bars that played the soundtrack for a new era: swing and jazz, introduced to locals by American servicemen.

Totsuko set up its offices in the Gotenyama neighborhood of Tokyo. Long ago, the hills of the area had been a sylvan retreat for Japan's aristocracy. Hokusai captured the scene in an 1832 woodblock print. It showed a spring cherry blossom viewing party overlooking the tiled rooftops of what was then a low city of paper and wood, Mount Fuji visible in the distance under a cerulean sky. In 1947, the neighborhood was as pockmarked by the scars of war as the rest of the city. Totsuko occupied an old warehouse in such disrepair that employees needed to open umbrellas over their desks if it rained. On the other hand, if it was sunny, they had to thread their way through freshly laundered diapers fluttering from neighbors' clotheslines: the first signs of a postwar baby boom. To power their sole vehicle for making deliveries, Ibuka and Morita—the only employees with driver's licenses—bartered with GIs for gasoline illicitly siphoned out of army jeeps.

Totsuko's first original product was a tape recorder. It was inspired by a glimpse of an American model that Ibuka had seen on a visit to NHK, the Japanese national television broadcaster, which was then under the control of the occupation forces. Ibuka convinced the Americans to allow his engineers to examine this exotic device, then had his men set about making their own. Ibuka was unable to procure plastic tape due to ongoing postwar material shortages, so he and a wizard of an engineer named Nobutoshi Kihara pinned long strips of Japanese *washi* paper to the lab's floor, then handcoated it with a slurry of glue and magnetic powder that Kihara literally cooked up in the company kitchen with a cast-iron frying pan. Primitive but ingeniously designed, the 1950 G-type Tapecorder was but the first of many recorders to come, a cornerstone of the firm's consumer-electronics empire. But the first product to put Totsuko on the map was that little transistor radio, released under their new brand name of Sony in December of 1957.

Morita and Ibuka invented the word as a play on *sonus*, the Latin for sound, and the bright-sounding word "sonny," as in "sonny boy," a turn of phrase picked up from American servicemen. Sony was concise and easy to pronounce in multiple languages. That it didn't sound even remotely Japanese was either an added plus or the entire point.

Today we most closely associate the transistor with integrated circuits and computers, but its first widespread commercial use was in miniaturizing the radio. Until the creation of the first transistor at Bell Labs in 1947, complex electronic devices depended on bulky and fragile vacuum tubes. As a result, radios were heavy, furniture-like appliances that sat in one place and obliged those who wanted to listen to gather around them. Transistors—simpler, cheaper, smaller, and more efficient—promised to revolutionize the electronics industry, if anyone could figure out a way to mass-produce them. The technical hurdles were significant enough that some worried the innovation might remain a laboratory curiosity.

When Ibuka learned of the transistor's existence on a visit to the United States in 1952, he immediately grasped the new invention's potential. The following year, he sent Morita to Western Electric, the company that owned Bell Labs, to negotiate a license to manufacture transistors. Even with the support of the same scientists who created the transistor, Sony's engineers struggled to craft one that could be reliably made in large quantities. Through years of trial and error, they virtually reinvented the device from the ground up; their laboratory experiments proved so ahead of the curve that one of the team's members, the physicist Leo Esaki, would go on to win a Nobel Prize based on discoveries he made during the course of the project.

Sony wasn't the first to get a transistor radio to market. The very first was produced by a tiny Indianapolis company called Regency, whose three-by-five-inch TR-1 hit American shelves in Christmas of 1954. A high defect rate meant few of the transistors the factory manufactured were actually usable, forcing Regency to retail the radios for $49.99—the equivalent of more than $400 in modern currency. Adding insult to injury, it sounded worse than standard vacuum tube models. Nevertheless, Regency sold a hundred thousand of them in the first year: respectable enough figures for a novelty product, but only the merest drop in the bucket for a nation home to some ninety-three million radio sets. Instead it was Sony's "pocketable" TR-63, released in late 1957, that would turn the transistor radio into a mass social phenomenon.

It was only slightly larger than a pack of cigarettes, but "pocketable" was an exaggeration. In Japan, Morita had special dress shirts tailored, with subtly oversized shirt pockets, for his salesmen. Still, it was noticeably smaller than the Regency model—and ten dollars cheaper, to boot. It also came in a rainbow of fun colors: black, red, yellow, and green. The tiny radios were an instant hit, the first must-have electronic product of the postwar era. Rhapsodized in songs from the Beach Boys to Van Morrison, transistor radios were the iPods of their generation: a metaphor for fun and independence, made in Japan. Within two years of the debut of the TR-63 and its successor the TR-610, Sony and other Japanese rivals were exporting six million transistor radios to America annually. At the peak of the phenomenon in 1969, Americans were scooping up more than twenty-seven million transistor radios every year. It was a rare American home that didn't have at least one, and many even more than one. In a little over a decade a technological triumph had been transformed into an unremarkable commodity.

As for the transistor itself, it would go on to become the most widely manufactured object in human history. A single modern computer chip can contain billions of them. The semiconductor industry analyst Jim Handy estimates that, altogether,

A 1957 airlift of TR-63s from Japan to the United States

thirteen sextillion have been produced since the day of their inception in 1947. A sextillion is one followed by twenty zeros—meaning there are many more transistors on Earth than there are stars in the Milky Way.

MORITA WAS FAR from the only Japanese person doing business deals in America in the mid-fifties, but most of them did so through long-established Japanese trading companies that specialized in helping manufacturers export their products abroad. Their expertise in shipping and clearing customs, handling logistics and distribution, and serving as the face of foreign corporations abroad was a godsend to firms without any experience doing business in foreign lands. And there was certainly money to be made partnering with these powerful and connected intermediaries. But Morita, born into wealth, dreamed of more than just financial reward. He wanted a powerful and connected company of his own. Bucking convention, he left his family behind temporarily to move to New York City. His goal was to master American business customs, without any help from the trading companies at all. It was unheard of for a Japanese executive at his level to uproot himself in this way.

Predictably, it was hard going at first. Morita spoke hardly any English, and due to the difficulties of wiring money internationally in the fifties, he had barely any cash. He stayed in cheap hotels and took his meals in automats, those fanciful vending-machine cafeterias of the pre–fast food era. But Morita was a fast learner, and as he made friends and business partners, he soaked in their advice and knowledge: Better to eat in fancy restaurants to learn about the service. Better the cheapest room in the best hotel than the best room in a cheap hotel. You're the face of a prestigious company. Image matters.

Yet he wasn't afraid to get his hands dirty. When thirty thousand of the latest transistor radios arrived at a New York warehouse in 1960, Morita traded his suit for overalls and helped unload the trucks. At the end of a very long day, one of the workers inadvertently triggered the burglar alarm. Instantly surrounded by guards dispatched from the security company, Morita and his grubby-looking crew undoubtedly feared they'd spend the night in jail. Fortunately, another employee arrived with the combination to the safe, which contained all the documents proving they were who they said they were. At least they knew the alarm worked.

In spite of it all, Morita loved the United States. He loved the openness, the progressiveness, the neon energy of New York City. He worked long hours, but he reveled in his free time, too. He went to concerts and museums. He took in Broadway shows like *My Fair Lady*. He dined at the finest restaurants. And most of all he walked. He walked all over the city, but his favorite spot was Fifth Avenue, where he could soak in the ambiance of what were then the top purveyors of American refinement and sophistication. Tiffany & Co. Cartier. Saks Fifth Avenue. Bergdorf Goodman. Before long, a plan formed. Sony would have a showroom here, too. As he looked around for a suitable spot, he noticed something. The flags of many nations were fluttering along the avenue, but nary a Japanese one was in sight. They had all come down after Pearl Harbor.

Transistor radios and tapedecks remained the staple of Sony's product line, but Morita hungered for a true flagship product to announce the showroom's presence to the world. Fortunately for him, Ibuka's band of merry engineers were hard at work on the firm's latest innovation. Shortly after the debut of the TR-63 transistor radio, Ibuka had the crew apply the same technology to television, successfully shrinking the normally furniture-sized television down to a (semi-) portable thirteen pounds. The TV8-301 definitively cemented Sony's reputation for creating stylish, miniaturized consumer electronics. With its rounded, space-age housing it looked somehow futuristic and timeless all at once, but it was hideously expensive and so prone to malfunction that it was nicknamed the "frail little baby." Ibuka was already putting the finishing touches on a more durable and moderately priced successor, the TV5-303. It was the perfect product for launching the new venture.

Opening day on Fifth Avenue was pandemonium, the tiny space thronged by more than four hundred guests and local dignitaries, with huge crowds pouring into the streets. Flying from the façade, above the SONY logo, was the Japanese *Hinomaru*, fluttering right alongside the Stars and Stripes. It was the first time a Japanese flag had flown in the city in more than twenty years. If there were any concerns over bad blood from the war, they dissipated over the next few days as thousands of New Yorkers made their way through the space for a glimpse of the tiniest TV anyone had ever seen.

The showroom was just the beginning. Behind the scenes, Morita ensured that the very first TV5-303 off the production line went to Frank Sinatra, establishing a precedent of courting American celebrities that would continue in the decades to come. Ibuka the engineer grappled with miniaturization as a fascinating technical puzzle; Morita the marketer keenly saw its potential for elevating personal electronics into a form of fashion—or even a new form of lifestyle.

Forging friendships with movers and shakers including David Rockefeller, *Vogue* editor in chief Diana Vreeland, fashion designer Bill Blass, Motown songwriter Jimmy Levine, and the composer Leonard Bernstein, among many others, he reinforced the connection between Sony's high-tech products and the nation's cultural elite. Morita spent increasing amounts of his precious free time studying American print and television advertising. He shot footage of the glorious signage of Broadway and Times Square for hints about how to sell Sony's brand in Japan. Then, after catching one of Doyle Dane Bernbach's classic "Think Small" ads for the Volkswagen Bug, he hired the agency to craft Sony an image for the U.S. They unveiled an edgy print campaign showcasing average Joes and Janes with "micro-TVs" in unexpected places ranging from barber chairs to fishing canoes to nudist camps. The trifecta of cutting-edge consumer gear, hip customers, and slick advertising established a new paradigm for pushing high-tech gadgets on average citizens. More than any other company, Sony drilled into the global consciousness the idea that, when it came to electronics, smaller meant better. This would turn out to have some surprisingly profound effects on the way we listened to music, transforming popular culture and spawning new countercultures.

The portable transistor radio transformed music culture by freeing young listeners from the shackles of parental approval, letting them mainline rock and roll in the privacy of their own rooms. "It opened my world up," says the engineer Steve Wozniak, who went on to play the role of Ibuka to Steve Jobs's Morita at Apple Computer. "I could sleep with it and hear music all night long." They listened to newfangled forms of music with titles that mystified the grown-ups, like 1954's "Rock Around the Clock"—the first song with "rock" in its title. Through their musical choices over the years to come, young Americans would construct the soundtrack for an ideological rebellion, most obviously in the form of the protest rock that sustained student activists of the sixties. But while portable radios fostered a newfound sense of independence, listeners still remained entirely dependent on gatekeepers—the radio stations and the deejays—for their listening choices. And so it would remain for many years to come.

THE OFFICIAL STORY is that the Walkman emerged out of a conversation between Ibuka and Morita in early 1979. "The idea took shape when Ibuka came into my office one day with one of our portable stereo tape recorders and a pair of our standard-sized headphones," wrote Morita in his memoirs. "I asked him what he was doing, and then he explained, 'I like to listen to music, but I don't want to disturb others. I can't sit there by my stereo all day. This is my solution—I take my music with me. But it's too heavy.'" Ibuka's gadget of choice was then Sony's smallest tapedeck, the TC-D5 field recorder. Intended for recording-industry professionals, it was the size of a box of breakfast cereal and weighed close to five pounds, even without batteries—necessitating the use of a heavy nylon carrying strap.

Morita recalled a recent visit to the United States, where he saw—or more to the point, heard—a new phenomenon gripping New York City: the boom box, the street name for the battery-powered portable tapedecks produced by his own and rival firms. Even larger than the TC-D5—some were easily more than double its size—they were affordable and very, very loud. In the late seventies they had developed an unexpected following among inner-city youth. Carried into the streets perched on a shoulder, or positioned on a corner to spark a break-dancing battle, they provided a new urban sonic backdrop designed to provoke. "Back then, the black man wasn't being heard in society," wrote the hip-hop historian Adisa Banjoko. "When he's got his boom box in his hand, you're forced to hear him." Critics disparaged them as "ghetto blasters," but Morita put two and two together: People wanted to take their music with them. And so he directed his staff to prepare a prototype of a miniature stereo cassette player.

In fact, the story is more nuanced. According to several sources inside the company, a prototype already existed, constructed by an unnamed young Sony engineer as a playful experiment. Ibuka's request simply rekindled this whimsical personal project back to life. The tape recorder division quickly whipped up a more polished sample from an existing product called the Pressman. Intended for journalists to record interviews and press conferences onto cassette tapes, the Pressman played back monaural sound over a single tiny internal speaker. (Apollo astronauts had carried a similar, earlier Sony model with them to record notes on the moon missions.) Modifying it to play back two-channel stereo music over a pair of headphones required gutting nearly every feature inessential to playing back music. Out went the internal speaker and the recording function.

This caused a great deal of consternation within the ranks. Despite Ibuka and Morita's enthusiasm, the concept upended decades of conventional wisdom. It was a tapedeck that couldn't record, a portable listening device without a speaker, and even more startling, a piece of consumer gear that actually obligated users to wear head-phones. You know who wore headphones in 1979? Telegraph opera-tors wore headphones. Submarine sonar operators wore headphones. Airplane pilots wore headphones. Nobody else save a few crazed hi-fi nerds did, and those obsessive techies weren't exactly trendsetters. (Not yet, anyway.) Further complicating things was an unfortunate social prejudice against the handicapped; anything you put in your ears to hear with, headphones included, was associated with im-paired hearing or deafness in Japan. (Perhaps this was true abroad, too; a 1960 ad for a Zenith transistor radio in *Life* magazine adver-tised its "private listening attachment" rather than using "earpiece" or "earphone.") As a result, nobody at Sony was willing to sign off on the gadget, and the fact that neither Ibuka nor Morita pushed it through testifies to their own ambivalence on the matter.

Then again, you have to remember the state of the art in head-phones at the time. They were complicated plastic-and-rubber con-traptions that resembled earmuffs more than audio gear. If you were lucky, each ear-swallowing cup was the size of a hockey puck. If you were unlucky, they were closer to the size of a softball cut in half. Or maybe they just felt that way: The average set tipped the scales at four hundred grams, or around a pound. (A pair of wireless AirPods weigh just four grams each.) This was fine if you were lounging around mission control, but they defeated the purpose of creating a truly portable stereo system.

Yet the headphones were key to the enterprise. They *were* the enterprise, even more than the Walkman was. Tapedecks had con-tinued to shrink in size—the TC-D5 field recorder and the Press-man were proof of that—but for the most part, headphones had remained defiantly gargantuan. In the mid-seventies, headphones were such a niche business that statistics are scarce. Today, head-phones represent a ten-billion-dollar-a-year industry, far bigger than music players themselves. iPod sales have dwindled to the point that Apple stopped reporting their sales figures in 2014; yet that same year, they purchased the headphone company Beats by Dre for

$3.2 billion—at the time the single largest corporate acquisition in Apple's history. (Ironically, Beats by Dre rose to fame by successfully convincing young consumers that they wanted bulbous seventies-style headsets, of the sort preferred by deejays, instead of cutting-edge earbuds.)

So the Walkman's success depended on pairing the portable cassette player with an equally portable way of listening to it. As it turned out, another Sony division already had a pair of lightweight headphones in the works. Unlike standard models, they were "open-air," sitting atop the ears on pads of colorful foam rather than engulfing them in plastic and rubber. They were simpler and much cheaper to produce than the standard models. And best of all was their weight: just fifty grams—an eighth of a standard set.

The pairing of these tiny earphones with the cassette deck was the turning point for the product, a sudden jump from dream to reality. "I was shocked the first time I heard it," recalled the Sony designer Yasuo Kuroki. "How on earth was something this small putting out such powerful sound? Everyone knows what headphones sound like today, but at the time, you couldn't even imagine it, and then suddenly Beethoven's Fifth is hammering between your ears."

The first production model, officially called the TPS-L2, was a strange beast by modern portable-listening standards. Roughly the dimensions of a paperback book, it was significantly larger than even the old TR-63 transistor radio; there was no way it would fit in a pocket. Instead, users had to clip it to a belt or waistband, using an included faux-leather holster accessory. Even more surprisingly, it was intended both for solo listening and for use by two people, with ports for two sets of head-

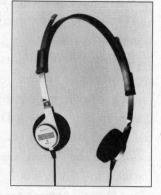

The "featherweight" headphones included with the very first Walkman were startlingly compact for their time.

phones. This last specification came at the request of Morita himself, who had discovered something we take for granted today: It was impossible to carry on a conversation while wearing the device. In an effort to offset the isolating nature of listening to music on headphones, he ordered the head engineer to add the second headphone jack and a bright orange button, dubbed the "hot line," that would mute the music and allow tandem users to talk to each other via a microphone hidden in the housing—one of the few components remaining from the device's origin as a recorder for journalists. (Hinting at romantic possibilities, Kuroki playfully labeled the twin headphone jacks GUYS & DOLLS on the very first production run, a joke that was quickly dropped in favor of a more straightforward A and B.)

But a bigger concern remained: Would it sell? Much as he loved the TPS-L2 personally, Morita agonized over the budget and details, calling in the heads of various departments to give him their takes on how many units they might move. Nobody had a clue. No company had ever released a product like this before. Reluctantly, Morita acquiesced to Kuroki's request to convene a focus group. This was extraordinary. Morita deeply mistrusted customer surveys, and Sony prided itself on never consulting consumers in developing new products.

"The public does not know what is possible," he wrote in his memoirs. "We do."

Yet here, for once, Morita cast his lot with the public. Five prototypes were loaded up with tapes of recent hits and shown to groups ranging in age from middle schoolers to college students. As a hundred of these testers cycled through headquarters over the course of the next ten days, Kuroki noticed two things. One was that the young men and women responded to the device instinctively, knowing what to do with it even without having been given instructions of any kind. The other was that at least one in five quickly lost themselves in the music, bobbing their heads and tapping their feet. It wasn't much to go on, but it seemed promising, anyway. Kuroki worked up a sales estimate based on the number of students in Japan at the time. He figured, conservatively, they could sell sixty thousand Walkmans before the novelty faded. But it turned out the factory couldn't possibly produce that many in time. Morita decreed that the first run would be just thirty thousand. It was a testament to how little expectation surrounded the product. By comparison, the first run of the old TR-63 transistor radio way back in '57 had been a hundred thousand units. The most popular products, such as the Trinitron TV series, had annual production runs in the millions.

Kuroki suggested naming the gadget the Hot Line, after the functionality that allowed one user to talk with the other. Tohru Kohno, head of the promotional team, immediately pushed back. "That's a function, not a product name," he argued. "Let's call it 'Walkie.'" The team even worked up a logo, with the *a* sprouting little walking feet. Then they learned Toshiba had already copyrighted the word. Kohno really didn't want to abandon it, so he fused "Pressman" with "Walkie" to make "Walkman." "It was the first portable stereo of its kind, so I knew the product would be hard to understand," he told me over coffee in downtown Tokyo. "I wanted a name that would teach customers what it was." Morita was cool on the idea but didn't have anything better. Walkman it would be.

A gala release event, thrown for the press in Tokyo's iconic Yoyogi Park, generated approximately zero headlines. An oddball advertising campaign centering on a spandex-clad Caucasian blonde leading a Japanese geezer around by the headphone wire failed to stir the nation's passions, or at least their electronic ones. There was no grand plan, just an attempt to dazzle as best they could with limited resources. "We weren't given the budget to do much else," Kohno said, sighing. For a product that would so profoundly transform the way we listen, the Walkman's debut in July of 1979 was heralded by near total silence.

THE WALKMAN'S ARRIVAL coincided with the beginning of a wild ride for both Japan and the West. An oil crisis sparked by the Iranian Revolution sent fuel prices skyrocketing around the world, triggering chaos. Panicked Americans swarmed gas stations, leading to strict fuel rationing and long queues of customers that looked like something out of the Soviet Union. Conspiracy theories swirled that the crisis had been manufactured by the press, the oil companies, the politicians. Frustration erupted into violence when two thousand furious truckers occupied downtown Levittown, Pennsylvania, barricading its main street with flaming tires and vehicles in protest of spiraling fuel costs.

Across the Pacific, Japan was thriving. It had emerged as the top supplier of the world's cars and manufacturing electronics, producing products that delighted customers even as they stoked resentment among American autoworkers, businesspeople, and policymakers. Thanks in large part to those exports, Japan rose to become the world's second-largest economy in 1978—an incredible triumph for a country whose major cities had been bombed-out piles of cinder just thirty years earlier. Where police had failed to snuff the student protests of the previous decade, prosperity succeeded: Citizens enjoyed an enviable combination of rapid economic growth, low inflation (just 3.8 percent, compared to America's 13.3 percent at the time), low unemployment, and high job security. Gleaming metropolises, rebuilt after the war, proved to be city-sized petri dishes for new trends and fads. Their inhabitants were largely well off, highly educated, and possessed of both disposable income and a desire for leisure (even if perpetually harried citizens barely had time for it). Desperately craving quick fixes of fun and escape amid stressed-out lives in overpacked cities, Japanese citizens were uniquely positioned to appreciate the appeal of a fantasy-delivery device like the Walkman. Just as the karaoke machine allowed grown-ups to escape into the fantasy role of professional entertainer, the Walkman offered the promise of a personally curated soundscape wherever you went. It is no coincidence that it debuted at precisely the moment Japanese creators were perfecting another form of electronic escape: the video game.

The Americans had invented this new form of leisure. The first hit arcade game, *Pong*, debuted in a shabby Sunnyvale, California, bar in September of 1972. It was created by Al Alcorn, an engineer at a Silicon Valley start-up called Atari, a company that took its name from the Japanese word for cornering an opponent in the game of Go.

Even by the technical standards of the day, *Pong* was primitive. The gameplay consisted of a glowing pair of oblong "racquets" and a square "ball" bouncing across the inky depths of a black TV screen; the only rules provided were the words INSERT COIN and a Zen koan–like AVOID MISSING BALL FOR HIGH SCORE. For the price of a quarter, two players could face off in a video ping-pong battle—the first public virtual sport, though the era of stadium-filling professional gaming bouts lay many decades in the future.

In spite of its simplicity, *Pong* proved fiendishly addictive. Over the next two years, Atari shipped thousands of *Pong* machines to venues throughout the United States, and it quickly emerged as one of the most profitable coin-operated games ever made. Fifty dollars a week was considered a good take for a pinball machine; the best *Pong* machines regularly brought in two hundred dollars. The only problem was you needed two people to play it. Atari's co-founder Nolan Bushnell had the germ of an idea for a single-player sequel called *Breakout*. It was, essentially, a version of *Pong* turned on its side, in which players would use the paddle and ball to knock out a wall of blocks at the top of the screen.

By this time, game manufacturers had moved from those early hardwired designs to using programmable integrated computer chips. The chips were, at this early stage of their development, very expensive and prone to burning out, which necessitated a steady supply of replacements. To keep costs down, Bushnell challenged his staff to devise a version using fewer chips than normal. He set a baseline of fifty chips, and offered a hefty bonus for every chip below that number that a designer managed to omit from their design.

In a story now enshrined in Silicon Valley lore, a young employee by the name of Steve Jobs, recently returned from a pilgrimage to

India, volunteered for the mission. By some accounts he was still dressed in saffron robes and sporting a shaved head. He didn't do any of the work himself. Instead, he subcontracted it to none other than Steve Wozniak, the very same person who had spent his childhood nights enchanted by the transistor radio. Now twenty-three, Wozniak had blossomed into a crack electronics engineer. He worked days at Hewlett-Packard. Nights he spent hanging out with Jobs, whether in the garage or at the Atari offices. ("I knew that Jobs and Woz were fast friends and Woz worked days at HP," said Bushnell in a 2015 Reddit post. "If I put Jobs on the night shift, I'd get two Steves for the price of one.")

In spite of there being no particular deadline, Jobs planned to take another sabbatical from Atari and gave Wozniak just four days to complete the project. Working for seventy-two hours straight, Wozniak culled the *Breakout* design down to twenty-five chips, earning Jobs a $5,000 bonus. Jobs then turned around and paid Wozniak, who was unaware of the original terms of the challenge, $750 for his efforts. Wozniak only learned of the deception when Bushnell offhandedly asked what he planned to do with his share of the windfall. And Wozniak's ingenious workarounds were so complex that they couldn't be replicated in mass production anyway. The final version ended up using one hundred chips.

Bushnell knew that Japan had a long history of amusement machines. Pinball and other electro-mechanical games of skill were popular there. As was pachinko, which was invented in Japan in the thirties and rose to popularity as a cheap diversion in the late forties. Pachinko is a form of gambling based on vertical, wall-mounted pinball machines. Players launch a stream of tiny metal balls into the playing field to cascade down through a maze of pins. The object is to land as many of the balls in special receptacles, resulting in a payout of more balls. The balls can then be exchanged outright for prizes, but more often are quietly exchanged for cash—a quasi-legal arrangement that has long been tolerated by the authorities. Regulations set the stakes deliberately low; high rollers might be lucky to net the equivalent of a few hundred dollars over a long day of play. But the profits for operators are considerable: According to one estimate, so many Japanese adults play pachinko today that the industry constitutes roughly 4 percent of the nation's entire GDP—more than the take of all the casinos of Las Vegas and Macau combined.

Breakout wasn't a form of gambling, of course. It was simply a video game. But Bushnell, figuring that high-tech Japan might find arcade games as compelling as Americans did, forged a relationship with a Tokyo-based amusement company called Namco. Founded in 1955 by a shipbuilding-engineer-turned-entrepreneur named Masaya Nakamura (the firm's name stood for "Nakamura Manufacturing Company"), Namco specialized in designing children's rides for amusement parks and department-store rooftops, urban play-spaces where customers could drop off the kids while they shopped.

Nakamura was quick to realize the value of Atari's products. He received the first delivery of *Breakout* machines in 1976, localized as *Burokku Kuzushi*—"blockbuster." As word spread throughout the amusement industry about these mysterious "television games" (as they were locally known) that turned thousands of yen in profit a day, the machines proliferated through bars and coffee shops in what Japanese came to call "the block-busting fad."

The only issue was that Atari had only shipped a few dozen *Breakout* cabinets to Japan. The rest were forgeries, produced illegally in local workshops with ties to the yakuza. Perhaps this shouldn't have come as a surprise; the cash-based business model of quarter-munching (or rather, hundred-yen-coin-munching) machines closely resembled pachinko, an industry that itself had deep ties to the underworld. That customers' coins were increasingly going into video games instead of the mob's pinball-based gambling machines could hardly have escaped notice. Nakamura dealt with the problem by fighting fire with fire, flooding the market with his own unlicensed copies of the game. It infuriated Bushnell but successfully protected Namco's share of the market. The problem of copycats would plague the Japanese game marketplace for decades to come.

Not all of the *Breakout* copies flooding the market were from gangsters, nor were all of them clones. More ambitious programmers offered variations, and even slight improvements on the basic idea. The most radical of them was something totally new: Tomohiro Nishikado's *Space Invaders*. Released in the summer of 1978, it represented the first step in transforming video games from simple ball-and-block diversions into something cinematic. In Nishikado's game, the racquet was replaced by a tiny spaceship, and the blocks took the form of space creatures descending the screen. No longer were you some nameless salaryman whiling away the hours by twiddling knobs in some smoky back room. You were a starship pilot! Or maybe a tank commander? The monochromatic lozenge shuttling across the bottom of the screen left some room for interpretation. Whatever you were, you were no longer *you* but a hero defending a city from relentless waves of alien intruders, looming over your head like the deadlines you were shirking by being there in the first place.

It had responsive controls. It had charming graphics—the jagged

Space Invaders lived up to its name as "Invader Rooms" proliferated through the cities and countryside.

little aliens were, arguably, the first recognizable characters in the world of video games. It offered the novelty of immersion in another world. It all combined to make *Space Invaders* a . . . well, blockbuster. Out went the paddles and balls. In came the "Invader Rooms," the prototypes of later video game arcades. They proved so popular—and profitable—that the machines began to appear in nearly any location that could host the tabletop-shaped and -sized contraptions. (Stand-up cabinets of the sort associated with American arcades were a later innovation.) Coffee shops threw out their old Formica tables for *Invaders* tabletops; some even began dispensing their signature beverage for free, as customers spent far more in a gaming session than they would have on the drink. The machines sucked in so much money that the nation began to experience a shortage of hundred-yen coins.

As the fad continued, *Invaders*-related social problems began making headlines. "Critics say noisy space invaders keep earth people awake at night, ruin eyesight, encourage juvenile delinquency, and damage Japanese moral fiber," explained one news report. Across the country, children were caught stealing money and shoplifting to feed their *Invaders* habits. In one particularly egregious week, fifty Tokyo middle schoolers were taken into custody for jimmying open machines or using coin-sized metal slugs to steal free plays. The metropolitan police issued an alert to parents requesting they keep their children away; PTA groups began patrolling the streets after school to intercept kids before they slipped into Invader Rooms.

For a time in 1978 it felt as though society had grown oversaturated by *Invaders*, and in a sense it had. For, in a new twist, the machines became equally popular beyond Japan's borders. Exported throughout the world, *Space Invaders* sparked frenzies nation by nation, city by city.

By 1982, according to one estimate, players around the world had dropped the equivalent of one billion quarters into the machines. Kosuge's jeep never made it beyond the borders of occupied Japan; exported anime largely remained a rarity in the West; the karaoke

Simple yet instantly recognizable, the Invaders proved the first superstar characters of the video game era.

machine was still mainly a domestic phenomenon; Hello Kitty was only then making its first inroads into the hearts and minds of children abroad. *Space Invaders* was something else altogether: the first Japanese fantasy to grip the globe. Despite the misgivings of cutie-game naysayers, *Invaders* paved the way for *Pac-Man* fever and *Donkey Kong* mania. While in Japan games remained limited to arcades and coffee shops, abroad they spread into supermarkets, convenience stores, even unexpected locations like dentists' offices and funeral parlors; it seemed few spots save for places of worship could resist the siren song of *Space Invaders* and *Pac-Man* machines.

Just a decade after *Pong*'s debut in that smoky California tavern, game designers from Japan were giving the Americans a serious run for their money and mindshare.

"WE JUST GOT back from Paris and *everyone's* wearing them," enthused Andy Warhol in 1981. The response was in answer to a question about his strange headgear: a pair of tiny Sony headphones connected to a TPS-L2 Walkman on his hip. Always at the forefront of trends, Warhol was another American, like Jobs, who instinctively grasped that the device represented more than just another new gadget. Over the next few years, candid photos of the pop artist would show him sporting the distinctive headphones on the street—and even at the dinner table with fellow celebrities like the writer William S. Burroughs.

The Walkman had arrived. It was Morita who had cracked the code. The fundamental problem was simple. Private, portable listening was something so new that the concept couldn't really be explained; you had to experience it.

Karaoke inventor Daisuke Inoue introduced the world to the karaoke machine by paying bar hostesses to sing on them in front of potential customers. Now Sony did something similar, hiring fashionable young couples to stroll through Tokyo's hip Ginza neighborhood, ostentatiously listening to their Walkmans and offering passersby a "hit" on their headphones.

It took a few months, but it worked. The initial production run of thirty thousand Walkmans went on sale in July. It sold out by September. The shortage was temporary—Morita quickly doubled, then tripled the manufacturing runs every month—but scarcity, too, worked in the company's favor. It transformed the little stereo from a commodity into a coveted status symbol. Movie stars flaunted theirs in fashion magazine spreads and on TV shows. "One day, nobody in Tokyo had a Walkman," Peter Barakan, a music-industry veteran who lived in Japan at the time, says. "The next, everyone had one. It was quite literally that quick."

In Japan, the Walkman took off among Japanese students and other young consumers first. But things would play out differently in the West. Although the TPS-L2 wouldn't arrive in the United States and Europe until February of 1980, jet-setters were already well aware of Sony's handiwork. In classic fashion, Morita had been handing them out like candy to visiting dignitaries. The entirety of the Berlin and New York Philharmonic orchestras received them when they played Japan. Sports stars Vitas Gerulaitis and Björn Borg picked them up on the tennis circuit. Movie celebrities and rockers quickly followed suit as they visited Japan on their tours. Paul Simon ostentatiously wore his to the 1981 Grammy Awards. The Walkman quickly became a standard Hollywood gift-bag item. Disco queen Donna Summer handed them out by the dozen as Christmas presents. (Not all were happy with this turn of events: In an interview with the press, the manager of the upscale Manhattan department store Barneys declared the devices "the disease of the eighties.")

Warhol instinctively grasped another unexpected facet of the Walkman. Being seen with one was even more important than what you listened to on it. When you did listen, chances are it wasn't even that hip. (Warhol himself listened nearly exclusively to opera.) The earliest adopters of what *The Wall Street Journal* enthusiastically called "the middle- and upper-class answer to the [boom] box" were wealthy, white, and nearing middle age, listening only to "the softest schmaltz and classical music." But that would change very soon.

IN 1981, A then-unknown Vancouver writer by the name of William Gibson wore his Walkman downtown. He was listening to Joy Division for the very first time. "It gave Vancouver a kind of weird totalitarian grandeur it hadn't previously had for me," he wrote years later. "I didn't take that thing off for a month." On one of his outings, he spotted a poster advertising an Apple desktop computer. *What if the information this machine processed could be accessed with the under-the-skin intimacy of the Walkman?* he wondered.

Gibson grasped just how profoundly the immersive experience of the Walkman could alter human consciousness. Still, there were mainstream fears to go along with Sony's new fantasy. In providing the earliest Walkmans with two headphone ports and the "hot line" function, Morita attempted to preemptively address what he correctly predicted would be the greatest criticism levied against Sony's new invention: its isolating nature. The first Japanese ads highlighted couples using the device. "Turn any street into a paradise," jingled one, featuring a pair of ladies looking like they'd just walked off an audition for Cyndi Lauper's *Girls Just Want to Have Fun* video. But, in Japan and around the world, it quickly became apparent that most users weren't interested in sharing their musical selections. They craved escape. "It's nice to hear Pavarotti instead of car horns," explained Warhol to *The Washington Post* in 1981.

A Japanese musicologist named Shuhei Hosokawa dubbed this voluntary isolation "the Walkman Effect." His work explored how plugging in to a personally curated soundscape meant dropping out of the shared sonic background that had traditionally bound city-dwellers together: cars, construction, sirens, snatches of conversations overheard. Yet while there was a narcissistic element to auditory escape, Hosokawa pointed out that marrying a soundtrack to daily life was also additive. The Walkman was less about shutting out the world than it was about transforming familiar streets into virtual movie sets. If the karaoke machine made you a star of the stage for the duration of a song, the Walkman made you a star of your daily surroundings for the length of a cassette. Or one side, anyway, until you needed to flip the tape.

For some Americans, the most concerning part of the Walkman was the Sony logo. Tastemakers like Warhol and technophiles like Steve Jobs were the rare exceptions who didn't fear the invasion of Japanese products. As Americans tried to fathom how a supposedly defeated Japan could re-emerge to challenge their nation, all that postwar condescension morphed into fury. Newspaper op-eds by economic pundits compared Japanese business practices to the attack on Pearl Harbor; academic titles such as *Japan as Number One* and *The Enigma of Japanese Power* crept up bestseller lists. As Japanese cars and consumer electronics flooded the American marketplace, "Japan-bashing" rhetoric gave way to hyperbole, with tragic consequences: a pair of unemployed autoworkers in Detroit mistook a

Not long after its debut in America, the Walkman took off among all walks of life, as seen in this 1981 scene on the New York subway.

Chinese man for Japanese, beating him to death while screaming, "It's because of you little (expletives) that we're out of work!"

Morita, for his part, tried to keep a low profile during this difficult time for the United States–Japan relationship. He had long since moved back to Japan, stepping down from day-to-day responsibilities to serve as chairman of the board. Sony's ambitious purchases of Columbia Records (home of Bruce Springsteen's *Born in the U.S.A.*) and then of Columbia Pictures stoked concern among U.S. citizens. Other firms' purchases of all-American icons, such as Mitsubishi's acquisition of Rockefeller Center and Nintendo's of the Seattle Mariners baseball team, stoked simmering tensions into an incandescent rage. American firms did everything they could to fuel it. "Imagine a few years from now," cheerily invited a 1990 ad for General Motors. "It's December and the whole family is going to go see the big tree in Hirohito Center!"

Popular entertainment offered no escape. Ridley Scott's 1982 film, *Blade Runner*, portrayed a crumbling American landscape framed in triumphant Japanese neon, with coquettish geisha popping pills on building-sized video screens. William Gibson went on to write *Neuromancer*, a 1984 novel set in a near-future dystopia dominated by Japanese megacorporations. It won the Nebula Award and turned a generation on to the pleasures of the emerging genre of cyberpunk. Hollywood's go-to bad guys became monster salarymen such as Mr. Fujitsu, the unforgiving Japanese boss who heartlessly fires Michael J. Fox's Marty McFly via fax machine in *Back to the Future Part II*.

The 1993 film *Rising Sun* represented the crescendo of this demagoguery masquerading as entertainment. Based on a novel by Michael Crichton of *Jurassic Park* and *Westworld* fame, it portrayed a Los Angeles divvied up between contemptuous Japanese companies and fearsome yakuza mobsters, with Americans relegated to service roles as interpreters, crooked cops, or whores. So it was that Generation X came of age surrounded by grown-ups who insisted that our futures lay in the hands of a high-tech empire where human needs ran a distant second to the needs of faceless Japanese conglomerates.

To which we simply shrugged, hitting play on our Walkmans as we picked up our Nintendo controllers or queued up another anime on our VCRs.

The Walkman itself escaped much of the wrath being focused on Japanese products such as cars, televisions, and computers. Part of this was because the Walkman represented such a breakthrough that there was almost nothing available in the West to compete with it. But a bigger reason was that, as successful as the Walkman was as a product, it functioned purely as a vehicle for the user's own personal tastes in music. It served up familiarity and comfort. Even the most devoted fan of the device wasn't obliged to consume actual content made in Japan. The Walkman's marketing whiz, Kuroki, lamented this difference between "hard" and "soft" technologies. Japan, he felt, mastered the art of separating global audiences from their money with cold, hard machinery but failed to truly grasp the global imagination with soft cultural products like song or story.

That was about to change. In fact, everything was about to change.

IN 1989, FOR a festive celebration of its fortieth anniversary, the Japanese TV station TBS hit upon the idea of paying the Soviet Union $14 million to send a reporter up to the Mir space station. Heavily promoted and sponsored, the idea was to boost Japan's second most popular network's image by beaming back a series of nightly weeklong specials from orbit. It was a testament to how wealthy Japan had grown that a Japanese TV station—and not even the top station—was able to assemble the cash to buy itself into a Cold War superpower's space program.

Soviet flight doctors winnowed a pool of hundreds of applicants from the broadcaster's employees down to two final candidates: Ryoko Kikuchi, a twenty-six-year-old camerawoman whose hobbies included mountain climbing, cycling, and skiing, and Toyohiro Akiyama, a forty-eight-year-old senior editor whose hobbies included chronic overtime and a four-pack-a-day cigarette habit. This was

Japan of the late eighties, when salarymen ruled the world. Was it any surprise when TBS picked Akiyama for the job?

It was the first commercial spaceflight in human history. On December 2, 1990, Japan's first man in space rocketed into the heavens from a launchpad surrounded by Minolta billboards, atop a Soyuz booster incongruously festooned with the logos of a Japanese electronics maker, a credit card company, and a sanitary napkin manufacturer. Once they hit orbit and docked with the station, the Russian cosmonauts obligingly swapped their spacesuits for TBS T-shirts. One small step for a salaryman, one giant leap for corporate branding.

Akiyama came back down to Earth six days later. His arrival coincided with a similar plunge for the Nikkei stock exchange. Already in free fall, by the end of the year the Japanese stock market racked up a collective $2 trillion in losses. "The Bubble Era," the peak of Japan's clout in the global economy, was over. The Lost Decades had begun.

6

EMPIRE OF THE SCHOOLGIRLS

Kitty Goes Global

You learn much more about a country when things fall apart. When the tide recedes, you get to see all the stuff it leaves behind.

—TIMOTHY GEITHNER, U.S. SECRETARY OF THE TREASURY, ON JAPAN IN 1990

—EMOJI TRANSLATION

IT IS THE turn of the millennium. The Japanese economy is in ruins. The unemployment rate has soared beyond 15 percent, leaving millions of able-bodied citizens out of work. Disillusioned teenagers, painfully aware of the grim futures awaiting them, are in open rebellion against their parents and teachers. Desperate to prevent the sort of societal unrest that marred the sixties, the Japanese government unveils an audacious program dubbed the New Century Educational Reform Law. Every year henceforth, one graduating high school class will be selected at random and sent to a deserted island. Military encirclement prevents escape; remote-controlled explosive neckbands ensure compliance. The first class is assigned a variety of weapons and a simple set of rules: kill or be killed. The lone survivor is allowed to return, serving as both entertainment for the masses and an abject lesson to other rebellious youths. Soldiers parade the first "winner" before a mass-media scrum. Sitting in the backseat of a military jeep, dressed in a tattered school uniform and clutching a stuffed doll, is a fifteen-year-old schoolgirl. She raises her blood-spattered face to the cameras and smiles.

Such was the opening scene of the 2000 blockbuster film *Battle Royale*, directed by Kinji Fukasaku and based on a hugely controversial 1999 novel of the same title. (Plot sound familiar? The author of *The Hunger Games* swears never to have heard of the Japanese movie or novel.) *Battle Royale* was far from the first dystopian horror film to sweep Japan. The suffering of citizens amid the rubble of society had been a staple of Japanese entertainment from 1954's *Godzilla* to the apocalyptic 1988 sci-fi anime *AKIRA*. Even Hayao Miyazaki, that bastion of socially conscious family-friendly fare, plumbed the topic of fallen civilizations in his breakthrough 1984 epic, *Nausicaä of the Valley of Wind*. But there was something distinct about *Battle Royale*: the schoolgirls. Some of the film's most arresting scenes centered on the female leads, such as the scenery-chewing, knife-packing Chiaki Kuriyama, who fends off the advances of an aggressive schoolmate by stabbing him repeatedly in the crotch. The idea of plushie-clutching schoolgirls surviving a combat situation, rather than the musclebound jocks you might expect, captivated audiences both domestic and foreign. Kuriyama went on to play a similarly shocking role as a supercute schoolgirl assassin in the 2003 film *Kill Bill: Volume 1*, whose director, Quentin Tarantino, cites *Battle Royale* as his favorite movie of the new millennium.

That this dark fantasy resonated so deeply was a testament to trying times. While real-life Japan in 2000 wasn't in nearly as bad shape as the fictional Japan of *Battle Royale*, the nation was in serious trouble. It had been ten years since the epic stock-market crash of December 1990. Over the next decade, Japan's incredible postwar economic miracle sputtered, then ground to a jarring halt.

The roller coaster of financial glory and catastrophe began in September 1985, when Japan and five other nations signed an agreement called the Plaza Accord in New York. Devised by an American government desperate to remedy a trade deficit with Japan and Europe, the idea was to depreciate the dollar against other currencies so as to make U.S. exports more competitive abroad. But every action has an equal and opposite reaction. Devaluing the dollar also had the effect of making other currencies, including the yen, go further in the States. Japanese companies, riding high on what was then the world's second-largest economy, went on a buying spree.

Rockefeller Center in New York City. The Pebble Beach Golf Club. Universal Studios. Columbia Pictures. One after the other, American icons fell into the hands of new Japanese corporate overlords. Freshly minted Japanese multimillionaires dueled in bidding wars for trophy acquisitions. Paper baron Ryoei Saito edged out another Japanese rival to pay a record-breaking $82.5 million for Van Gogh's *Portrait of Dr. Gachet,* then sparked international fury by declaring his intention to have it cremated with him when he died. (He quickly claimed it was a joke; the painting remains safe today.) Housewives flush with cash from their salaryman husbands' bonuses sipped on $500 cups of coffee sprinkled with gold dust. And the real estate market went absolutely wild. At its peak, frenzied speculation inflated the value of all of the land in Japan to $18 trillion, four times the value of all property in the United States. The grounds of the Imperial Palace in the heart of Tokyo, a patch of greenery just a third the size of Central Park, were valued more than all the land in California, all on their own. Nobody called it a bubble at the time. Everyone expected the good times would keep rolling on.

Even today, nobody is precisely sure why everything collapsed; there was no singular cause, but rather a complicated confluence of factors. What is certain is that the Nikkei stock index peaked in December of 1989, then began a rapid slide downward. In the fall of 1990, real estate prices followed. Organizations and individuals who had taken out massive loans suddenly found their real estate assets totally underwater, worth far less than the mortgages they had eagerly signed to pay. Businesses began going bankrupt. Corporate and individual investment ground to a halt. By 1992, when the Nikkei had plunged to just 60 percent of its peak, it was clear that there would be no return to the glory years. The economists solemnly declared that it had been a mirage—or, in financial parlance, a bubble. And the bubble had most definitely popped. Fortunes had been lost and lives had been ruined. Dreams gave way to depression, both of the financial and of the emotional varieties. Suicide rates spiked to some of the highest known in the developed world.

One of the most keenly affected was Sanrio's Shintaro Tsuji. His firm had grown steadily throughout the years, a seeming rock amid turbulent times. Then came the crash. By September of 1990, Sanrio had lost eighteen billion yen—roughly seventy-five million dollars at the contemporary exchange rate. "Stock-Crazed Rogue CEO Drives Sanrio Deep into Red," trumpeted one magazine headline—a shocking comeuppance. It turned out that Tsuji had been engaging in a popular form of financial speculation the Japanese called *zaiteku*, a bubble buzzword among the executive class meaning "financial engineering." As many a Japanese CEO had, Tsuji plowed his firm's cash reserves into stocks, real estate trusts, and other high-risk, high-return corporate investment schemes. During the bubble this risky strategy had paid off handsomely; for a time, Tsuji's profits from trading exceeded Sanrio's income from its products and licenses. Emboldened, he launched an audacious plan to build a Sanrio theme park, to be called Puroland, on the outskirts of Tokyo. But as the stock market crumbled, so did Tsuji's positions. Almost overnight, the firm Tsuji had painstakingly built over decades lost 90 percent of its value. "I couldn't sleep without sleeping pills," he confided in his memoir. At one point, he even contemplated suicide.

These were dark times indeed. Amid real-life economic dystopia, Japanese youth turned increasingly inward toward fantasy, fueling the rise of new cultures and subcultures: the growing embrace of video gaming as a mainstream leisure activity; the appearance of wild fashions and elaborate cosplay in public spaces; the proliferation of mass gatherings for those who embraced anime and manga less as entertainment than as a lifestyle. Yet there was no better image of survival than that of the Japanese schoolgirl. Using every tool at her disposal, young women transformed themselves, *Sailor Moon*–style, into tastemakers who blazed a path for Japan through the Lost Decades. Salarymen built Japan, Inc. As it crumbled around them, young women picked up the pieces. They re-envisioned adulthood by unabashedly consuming things they were traditionally expected to abandon as they grew up, from girls' comics to Sanrio products. In embracing emerging new technologies far earlier than cautious grown-ups, they almost single-handedly upended entire industries. The karaoke scene was the first to be so disrupted, followed closely by the music industry as a whole. Then, as schoolgirls threw themselves into newly developing forms of digital communications, they recast a host of cutting-edge technologies into tools better suited to this strange new era. Text messaging; the perfection of the online "language" of emoji; even, arguably, the foundations of social media. A great many things we global citizens take for granted in our constantly connected digital lives were pioneered by schoolgirls on the streets of Tokyo.

Their appearance on the scene heralded a dramatic societal shift. Consumers were evolving from passive recipients of the things makers gave them into a new sort of creative collective in their own right. Men and their factories made Japan an economic tiger; now, in the 1990s, girls were recasting Japan as a cultural superpower in their own image. And they did it under the Jolly Roger of another feline: Hello Kitty.

AFTER RELUCTANTLY TAKING charge of Hello Kitty in 1980 at the age of twenty-five, Sanrio's Yuko Yamaguchi spent the next fifteen years re-envisioning both the character and herself. The ambitious young graphic designer had joined the company in hopes of forging opportunities that didn't exist for women in mainstream Japanese companies. She found them, but—wait a second. Fifteen years? What was a (gasp!!) forty-year-old woman still doing at Sanrio, the company that ushered women out the door the moment they married? Times had changed, that's what.

Yamaguchi found opportunity aplenty within the bailiwick of design at Sanrio, but quietly fumed about the company's cavalier attitude toward retaining its female talent. On the surface, everything looked great. Sanrio's female staff weren't forced to serve tea to the men as they were at other big Japanese companies of the day (or, at least, not after their first year or two). And once they established themselves, they were given great latitude to propose designs or manage product lines or handle whatever their specialty might have been. But that relative freedom didn't translate to upward mobility in the ranks of the company. Over the years, Yamaguchi watched talented woman after woman quit out of frustration. Eventually she had had enough. A few years after taking charge of Kitty, she marched into a managing director's office and told him that if the company didn't start moving qualified female staff into managerial roles, she'd quit on the spot. The tactic worked. Shortly thereafter, all the women who'd been there longer than her suddenly got promotions. And by the mid-nineties, Yamaguchi was no longer simply Kitty's designer. She was the manager for a two-dimensional talent, the flesh-and-blood oracle for a voiceless kitty-girl.

Dyeing her hair with shocking pink highlights and often wearing vividly patterned baby-doll dresses, Yamaguchi toured the country relentlessly. Her destination was inevitably one of Sanrio's Gift Gates, of which there were now more than a thousand operating in Japan, steadfastly maintained even amid the financial apocalypse unfolding at Sanrio HQ. There she would sit at a table and interact with young Kitty consumers. The events started simply as a form of PR outreach. Over the years they developed into something more: a way for Yamaguchi to observe trends among Kitty's fans in real time, helping her keep the character fresh in the face of constantly evolving tastes. In many ways she was a celebrity in her own right, at least among those who loved Sanrio's products.

Thanks to these events, Yamaguchi had already noticed a subtle aging up of Kitty's traditional demographic. Like all Sanrio's mascots to that point, Hello Kitty was created to appeal to kindergarten and elementary school girls. That is who had supported her during

Hello Kitty's "manager," Yuko Yamaguchi, at a Sanrio Gift Gate

the boom of the late seventies and a subsequent one in the mid-eighties. But as the nineties rolled around, junior and senior high schoolers began appearing amid the little girls and mothers who had traditionally formed the bulk of the participants at Yamaguchi's sessions. Raised on Kitty, they either refused to graduate from this childhood pleasure as they aged or returned to her as older girls. So it wasn't particularly shocking to see a group of high schoolers standing in front of her table one afternoon in 1995, as she recounted in her memoir *Tears of Kitty*.

Something about these teens was different. They wore sailor suits, the style of uniform seen in high schools throughout Japan: white blouse adorned with a wide blue collar, red neckerchief, blue pleated skirt, and knee socks with loafers. But these weren't standard issue—they had been subtly modified. Their *ruzu sokkusu* ("loose socks"), as the style was known, were thick and puffy as legwarmers, sagging around the ankles and pooling over their shoes like wax dripping from a candle. The skirts had been shortened enough that you could practically see the curves of the girls' backsides. Yamaguchi recognized the look. These were the much-rumored *kogyaru*—"kogals." Teen slang for "high school gals," they were fashion-obsessed delinquents from the streets of Shibuya, where all the cool kids in Tokyo and everywhere else in Japan aspired to hang out. The kogals were essentially version 2.0 of the *gyaru*, those party girls of the glitzy bubble years. The party was long over, but the new generation kogals hungered for the same Burberry scarves and Vuitton handbags they'd seen their older sisters flaunting during those epic eighties boom days. The problem was that there wasn't much money to go around anymore.

Shibuya was located adjacent to Tokyo's fashion district of Harajuku. It was a grubbier, lower-rent, teen-focused hangout, packed with bars, fast-food chains and cheap ramen joints, fifty-yen (as opposed to the usual hundred-yen) video game arcades, karaoke boxes, and department stores specializing in low-cost cosmetics and fauxbling accessories. In short, everything a schoolgirl needed to strut her stuff down Center Street, Shibuya's main drag, the neon-lit, graffiti-tagged urban canyon at the heart of the neighborhood—all of it bathed in the redolent aroma of cigarette smoke, shallow sewers, and stale beer from the piles of empties growing on the curbs outside the all-night convienence stores.

Yamaguchi had seen the three earlier, talking among themselves before the event had started. When the designer walked by, she'd overheard a phrase that sent a shiver down her spine: *enko*. Short for *enjo kosai*. It meant "compensated dating."

The word was all anyone was talking about that year. There'd been a series of articles about it in the popular news weekly *Shukan Bunshun*. Investigative reporter Katsushi Kuronuma scandalized society with an exposé of an underworld of dating services that charged men a fee to browse voice messages left by potential partners. Although they were officially intended as a matchmaking service for grown-ups, a subset of teens realized that these "telephone clubs" provided access to wealthy men. Young girls coveting status symbols left messages offering companionship by the hour in exchange for designer bags or expensive jeans, often specified down to the color and size.

Sometimes it really was just companionship in the form of a dinner out on the town. Other times it went further. This wasn't called prostitution, a label all parties desperately wanted to avoid. Instead it was euphemistically referred to as *enjo kosai*. Kuronuma's piece had been straightforward investigative journalism, but once the story broke, the tabloids had a field day with the image of Hermès-hungry schoolgirls flaunting themselves to horny, hard-up salarymen. Those same salacious headlines provided other girls with a template for imitation, fueling behavior that was picked up again by reporters hungry for titillating content. It was a vicious cycle.

Yamaguchi sat at her table, her arms around a large Hello Kitty plushie, trying to figure out something to say to them. The girls stood quietly before her in their heavy makeup and micro-miniskirts, waiting for autographs. Yamaguchi wanted to yell at them, to tell them she'd heard, to tell them to stop. Instead she found herself blurting out a question she never dreamed she'd be asking, let alone with a Hello Kitty in her lap.

"Why do you sell yourself to men?"

The question hung in the air for a moment. Yamaguchi suspected they thought Kitty herself had asked it. The girls didn't make eye contact. Finally, one of them broke the silence.

"Because I want a name-brand wallet. They're made of cool materials. They're kawaii."

Yamaguchi thought this over for a moment. Then she made a proposal: She'd make a Kitty wallet just for them. It would be pink, and finished just like an expensive brand. But it would feature Kitty, and be priced right, so nobody would have to do anything weird to buy one. The girls' faces lit up.

The wallet debuted in 1996, together with a host of other accessories: a handbag, a cellphone holder, a coin purse. They were made out of quilted faux leather in a pastel pink. They didn't look anything like that first Petit Purse of decades earlier, cheap and designed for tiny hands. They looked like something a big fashion brand might make, with one big exception: Right where you might expect some famous logo was Kitty's placid face.

So many of Yamaguchi's grown-up Kitty accessories sold in 1996 that she literally flipped the firm's fortunes, improbably converting a projected 340-million-yen loss into a 2.8-billion-yen profit. The new fashion line tapped into something no one, not even Kitty's manager herself, had imagined existed: a latent demand for elementary school characters among the teens and even grown women of Japan. Eighties gals had craved glamour and sophistication. The kogals of the nineties craved it, too—but recast in the comforting form of a fondly remembered icon from their childhoods, one that could also serve as an unspoken visual code for bringing like-minded friends together. Years later, the journalist Kazuma Yamane would call this new evolution of fancy goods "communication cosmetics."

Looking back, it makes perfect sense: a fantasy of having your cake and eating it, too, basking in a childhood pleasure while still looking stylish enough for a grown-up night on the town (or at least an afternoon out on Shibuya's Center Street). Left unsaid in all the media coverage—and the surprise at Sanrio's unexpected resurrection from the financial dead—was the fact that it never would have happened save for Yamaguchi's chance encounter with a clique of schoolgirls seeking sugar daddies.

NOT ALL SCHOOLGIRLS aspired to sugar daddy relationships, of course; despite media hype to the contrary, "compensated dating" remained firmly on the fringes of polite society. For the average Japanese teen, as for the average Western one, it was the rock star who occupied a central role in their leisure and fantasy lives.

It is 1996, and the king and queen of Japanese pop are on a date. He is the multimillion-selling superproducer Tetsuya Komuro. She is his protégé and star of the moment, the vocalist Tomomi Kahara. Already popular when she met Komuro, with him she recorded her first solo album, *Love Brace*. Just a week after it was released, in June of 1996, it sold a million copies. Now the pair are celebrating with a date on the town, documented by the eager cameras of the country's most popular music show, *Utaban*. Will the pair pick a fancy restaurant and open a bottle of champagne? A night out at one of Tokyo's famed discothèques, bathed in lights and adulation? Perhaps a romantic retreat at one of the city's upscale hotels?

None of the above. The twenty-two-year-old Kahara has insisted her boyfriend take her to Sanrio Puroland.

Almost complete when Sanrio announced their horrific losses in the stock market in the fall of 1990, the theme park opened in December of the same year. Incorporating input from designers who had worked on attractions for Universal and Disney, Tsuji envisioned Puroland as "a land of love and dreams," a pastel wonderland for elementary school girls, complete with simple rides, stage shows, actors clad in Sanrio mascot suits, and of course numerous gift shops. Initially, it was a costly failure. Already far smaller in size than its intended rival, Tokyo Disneyland, which opened in 1983, it was also by nature more tailored to the tastes of little girls—further limiting the pool of customers. The park hemorrhaged money for the first three years of its existence; critics derided it as "an expensive box," all packaging and no substance, a true low blow in a nation as serious about presentation as Japan. Tsuji began tweaking the shows and attractions to better suit a broad spectrum of tastes—or perhaps his own personal ones. "If the dancers aren't sexy, fathers won't come to see the show," he explained matter-of-factly to American journalists. "We can't do dirty shows or show breasts, but we can show thongs." Finally the park began turning a modest profit. But in truth, it wasn't because of thongs or fathers. It was because of teenagers and young women. Women like Kahara.

As the cameras roll, the young, presumably fabulously wealthy vocalist strolls arm in arm with an actor in a furry, life-sized Hello Kitty costume. Then she raids the gift shop and fills basket after pink basket with seemingly every Sanrio product ever made. Stationery. Housewares. Enormous plush dolls. All of it goes into a series of giant plastic bags that are hustled out by a coterie of black-suited handlers like kawaii bagmen. Although Kahara is a seemingly healthy, grown woman, her every utterance, her every gesticulation, is made in the manner of an overstimulated preschooler: knees bouncing, arms swinging, making little squeaks and bunny hops out of sheer excitement. Onstage, Kahara is a formidable presence: focused, driven, delivering love songs in a voice high pitched but well within adult register. Here in public, however, she is kawaii personified: a flesh-and-blood version of the products on the shelves. Whether she's putting on an act or simply someone in touch with her inner child, the rift between the two personas is jarring. A grown woman at the peak of her artistic powers behaving like an overgrown toddler was at odds with the perception of a diva—at least compared to the global trendsetters of the day, sultry Western singers such as Madonna, Celine Dion, or Toni Braxton.

Or was it? There's something about Kahara's performance at Puroland that is oddly reminiscent of a certain group of femme fatales from the early nineties: the riot grrrls, a very loose collective of all-girl bands that emerged in the era of grunge. These lo-fi pioneers, who orbited around a punk group named Bikini Kill, heralded a new constellation of female talent who sang for themselves instead of the boys. In an era that was dominated by aging arena rockers, graying hair-metalists, and nihilistic grunge acts, the grrrls injected a breath of fresh air into the American rock scene.

Superficially, of course, a riot grrrl couldn't be more different from a kawaii Japanese idol. Grrrls were raw, ironic, aggressive, anticute. Idols like Kahara were (and are) carefully managed, plastic and comforting. Yet the riot grrrls were no strangers to childhood imagery themselves. Bikini Kill's Kathleen Hanna often performed in barrettes and pigtails; Babes in Toyland deployed literal dolls in their videos; Courtney Love dressed in tattered baby-doll dresses while screaming ragged songs about abuse and sexism. Ignoring the message of empowerment in favor of the titillating presentation, sexist critics derided the look as "kinderwhore" and the riot grrrls as perpetually aggrieved man haters. What they really were was a jolt to the establishment of the traditionally testosterone-saturated industry of rock and roll. Kogals, dressed in their own versions of kinderwhore outfits, defiantly refusing to give up their childhood pleasures, and squeezing pocket money out of salarymen, represented much the same to Japan on a society-wide scale. And Kahara in particular, who whiplashed between sexy singer onstage and overgrown preschooler openly declaring love for Hello Kitty on prime-time network television, almost single-handedly made kiddie stuff cool for a new generation of teenage fans.

Kogals weren't countercultural rebels in the sense of the student protesters of a generation earlier, nor were they punks flipping a finger at polite society. They chipped away at the foundations of a male-dominated consumer culture in a passive way, simply by consuming the products they liked. This proved surprisingly disruptive—even more so, arguably, than the efforts of the riot grrrls. One of the first major businesses to be turned on its head by schoolgirl sensibilities was the karaoke industry, long the realm of the salarymen who crooned in the smoky companionship of by-the-hour hostess clubs. In the early nineties, girls flipped the karaoke demographic from old and male to young and female virtually overnight. As a result, both karaoke and the entire Japanese music industry would come to revolve around their tastes.

This sea change wasn't anything that could have been planned or predicted. It was the unexpected result of a new technology: digitized, streaming karaoke on demand. Storage had always been a problem for karaoke; formats changed quickly, and it cost a fortune to update one's collection of 8-track tapes into cassettes or CDs. For a while—roughly, the late eighties into the early nineties—laserdiscs reigned as the ultimate karaoke delivery system. They looked like overgrown DVDs: gleaming silver platters the size of a vinyl record. Although the medium was analog rather than digital, laserdiscs worked pretty much like DVDs. They stored music and videos, and allowed users to skip from track to track at the press of a button. The largest laserdisc "carousels" were contraptions the size of refrigerators, accommodating as many as 144 of the platter-like discs—throwbacks to the jukebox era of musical furniture. Yet even this wasn't enough to keep up with the constantly expanding catalog of pop music, for it took months to license, master, press, and distribute a CD or laserdisc. For most of karaoke's early existence, there was no way to sing a recent hit.

The fix for this problem wasn't exactly rocket science, but it was close. It was the creation of a plasma physicist by the name of Yuichi Yasutomo. His invention of *tsushin karaoke* (literally, "communication karaoke," or in more modern parlance "streaming karaoke") in 1992 inaugurated the world's first truly popular digital music-delivery service. Originally intended for karaoke pubs and their middle-aged patrons, it took off among teenagers instead, a trend that would profoundly shift the Japanese pop music scene as a whole. Ironically, the invention was created by someone without much of an interest in karaoke at all.

"I never, ever sing," Dr. Yasutomo says in the meeting room of his downtown Nagoya office. Long since retired from the industry, he coaches start-ups in a tech incubator. "The only time you'll see me with a mic in my hand is if someone tricks me into it. Sorry." A low talker with a wry, self-deprecating sense of humor, he grows visibly excited as he sketches out the schematics for his karaoke-on-demand

Yuichi Yasutomo, streaming karaoke pioneer

system on a whiteboard for me. "I never made anything off this beyond my base salary," he says, laughing as he draws. "My wife is always like, 'What's wrong with you?'"

Plasma physics and karaoke seem an unlikely match, but by the eighties, karaoke was a huge business. In much the same way that pornography spurred the development of its own host of communication technologies in the United States—the Polaroid camera, the VCR, cable TV, premium-rate telephone services, and the Internet all owe their widespread adoption in part to the popularity of smut— Japan's karaoke industry spurred the development of audio-video technology there. This was particularly true for storage media and content-delivery systems, with increasingly high-capacity formats capable of serving up as many songs to customers as quickly as possible. But karaoke's influence could be felt outside of the music industry as well. The earliest incarnation of Nintendo's Family Computer, or Famicom, precursor of the Nintendo Entertainment System—incorporated a microphone into one of its control pads in anticipation of software companies releasing karaoke cartridges; and without karaoke we'd likely never have seen the Sony PlayStation, either. Sony's executives, reluctant to commit the vast sums of money required to compete in the ferocious home video game "console wars" of the 1990s, only gave it the green light because they believed as many or more customers would purchase the consoles as singing machines as they did for gaming.

Yasutomo was long interested in computers, which he used extensively in the course of his physics studies. After completing his PhD, he joined a Nagoya-based printer manufacturer (formerly a sewing machine company) by the name of Brother. His first project was designing for them a vending machine for software. A nationwide network of TAKERU kiosks allowed users to download programs to floppy disks, saving software companies the cost of manufacturing, storing, and distributing packages. They were, in effect, like websites you had to physically visit. But this was far ahead of the curve, and Brother had a hard time turning a profit. So Yasutomo came up with the idea of giving the machines a double life. By day they would vend software as usual. But after hours, once the computer shops closed, the machines would quietly transform into karaoke servers, using modems and telephone lines to reach out across Japan and serve up the latest crop of songs to yet-to-be-developed digital karaoke machines. Theoretically, any bar, coffee shop, or karaoke room that purchased one of them would never have to purchase physical media ever again.

Emphasis on the "theoretical." Today we take the digital distribution of all sorts of content for granted, but this was long before the Internet made such things part of daily life. It was all the more remarkable for the technology of the day. Thanks to the limited capacity of telephone lines, Yasutomo couldn't transmit actual digital recordings. Instead, the songs would need to be rendered in a computer format called MIDI, which was like digital sheet music. A MIDI file wasn't a song itself but rather instructions for a computer to synthesize it locally. Unfortunately, MIDI didn't sound anywhere near as good as an actual recording, and a lot of people thought his system was crazy. ("What is this plinky-sounding shit?" thundered a karaoke executive to whom Yasutomo demoed the system.) Nor was the system capable of serving anything beyond the music and lyrics—there would be no accompanying videos, as had become commonplace in laserdisc-equipped clubs. It was all about convenience; once a song was digitized, it could essentially be distributed to any and every computerized karaoke machine instantly.

Another tiny problem: The songs would need to be rendered into MIDI format by hand—thousands upon thousands of them. Undaunted, Yasutomo hired a hundred data-entry specialists, forty of them kids from a local college of music. Hunched over their keyboards, wearing earphones, the team members listened to songs, entering the music into their computers bar by bar. It was slow, tedious work. There were no apps or tools to assist them. The start-and-stop process of listening to a snippet of a song, transcribing it into MIDI, listening to the output, and correcting the code meant even a simple song might take a week to process. More complicated tunes could take a month. Altogether, the effort took a year and a half of round-the-clock data entry. It cost Brother six hundred million yen—close to five million U.S. dollars at the time. It also cost Yasutomo his high-frequency hearing range, wiped out by countless hours spent listening to plinky-sounding songs as he managed the entire process.

The first version of his streaming karaoke machine arrived in 1992. The middle-aged *enka* crowd, crooning old-school ballads on those gleaming laserdiscs in their hostess clubs, could have cared less, and Brother had a hard time convincing many outlets to purchase their new streaming karaoke machine. It was the second edition, released a year later in 1993, that really changed the narrative. The reason was simple. Instead of the *enka* standards preferred by karaoke's traditional middle-aged fan base, Yasutomo followed the advice of younger assistants and packed the database with up-to-the-minute hits from the J-pop charts instead.

Suddenly, queues formed outside karaoke boxes advertising his machines. The kids didn't care that the music sounded plinky; it was their music. Finally, they could sing the songs they wanted to sing. Within two years, more than 60 percent of karaoke venues shifted from discs to streaming systems made by Brother and its rivals. But something even bigger than market share was at play.

Streaming karaoke machines tracked every song that consumers chose to sing, as they were being sung. The ostensible reason for this was tallying playbacks for calculating royalties, but it also transformed each participant's selection of song into a vote. No longer was a karaoke song a shout into the void. Very quickly, record labels realized that they could use the royalty data to play "moneyball," sifting through to see what kind of song worked best with what kind of singer, what kind of songs resulted in hits. Depending on how granular your report was, you could even make predictions about who was singing based on demographics. If you knew a machine was located in a love hotel, for example, and a creaky old *enka* song was followed by a teen idol song, you could be pretty sure some "compensated dating" was going on.

So it happened that Yasutomo accidentally invented "big data for music," as he now calls it. Before on-demand karaoke, only a handful of Japanese singles had ever sold a million copies. After its debut, ten such hits appeared in 1993. Two years later, the number had risen to twenty. Twenty million–selling songs a year! In the United Kingdom, by comparison, only twenty-six singles sold a million copies during the entirety of the nineties. This was unprecedented stuff for *any* nation's music industry, let alone one supposedly in the midst of a hideous economic recession. And it was all thanks to karaoke—or more precisely, to the young people eagerly incorporating it into their social lives.

Schoolgirls were among streaming karaoke's most avid early adopters. It was a cheap social activity and a way to connect with their idols—divas like the Kitty-obsessed Kahara. In fact, in many ways, she owed her career to streaming karaoke. Her boyfriend/ producer Komuro was one of the first to realize that networked karaoke machines weren't simply music dispensers. They represented a direct line into the hearts of young fans. To the incoming data from thousands of Yasutomo's karaoke machines he and his label, Avex, added on-the-street surveys and focus groups of high school girls. They used it to guide them in everything from what sort of singles to cut to the lyrics of the songs to the very outfits that the performers would wear onstage. What young fans wanted, it became clear, were idols who looked and sounded a lot like them. In the West, it was punk rockers armed with elemental chords who tore down the invisible walls between pro and amateur, between creator and consumer. In Japan, it was schoolgirls and streaming karaoke. Singability began affecting the songwriting process before a single note was even laid down in the studio. As far back as the seventies, the *hiki-katari* sing-along artists realized that karaoke would eat their lunch. They'd been right about that, but nobody could have imagined that it might eat into the careers of professionally trained singers, too.

As J-pop artists came to be selected not by inherent talent but rather the ability of the average schoolgirl or schoolboy to mimic them, squeaky-cute vocalists like Kahara and wholesome boy bands with names like SMAP, Tokio, and Arashi displaced traditional rockers and vocalists on the pop charts. This arrangement made fortunes for karaoke-savvy kingmakers like Komuro. "You don't always need to be number one," opened SMAP's massive 2003 hit, "The One and Only Flower in the World." It was intended as sonic comfort food, a song of love and acceptance, but they might as well have been singing about Japan, slogging through a recession so prolonged that some were beginning to wonder if it might ever lift.

THE YEAR 1995 was the roughest yet. In January, an earthquake leveled large parts of the city of Kobe. The government so thoroughly dithered its response, waiting more than seventy-two hours to dispatch Self-Defense Force rescue crews to help, that a local yakuza gang stepped in to distribute food and supplies to trapped citizens. Just a few months later, in March, an apocalyptic death cult called Aum Supreme Truth released handmade nerve gas in a crowded Tokyo subway station. The terrorist attack killed thirteen, grievously injured fifty, and sickened a thousand more. Taken together, the incidents raised disturbing questions about just who, if anyone, was really in charge anymore.

The backbone of Japan's domestic and export consumer economy—high-tech manufacturers such as Hitachi, Toshiba, Mitsubishi, and NEC—were shedding catastrophic amounts of market share to Asian rivals. When President Bill Clinton made a trip to Asia in 1998, something happened that would have been unthinkable just a few years earlier: He skipped Tokyo. As American political and business leaders eagerly turned their gaze to newly ascendant China and South Korea, the same Japanese politicians who had railed against Japan bashing began fretting about what they called "Japan passing."

Prolonged economic unease had a profound effect on young citizens, and the mass media eagerly chronicled a perceived crumbling of society. Terms like *hikikomori* (a coinage for young shut-ins who refuse to attend school or even leave their homes) and *gakkyu hokai* ("classroom chaos") entered the popular lexicon. College grads, both male and female, desperately cast about for jobs in the midst of a hiring freeze so pronounced that it is now called *shushoku hyogaki*— the Ice Age of Employment. Many millions never launched careers at all. The kids, it seemed, weren't all right.

It felt like everything had gone topsy-turvy, that a once-great nation was coming apart at the seams. Unable to attain the milestones of adulthood, Japan's youth increasingly turned from mainstream culture to subcultures. Increasing numbers of young men and women immersed themselves in vibrant fantasy worlds, fashioning new identities for themselves as super-connoisseurs of manga, video games, and anime. The most striking changes, and the ones with the most global impact, played out in Tokyo's fashion centers of Shibuya and Harajuku, where schoolgirls and young women fashioned new identities and forged new styles of communication. Among their tools were text-capable pocket pagers, mobile phones, and access to one of the world's earliest mobile Internet providers. Grumpy grown-up critics framed these endeavors as a shirking of responsibility, an infantilization of a once-proud society, a great dropping out. But those in the thick of it knew they were plugging in to something new.

Interconnected like never before, sophisticated young consumers with an unceasing hunger to connect formed new social networks that transformed Japan's city streets into petri dishes for cultural innovation. In an economy bloodied by the burst of the bubble, the nerds and the schoolgirls were the last consumers standing. *Battle Royale* may have been fiction, but maybe only by a little bit.

IN THE WINTER of 1996, fifty-one years after Kosuge's jeep went on sale in Kyoto, a strange new product appeared in Tokyo. It captured the zeitgeist in much the same way that Kosuge's scrap-tin jeeps had, and thousands queued up outside of Japan's many toy shops for their chance to own one of the prized new playthings. This time, however, the toy wasn't made of junk. In many ways it represented the cutting edge of electronic engineering: a silicon computer chip driving a postage stamp–sized mini liquid crystal display, these high-tech innards sheathed in a colorful plastic housing designed to appeal to schoolgirls. It was called the Tamagotchi.

A portmanteau of the Japanese words *tamago* (egg) and *uocchi* (watch), the palm-sized electronic Tamagotchi resembled a portable video game, but the point wasn't beating a puzzle or fighting enemy invaders. On a miniature black-and-white screen "lived" a tiny blob that demanded continuous attention, just like a real critter. If properly fed, watered, and cleaned up after—they "pooped" just like real critters, too—a Tamagotchi would "grow" through a series of phases into an adult, its final appearance, attitude, and constitution depending on just how you nurtured it through infancy and adolescence. The trick was that there was no Off button. From the moment you removed your Tamagotchi from the package, you were responsible for the life of this tiny digital creature, beholden to its beeps for attention and sustenance. If you left it alone for too long at any point, for any reason, it would wither and die, its expiration marked by the pathetic scene of a ghost hovering over a tiny pixelated grave.

Defecation and death don't exactly sound like a recipe for good times, let alone a hit product. But entrepreneur Akihiro Yokoi felt otherwise. The idea for the toy came to him early in 1995. A former employee of the toy giant Bandai, he ran a design company called Wiz. Like Kosuge's tin-toy studio decades earlier, Yokoi's firm didn't actually sell toys; it sold ideas for them to bigger manufacturers, chief among them his former employer. Yokoi's latest emerged from his love for animals. He kept cats, dogs, and a parrot at home, and the centerpiece of the Wiz offices was a three-hundred-gallon salt-water tank filled with exotic tropical fish. What he hated was leaving them behind whenever he had to travel. The Tamagotchi, as he and his staff developed the idea over the next few months, was a pet that you could carry with you anywhere, anytime, in the form of a specially designed gadget—caring for it from egg to adulthood.

His collaborator was Aki Maita. She was a thirty-year-old Bandai marketing specialist when Yokoi's proposal came across her desk in the summer of 1995. It featured a cartoon of a man leaping into action with the Tamagotchi strapped to his wrist. Another illustration set the Tamagotchi atop a stand, flanked by a little figure of a caveman. These were decidedly boyish fantasies. Maita loved the idea but thought the proposal appealed to the wrong audience. She thought it should be fancified for little girls. After many meetings, Yokoi and Maita's teams began refining the design of the toy.

To keep costs down, a Tamagotchi's screen had to be tiny: a little rectangle just sixteen by thirty-two pixels. The bobbly-head-tiny-body philosophy that gave rise to Kitty and Mario had the power to breathe life into the barest of design elements. But kawaii alone was old hat now. Yokoi cast about for something fresh and new. Flipping through girls' fashion magazines for inspiration, he noticed something interesting. A lot of the illustrations in their pages were deliberately primitive. They looked less like graphic

Aki Maita and the Tamagotchi

design and more like something the parent of a preschooler might proudly display on their refrigerator. He'd seen this kind of thing before, usually deployed in four-panel comedy manga, but it seemed to have become the default graphic style of the girls' magazines. Aficionados called practitioners of the style *heta-uma*—really good at drawing badly. Hello Kitty was cute, but so too was she a slick piece of graphic design. Ditto for Mario, refined from his blocky origins into a clearly defined cartoon character as game technology improved over subsequent sequels. Part of the charm of *heta-uma* characters was that they looked like something consumers might actually doodle themselves.

But *heta-uma* in fact took a great deal of skill to pull off. Yokoi convened an in-house talent competition similar to the one Sanrio had used to determine Kitty's manager in 1980. The winning illustration came out of nowhere, from a freshly hired designer named Yoko Shirotsubaki. Then twenty-five, she was only a little older than the schoolgirls whom the product was designed to target. She'd managed to change jobs some thirty times in the four years between graduating from art school and landing at Wiz, dabbling in everything from retail sales to waitressing at a lesbian bar in Kabukicho, Tokyo's red-light district. Her vision of the Tamagotchi was even more stripped down than Mario or Kitty. It looked like something the famed eighteenth-century biological taxonomist Carl Linnaeus might have drawn had he worked for Sanrio, an evolutionary tree of little blobs that Shirotsubaki had managed to clearly differentiate using only the vaguest of features: dashes or dots for eyes, some with tiny ears, or the hint of what seemed to be a beak—or were those lips? Was that one a starfish? Or some kind of one-eared bunny? They were deeply weird yet instantly recognizable at the same time.

Now that they had their characters, all that remained was to perfect the Tamagotchi's external appearance. For this, Maita and her co-workers began canvassing the streets with mock-ups of plastic shells, inviting passing kogals to comment on which shapes and colors they liked best. Their first destination was Harajuku, the city's fashion district. Located just one stop away from Shibuya, where the kogals congregated, Harajuku's high-end boutiques radiated an aspirational sophistication, making it a sort of Oz for schoolgirls. The neighborhood's main drag of Omotesando Boulevard, lined with towering ornamental zelkova trees, was and is home to the flagship outlets of Chanel, Hermès, and the other foreign luxury brands they so coveted. But the real heart and soul of Harajuku lurked just out of sight, behind the façades of high fashion.

In contrast to the bling of Omotesando's boutiques, Harajuku's backstreets were a twisting maze of alleys and dead ends. The most famous was Takeshita Street, a sort of urban boardwalk where tiny shops hawked cheap fashions, sugary foods, and posters of pop singers from around the world to eager teens. As one penetrated deeper into the labyrinth, the luxurious foreign influence evaporated. In its place one could bathe in a strange aura from countless tiny domestic boutiques that supplied seemingly bizarre accessories to the tiniest of niches. Within the confines of what everyone called Ura-Harajuku—the "Harajuku underground"—even the meekest of classroom dwellers were empowered to reimagine themselves in a riot of ever-changing identities, from beach Barbie gals in thick platform heels to black, frilly Gothic Lolitas who resembled Alice in Wonderland after a homestay with *The Addams Family*. So too the boys, in fashions ranging from fifties greasers in denim and leather to androgynous Visual-kei glam rockers decked out in fabulous sequins and *Dragon Ball*-style hair. So transformed, they bided their time for the weekends, when fashion freaks from all over Japan poured in to dance in the streets that were closed off to traffic. Harajuku was more than a neighborhood. It was a state of mind.

In other words, this was the perfect crowd upon which to test something as weird as the Tamagotchi. At the peak of Japan's summer season in August, Bandai employees canvassed the streets of Harajuku and Shibuya for as many young women as they could get to respond—from middle schoolers to office workers—showing them mock-ups of potential Tamagotchi housings. Some were circular, others rectangular, still others oval. Over subsequent rounds of survey and modifications, an egg shape emerged as the most popular. Maita knew they were on the right track when girls finally began asking if they could keep the colorful samples. The Tamagotchi was almost ready to leave the nest. But these surveys merely identified whether respondents thought the product's exterior looked cute or not. Nobody knew if customers would actually pay money to clean up digital pet poop. For the answer to that heretofore never-contemplated question, they could only release the product and wait.

EVEN BEFORE MAITA hit the streets, one of her first suggestions had been taking the Tamagotchi off the watchband and putting it on a keychain. The reasoning was twofold. First of all, kogals loved to attach keychains and other tchotchkes to their handbags. But an even bigger consideration was that while a girl might or might not carry a wristwatch, she wouldn't be caught dead leaving home without her "pocket bell"—Japanese for pocket pager. Making the Tamagotchi a handheld object rather than a watch would more closely align it with this indispensable accessory.

For those who may not remember, pocket pagers were products of the pre-cellphone era. They were little devices roughly half again as large as a matchbox and maybe twice as thick, with a tiny black-and-white LCD display along one edge. Originally intended as a way for doctors and businessmen to stay in contact with their offices in an era before cellphones, their only function was displaying the numbers of people who'd called you. Every pager came with its own telephone number, which you'd give out to anyone with whom you wanted to keep in touch. If they needed to reach you when you were out, they would instead call your pager, which would in turn prompt them to key in a callback number. Your pager would then display that number and beep to alert you. (Thus their nickname, "beepers.") As prices for a subscription dropped rapidly in the early nineties, suddenly nearly anyone could afford them. Young female office workers were among the first non-specialists to embrace this newly affordable communications technology, to the point a primetime soap opera called *Why Won't My Pager Beep?* emerged as one of 1993's most popular television shows. Perhaps inspired by these "office ladies," teenage girls began signing up in droves. In 1993, only a tiny percentage of Tokyo's high school girls owned a pager. By 1997, one out of every two did. They called each other *berutomo*—"pager pals."

Pagers were a big thing among American youth in the early nineties, too. The difference was the demographic. In the States, they weren't associated with schoolkids. They were associated with drug dealers, pimps, and rappers. But even they used them like any respectable doctor or lawyer would: for receiving phone calls. It was in Japan that some unsung outside-the-box thinker repurposed them as makeshift proto-texting devices. We'll never know who dreamed up this particular life hack, but chances are it was a schoolgirl, for they were the true power users of this new lexicon.

They were aided in their endeavors by a peculiarity of the Japanese language that allows numbers to be read phonetically. This allowed you to type in strings of numbers that could be read as words, if the person you were paging knew that was what you were up to. Instead of a callback number, you'd instead enter 3341 (*sa-mi-shi-i*)—"I'm lonely." To which your recipient might reply, 1052167 (*do-ko-ni-i-ru-no*)—"Where are you?" Your answer, 428 = "Shibu-ya." It was kludgy and indirect; in the earliest iterations of the technology, the numeric code would take the place of the callback

Pocket pagers, along with lipstick and business cards, were dubbed the "holy trinity" of must-have items for young women in the nineties.

number, so it was necessary to discuss things ahead of time for a recipient to know who was messaging. Still, the hugely popular practice represented an early form of mobile texting, and Japanese schoolgirls were the first people on the planet to incorporate this now-common habit into their daily lives.

They texted so furiously, in fact, that schoolgirl users quickly began outnumbering the salarymen users. This sparked a peculiarly localized mid-nineties Japanese telecom tech race to rush out new products designed specifically for girls. Season after season, makers debuted new sets of features for an increasingly tech-savvy and discriminating crew.

"Print Club" booths, originally intended for salarymen to print photo stickers of themselves for use with business cards, were another technology repurposed by nineties schoolgirls. They swapped selfies with friends to compile literal "face books" of their social circles.

The ability to display alphabetical and Japanese scripts; then kanji characters; and later, rudimentary graphics in the form of hearts and smiley faces, the ancestors of modern-day emoji—all these functions were incorporated into pagers specifically to appeal to Japanese schoolgirls. By the peak of the phenomenon, in 1996, ten million beepers were circulating on Japanese streets. The majority of them were being used by women, and the majority of the women were under twenty years old. In their life-hacking of devices not originally intended for them, schoolgirls transformed from consumers into innovators. In layman's terms, they were the nation's power users and tastemakers for mobile technologies, and the entire Japanese tech industry knew it.

In a certain sense, the Tamagotchi can be thought of as a beeper minus the telecommunications technology, packed with an army of super-kawaii mascots instead of telephone numbers.

. . .

IT IS EARLY 1997. The Tamagotchi is more than a hit—it's a full-blown fad. Bandai can barely keep up with demand; shortages are constant, as are the lines that form outside every toy store that gets even a handful of the gadgets in stock. At the toy shop Kiddyland, located in the fashion district, the lines sometimes stretch all the way up Omotesando to Harajuku Station, five blocks away.

Emma Miyazawa is eight years old. Like most little girls her age, she desperately wants a Tamagotchi of her own. She can't get her hands on one, because they're sold out nearly everywhere. But Emma has a trick up her sleeve. Her grandfather is Kiichi Miyazawa, the former prime minister of Japan.

Emma's birthday is coming up. She tells Grandpa that what she'd really like is a Tamagotchi. Kiichi has lots of time on his hands now that he's retired. Would she like him to take her to the toy store? She would. And so it was that a limo bearing Emma, Grandpa, and an armed member of the Japanese secret service pulled up to the curb outside of the Harajuku Kiddyland on a winter afternoon.

Kiichi, once the most powerful man in Japan, surveyed this corner of his former domain. The line was already hundreds long by this point, with a knot dozens deep clustered around the entrance. Things didn't look good. But Kiichi had seen and survived worse. George Bush the elder had vomited in his lap during an official dinner. Compared to that, this scrum was nothing.

Taking Emma by the hand, Kiichi strode purposefully to Kiddyland's door. Years later, Emma recalled hearing the family name burbling throughout the crowd, and the people parting "like the Red Sea in *The Ten Commandments*." It was the first time that she realized just how different her grandfather was from other men.

Presently the trio reached the head of the line. Mustering the gravitas only a former head of state can bring to bear, Kiichi addressed the clerk who stood guard over the latest jewels of Japan's pop-cultural kingdom.

"One Tamagotchi, please."

The Kiddyland employee looked at the former prime minister for a moment, then the queue of eager citizens stretching far behind him.

"Sir, I'm afraid I'm going to have to ask you to get in line." No exceptions, not even for a former prime minister. Such was the demand for the Tamagotchi at the peak of the craze.

After the little digital eggs spread through Japanese society at large, they leapt the nation's borders to colonize North America and Europe. Within two years of its debut, forty million Tamagotchis would be living, eating, and soiling screens around the globe, earning its co-creators the 1997 Ig Nobel Prize in Economics ("for diverting millions of man-hours of work into the husbandry of virtual pets.") The series is still going strong, in fact. As of this writing, the current number in circulation is more than double that. One of the reasons for its longevity, fittingly, is evolution. In a great circle of kawaii culture, some of the latest iterations actually incorporate Sanrio characters into the action, letting players create supercute fusions of traditional Tamagotchis and Hello Kitty—though, predictably if a little disappointingly, with functionality limited so as to avoid untoward situations. A traditional Tamagotchi might poop or pass away, but the question as to whether Kitty has a functioning digestive tract or an afterlife will remain a mystery for the time being.

JAPANESE POP MUSIC, unlike so many other cultural exports ranging from food to comic books, failed to find much of a foothold in the West. Chances are you've never heard of Kahara, or even more successful kogal favorites like Namie Amuro, Ayumi Hamasaki, or Hikaru Utada. The cynical sort might say it is because they are products of a system designed to reward mediocrity, but there is no actual shortage of musical talent in Japan. Idols rule because mainstream Japanese pop is the product of a database that emphasizes pleasure and escape over virtuosity and artisanship. ("You don't need to practice singing and dancing," the former AKB48 idol

Rino Sashihara told a group of schoolchildren on the long-running variety show *Waratte Iitomo* in 2013. "Most idol fans are old men, these days, and they think girls who can't dance are cuter.")

In virtually every other way, however, schoolgirl tastes wormed their way into the fabric of daily life all over the world. The Tamagotchi, silly though it may be, encapsulates how much we take for granted, as our always-connected, digitally enhanced daily lifestyles emerged. These schoolgirls were the first to collapse a gadget's value into a single criterion: *How does this connect me with others?* It was the first appearance of schoolgirl tastes on the global scene, the first export of Japan's kawaii culture in a non-Kitty context. It also heralded a profound shift in the way trends spread around the globe.

This peculiarity of the Japanese marketplace could throw even the savviest foreign companies for a loop. When Apple launched the iPhone in 2007, it proved an instant hit across the globe, with one glaring exception: Japan. There and there alone it flopped, because Apple had neglected to include emoji.

Although "emoji" is usually and quite naturally pronounced in America like "email" or "emotion," which it resembles in English, the word is actually a combination of two Japanese words: *e* (pronounced "eh"), meaning picture, and *moji*, meaning letter or character. A better translation might be "pictogram." But, like those for other uniquely Japanese inventions—samurai, sushi, haiku, kaiju—the loanword has stuck.

The little glyphs debuted on Japanese mobile phones in the late nineties, a natural fusion of texting and kawaii illustration culture. As young women eagerly peppered their missives with little hearts, smiles, and weeping faces, they elevated the emoji from a form of visual punctuation into a new grammar for online communication. By the early twenty-first century, emoji were no longer an optional feature for the female cellphone users of Japan; they were critically necessary for text communications. Yet cellular texting and data services of the day weren't designed for compatibility among competitors' platforms. Rival companies had no incentive to cooperate or standardize, so every company coded its emoji somewhat differently; one carrier's smiley might well be another's frown. Thus, when it came to picking a cellphone, boyfriends and husbands tended to follow the lead of the ladies in their lives. If a phone didn't take off with female customers in Japan, it didn't take off, period. Apple's belated realization of the emoji's importance launched a complicated, multiyear cooperative effort with Google to standardize the little icons for international use. The debut of emoji on the iPhone virtual keyboard in 2011 transformed the rest of humanity into Japanese schoolgirl-style texters.

At the turn of the millennium, the cultural epicenters of Hollywood, New York, London, and Paris still reigned as the world's trend factories. But trends like texting with emoji and products like the Tamagotchi represented new eddies in the flow of pop culture globally. Things that Japan's youth found interesting were increasingly things that young people all over the world found interesting. And while the Tamagotchi fad faded, it paved the way for an even more popular wave of digital and pocket-sized monsters. That egg-shaped gadget designed for schoolgirls was but a taste; its successors would decisively Japanize the global imagination. The story of how that happened involves a little detour into a far less fashionable part of the city, filled with a far less fashionable crowd of people.

7

A NEW ANIME CENTURY

otaku
/əʊˈtɑːkuː/

People who are interested in a particular genre or subject, are extraordinarily knowledgeable about it, and are lacking in social common sense.

—*KOJIEN* (JAPANESE DICTIONARY), SIXTH EDITION (2008)

The vast majority of Japanese animation is made by humans who can't stand looking at other humans.

—HAYAO MIYAZAKI (2014)

ON JULY 18, 1997, a strange advertisement appeared in the pages of the *Asahi Shimbun* newspaper. It was sandwiched in between previews for other films: the late Osamu Tezuka's smiling face pitching a new *Jungle Emperor* to the left, an anime called *Tamagotchi: The True Story* to the right. But this ad didn't resemble those perky exhortations at all. In stark contrast to their colorful enticements, it was a wall of text. A disordered series of fragmentary statements, thirty-three in all. A sampling:

A sea of despair . . . The cruelty of strangers . . . A desire for nothingness . . . Separation anxiety . . . Dangerous thoughts . . . Isolation . . . Doubts of worth . . . Empty days . . . A yearning for destruction . . . The end of dreams.

And then the punch of the final line: *So why are you here?*

What was this laundry list? Symptoms? A suicide note? An unusually provocative ad from the author of a self-help book? It was none of these things. The phrases sat atop the logo for an animated film called *The End of Evangelion*. This was an advertisement for a cartoon.

Sure seems like a bummer of a PR move for a summer movie. Yet it worked. Crowds of young fans mobbed theaters, queuing up by the hundreds weeks ahead of the film's release to purchase presale tickets. *The End of Evangelion* would go on to become the fourth-highest-grossing film in Japan that year. (The number one spot went to another anime: Hayao Miyazaki's *Princess Mononoke*, significantly outperforming Hollywood hits like *Independence Day* and *Speed*.) Later, *The End of Evangelion* would win the 1998 Japan Association of Theater Owners' award for "Most Talked-About Film." Somehow, the feel-bad movie of the season had become a sensation.

That the outcasts of society might identify with as lonely and impotent a protagonist as *Evangelion*'s young Shinji Ikari wasn't surprising. That young people all over Japan saw themselves in him, or in one of the show's other, equally emotionally damaged characters, certainly was. As *Evangelion*'s dark fantasy gripped the nation, alarmed newspaper headlines opined about "the fad that reflects a sick generation." If they were being more honest, they would have written about a sick country. The Japan of 1987 had been ascendant in every way. The Japan of 1997 was a case study in the effects of prolonged economic depression—both societally and at a personal level. Little had changed after the terrorism and natural disasters of 1995; young citizens still struggled with planning for a future that, amid an ongoing recession with no end in sight, looked increasingly bleak.

The End of Evangelion was the continuation of a television series, launched in 1995, called *Neon Genesis Evangelion*. Set in 2015, fifteen years after a mysterious cataclysm in the Antarctic has halved the Earth's population, the show starred a gloomy middle schooler named Shinji Ikari. He has had a horrible childhood. He never knew his mother. His father absconded when he was a baby. As the story begins, Shinji is summoned to the futuristic fortified city of Tokyo-3 by his long-absent father, Gendo. It turns out that Dad hasn't been around because he runs a shadowy paramilitary organization called NERV. It has constructed a series of giant biomechanical organisms called Evangelion units that can only be controlled from the inside, by teenagers whose nervous systems perfectly synchronize with those of the giant creatures. The reason Gendo has called Shinji isn't because he wants to see him but because he's short a pilot. There's a race of monstrous beings called Angels attacking Earth, and only the Evangelion machines can stop them. By the way, one's heading toward us right now.

Traumatized by years of psychological and physical neglect, Shinji summons the courage to refuse his father. As if on cue, Dad has a gurney wheeled in bearing a beautiful young girl wrapped theatrically, fetishistically, in white bandages: the previous pilot. If she has to go back in, she'll die, and it's all going to be Shinji's fault. What else can he do? Predictably, the Angel beats him to a pulp, his father watching emotionlessly all the while. Sent into battle again and again over the course of the series, Shinji finds his masculinity constantly challenged by more competent women and the occasional cybernetically enhanced penguin. Living on the verge of total mental collapse, his only escape is curling up on his bed with his Sony SDAT, a high-tech descendant of the Walkman. The titanic and menacing Angels take increasingly weirder and more personal forms; one isn't giant-sized at all, but worms its way into Shinji's life in the guise of a friendly classmate. Abandoned by grown-ups in a world ravaged by crises beyond his control, Shinji is completely unprepared for whatever is to come, yet the future rests entirely in this fragile young man's hands. All we can do is watch in agony as he blunders his way along.

Evangelion was the latest creation of an animation studio called Gainax, an organization that was, much like Shinji himself, constantly running on the brink of collapse. Its members met through college anime fan circles, where they honed their skills by creating a series of handmade animated shorts for projection during the opening ceremonies of the Nihon SF Taikai (Japan Science Fiction Convention). One in particular, the *Daicon IV Opening Animation* from 1983, truly put them on the map. The untitled five-minute film featured a sexy Playboy Bunny–style girl in fishnet stockings soaring through the air above a cast of characters assembled from decades of

Japanese and Western pop culture. Big shots like Godzilla and Ultra-man and Darth Vader and Yoda were joined by hundreds of popular cartoon, television, and movie characters in split-second cameos throughout. It was a fantasy collage culled from the mental database of anime fans, decanted into a visual spectacle anyone could enjoy (even if you had to be an eagle-eyed nerd to actually get all the references, which was precisely the point).

It looked startlingly professional for something that had been created by just twelve obsessive fans pulling all-nighters in a dingy room in an old textile factory. All of it was gloriously unlicensed, including its soundtrack of the Electric Light Orchestra hit "Twilight." This precluded any sort of official distribution of the film, but so too did it give the production a thrillingly illicit pedigree. Over the years, as fans quietly passed copies among themselves on film reels and videocassettes, like some sort of visual drug, it burnished the image of anime as something more than just the moving equivalent of manga. This was a punky, lawless, underground art form. The crew went pro in 1985 under the name of Gainax.

Neon Genesis Evangelion was, in many ways, like that early fan film: a pastiche of references and callbacks to old anime and sci-fi shows, artfully redesigned and remixed into something new. It gripped young people like no other anime show in recent memory, perhaps like no other show of any kind in history, speaking directly to them in a visual language that had grown startlingly sophisticated in the three-plus decades since the debut of *Mighty Atom* in 1963. The staff was so perpetually behind schedule that the final two episodes aired as little more than rough pencil sketches. When these failed to deliver the answers to the mysteries teased by earlier episodes, grown-up fans exploded.

It's tempting to call the *Evangelion* phenomenon a society-wide case of adolescent escapism—a retreat into fantasy amid trying times. But even the show's most obsessive fans weren't really dropping out; they were essentially reanimating the zeitgeist in their own image.

Evangelion's creator and director was a scraggly-haired, bearded, perpetually sunglasses-clad, clinically depressed thirty-seven-year-old named Hideaki Anno. He knew his audience well, because he was one of them: an *otaku*. Coined in 1983, the word described someone so obsessed with pop culture—sci-fi shows or anime or manga or idol singers, or all at once—that it becomes the axis of their entire existence. It was no surprise that Anno's vision of what anime should be might resonate with die-hard anime fans. But now his work was appealing to audiences at large, rivaling the popularity of mainstream maestros like Hayao Miyazaki (who had in fact, years back, given Anno one of his first jobs in the industry).

The surprise success of Anno's television show and later films heralded a coming-out for a medium long derided as kid stuff, but it also represented a great coming-out for the otaku themselves, long disparaged as overgrown children, and even at one point as criminals, by society at large. To average observers, their moment in the sun might have seemed to come out of nowhere, but of course that wasn't the case at all. It was the culmination of numerous political, social, and subcultural threads. One was, of course, the crumbling of Japan's economic power. Another was the sense of abandonment young citizens felt in this strange new world, stripped of the safety nets like lifetime employment that had sustained their fathers' and mothers' generation. But perhaps most of all it was the realization of a long-forgotten dream from the beginning of the eighties. A dream in which society recognized anime as more than kid stuff, as a new form of expression for young people everywhere. Long forgotten, that is, to everyone save the otaku themselves.

WHEN THE FIRST rays of the sun crept over Tokyo's business district of Shinjuku on a chilly winter morning in February of 1981, dawn broke upon hundreds of young men and women huddled in blankets on the east side of the station, shivering atop the cold concrete. At first glance the scene resembled those grim days just after the war's end. But this spot was some tony real estate, just a few blocks from

Sanrio's very first Gift Gate. These weren't refugees; they were anime fans waiting for a special event to begin. Many were dressed in costumes far too flimsy for the cold weather. They didn't care about the cold. They were here because they were crazy about a 1979 TV series called *Mobile Suit Gundam,* and today was the day of a special promotional event.

Gundam was an animated sci-fi fantasy set in the far future. Overcrowding of the planet had driven humanity to migrate into giant space colonies. Gundam was just one of many giant robotic weapons called "mobile suits," piloted by soldiers in an epic conflict unfolding between the earthlings and the "spacenoids." Rather than the standard justice-trumps-evil fare of kids' cartoons, the story offered good guys and bad guys on both sides. Instead of a traditional, aspirational, gung-ho macho protagonist, *Gundam* centered on a gloomy, introverted fifteen-year-old computer whiz named Amuro Ray who didn't want to fight anyone at all. Forced to pilot Gundam into battle by grown-ups with little regard for his opinion on the matter, Amuro finds that his unexpected skill in combat brings him no satisfaction— only more emotional trauma. Yet amid the darkness is a ray of hope. As the war reaches a terrifying crescendo, Amuro emerges as one of a new species of clairvoyant "newtypes," evolved for life among the stars rather than the surly bonds of planet Earth.

The show was designed, as were most animated television shows of the seventies, for one explicit purpose: to sell robot toys to children. In this it failed. The toy manufacturer that sponsored the series expected its creator, the animation director Yoshiyuki Tomino, to make a show suitable for elementary-schoolers. What he delivered instead was dark and brooding, seething with pubescent angst— a defiantly antiestablishment, antiauthoritarian, anti-everything portrayal of a war in which everyone, even the supposed victors, loses. In short, it was a gekiga for the living-room screen—which was entirely fitting, as Tomino had penned and directed many episodes of the animated *Ashita no Jo* for Osamu Tezuka's Mushi Productions.

It is tempting to call Tomino's creation Japan's answer to *Star*

Wars, which debuted in Japanese theaters in the summer of 1978. George Lucas's film blew the minds of Japanese audiences in much the way it had American ones, sparking a local craze for epic space dramas. The influences on *Gundam* are obvious: the space-opera setting; the "beam sabers" wielded by the giant robots; the Vader-esque helmet and mask worn by Amuro's sworn antagonist, Char Aznable. And the love affair was mutual. The films of Akira Kurosawa are what led Lucas to incorporate Japanese motifs into his films in the first place. In fact, the original draft of the *Star Wars* script bears a striking resemblance to Kurosawa's 1958 samurai adventure, *The Hidden Fortress.*

But *Star Wars* was, at its heart, a throwback to old thirties sci-fi serials like *Flash Gordon,* filtered through American new wave filmmaking sensibilities. Its conflict ended in triumph. *Gundam* was a war story as could only be told by someone on the losing side. Its politics were guided by the fact that many of the staff members were former student radicals. This wasn't uncommon; unable to find "normal" jobs after the collapse of the protest movement in the early seventies, large numbers of disillusioned former students filtered instead into the manga and animation industries.

Gundam was a production with a vision, well written and stylishly designed. It was also a terrible children's show. Allusions to World War II? Complex politics? Nerdy heroes who didn't want to fight anyone? Little kids tuned in expecting a rock-'em-sock-'em-robot show, grew confused, and tuned out in droves. Even worse, they didn't buy the sponsoring toy company's products—which was, at the time, the only true measure of a show's success. Finally the toy company did the unthinkable. They pulled the plug midway through. Originally slated to run for a full year of fifty-two episodes, *Gundam* would now end on episode forty-three, forcing the director to rush together a hasty conclusion to his series. The final episode aired on January 26, 1980. Many a popular show had quietly ended after a successful run. *Gundam* was anything but successful. That should have been the end of things, but it wasn't. For it turned out that people were watching after all—just not the sort of people who bought toys. In *Gundam*'s awkward teenage protagonists a generation of young Japanese men and women saw themselves. And they were furious about their favorite show's cancellation.

Which brings us back to that Sunday morning in 1981. As the first trains of the day began pulling into Shinjuku Station, they disgorged growing numbers of young people into the station's square. They were drawn here by a singular purpose: attending an event called the Anime New Century Declaration. In spite of the grandiose title, which sounded like something a Martin Luther cosplayer might have nailed to the door of a television station, it was a promotional effort conceived to spread the word about a new movie based on *Gundam*. For in the months since its cancellation, fans had mounted a concerted campaign in the pages of the nation's anime magazines to get it resurrected. "The true theme of *Gundam* is a renaissance for humanity!" declared one impassioned nineteen-year-old fan. "We need new ways of thinking, new forms of perception, as is obvious from a look at modern Japanese politics."

The campaign worked. A film company took note of this unusual interest and financed a feature-length movie based on the series. Promising to tie up the ends left loose by the television show's early demise, it was due to open in March of 1981, a month after the Anime New Century Declaration.

The organizers had hoped, optimistically, to attract a thousand fans. After losing count midmorning at eight thousand with no end in sight, they began to grow increasingly alarmed. So too did the police. The last time the authorities had seen this many kids amassing in Shinjuku, armored riot cops had to brave a hail of bricks and Molotov cocktails to get them out. But it had been many years since the Shinjuku Riot of 1968, and well over a decade since the implosion of the student protest movement. This crowd sure fit the demographic, but it wasn't showing any signs of agitation. It was just big—dangerously so, a sea of young humanity spreading from the stage, spilling into the side streets and railway underpasses around the station. Mostly male, the crowd was dotted here and there with female faces. The ages ranged from junior-high-schoolers to those who looked to be college graduates. Aside from a handful of cosplayers, they were dressed in the jeans and coats and caps one might expect on a chilly day. Were it not for the fact that thousands were packed in like sardines, they would have blended into any city scene in the country.

By twelve-thirty something had to give. Those in the front rows, who had spent all night in the cold staking out their spots, were in danger of being crushed against the stage by later arrivals. The ropes intended to corral the crowds had long since been trampled underfoot; in desperation, organizers linked arms in a human chain to

Yoshiyuki Tomino's commanding presence onstage added to the mystique for legions of *Gundam* fans.

keep those in front from tumbling like dominoes. Cries of "Stop pushing!" and "Give us room!" began to echo through the crowd as a never-ending flow of young fans poured out of Shinjuku Station's many exits. It was only a matter of time before someone would get hurt. A man strode out on stage, grabbed a microphone, and barked out a command.

"Everyone, take it easy!"

Those who were there on that day speak of the awesome silence that descended over the crowd, now easily fifteen thousand strong. The man on stage was Yoshiyuki Tomino, the creator and director of *Mobile Suit Gundam*. Save for the fact that he stood before a giant two-story-tall cutout of the titular robot, he didn't look much like someone a crowd of teens would be predisposed to listen to. Thirty-nine, slim of build, with a rapidly receding hairline and a double-breasted suit, he almost looked like a salaryman—*almost*. The gleaming gold buttons, flaming-red tie, and half-tinted aviator shades hinted that this was something else. Tomino thrust a righteous finger at the crowd. "This is more than an event. It's a *matsuri*," he declared, using the word for a traditional Japanese festival. Annual religious celebrations associated with Shinto shrines, *matsuri* were as much about gathering to drink, dance, and feast with neighbors as thanking the gods; some grew quite raucous as the participants got into the spirit (and spirits). There was no drinking here today; Tomino meant it symbolically. "I appreciate the passion that brought you here today. But you know what will happen if someone gets hurt? They'll say, 'That's anime fans for you. Just a bunch of idiots who run wild when they get together.' If we want to make this a success, we can't give them anything to talk about us behind our backs."

By "they" Tomino meant grown-ups; society at large. This wasn't idle pandering, though. He had a point: A culture war had long been unfolding between Japan's old and young adults. In the sixties, the psychoanalyst Takeo Doi famously dubbed student protesters *amae* (something like "spoiled rotten"): a generation of overgrown toddlers squalling for attention. By 1981, the student movement was ancient history, but now the mass media was having a field day with the work of a Keio University professor named Keigo Okonogi. In a series of articles and later a bestselling book, he excoriated Japan's latest crop of young men and women as uninvolved, apathetic, addicted to simple pleasures like video games and comic books, committed to nothing at all save maintaining a permanent state of adolescence. "Society embraces an increasing number of people who have no sense of belonging to any party or organization but instead are oriented toward nonaffiliation, escape from controlled society, and youth culture," he wrote. "I call them the 'moratorium people.'"

The attendees of the Anime New Century Declaration, teens on the cusp of adulthood who still watched cartoons, could well have been poster children for this widely shared youth-bashing narrative. Whether taking to the streets in protest or quietly watching cartoons indoors, it seemed, kids couldn't win. No wonder they loved Tomino, with his portrayals of shifty adults manipulating young people for their own twisted ends.

Yet this crowd was anything but spoiled or apathetic. And they were certainly affiliated with something: Tomino's vision. Tomino was in fact precisely whom they had come to see, the architect of the fantasy that had compelled so many of them to gather. They were here to pay respect. Thousands of fans stopped moving and took a big step back. The staff members breathed a sigh of relief as their human chain finally went slack. There would be no incidents for the grown-ups to talk about that day.

The event kicked off as planned at one o'clock. For the next two hours, a parade of designers, animators, and staff members addressed the crowd. Animators traditionally worked long, lonely hours in dark rooms, sketching and inking their frames with little in the way of public recognition. This was the first time many fans saw the faces of the artists who created their favorite show. As they introduced themselves, the crowd roared, giving creatives who had long toiled in the shadows a hero's welcome. The young men and women gathered in Shinjuku were every bit as passionate and engaged as the protesters of a generation earlier. That grown-ups didn't understand the object of their energies didn't bother them in the slightest; in fact, maybe that was the entire point.

A group of fans dressed in handmade costumes as characters from the show were invited up onstage—the first widely seen public display of what Japanese would soon call "cosplay." (The very first known Japanese cosplayer, a woman named Mari Kotani, marched around the 1978 Japan Science Fiction Convention dressed as the protagonist of Edgar Rice Burroughs's *A Fighting Man of Mars,* but the term "cosplay" wouldn't enter the Japanese lexicon until 1983.) In an impromptu performance, the elaborately dressed participants reenacted their favorite *Gundam* scenes while the actual voice actors from the show recited their lines. Finally, a young man and woman—also in costume—took the microphone to recite the event's signature statement. In front of a crowd that is now estimated to have approached twenty thousand, they read in unison, the giant cutout of Gundam standing behind them. Soon, the closing lines rang out over Shinjuku: "We the assembled have gathered here to declare the start of a new era. Our era. A new anime century."

Precious little footage and few photos exist of the event, which was largely ignored by the mass media at the time. Today it is remembered less as a promotion for the movie than a great coming out, a Woodstock for the teenage anime fans of Japan. In the weeks to come, they would continue to make themselves heard in other ways. One of the biggest was through their wallets. A hundred thousand tickets sold before *Mobile Suit Gundam* even opened; as the big day approached, scenes similar to the Anime New Century Declaration spontaneously repeated in cities across Japan. Fans camped out days before the first showings, clustering around portable televisions and boom boxes, transforming urban streets into impromptu festivals. At one theater in Shinjuku, a line of six hundred fans snaked around multiple city blocks. "I want to see the movie," one young man told an *Asahi Shimbun* reporter, "but I just love the scene here in line!" The movie went on to gross 1.8 billion yen at the box office, shattering records for an animated film.

In the wake of this unexpected mega-success, the studio green-lit two sequels. The third film in the trilogy nearly doubled the box office take of the first, and a series of novelizations penned by Tomino crept up bestseller lists. Subsequent rebroadcasts of the original television show hooked legions of new fans, leading the show's new sponsor, a toy company called Bandai, to sell an astounding thirty million plastic model kits of the show's many and varied robots. Suddenly the little kids who'd ignored *Gundam* during its initial run couldn't get enough. Supply ran so low and demand so high that riots broke out at toy stores, sending several unfortunate children to the hospital. *Gundam* was more than a cartoon. It was mass hysteria.

THE 1963 DEBUT of *Mighty Atom,* Japan's very first animated television series, revolutionized the way children entertained themselves, tuning in to watch cartoons and buying branded products of the characters with which to play. But the appearance of large numbers of adolescent anime fans of both genders in the late seventies and early eighties would have an even bigger impact on the nation and the world at large. In the sixties, furious students used the gekiga they loved as symbols of their protest movement. In the eighties, gekiga, manga, and anime *were* the movement. At first, these teenage anime fanatics were regarded with amusement; then—as their numbers grew over the course of the decade—as unsettling aberrations. By the end of the eighties they would be framed as the very scourge of society. In spite of it all, they would profoundly transform mainstream tastes. As the sensibilities of sophisticated young fans helped shape Japanese comics and cartoons into a seasoned art form, they found eager audiences abroad, thanks to the emergence of new technologies: first videocassettes, then cable television, and later the Internet.

Tomino didn't set out to launch a global youth movement, but he came with impeccable anime credentials. Born in 1941 just a month before Pearl Harbor, he spent the first few years of his career writing *Mighty Atom* scripts at Tezuka's Mushi Productions. In 1968 he went freelance. At first, he specialized in storyboarding the visual sequences of cartoon episodes (including more than a few for *Ashita no Jo*), and then he proved himself a proficient journeyman director. The work took him to different studios, bringing him into contact with many up-and-coming talents.

One of them was a young Hayao Miyazaki, with whom Tomino developed an intense professional rivalry. In 1978 Tomino was hired to draw the storyboards for a new series Miyazaki was helming called *Future Boy Conan*. But no sooner did Tomino turn them in than Miyazaki redrew the entire thing from scratch. It was nothing personal—Miyazaki was a notorious control freak, no matter who handed in the work—but it stung. Tomino swore creative revenge. It would come in the form of *Mobile Suit Gundam*. By this point Tomino had directed a great many episodes of animation and even helmed a few series himself. *Gundam* was the first that he was charged with helping create from the ground up. Even he was unprepared for its surprise second life as a polestar for Japanese teens.

In the years after the Declaration, fans and observers grappled with what to call this strange new generation of grown-up (or nearly so) Japanese who threw themselves into pop-cultural pursuits with a focus bordering on total obsession. Most fans referred to themselves as "maniacs." Others, tellingly, preferred self-deprecatory terms such as *byoki* ("sickos") or *nekura-zoku* ("the gloomy tribe")—punkishly reveling in the negative societal perception of anime fans. The bestselling fantasy novelist Sumiyo Imaoka (best known by the pen name Kaoru Kurimoto, here writing under the alias of Azusa Nakajima) disparagingly called them "hermit crabs," observing that "no matter where they go, they cart around tons of books, magazines, fanzines, and scraps stuffed into huge paper bags"—physical databases of the ephemera the most dedicated used to establish their personal identities, for a life without anime and its trappings was unthinkable for them. It *was* their lives.

The personal collections of *Gundam* superfans, chronicled in the pages of anime and mainstream news magazines, were the stuff of legend. The girls tended to accumulate massive quantities of imagery of the male characters, particularly the beautiful young men, designed by the series's lead artist, a former sixties radical named Yasuhiko Yoshikazu. Boys were hyperfocused on the female characters and the mechanical designs of the robots and spacecraft, hoarding absurd quantities of model kits and other merchandise. Some filled every square inch of their living spaces with reference books and portrayals of their favorite characters. There was no precedent for this kind of behavior in the postwar era, or Japanese history as a whole, or anywhere on the planet, for that matter. Americans had no shortage of die-hard Trekkies and *Star Wars* fans, but theirs was more a scene of camaraderie over a shared interest. Anime hyperconnoisseurs used the information and merchandise they hoarded to create entirely new identities outside of the mainstream. Some of the most ardent fans declared that they had a "2D complex"—more of a romantic attraction to illustrations than human partners. It was 1983 when a young journalist by the name of Akio Nakamori finally coined the term that would define this motley new generation of obsessive pop-cultural enthusiasts: *otaku*.

Nakamori, then twenty-three, had been assigned to cover Comic Market. Since its founding in 1975, it had grown into a biannual event that played host to as many as ten thousand visitors. Just as in its earliest days, the majority of the content there consisted of *yaoi*: those erotic parodies featuring homosexual hook-ups between the male characters of popular manga, drawn by and for women. But right around 1979, something interesting started happening. The boys began pushing back. A new genre of illustrated fan fiction began sweeping Comic Market: *lolicon*, short for "Lolita complex," a genre involving supercute, underage-seeming female cartoon characters in sexual situations. It all started as a joke. "I couldn't understand why *yaoi* was so popular at Comiket," explained Hideo Azuma, widely credited with producing the first *lolicon* comic, in a 2011 interview. "It felt like eighty percent of the content there was dominated by *yaoi*." His fanzine, *Cybelle*, was filled with parodies of Tezuka-style cuties in compromising situations. It also contained several spirited, tongue-in-cheek essays defending the genre; one waxed ecstatic about the joy of underaged female characters in the eleventh-century classic *Tale of Genji*; another profiled Lewis Carroll and Vladimir Nabokov alongside illustrations of the heroines from *Alice's Adventures in Wonderland* and, of course, *Lolita*. This was highbrow stuff for smut, and the strange little booklet, hand-stapled from Xeroxes and clad in a featureless black jacket, sparked a flood of *lolicon* content in the years to come. "We did it half for fun, and half to mess with people's heads," recalled Azuma. "I always drew knowing what I was doing was 'wrong,' but the younger ones who followed drew it because they actually loved it."

The idea of illustrated pornography was nothing new in Japan. Hokusai and his cohorts thrilled the world with explicit sexual prints way back in Victorian times. (In turn-of-the-century Paris, inviting a woman to see your collection of Japanese "etchings" was the "Netflix and chill" pickup line of its era.) Nor was the idea of cartoon nudity an underground phenomenon. The third *Gundam* movie, which opened in 1982, included a scene of a female pilot named Sayla Mass getting out of the bath after a long mission. (That a futuristic space battleship might come equipped with such a facility went unquestioned in a nation as obsessed with cleanliness as Japan, land of public baths and automatic bum-cleaning Washlet toilet seats.)

In a shot just under fifteen seconds long, Sayla is startled by an alarm, emerges from the water, wraps a towel around herself, and moves into the adjoining compartment—exposing her cartoon breasts for the briefest of instants. It wasn't the anime world's first moment of nudity, but it was by far the most seen, and the moment had a profound effect on the fantasy lives of male anime fans. Some even smuggled cameras into theaters to snap keepsakes of the moment. "Tomino did not realize the impact that it would have to show this character nude onscreen," explained the psychologist Tamaki Saito of this now-legendary moment in anime history. "He simply wanted to make his characters more realistic and human. But he inadvertently stimulated desire for a fictional character."

Desire for fictional characters was Comic Market's stock-in-trade. When Nakamori arrived, he was shocked to discover the hall packed with more than ten thousand participants shopping for illustrated fanzines. "Like those kids—every class has one—who never got enough exercise, who spent recess holed up in the classroom," he wrote in a now-infamous essay published in 1983. "The boys were all either skin and bones, as if borderline malnourished, or squealing piggies with faces so chubby the arms of their eyeglasses were in danger of disappearing into the sides of their brow; all the girls sported bobbed hair and most were overweight, their tubby, treelike legs stuffed into long white socks." (Body-shame much?) Above all, what struck him was the strange way in which they addressed one another.

Unlike English, Japanese has many ways of saying "you," depending on the age and gender of the person you're addressing. Rather than the standard casual forms of address teenagers used, Comic Market's attendees preferred a rarefied, formal, distancing honorific more commonly heard from matronly old ladies: otaku. It's a little tough for English speakers to understand how deeply weird this sounded coming out of the mouths of teenage boys and girls, something akin to unironically using "thee" or "thou." Otaku represented a kind of code word for those in the know. But it wasn't intended to draw people together. Otaku was the linguistic equivalent of the proverbial ten-foot pole, deployed by people more interested in cartoons than they were in one another.

"That's what we'll call them from now on," concluded Nakamori's essay, forever cementing the strange form of address as a title. Though intended purely as a dig at a bunch of kids he thought were freaks, this new application of otaku filled a need, quickly spreading through fan communities and the handful of observers who cared enough to acknowledge their existence. ("It was like, finally, we had a word for them," as a journalist friend of mine recalled.) Still, the term remained underground, unknown to the average Japanese, who was far more interested in the trappings of Japan's ascendance as an economic power than in superfans who subsisted on a diet of pop-cultural junk food. It wasn't until the turn of the decade that a terrible event dragged the otaku out of the shadows of subculture and into the harsh light of mass-media scrutiny.

In 1989, a young man by the name of Tsutomu Miyazaki was arrested for the abduction, rape, and killings of four elementary school girls in a Tokyo suburb. The Japanese press, desperate for a way to explain the inexplicable horror of Miyazaki's heinous crimes, seized on the presence of thousands of videotapes of horror movies, anime shows, and manga in his cluttered bedroom to paint him as "an otaku murderer." Given the immense popularity of all sorts of illustrated entertainment among young Japanese, the connection was a stretch. But the appellation stuck. Now everyone in Japan knew the word "otaku"—and it was a four-letter word.

And so it was that the superfans went back underground for years. The new anime century would have to wait. But it was coming, whether the critics of the otaku wanted it or not.

WHAT WAS IT about the year 2019 that so enchanted the fantasy-makers of the eighties? Director Ridley Scott's 1982 sci-fi epic *Blade Runner* is set in 2019. And who could forget the 1987 Arnold Schwarzenegger vehicle *The Running Man,* centered around the preposterous premise of a reality TV star launching a political revolution. So too was 2019 the setting for a 1988 animated film from Japan that would profoundly affect the global fantasyscape. It was an otaku favorite called *AKIRA.* While the otaku themselves lay low in Japanese society, this sophisticated sci-fi pop-fantasy would play a key role in introducing their tastes to audiences abroad.

It was based on a long-running manga of the same name by the artist Katsuhiro Otomo. His appearance on the comic-book scene in

Japan in the late seventies cleft the history of manga there in much the same way Osamu Tezuka's *Shin Takarajima* had redefined manga in its day. There was pre-Otomo and post-Otomo, his work neither manga nor gekiga but a new form of illustrated hyperreality, showcasing an almost absurdly detailed level of draftsmanship that none had brought to the page before, in Japan or anywhere else. Born in 1954, he devoured the work of Tezuka and the gekiga revolutionaries of the sixties, leaving his rural hometown for Tokyo to launch his own career in 1973. Then nineteen—pudgy, shaggy-haired, and sporting thick-framed Coke bottle glasses—the country boy drank in the cityscape in all its forms. His early works dealt almost exclusively with the seamy side of urban life: criminals, cops, drug users, would-be revolutionaries, dive-bar hostesses, go-nowhere garage bands. When he won Japan's Science Fiction Grand Prix a decade later in 1983, it was the first time the prestigious literature prize so recognized a manga creator. (Otomo's reception seems to have given the notoriously insecure Tezuka the vapors. Upon meeting Otomo around this time, he reportedly blurted out that "I could draw like you if I really wanted to.") *AKIRA* was the very first Japanese manga to get a marquee release in American comic-book stores, translated and colorized by Marvel Comics to great acclaim in 1988.

The theatrical version of *AKIRA*, directed by Otomo himself, was in many ways a product of the Anime New Century Declaration. Part of a new wave of ultra-high-budget theatrical anime films targeting young adults that were produced in the wake of *Gundam*'s surprise success, it was funded in part by Bandai, the same company that had profited so handsomely off of model kits. But *AKIRA* represented a totally new business model, one fueled by the rise of another Japanese innovation: the videocassette recorder, better known as the VCR. The technology was in its infancy when *Gundam* first aired, but by the mid-eighties it had firmly entrenched itself in homes worldwide. The videocassette enabled a totally new system for content delivery. Now, producers could cut out the middleman of television stations altogether and sell anime directly to growing legions of adolescent fans, either after a theatrical run or as direct-to-video products. The advent of the VCR meant that anime was no longer the medium: It could be packaged and sold as a product in its own right.

AKIRA debuted in its home country in 1988 and in American art-house theaters on Christmas Day 1989. At more than one billion yen (nine million U.S. dollars), it was the single biggest-budget anime feature Japan had ever produced. But a limited, art-house release was the best any non-Disney animated film could hope for in the United States of the era. Budget and artistic intention be damned, the American mainstream saw anything animated as kid stuff. (Tellingly, some film critics invoked comparisons to Tezuka's old sixties *Astro Boy* cartoons in their reviews, highlighting how little by way of comparison had arrived in the United States in the two decades since.)

AKIRA would definitively prove cartoon naysayers wrong, having much the same effect on U.S. teens and young adults that Tezuka's *Shin Takarajima* had had on Japanese manga readers forty years earlier: opening their eyes to the potential of animated fare as a storytelling medium. Its impact was even further heightened by the fact that it seemingly came out of nowhere, from a foreign land. Japan had long been hailed as the planet's premier maker of things—everyone knew big names like Sony and Toyota and Mitsubishi—but when it came to content, Japanese hits were largely confined to the world of home video games, a genre that remained firmly in the realm of the schoolchild at the time. AKIRA took the first real step outside this limited sphere, suggesting that Japanese creatives could be cutting-edge visual storytellers as well as top-notch programmers.

In an eerie coincidence, the film was set on the eve of the 2020 Tokyo Olympics. But in virtually every other way, the 2019 of *AKIRA* is not the 2019 that humanity experienced. It is a 2019 thirty-one years after World War III—a conflict sparked by the surprise detonation of a weapon of mass destruction over downtown Tokyo: a giant black bubble swelling to encompass the city, then annihilating it (another eerie coincidence that turned out to be true in symbol if not in actual fact, as real-life Japan's economic bubble popped). In the decades after, survivors rebuilt the city into a gleaming new metropolis called Neo-Tokyo. It is dazzling and gloriously dense, its skyline dominated by massive buildings and spotlights and neon, nothing organic in sight, high-tech vehicles squealing along ribbons of asphalt threading through an urban space on a scale never before seen. Yet Neo-Tokyo is also a very unpleasant place to live. It is beset by venal politicians, terrorized by teenage dropouts and radicals clashing with armored police. In other words, it is a lot like late-sixties Tokyo.

It emerges that the city's earlier destruction was the result of a little boy named Akira. He was raised by the Japanese government in a secret parapsychological project to create weapons out of psychic children. After Akira wiped out the entire city and triggered World War III, his keepers locked him away in cold storage. But thanks to the government never learning its lesson, thirty-one years later—in 2019—history is on the verge of repeating. As experimental drugs transform a juvenile delinquent named Tetsuo into an uncontrollable superhuman, Neo-Tokyo is about to explode—unless Tetsuo's old biker buddy, Kaneda, can stop him first.

Truth be told, *AKIRA* wasn't really about the story, condensed from thousands of pages of manga into an overly convoluted plot that was further garbled for foreign audiences by a lackluster translation. What drew in fans, both domestic and foreign, was the sheer energy exploding onscreen. Motorcycle gangs. Terrorism. SWAT teams. Orbital laser platforms. Designer drugs. A pounding musical score interweaving the sounds of traditional *matsuri* festival chants and drums. It was pure rock and roll in cartoon form. Writing about the film without sound and imagery is, as the old saw goes, like dancing about architecture. The saying is particularly apt because *AKIRA* was as much about city as it was about story, with Neo-Tokyo playing as key a part as any of the human characters. The obsessive attention to detail exposed a new generation of young Americans to uncompromising Japanese *shokunin* craftsmanship, expressed here in the form of anime's ink and celluloid.

WHEN *AKIRA* ARRIVED in that handful of art-house theaters in America on the cusp of the nineties, there was nothing even remotely comparable to it available in the States. The animated fantasies of 1980s America inevitably took the form of after-school and Saturday-morning cartoons, most of them intended as thirty-minute commercials for toys. But these, too, had a strong Japanese connection. Starting in the late sixties, the Federal Communications Commission stood watch over the children's television industry, promoting rules that shielded young viewers from anything smacking of commercial content. In 1982, President Reagan's staunchly anti-regulation FCC commissioner upended all of that. With a flick of his pen, the lawmaker allowed American toy companies to produce television shows based on the toys they sold. There was just one problem: Change had happened so quickly that none of the toy makers had any content ready to go.

Their counterparts across the Pacific did. The very first show to take to the airwaves was *Pac-Man*, hastily animated by Hanna-Barbera and based on the smash-hit Namco video game character. In the years to come, American toy companies relied heavily on Japanese anime studios to craft the cartoons used to pitch their products. *G.I. Joe*, based on a wildly popular 1985 toy series about a "real American hero" (as the theme song goes), was animated in Tokyo by Tezuka's old nemesis, Toei. The story of *The Transformers* was written by Americans, but its merchandise was based on a Japanese toy series called *Diaclone Car Robots*. While the grown-ups running the country fretted about imported Japanese vehicles and electronics disrupting local marketplaces, deregulating children's entertainment effectively handed Japanese creators the keys to the hearts and minds of young Americans. As our airwaves filled with Japanese content, so too did our toy stores fill with Japanese delights—no longer simply made in Japan to American specifications, as Barbie had been back in the fifties, but made in Japan for Japanese kids, and imported to America on their own merits: mysteriously alluring Sanrio products, puzzle-like transforming and combining robots, and the literally game-changing Nintendo Entertainment System. By the time *Mighty Morphin' Power Rangers* arrived, in 1993, Japanese toy makers were flush with newfound confidence. "We knew they would appeal to kids in America, just as they did in Japan," boasted the show's marketing supervisor, Katsumi Murakami. "We were right."

The Japanese called this cooperation among toy companies, anime studios, and television stations the "media mix." In its original incarnation in its home country, the media mix treated anime as nothing more than a vehicle to sell products to children. *Gundam* upended the paradigm by proving anime could just as successfully appeal to teens and young adults who didn't buy toys. *AKIRA* heralded a totally new approach in which anime was no longer a tool for merchandising but was *itself* the product. In comparison to *Gundam*, little in the way of merchandise was produced for *AKIRA*, because everyone from the director himself down to the fans in the movie theaters knew the whole point was losing yourself—and perhaps finding yourself—in that richly imagined animated world.

Viewed only from its performance in a handful of tiny repertory theaters during its initial theatrical run abroad, the film could charitably be described as a cult hit. It was on video that *AKIRA* truly found its foreign audience: tapes and discs passing from viewer to viewer in much the same way Anno's fan-made anime short had been passed among Japanese fans in the early eighties. It was a tantalizing hint that cutting-edge entertainment might no longer be the sole purview of the Hollywood machine. The Walkman had given the world a taste of being able to choose what and when and where to listen to their favorite audio content. New technologies such as VHS, DVD, and, later, streaming media let audiences do the same with videos—among them increasing amounts of imported anime.

With ever more Japanese fantasies, in the form of toys, cartoons, and video games, available in the American marketplace, the pop-cultural tastes of the two nations began to swirl and merge—often in unexpected ways.

I WAS FIFTEEN when I first saw *AKIRA* in a run-down theater in Washington, D.C., in 1990. The impact on my friends and me was instantaneous and electrifying. In spite of the fact that we were watching a cartoon, it somehow felt *more* real than filmed entertainment. What was going on inside those gleaming towers and street-side shops? The backgrounds were drawn with enough detail to hint at their own individual dramas unfolding within. From the piles of trash meticulously rendered in the alleyways to the fact that the characters actually looked Japanese, with almond-shaped eyes and olive skin and black hair, instead of the wild abstractions of the average anime (or Western cartoon) character, it felt less like a fantasy than like some mysterious documentary that had materialized out of the future.

The critical and popular success of films like *AKIRA* and later arrivals like 1995's *Ghost in the Shell* represented a coming-out for a tiny but growing American anime-fan scene. The 1996 Anime Expo in Anaheim welcomed close to three thousand visitors, double the number of attendees from its inception in 1992. (A respectable showing, to be sure, but still behind the curve compared to the love manga and anime received in their home country; the summer 1996 Tokyo Comic Market was mobbed by 350,000 manga and anime fans.)

Anime Expo's guest of honor that year was none other than Hideaki Anno, whose *Evangelion* had percolated among American fans almost from the moment of its Japanese debut, first in the form of bootlegs taped off Japanese TV (often only available for rent at Asian markets in the States), then as official English-language releases on videocassette. When Anno addressed the crowd, he received a hero's welcome, and *Evangelion* took the festival's prize for best TV series. (Reveling in the attention, Anno gleefully teased foreign fans who begged for hints about the show's cryptic ending with an English "Too bad!") Though entirely made in Japan, Anno's sci-fi fantasy of lost young boys and heartless adults seemed to resonate with American audiences, too.

Meanwhile, back in Japan, using what was then a new medium of online chat rooms and bulletin boards, *Evangelion* fans vented their frustrations about the show that had strung them along for most of a year. In English, the show was called *Neon Genesis Evangelion,* but its Japanese title was *New Century Evangelion,* a clear nod to that seminal eighties otaku moment in Shinjuku. Viewers hoped for some kind of redemption for the show's tormented hero; what they got instead were even more questions. "Anno wanted his characters to start from a damaged place and change," said Michael House, a translator who worked at Gainax during the production of *Evangelion,* to me. "But they were too damaged for that to happen in any believable way. And instead of anyone getting better, they got more screwed up as things went on." (Anno has been even more blunt about the situation in interviews. "The protagonist Shinji is me," he confessed to the *Asahi Shimbun.*) Some fans worked themselves up into such a lather over the lack of resolution that they posted death threats against Anno—an early instance of what we now know all too well as "toxic fandom." (Unruffled, he incorporated screenshots into a montage sequence in *The End of Evangelion.*)

In Japan, anime isn't a genre but rather a medium. There is anime for the very young—the long-running *Anpanman,* a superhero whose head is modeled on a Japanese pastry called an *anpan,* is so popular among the toddler set that he briefly dethroned Hello Kitty in the role of Japan's top-grossing character of 2002. There is anime for elementary-schoolers (the atomic-powered robot cat *Doraemon,* another big-headed super-kawaii cultural icon). There is anime for teens (such as *Gundam* or *Evangelion*) and anime for older audiences (for example, the contemplative 2016 film *In This Corner of the World,* set near Hiroshima just before the atomic bombing). There is educational anime watched in schools, and erotic anime watched, hope-fully, in private. In Japan, anime is so widely accepted that it regularly outperforms big-budget fare from Hollywood at the box office: Director Makoto Shinkai's 2016 teen romance *Your Name* skyrocketed to the fourth-highest-earning film of all time in its home country, edged out only by the likes of *Frozen* (number three) and *Titanic* (number two).

And as for number one? Japan's top-earning filmmaker of all time is an animator, too. His name is Hayao Miyazaki.

IT IS 2003, the night of the seventy-fifth annual Academy Awards ceremony, and it seems that cohost Cameron Diaz would rather be somewhere else. She's been saddled with the task of delivering the least anticipated award of the ceremony: Best Animated Feature Film. The Academy only reluctantly added the award the year before, under mounting pressure from big-budget cartoon producers such as Pixar and DreamWorks SKG (whose *Shrek* claimed the new category's first award). Until that point, animated features were forced to go head-to-head with live-action fare for Best Picture, almost always to their detriment; the sole animated film to be so nominated over the many decades of the Academy's existence was Disney's 1991 *Beauty and the Beast*. It lost.

After a somewhat puzzling introduction ("Once, parents took their children to see animated features; today's has reached such a level of sophistication that children take their parents"), Diaz went right into the nominees. The list was filled with the Hollywood names you might expect: 20th Century Fox Animation's *Ice Age*, Disney's *Lilo & Stitch*, DreamWorks' period drama *Spirit: Stallion of the Cimarron*. Then came a literal dark-horse contender: Hayao Miyazaki's *Spirited Away*.

It won.

This was a seriously strange turn of events for a film that its own producer claimed was initially rejected by U.S. distributors as unsuitable for American audiences. *Spirited Away* portrayed the strange adventure of Chihiro, a ten-year-old girl from the suburbs of modern-day Tokyo who journeys through a strange fairy-tale world to rescue her parents. Set in a mysterious bathhouse that serves a motley crew of creatures inspired by local folklore and religion, it was by nature and design an unrepentantly Japanese film, packed with hidden subtexts about the sad state of the environment and the hurdles facing young women in society.

Miyazaki wasn't in the audience for this unexpected triumph. He wasn't even in America. He didn't make a speech or hold a conference after the fact. "It is regrettable that I cannot rejoice from my heart over the prize," he finally wrote in a statement to the press, "because of the deeply sad events taking place in the world." He was referring to the American war in Iraq. Progressive causes were intertwined with his art; he had been a union organizer at Toei from almost the very earliest days of his career. Later, in the wake of the meltdowns of the nuclear reactors caused by the great Tohoku earthquake of 2011, he ordered his company, Studio Ghibli, to fly banners declaring their opposition to nuclear power, and he remains a vocal critic of the American military presence in his country.

It's easy for the politically outspoken to alienate those not of their beliefs, but in Japan Miyazaki is regarded as something akin to a national treasure. Non-Japanese feel as though he is speaking directly to them, as well. "When I first saw *Totoro*," enthused the late film critic Roger Ebert, "I knew that no one would ever again have to explain those shelves of anime to me." *Vice* enthused about "The Universal Appeal of Hayao Miyazaki." Even amid seemingly never-ending political tensions between Japan and China, *Spirited Away* set a new box office record when it was belatedly released on the mainland in 2018. Miyazaki no longer belongs to Japan. He belongs to the world.

For his part, Miyazaki claims to be baffled by the popularity of his work in America and other foreign countries. But perhaps it shouldn't come as a surprise, because the director's approach dovetails neatly with that of another name-brand Japanese creator with impeccable international tastemaker credentials, Haruki Murakami.

In its broadest strokes, Miyazaki's work—and *Spirited Away* in particular—feels like a page out of the Murakami playbook: a magically inflected reality, where outsider protagonists find themselves unwittingly slipping into supernatural realms that lie just beyond the peripheries of our own. Miyazaki's films, like Murakami's books, maintain a distinctly Japanese aesthetic without demanding any particular knowledge of Japanese culture to enjoy them.

Yet this is precisely why Miyazaki's work, beloved as it is, successful as it is, stunningly beautiful as it is, doesn't really represent anime as a whole. Miyazaki works outside the usual channels of production and creates films quite different from the usual anime fare. Its accessibility and universality and all-around virtuosity make it unimpeachable—the sort of thing that cuts across generational, cultural, and even political lines. Everyone loves Miyazaki; he is in many ways a genre of one. Tellingly, Studio Ghibli chose to shutter its animation studio rather than name a successor after Miyazaki announced his retirement—for the seventh time—in 2013. (They reopened their doors after his seventh un-retirement, five years later.)

IT'S TEMPTING TO frame Miyazaki's triumph as a culmination of everything Japanese animators had been working for—as anime's long-awaited moment in the limelight. It was, in a sense. Tezuka craved international recognition for his work, but he never achieved anything on the scale of an Oscar win before his death from cancer in 1989. After Miyazaki's triumph, 2003 proved a watershed year for Japanese fantasies, as Hollywood tastemakers began incorporating anime directly into their films. The Wachowski siblings enlisted an army of Japanese animators to create the direct-to-video anthology film *The Animatrix;* Quentin Tarantino commissioned a brutal anime interlude for *Kill Bill: Volume 1.* American animation studios launched Japan-styled content, led by hits such as *Avatar: The Last Airbender* and *Teen Titans.* Anime was no longer subculture, it seemed, but culture writ large.

Or was it? After this flurry of experimentation and cross-cultural productions, anime quickly settled back into the subcultural niche it had long occupied. Even after Miyazaki's epic absentee win, admitting you liked anime felt more like a confession than a brag, more likely to elicit winces than high fives. When anime fans appeared in mainstream media, it was more likely than not as the butt of a joke—think James Franco's character on *30 Rock* introducing his "girlfriend," Kimiko: a body pillow with a sexy anime girl drawn on it. In the nearly two decades since *Spirited Away*, no animated film from Japan has ever claimed another Oscar; American anime fans remain defensive enough about their reputation that the website Kotaku felt the need to run a piece in 2018 entitled "It's Time to Stop Acting Like Nobody Watches Anime." But that eternal outsiderness is precisely what makes anime *anime:* its nerdiness, its pubescent energy and adolescent angst, its gleeful disdain of social sensibilities around violence or age-appropriateness or gender, its utter inexplicability to those not in on the joke. Anime's inherent alienness, more than its universal appeal, is what makes anime so appealing to the sorts of people who identify with it so closely. In America, anime is and always has been a medium for outsiders.

Miyazaki and other vets like Tomino, born before World War II and raised in its aftermath, dedicated themselves to using the art of animation to appeal to mainstream audiences. Artists like Otomo and Anno represented a new wave of fans, who had been raised reading manga and watching anime since birth. They dedicated themselves not to animation per se but rather the art of anime; and while they, of course, craved success, so too did they feel a need to appeal to those like themselves through parody, pastiche, and homage. It was the natural extension of hyperfan sensibilities cultivated in places such as Comic Market, a new form of anime created by and for anime connoisseurs. Hideaki Anno, a hyperfan himself turned pro, provided the role model for a new generation of Japanese cartoon creators whose dreams revolved around the content of their youth.

In the end, however, it would not be Miyazaki or Tomino who would truly bring anime into American living rooms. Nor would it be Otomo or Anno, for their work was never broadcast on the mass medium of television here until long after their Japanese debuts. A completely different sort of program would capture the hearts of young Americans and usher in a global anime century. It came out of left field, for it wasn't based on a toy series or manga. It was a program in both senses of the word: an anime based on a video game. And that game was crafted by a man as obsessed with his chosen medium as Otomo and Anno were with illustrated entertainment. His work would play an even bigger role in Japanizing global fantasies. His name was Satoshi Tajiri, and his game was called *Pokémon*.

8

GAMING THE WORLD

The Famicom & Game Boy

I think video games are evil.
—YOSHIYUKI TOMINO, CREATOR OF *MOBILE SUIT GUNDAM*

Video games are bad for you? That's what they said about rock and roll.
—SHIGERU MIYAMOTO, DESIGNER OF *SUPER MARIO BROS.*

IT IS JULY of 1999 at the Mall of America. On this particular summer morning, the first thing a visitor would notice were the lines; queues of children, thousands long. The second was the noise, or rather the lack thereof. With fifty-five thousand boys and girls between the ages of seven and fourteen making their way there that day, you might expect utter pandemonium. The noise level never rose above a loud murmur, for these children were facedown in their Game Boys or paging through binders of cards, preparing for an epic battle unfolding on tabletops set up throughout the mall. Who among them would walk away with the coveted title of Pokémon Master?

Minneapolis was the first stop on the Pokémon League Summer Training Tour: a promotional campaign for what had emerged, over the span of just ten months, as the world's most popular video game, card, and cartoon series. The Mall of America scene would repeat over and over in major cities across the United States.

The idea that children all over America might fall in love with a mass-media franchise was, of course, nothing new. Nor was the use of the game's Japanese pedigree as a selling point—Sony had used that same angle to sell millions of copies of *Final Fantasy VII* in 1997.

But the sheer scope of *Pokémon*'s popularity was something altogether unique. It ensnared virtually every child and preteen in the nation, forcing countless middle-aged parents to master a new argot of Pokédexes and Poké Balls, Charmanders, Bulbasaurs, Lickitungs, and Pikachus. By now, everyone knew Japan's toy makers were good at their jobs. That they had *this* kind of cultural clout was shocking— to Americans and Japanese both.

Pokémon debuted in Japan in 1996 as a Game Boy cartridge and nothing more. Truth be told, Nintendo didn't have particularly high expectations for the title. In the game industry, six years was considered a long run for a game console. The Game Boy, close to eight by that point, was already considered a dinosaur. And *Pokémon* itself was . . . well, even Nintendo thought it was a little weird. That was precisely why they'd relegated it to an old system at the end of its life span rather than using it as a launch title for a cutting-edge new one. The Game Boy wasn't even cutting edge when it first came out in 1989. Its creator, the veteran engineer Gunpei Yokoi, had so worried about how the system's blurry, sickly green, unilluminated LCD screen would fare against the color screens of rival handhelds that he'd been diagnosed with malnutrition during its development. Nintendo figured *Pokémon* might be a pleasant way to put the old Boy out to pasture.

Pokémon wasn't much like the run-and-jump "platformers" à la the *Mega Man* or *Super Mario* series, shoot-'em-ups such as *Contra,* or puzzle games in the vein of *Tetris* that came to dominate video gaming in the years since home consoles and handheld systems had displaced arcades as the epicenters of young gamers' lives. In fact, it was downright meditative. The game's ten-year-old protagonist journeyed through a fantasy world collecting strange creatures called Pocket Monsters, abbreviated to Pokémon. Players nurtured them into stronger forms similar to Tamagotchi, though here the purpose was grooming them for battle. So too could children trade their Pokémon with friends via a special Game Link Cable, a physical wire that was the easiest way to connect two Game Boys in the era before

Wi-Fi. Even the fights were unlike those of other games. One hundred fifty-one Pokémon of differing attributes squared off in what amounted to a glorified game of rock, paper, scissors. Nobody ever got hurt or died; at worst a monster fainted. Nervous about the game's untested creator, Nintendo assigned *Mario*'s Shigeru Miyamoto to mentor the young man during the development process, which dragged on for six years. Even once the game was finally ready for release in Japan, recalled Miyamoto, "I was told that this kind of thing would never appeal to American audiences."

Then something unexpected happened. Without any marketing at all, word of *Pokémon* spread across Japanese playgrounds. Over the next few months, sales continued to climb. This forced Nintendo to reconsider the strange little game. They scrambled to partner with companies that might help them cross-promote the title by making anime and manga, then plotted to release the game abroad. When the English editions, split into two cartridges called *Pokémon Red Version* and *Pokémon Blue Version*, hit America in late 1998, they arrived as part of a fully formed multimedia extravaganza consisting of the games themselves, a cartoon show, and a collectible card game that allowed kids to play even without a Game Boy. Just twelve months later, at the end of 1999, Nintendo announced that the series had earned $5 billion—roughly a cumulative equivalent to the size of the entire U.S. game industry that year—all by itself. America—no, the world—had never seen anything like this before. Well, maybe *Star Wars*, but that was a Hollywood spectacle, not some silly monsters from Japan. "Pokemania," *Time* declared it in a cover story dedicated to the phenomenon. "A pestilential Ponzi scheme."

It was a business success the likes of which Nintendo had never dreamed—not at first, anyway—but it was also something more: a truly *Pokémon*-esque moment, in which Japan the nation evolved into Japan the fantasy superpower. So too was it proof that the string of made-in-Japan pop-cultural hits that seized the hearts of Western children the decade before weren't lucky breaks but the result of canny craftsmanship. *Time*'s breathless coverage echoed the treatment of *Space Invaders* by the Japanese press twenty years earlier: a cataloging of sins ranging from alleged racketeering (a New Jersey parents' group suing the American distributor for artificially limiting the supply of Pokémon cards) to the promotion of juvenile delinquency (cases of muggings and stabbings over the game). What the critics inevitably missed was that *Pokémon*'s success hadn't come out of nowhere. It could be traced to cultural streams that had been flowing since the end of World War II, now merging into a raging flood.

The Game Boy itself, now improbably relevant again in 1998, was an heir to both Japan's toy-making traditions and the trail blazed by the Walkman; even its name was an obvious nod to this hallowed founding father of portable electronic gadgetry. The monsters that paraded through its virtual world were downright kawaii: big headed, soft, and cuddly; even the critics at *Time* were forced to acknowledge Pikachu as "the most celebrated icon since Hello Kitty."

Pokémon the game was accompanied by an anime of the same name. The television show, rushed into production in Japan after the surprise success of the game there, was ready for broadcast almost in unison with the game's release in America. It proved so popular in America that when Warner Bros. announced it would release an English translation of *Pokémon: The First Movie: Mewtwo Strikes Back,* their switchboard was inundated with seventy thousand calls a minute from children and parents desperate for tickets. The film opened on a Wednesday in 1999; so many kids cut class to see it that *The New York Times* dubbed the phenomenon the "Pokéflu." It made ten million dollars on opening day, then went on to sell ten million home videos.

And then there was *Pokémon*'s creator, Satoshi Tajiri, just thirty years old when the game was released in Japan. "Tajiri is the kind of person the Japanese call *otaku,*" wrote *Time* in what was undoubtedly many Americans' first exposure to the term. "They know the difference between the real and virtual worlds, but they would rather be in a virtual world." Tajiri's first exposure to video games came at age thirteen, when *Space Invaders* arrived in his neighborhood. He grew so obsessed with the game that he began skipping classes to play; his exasperated parents saw the pastime of video gaming "as sinful as shoplifting," as he later put it. After graduating from a vocational college, he co-founded a company dedicated to creating ideas for video games and selling them to bigger companies—a sort of digital version of the toy think tank that Kosuge had run back in the prewar era. The sale of *Pokémon* to Nintendo, and its smashing success, represented a vindication for both himself and everyone like him. The otaku were enjoying a newfound renaissance in their home country thanks to the unexpected mainstream success of *Evangelion,* and now one of their lot was being heralded by the mainstream American media as a sort of multimedia Svengali. The Anime New Century Declaration was looking to be, if anything, a gross understatement.

We'll get to the mechanics of how Pokemania took both Japan and America by surprise, but first we need to explore one of the primordial precursors of the global phenomenon. It arrived in 1966, as a fad that swept Japanese kids with every bit the force that *Pokémon* would three decades later. Those of a certain age still remember it fondly. It was the Year of the Kaiju—"kaiju" being the Japanese word for "giant monster."

JAPAN WAS IN serious trouble. Its cities were under constant attack, citizens fleeing in terror as buildings collapsed around them. The best pilots were no match for the enemy, far larger and more powerful than they were. Only a miracle could save the nation now.

It sounds like mid-1945 and the final days of war, but we are in fact talking about the summer of 1966—and the nation's most popular television show among the schoolyard set. The nation-saving miracle came in the form of *Ultraman.* The first episode aired at seven P.M. in July of 1966. When the dust cleared half an hour later, Japanese entertainment would never be the same. Gargantuan laser-breathing sea creatures. Boiling lakes and flaming forests. High-tech submarines and fighter jets. All of this within the first ten minutes; then things really heated up. Enter Ultraman, giant-sized alter ego of pilot Shin Hayata. Human enough to be on our side, monster enough to judo-throw a kaiju into a conveniently placed skyscraper, meticulously engineered by special effects craftsmen to collapse just like the real thing. Ultraman was invincible—but only for three minutes, at which point his energy ran out. (What seemed a narrative device was in fact a financial one, for staging the hero's epic battles consumed the lion's share of every episode's budget.)

Ultraman was dreamed up by Eiji Tsuburaya, a sixtysomething special effects wizard whose résumé read like a laundry list of greatest hits of Japanese film. He made propaganda films during the war; after, he brought to life the likes of Godzilla; Rodan; Mothra; Ghidorah, the Three-Headed Monster; and many other classic kaiju for other directors. A man who had experienced firsthand the destruction of his homeland had improbably repackaged the wholesale destruction of cities into his nation's most popular form of children's entertainment.

Marusan, of Kosuge's tin Cadillac fame, manufactured figures of Ultraman and also of nearly every single one of the kaiju that he battled during the course of the series. Molded out of a soft vinyl material to evoke monster skin and sculpted in a rounder, cuter form than what appeared onscreen so as to avoid scaring children, the toys leapt from the imagination of a man named Saburo Ishizuki. An early Marusan hire with a keen eye for new trends, the then thirty-year-old instantly grasped the hold monsters had on Japanese children. It was he who noticed how many kids watched their favorite show with a hand in front of their faces, peeking through their fingers in ecstatic terror as they waited for a kaiju to appear.

Japanese religion and folklore brim with an astounding variety of deities and creatures, products of a polytheistic belief system that encompassed, according to tradition, some "eight million gods." These ranged from divine presences on high, all the way down to less ambitious spooks content to leap out of shadows and startle passersby. In an era before science, they were the personifications of the inexplicable, the faces of unpredictable forces beyond human control. Richly varied in appearance and behavior, the weird pantheon laid the groundwork for the character culture of the modern era. Kaiju, written with the characters for "strange" and "beast," who menaced Japan's cities in their own multitude of weird forms, could be seen as offshoots of this long folk tradition—fairy tales for children raised in the modern, urban era.

Until Ishizuki came up with the idea of making his vinyl kaiju figures, the conventional wisdom was that kids either wanted to dress up like their heroes or buy stuff gussied up with the lead character's face—costumes, or *Mighty Atom*–branded candies that children had splurged their allowances on back in '63. Ishizuki's inspiration ushered in a totally new development in the way kids played: collectibility. A decade before George Lucas realized of *Star Wars* that "all the money is in the action figures" and three decades before *Pokémon* made "Gotta Catch 'Em All!" a global catchphrase, the children of Japan clamored for monsters to add to their growing collections. Other television

Marusan's very first kaiju figures were of characters from an earlier Tsuburaya series called *Ultra Q*, which laid the conceptual groundwork for *Ultraman*.

production and toy companies leapt into the fray. By 1967, the rubbery arms race was on. Anime was out; monsters were in.

While Americans and Brits experienced the Summer of Love, Japan was swept by the Year of the Kaiju. There were no less than seven monster shows on TV, while films like *Son of Godzilla* continued packing children into theaters. Suddenly, giant monsters were everywhere. Department stores staged elaborate shows featuring replicas of the same hero and monster suits used in the shows, bringing kaiju battles to life for crowds of hyper children. Eager to cash in on the trend, publishers rolled out lavishly illustrated guidebooks to the monsters, including everything from catalogs of their names and onscreen appearances to absurdly detailed anatomical exposés of their supposed internal organs (which included, in Godzilla's case, a "brain (not very large)," a "uranium pouch," and—of course—a "thermonuclear regurgitator").

This was more than simply kid stuff; kaiju fever touched all levels of society. Reporters shadowing the imperial family on a shopping trip downtown spotted the six-year-old crown prince, Naruhito, buying an encyclopedia of giant monsters at a Tokyo bookstore. The postwar fiction writer Yukio Mishima penned a wistful essay in which he declared, "I, too, am a kaiju, though one that spits poison gas rather than sulfurous flames. That gas is the stuff called 'novels.'"

When *Ultraman* was on, the kids wanted toy kaiju; when they played with their toy kaiju, they dreamed of *Ultraman*. The fad faded a year later, but giant monsters left an indelible imprint on the Japanese pop-cultural consciousness. In 1990, when Satoshi Tajiri drafted the proposal for *Capsule Monsters*—the idea that would evolve into *Pokémon*—the very first illustration he deployed to explain the combat system used a fire-breathing lizard called Godzillante, squaring off against a giant gorilla suspiciously reminiscent of King Kong. Though pocket-sized, the Pokémon have kaiju in their DNA—creatively in their monstrous appearances, conceptually in the idea of battling one another, and financially in their business model of constant variation and collectibility.

Not even politics were unaffected by kaiju fever: A spring 1967 May Day labor protest in Osaka featured "Amegon," a monstrous symbol of American influence.

· · ·

IT WOULDN'T BE until the eighties that computer technology advanced to the point where one might conceivably make a game featuring characters that could rival those of the silver and small
screens. The first was the 1980 hit *Pac-Man*, created by a programmer named Toru Iwatani. The name derived from the Japanese word
paku-paku, onomatopoeia for munching. The very first machines
went into Japanese arcades under the name *Puck Man*. Namco only
changed the title when some sage at their American export partner,
Bally-Midway Games, noted that English-speaking mischief-makers
would immediately vandalize the *P* into an *F*.

Pac-Man was the video game world's very first superstar. It had
intuitive gameplay and charming visuals: You were in a maze, gob-
bling dots while evading monsters, questing for "power pellets" to
energize yourself and temporarily turn the tables on them. It had the
game world's first truly recognizable protagonist in the form of its
pizza-shaped hero, plus a mix of colorful foils named Inky, Pinky,

Blinky, and Clyde. And it had a mesmerizing sonic backdrop: *wakka-wakka-wakka*. The mixture of simplicity, fun, and strategy elevated *Pac-Man* from a hit game to a societal phenomenon, one that swept arcades and homes and daily life, ensnaring men and women, young and old, around the world.

The American media called it "Pac-Man fever." For those of us who survived exposure, the synthetic strains of the prelude jingle retain a Pavlovian power to excite even now, decades after the fact. Hearing it meant you'd just invested a precious quarter, hard earned or begged from your parents, and The Game was about to begin. Your body ached with tension and excitement, a cocktail no grown-up beverage or substance could hope to match. You wondered: *How far will I get this time? What lurks beyond the legendary 256th level? Will I get to enshrine my initials on the high-score screen? Or squander the opportunity by inputting "ASS" instead?*

Pac-Man was the first video game character to leave the arcade and weave itself into the fabric of daily life. I, and my comrades-in-arms in the eternal battle against the ghosts, slept on *Pac-Man* sheets; dried our faces on *Pac-Man* towels; dressed in *Pac-Man* shirts; breakfasted on *Pac-Man* cereal; carried our sandwiches to school in *Pac-Man* lunch boxes; listened to *Pac-Man* on the radio courtesy of Buckner & Garcia's 1982 Billboard hit, "Pac-Man Fever"; played *Pac-Man* at home on our Atari 2600 game consoles; and, when we finally were forced by parents to turn those off, sought solace in Hanna-Barbera's *Pac-Man: The Animated Series*. Yes, I—we, a great many of us in that generation—did all these things. Those formative experiences made me the man-child I am today.

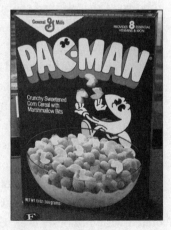

The breakfast of *Pac-Man* champions

But, for all its success, Pac-Man fever was just that: a fad. The game's cultural impact would pale in comparison to that of another title released the following year, in 1981. It was called *Donkey Kong*, and its sudden appearance at Nintendo of America's warehouse in Seattle, shipped there by the parent company in Kyoto, threw the company into chaos. First was the name: When the American sales managers heard it, they thought Nintendo president Hiroshi Yamauchi had lost his mind. *Donkey . . . what? Donkey Hong? Konkey Hong? What did it mean?* Try as they might, it made no sense to them. The best games Americans had to offer—and we were the pioneers, were we not?—showcased macho scenarios full of shooting and explosions, experiences that made players feel like superheroic space pilots or saviors of the planet from alien destruction. When the staff played *Donkey Kong*, they were horrified. This wasn't cool at all; it was downright cute. It looked like a goddamned kiddie cartoon! What red-blooded American boy would pay to play that? One manager reportedly hated *Donkey Kong* so much that he began looking for a new job.

I was eight when *Donkey Kong* hit American shores in 1981, and even today, looking back with grown-up eyes, it is difficult for me to fathom this initial outrage at such a colorful, playful experience. Amid the cacophony of beeps, blasts, and the ominous synthetic robo-voice that defined the audioscapes of those early arcade days, the pleasantly quarking susurrus that accompanied *Donkey Kong*'s ever-skyward quest drew my young friends and me like moths to a flaming barrel. We had found the first character that might dethrone the almighty Pac-Man as the object of our obsession. What the grown-ups at Nintendo of America initially pooh-poohed as cute we knew to be something else. It might not have been cool in the traditional sense of the word, as used by Americans, but it wasn't uncool, either. It was somehow . . . comfortable. It was our first exposure to kawaii design, though none of us had any idea at the time.

The arcade games we knew were housed in wooden cabinets decorated with gloriously over-the-top illustrations, intended as visual suggestions as to what the dots and blocks onscreen were intended to represent. Nuclear monsters hurling missiles; heroic spacecraft soaring over hostile alien landscapes; flying saucers unleashing their deadly payloads on the good citizens of . . . wherever. In *Donkey Kong* we'd found a game that didn't need them at all. With characters that actually looked like characters, a plucky soundtrack, and a boy-saves-girl story line, it felt like playing a real-life cartoon. Never again would abstract representations suffice. And Nintendo joined the ranks of video game companies whose arcade releases we tracked with the same passion the grown-ups around us poured into their old-person pursuits of music, movies, and television.

Donkey Kong's origins could actually be traced back to a cartoon. But the story begins with a warehouse full of unwanted circuit boards for *Radarscope*, an arcade game that didn't do particularly well in the United States. Nintendo president Yamauchi ordered them modified into something that might sell. The rescue mission fell to the same twenty-seven-year-old who'd made the dud: Shigeru Miyamoto. Introduced to Yamauchi by a family friend, Miyamoto had been hired as a graphic designer. At a top game company like Atari or Taito or Namco, a person with zero programming experience like Miyamoto would have been laughed out of the game division. At Nintendo, it didn't matter. All the technical aspects would be outsourced to the same firm that did the actual work of building Nintendo's arcade games: a manufacturer of television broadcasting equipment called Ikegami Tsushinki. Nintendo simply didn't have the capability to make arcade games itself—yet.

Miyamoto's manager, Gunpei Yokoi, came up with the core idea for the game after watching an old *Popeye* cartoon. In "A Dream Walking," animated by Fleischer Studios in 1934, Olive Oyl sleepwalks through a construction site. As Popeye and Bluto compete to rescue her from the girders of a skyscraper being built, they knock each other from level to level in a stalemate until the sailorman cracks his signature can of spinach. (This classic trope, incidentally, also inspired Toru Iwatani to incorporate the "energizer pellets" into *Pac-Man*.) Nintendo's negotiations for the rights to *Popeye the Sailor*

Man fell through, but the gameplay remained. Bluto became a gorilla, and Olive Oyl a blonde in pigtails. And Popeye became Jumpman, no longer a sailorman but an everyman clad in red cap and blue overalls.

Miyamoto originally wanted to call him Mister Video. "The idea was that he'd show up in all my video games, the way Hitchcock showed up in all his own films, which I thought was really cool, or how the same characters appear in so many different comics by Osamu Tezuka," he explained years later. Next they needed a title. Flipping through a dictionary for inspiration, he paired a symbol for stubbornness, Donkey, with the name of a favorite kaiju movie: *King Kong.* (The great-granddaddy of all giant movie monsters was considered a kaiju in Japan, thanks to his appearance in 1962's *King Kong vs. Godzilla.*)

"It's a good game" was Yamauchi's curt response to the critics at Nintendo of America. They had no choice but to sell it. The Americans did manage to extract one concession: They were allowed to rename the two human protagonists. The unnamed girlfriend became Pauline. Jumpman became Mario. This was an inside joke. The mustachioed character resembled Nintendo of America's landlord, Mario Segale, who supposedly interrupted the discussion to demand his rent for the firm's warehouse.

America's very first *Donkey Kong* machine debuted, just as *Pong* had a decade before, in a tavern. In similar fashion, its daily take in quarters astonished the Americans who had placed it there. In a sea of shooting and maze-running games, it seemed there was a latent demand for this totally new type of virtual experience, one that Miyamoto dubbed "the running-jumping-climbing game." By the end of 1981, Nintendo of America sold more than sixty thousand *Donkey Kong* machines, making instant millionaires of its founding partners and flipping the subsidiary from borderline insolvency to Nintendo's single most profitable unit. For years to come, Nintendo of America employees would introduce themselves to clients as being from "the *Donkey Kong* company." It made sense. Everyone in

America knew the game. Nobody knew who or what Nintendo was. But that was about to change.

Just a few years earlier, American makers had all but controlled the global arcade scene. Now the arcades were ruled by a triumvirate of games made in Japan—*Space Invaders, Pac-Man,* and *Donkey Kong.* It was like a planet-sized game of *Pong* playing out across the Pacific Rim. A motley crew of Japanese creators had served up a package of massive hits, right into the heartland of the American game industry. What happened next nobody could have guessed.

America flinched.

Today, industry insiders call it the crash. After a catastrophically oversized investment in a poorly conceived game based on the film *E.T. the Extra-Terrestrial,* the once-invincible Atari's fortunes went into free fall. The sudden turn of events spooked competitors, who exited the industry either by choice or by bankruptcy, one after another; by the end of 1983, the U.S. video game industry resembled the radioactive ruins at the end of a round of *Missile Command:* a multibillion-dollar marketplace reduced to just a hundred million over the space of a few months. The carnage all but ensured that no company would dare to produce a home video game console for the forseeable future.

No company in America, anyway. Ready, player two?

MASAYUKI UEMURA IS the architect of Nintendo's "Family Computer," better known as the Famicom in Japan and the Nintendo Entertainment System abroad. Released in Japan in 1983, its appearance in America and Europe two years later single-handedly revived a global gaming industry the vast majority of observers considered dead and buried.

Uemura was born in 1943 and raised in Kyoto, where he counted Kosuge's tin jeep among his childhood playthings. After graduating with a degree in electrical engineering, he worked at Hayakawa Electric (now Sharp) for several years before being recruited by Nintendo's Gunpei Yokoi in 1971. Today he serves as the head of the

Ritsumeikan University Center for Game Studies in Kyoto, one of only a handful of academic organizations dedicated to the preservation of home video game systems, software, and magazines. Video games are surprisingly ephemeral. As new forms of computer chips and consoles and televisions are continually devised for the consumer marketplace, old ones are unsentimentally relegated to the dustbin of history. But here in the Center for Game Studies, with its collections of vintage consoles and high-tech tools for extracting and archiving data from old cartridges and discs, time stands still for games. The pair of us sit in a communal research space, surrounded by the desks of graduate students and young professors investigating their own areas of expertise: early 3-D games, PC games, even paper-and-dice-based tabletop role-playing games. A vintage 1980s Famicom sits on the table between Uemura and me, its beige plastic yellowed with age now, attached to an equally archaic cathode-ray tube television. *Donkey Kong* plays silently on the screen. The air smells faintly of new carpet, old cardboard, and ozone. It reminds me of childhood, of countless basement rumpus-room gaming sessions, issues of *Nintendo Power* splayed open around us for tips.

Nintendo had never built a cartridge-based game system before the Famicom, Uemura explains. In a certain sense, it hadn't built any of its games at all. The guts of Nintendo's products—whether home products like simple plug-and-play *Pong*-style games or arcade machines—inevitably originated in the factories of high-tech manufacturers like Mitsubishi, Sharp, and Ricoh; the programming was done by specialists like Ikegami Tsushinki. Nobody at Nintendo was prepared for how steep of a learning curve awaited them.

Uemura began by purchasing samples of American hardware. He tore an Atari 2600 console and a Magnavox Odyssey[2] down to their transistors. He worked with a semiconductor laboratory to dissolve the plastic coverings on the systems' central processing units, photographed the circuitry, and blew up the images so he could trace the wiring patterns. After six months of poking through the guts of these rival machines, one thing was clear. None of it would be any help in building a new console. "All of it was already old-fashioned technology," he told me.

One of Uemura's team members proposed a tantalizing shortcut. They could repurpose the innards of their company's most popular arcade game: *Donkey Kong.* Miniaturizing an arcade game's circuitry into a tabletop size that was able to play not only *Donkey Kong* but other games, too, was a tall order from a technical standpoint. And then there was that inevitable other factor at play: an overarching directive from Yamaguchi that superseded nearly every other. "We had to make it as cheaply as possible," says Uemura with a laugh.

The Famicom arrived on Japanese toy store shelves on July 15, 1983. There were few inklings of its future success. Uemura describes it as "a product people expected absolutely nothing from." The boxy little beige-and-burgundy machine was released with little fanfare, and the response was tepid at best. "What's so interesting about it?" demanded a journalist of Uemura at the press conference announcing the product. "It doesn't even have a keyboard!" In America, the big game companies were pivoting from game consoles into home computers. In comparison to those ambitious new devices, the Famicom was deliberately, almost defiantly, toylike. Capping it all off, a rival company called Sega launched their own competing game console on the very same day. It had a keyboard.

"I was so deflated," recalls Uemura.

He'd built a system for Nintendo. What it lacked, at this moment, was a compelling reason to choose it over its competitors. Nintendo needed what we know today as a killer app: a game so enticing that it would compel consumers to purchase the game system simply to play it.

OF ALL THE twists and turns in the long career of Nintendo president Hiroshi Yamauchi, the single luckiest move may have been finding Shigeru Miyamoto. Born in 1952, Miyamoto grew up in a tiny village on the outskirts of Kyoto. His home had no car, no television, nor even much in the way of toys. He didn't need them; the countryside with its critter-filled rice paddies, streams, forests, and rolling hills became his playground. In interviews, Miyamoto often describes a particularly formative experience of discovering a small cave, the secrets of which he plumbed with the aid of a small lantern. The childhood moment has been burnished over many retellings into an origin story: "what the cherry tree was to George Washington, or what LSD is to Steve Jobs," as *The New Yorker* put it in a 2010 profile.

Donkey Kong proved that Miyamoto had a knack for creating compelling characters and game worlds. Yokoi tasked him with creating a sequel, *Donkey Kong Jr.,* and then another, *Mario Bros.,* which paired the hero with a brother named Luigi. But it was *Super Mario Bros.,* released in 1985, that would truly cement Miyamoto's reputation as a master gamesmith.

Donkey Kong had been a big hit, but *Super Mario Bros.* proved absolutely intoxicating to players. No longer was the action confined to a single screen; in search of a kidnapped princess, Mario sprinted through a world that scrolled out like a digitized fairy tale, complete with lava pits, secret rooms, castles, bridges, and monsters. It wasn't the first "side-scrolling platform game," as fans came to call the genre (*Pac-Land*, a side-scrolling version of *Pac-Man*, beat it to market by a year), but it was indisputably the best executed. Responsive controls, charming graphics, intuitive gameplay, an infectious soundtrack, a menagerie of funny characters, and most important, a sense of epic secrets lurking just out of sight. It coalesced into something more than just a game; it felt like a translation of the childhood imagination. That many players already recognized the protagonist from previous adventures only added to the sense that they were partaking of something much bigger than what was unfolding onscreen. Suddenly, the home game system was no longer just a plaything. It was a portal to mysterious worlds, a springboard to a new form of digital leisure far richer than the frenetic quarter-munching experience of the arcades.

Super Mario Bros. was truly a great game, but a healthy measure of its success was also due to fortuitous timing. It arrived seven months after the enactment of a new law that dramatically affected Japan's game industry. Parliament originally passed the Businesses Affecting Public Morals Regulation Act in 1948 to keep minors out of adult establishments such as bars, dance halls, porn shops, and gambling parlors. In 1984, lawmakers modified it to include the nation's twenty-six thousand video game arcades, whose rapid proliferation throughout the country greatly alarmed authorities. The new law took effect in February of 1985. Though fairly toothless (it merely precluded those under twenty from being in arcades after ten P.M.), it represented one of the first attempts on the part of a nation to regulate access to video games. Critics of arcades had pushed for similar ordinances in the United States and Europe, and a few municipalities enacted curfews or outright bans, but none was anywhere nearly as far-reaching as the Japanese law. To the chagrin of many who had lobbied for the change, it sent sales of home video game systems skyrocketing, sparking a society-wide Famicom boom. The pull of this newfound pastime of home gaming so permeated mainstream culture that a book called *Super Mario Bros.: The Complete Strategy Guide* topped the Japanese best-seller list two years running, in 1985 and 1986—a feat not even the likes of Haruki Murakami or J.K. Rowling has ever managed to duplicate.

When the Famicom officially launched in the United States and across Europe in 1986, redesigned as the Nintendo Entertainment System (NES), one of the key sales hooks was that it came bundled with *Super Mario Bros.* Thanks to the crash of the American game industry three years earlier, Nintendo made a beachhead virtually unopposed by domestic competition, and its eventual success set the stage for Japanese creators to monopolize the mindshare of children around the globe until the first years of the twenty-first century.

That video games might have the potential to transcend mere pastime was made abundantly clear on a crisp Tokyo day in February of 1988. As the first commuters arrived in Shinjuku early that Wednesday morning, they were shocked to find hundreds of people already there, patiently waiting in queues that snaked around buildings and entire city blocks, steam rising from their breath in the chill morning air. Similar sights were reported in other Tokyo neighborhoods and major cities including Osaka and Nagoya. They had staked out prime spots in front of major electronics stores for a chance to buy *Dragon Quest III,* the software company Enix's hugely anticipated latest release for the Famicom.

Dragon Quest III didn't feature the action-packed race for points typical of the previous generation's hits. It didn't have a score at all; it was a role-playing game that gave players free rein to quietly explore a fairy-tale landscape of castles and dungeons. The graphics were crude by modern standards, but the packaging and instruction manual were richly illustrated by artist Akira Toriyama, creator of Japan's best-selling manga, *Dragon Ball.* The whole production had a slick crossover appeal surpassing that of any video game seen to date.

The startling success of *Dragon Quest III* made director Yuji Horii an instant celebrity, the face of a new generation of high-tech creatives who took their job of building virtual worlds every bit as seriously as the craftspeople who had created the toys, radios, televisions, cars, and consumer electronics upon which Japan's postwar economic foundations rested. To them, the Nintendo Entertainment System was more than a game machine; it was a platform, their voice to the world.

As these creators unconsciously borrowed and incorporated the conventions of kaiju shows, anime, and manga into their game work, the NES and its successors functioned as a Rosetta stone for transmitting Japanese sensibilities to the world. It was through games, not television or manga or anime, that many foreign children would first encounter kawaii design, otaku-favorite robotic "mecha," or the idea of "powering up" into a supersized superhero like Ultraman.

NINTENDO SOLD SO many Nintendo Entertainment Systems that, by 1990, "playing Nintendo" was effectively synonymous with video gaming in the Western world. By 1993, Nintendo was making more money than all of Hollywood's top five studios put together, with more American children surveyed recognizing Mario than Mickey Mouse. Yet Nintendo's face abroad wasn't Uemura or Miyamoto, or even Nintendo of America's president—Yamauchi's son-in-law. Instead, it was a blond-haired, freckle-faced, bow tie–wearing twenty-something named Howard Phillips. Nintendo of America's "game master" served as the face of the company for journalists and on-stage at official events, taking on all challengers at public gaming forums and dispensing tips in the pages of the firm's house organ, *Nintendo Power*, where he had his own comic strip, *Howard & Nester*. Americans were hungry for Japanese games, but they weren't ready to embrace Japan just yet. That would take a few more years.

The debut of the Mega Drive, created by a former jukebox repair firm called Sega and released in Japan in late 1988, signaled the arrival of the first real contender to Nintendo's five-year hegemony of the home-gaming industry. Finished in glossy black and chrome, the Mega Drive fared poorly in its home country against the cherished Famicom and the PC Engine—another rival machine, created by the Japanese electronics firm NEC. But it didn't matter. By this point, it was obvious that the real battle for market share lay beyond Japan's borders. Nintendo had sold far more of its machines abroad than at home. In the States, for example, more children were playing Nintendo than watching the nation's biggest children's TV network, Nickelodeon. It was simple math: Games were hugely popular in Japan, but there were more children abroad. Echoing manga and anime fans of late-seventies Japan, a generation of foreign kids, raised on video games, refused to graduate from these supposed toys as they grew older. They instead demanded more sophistication.

Renamed "Genesis" for its 1989 American release, the Mega Drive handily outshone the aging capabilities of the six-year-old NES. Two weeks after the Genesis's debut, NEC leapt into the market with the TurboGrafx-16, an Americanized version of its PC Engine. For the very first time since launching the NES in 1986, Nintendo faced real competition for its products abroad. The console wars were on. A public battle for mindshare was something that could only have transpired abroad, for Japanese companies were notoriously reticent to engage in anything smacking of competitive advertising. The concept of publicly tearing down a competitor's product, so familiar to Western audiences from endless Coke vs. Pepsi–style showdowns, wasn't considered proper form in Japan.

To counter Mario, the frumpy middle-aged plumber, Sega introduced *Sonic the Hedgehog*, the creation of a twenty-five-year-old programmer named Yuji Naka. Sonic was a punky rodent who wagged a finger at the player on the title screen, then loop-de-looped through a lush tropical world at a breakneck speed even the fastest NES games couldn't hope to match. If *Super Mario Bros.* felt like playing a cartoon, *Sonic the Hedgehog* felt like mainlining one straight into your brain stem, delivering a potent dose of big-headed kawaii design and cool factor to Western fans. Echoing Nintendo of America's initial reaction to *Donkey Kong*, Sega of America's president initially thought building a game around a hedgehog was "nuts." Again the American tastemakers were proven wrong and the Japanese right, as millions of kids voted with their (or more accurately, their parents') wallets. Sonic's very existence stood in opposition to Nintendo's mainstream of gaming. There was no damsel in distress, only an instinctual need for speed; he even tapped a foot impatiently if the player left their controller unattended. Sonic gave the Genesis a hip, rebellious image that slotted perfectly into the "alternative" culture of the era, in which flannel-clad grunge heroes emerged as ironic foils to the slick arena rockers of the eighties. Sega did everything they could to play up the partisanship, running aggressive print and TV ads crowing, "Genesis does what Nintendon't!"

For no longer was the question *whether* you played video games. It felt like every kid played video games now. It was all about what *kind* of a gamer you were. At the height of the hot rod mania in the sixties, a vibrant subculture of car-crazed young Americans defined themselves with a new vocabulary forged from Detroit steel: Chevys and Fords, V-8 hemis and big blocks, kandy kolors and chrome. Now, nineties gamers did the same—with Japanese silicon. They plowed game-based idioms like "power up," "level up," "miniboss," "boss battle," "limit break," "cutscene," and "save point" into the English lexicon, hyperventilated over 8-bit versus 16-bit microprocessors, and turned tortured mistranslations from favorite games into inside jokes: A winner is you! All your base are belong to us! There was plenty to debate: Nintendo's polished gameplay set the standard by which all others were judged; NEC's TurboGrafx-16 represented the first system with a CD-ROM drive accessory for better music and sound effects; Sega's edgier attitude and sporty game library appealed to geeks and jocks alike. When the time came for me to move to college in 1991, the idea of packing my trusty old childhood NES never even crossed my mind. The Genesis went in before the school supplies. And so too did another little gadget called the Game Boy.

NINTENDO TOOK ITS sweet time creating a successor to the Famicom. Never a company at the forefront of technological innovation, it chose instead to follow a path established by Gunpei Yokoi, who espoused a design philosophy he termed "lateral thinking with withered technology." In plain English, it meant that when Nintendo developed a new product, they stuck with cheap and proven off-the-shelf components instead of gambling untold sums on creating cutting-edge new ones themselves. This seemingly retrograde mindset, completely at odds with the envelope-pushing attitudes of most tech companies, crystallized in the product for which Yokoi would be most remembered.

Released in 1989, his Game Boy did for video gaming what the Walkman had done for music in 1979. It wasn't the first portable gaming device, but it was the one that truly brought the concept of gaming on the go to the masses. No longer would gamers need to congregate in arcades or tether themselves to their home televisions.

With the Game Boy they could play anywhere, anytime. Similar to the Walkman, the Game Boy wasn't state-of-the-art technology. In contrast to the high-tech, full-color portable machines released by competitors, Nintendo's machine featured a monochromatic display with a noticeable blur whenever characters moved quickly. Industry insiders were unimpressed. "We called it the Lameboy," Rebecca Heineman, a co-founder of the American game developer Interplay, told me. The specifications may have looked lame to experts, but average users simply didn't care. Just as the ability to watch *Astro Boy* at home trumped the fact its animation was quite cheap looking— just as the Walkman's portability far outweighed the fact the earliest versions couldn't record music—convenience and content trumped all else. The Game Boy served up the fantasies we wanted, in minia-ture, starting with Mario and going right down the line of Nintendo classics. No competitor could hope to match that, no matter their devices' spectacular specifications. That's why the Game Boy never felt lame to my friends and me. It felt necessary.

For while the specs may have suffered, in nearly every other way the Game Boy was the superior product. It was stylishly neutral in design: neither masculine nor feminine, neither childish nor adult, neither high-tech nor retro. Rivals, clad in angular, jet-black plastic, virtually screamed *high tech*—the kind of things a teenage boy might use to impress his circle of friends. The Game Boy, on the other hand, was designed for comfort. Its smaller size (roughly that of a paperback book), its deliberately disarming name, its gray color scheme, and its gently rounded edges almost begged you to carry it along, settling into the palm of your hand as if by instinct when you did. It is tempting to describe it as kawaii. Meanwhile, it boasted a superior battery life, and—key for any portable electronic device—it was nearly indestructible. Truly, the things could take an unbeliev-able beating. One specimen, carried into Kuwait by an American soldier during the first Gulf War, kept working even after being melted to near oblivion in a terror bombing. (It was in fact still functioning as of 2019, on display at the Nintendo Store in Rockefeller Center.) But most of all, the Game Boy had the games. Popular characters, not technical specifications, made the Game Boy the single top-selling game system of the 1990s. Not only did it crush the handheld competition, it trounced even the consoles—the Super NES, the Genesis, and all the contenders to follow. In fact, if all its incarnations, such as the Game Boy Color and Game Boy Advance, are included, the Game Boy is the top-selling game machine of all time.

The console wars were a head-to-head competition over the specifications of cutting-edge hardware. The Game Boy represented a triumph of content and convenience over tech. Young gamers flocked to the Game Boy instead of competitors because of the fantasies it facilitated: scaled-down black-and-white versions of beloved NES classics like *Super Mario Land, Metroid, The Legend of Zelda,* and the *Castlevania* series. Grown-ups loved it for the game it came packaged with: *Tetris,* a gripping puzzle that had been developed in a Soviet computer lab (and licensed to Nintendo through a byzantine series of twists and turns reminiscent of a Cold War thriller). The textbook case of a killer app, *Tetris* made gamers out of legions who'd never dreamed of dropping a quarter or touching a controller before—including one President George H. W. Bush, who was photographed playing a Game Boy as he recuperated from a thyroid operation. It also proved incredibly popular among girls and women, who, according to one Nintendo of America survey, constituted 46 percent of all Game Boy users. "I have become quite a fan," admitted Hillary Clinton in a 1993 *Time* interview, explaining that she purchased her own unit so as not to monopolize Chelsea's. Globalization in a nutshell: a former president and a first lady playing a Soviet-made puzzle game on a Japanese game system. There is no indication that any of these instances of people in positions of power fiddling with foreign fantasies affected politics one way or the other. Or not yet, anyway—that's a story for our next chapter.

First Lady Hillary Clinton aboard
Air Force One, 1992

Intentionally or not, Nintendo had achieved something no other gaming company ever had: gender parity. Or perhaps it was better to say the Game Boy, despite its name, appealed to both genders because of its studied anti-machismo, so different from the edgy offerings of its rivals. "The combination of portability and kawaii design sensibilities meant that people actively enjoyed taking these things around with them," explained the *Guardian* in 2015—tellingly, not even bothering to explain kawaii to its audience.

"Nintendo understands that small things are cute and that cuteness pervades the whole experience. This is exactly what's going on in the smartphone sector with *Candy Crush, Fruit Ninja,* and *Angry Birds.*" Or, bringing things full circle, *Pokémon GO*, which was downloaded more than a hundred million times globally in just the first month after its 2016 release.

ARCADE GAMING WAS a shared public experience, with all the social interactions that entailed: physically going there, watching the moves of other players, finding opponents for head-to-head battles, mastering local etiquette such as when and where to lay a coin on the edge of the screen to secure the next play. Console gaming was, by definition, something you could do alone, without leaving the comfort of your own home. Already, by the peak of the bubble in the late eighties, Japanese social commentators noted with alarm the increasing numbers of children who chose to stay home and game by themselves rather than going out to play with other children, in articles with titles like a 1989 newspaper report called "How Information Society Warps Children" and books such as that same year's *A Childhood in Solitude: The Fate of the First Generation of Home Gamers*. But was the trend really about games, or society? Often lost in the criticism of technology was a sobering fact. As the Japanese real estate market boomed, playgrounds, forests, and even empty lots disappeared from cities and suburbs at a rapid clip. In a self-fulfilling cycle, the fewer opportunities children had for outdoor play, the more time they chose to spend in thrilling virtual worlds.

Pokémon creator Satoshi Tajiri was one of them. Born in 1965, he grew up in Machida, a commuter town located a forty-five-minute train ride from downtown Tokyo. As a little boy Tajiri spent as much time as he could outdoors. "There was still so much nature then," he recalled in a 2000 interview. "It felt like I was surrounded by living things. I'd catch tadpoles and crayfish and raise them at home." It wasn't until the cusp of his teens that he first noticed how much his town was starting to change. His old hunting grounds were disappearing, replaced by new housing developments and buildings. He was in junior high when his favorite fishing spot in front of the station disappeared. In its place was erected a video game arcade.

It is fair to say that Tajiri's encounter with this strange new establishment transformed his entire existence. "I couldn't catch bugs anymore, so I put all of that effort into *Space Invaders*." Passion begat obsession; his parents cried that he had turned into some kind of juvenile delinquent. Rather than the local high school, he chose a more distant vocational school that taught computer programming. Forced to attend a cram school to get his grades in shape for college, he deliberately picked one near an arcade so that he could dash over for a quick session of *Missile Command* during the fifteen-minute breaks between lessons. He began submitting articles to game magazines. Together with an illustrator friend he launched a fanzine filled with strategies for conquering arcade and console games. He called it what he called someone like himself: *Game Freak*. In 1989, the pair launched a game company by the same name.

Capsule Monster was one of their very first proposals. Nintendo

bought it with the proviso that Tajiri reshape the idea to their specifications. Those specifications were provided by Mario's creator
Shigeru Miyamoto. It was a dream come true for a game-obsessed
kid. "Ever since I was a teenager, playing *Donkey Kong,* he's always
been my role model," Tajiri told *Time* in 1999. "I'd memorize each
piece of advice he gave." He even named the protagonist's rival
Shigeru ("Gary Oak" in the English version) to commemorate the
challenges the pair faced together. Trademark difficulties resulted in
a last-minute name change to *Pocket Monsters,* later shortened to
Pokémon. By the time Nintendo finally approved it for release in
1996, the Game Boy for which it had been designed was regarded as
a technological antiquity. Nintendo envisioned the game as a sort of
send-off for the beloved device before launching a new and improved
version.

It had taken six years for Tajiri to develop *Pokémon,* but it was
really a product twenty years in the making. "It *is* my childhood," he
explained. "All of those experiences and memories went into the
making of *Pocket Monsters.*" The adults might have taken away his
fishing hole, but here inside the confines of the Game Boy he had
created a place where a child could run free and hunt for creatures to
their heart's content. As the architect of this world he could make
them better, even more compelling, than any real-life critter.
Through the expedient of "Poké Balls," the in-game device for capturing the Pokémon so that they could be trained into more powerful forms, he could provide an endless supply of them to the children
of Japan. Well, not exactly endless. The first edition of the game
contained 151 of them.

Nintendo's Gunpei Yokoi had compromised on many things when
designing the Game Boy, but one function he refused to live without
was the Game Link Cable for networking two of the devices together.
The Game Boy wasn't the first handheld to offer the option—Atari's
Lynx, as per its name, was designed to link with other Lynxes, too—
but sheer ubiquity meant that the Game Boy ended up being most

gamers' introduction to multiplayer gaming. These early communal game experiences were primitive by modern, surround sound, three-dimensional standards: head-to-head Tetris battles, tennis matches, racing games. They were also surprisingly, satisfyingly immersive—even if you had to be careful not to tangle yourself in the link cable when you got swept up in the action.

These early experiments in multiplayer gaming mediated simple forms of head-to-head competition through computers. But the next evolution would be Tajiri's. "That cable really got me interested. I thought of actual living organisms moving back and forth across the cable," he recalled. "I liked competition, too. But I wanted to design a game that involved interactive communication." There was no way to find all 151 Pokémon in the digital wilds of one's own Game Boy. The game was released in two cartridges, each containing partial menageries, and the only way to complete your "Pokédex" of monsters was through the act of trading—by linking up Game Boys. For the first time, children connected their machines together not only to battle (though they could and did that as well) but to commune over a shared interest in completing their collections. More than any other multiplayer game to date, Tajiri's innovation had the effect of channeling solo home gaming back into the public sphere. And he'd done something more.

In *Pokémon* Tajiri created a powerful new tool for navigating a Japan whose natural terrain had been wracked by the scars of unchecked urbanization, and whose societal fabric was being rent by the chaos of the Lost Decades. In a symbolic bit of flair, the game opened with the protagonist, Ash, playing a Super Nintendo on a television in his bedroom, then setting down the controller and heading out into the world—passing his mother along the way, who remains glued to her own television downstairs. This was a world in which kids would need to rely on their own wits, find their own comrades, and devise their own tools to navigate. Though Tajiri was already in his mid-twenties by the time the Lost Decades began, he never stopped feeling the pain of his lost childhood pleasures. That is what made the game so compelling to children experiencing similar things around the world.

Put another way, the enormous popularity of the video game he created carried the seeds for the digitization of socialization. They would blossom in new and unpredictable ways as more and more people all over the globe began connecting on a transformative new medium for communication: the Internet.

9

THE ANTISOCIAL NETWORK

2channel

The Internet is Serious Business.
—ANONYMOUS

We are what we pretend to be, so we must be careful about what we pretend to be.
—KURT VONNEGUT

TRAIN MAN IS your stereotypical otaku. At twenty-three he still lives with his parents, in a childhood bedroom overflowing with toy robots and figurines of anime starlets. He's never had a girlfriend or even been on a date. His hair is unkempt, and his clothes little changed from the styles his mother picked out for him as a kid. He works long hours at a tedious desk job. His precious days off from work are spent in Akihabara, Tokyo's epicenter for electronics and anime products. His nights are spent in front of his computer.

On the ride home one night, Train Man sees a young woman being harassed by a drunken salaryman. Uncharacteristically, he leaps to her defense. The drunk picks a fight. The conductor calls the police and the lout is arrested. When the ordeal is over, the young woman asks for Train Man's address so that she can send him a gift, a common courtesy in Japan. He stutters out his contact information, but cannot muster the courage to ask for hers in return. Humiliated, he trudges back to his bedroom and turns to the Internet for solace.

It is the night of Valentine's Day, 2004, when Train Man posts the glum details of his encounter on 2channel (pronounced "ni-channeru"), Japan's largest anonymous online bulletin board system. There is a forum there dedicated to the travails of men unlucky in love, with a long-running thread called "Men Shot in the Back" that chronicles tales of woe similar to Train Man's. In fact the Single Men board is one of the site's most popular forums, regularly attracting tens of thousands of posts daily from men without romantic prospects. At least they're trying. Fourteen years after the burst of the bubble, indicators such as the birth rate and even condom sales have plunged so low that Japan's top news magazine, *Aera*, recently published a story pleadingly titled "Young People, Don't Hate Sex."

The regulars call themselves Poison Men, because the kanji characters for "single" and "poison" happen to be homonyms in Japanese. The commentary on the Single Men board is sad and predictable and comforting. Train Man's post is but one of many in the thread, and the unceasing flood of incoming posts shunts his missive off the top page and into oblivion: just another night on the Single Men board. But then: the unexpected.

Forty-eight hours later, Train Man checks back in to report receiving a handwritten note and an exquisite pair of Hermès teacups from the woman. *A pair!* Could this be a sign? From the shipping label he has obtained her address and phone number, but again he finds himself paralyzed at the thought of establishing contact. "I can't call a woman on the phone! __| ̄ |○" he writes, the last bit being an emoticon illustrating the concept of being brought to one's knees, an onscreen expression of total surrender that punctuates many of the Poison Men's dispatches. Yet something about Train Man's plight resonates. For, suddenly, the thread blossoms into a rapid-fire coaching session. The lonely masses have found a human Tamagotchi.

Train Man gamely reports back with regular updates. Anonymous posters weigh in with more advice. Buoyed by their support, he summons the courage to call Hermès, as he has nicknamed the woman to preserve her privacy. They go on a date. Following the instructions of his anonymous online advisors, he gets a haircut, updates his wardrobe, and scouts out date spots. At one point he even puts his nerd knowledge to work, using his computer skills to impress his new girlfriend by fixing her PC. After two months of incremental progress, reported in painstaking detail, Train Man announces that he plans to propose to Hermès. More advice floods in from the hive mind—a collective, digital Cyrano de Bergerac. She accepts! The Poison Men erupt in celebration, congratulating the couple with a flood of posts filled with elaborate emoticon art. After thanking the participants, Train Man disappears from the boards, never to be seen again. He is no longer one of them. The end.

Or is it? Word of the dramatic thread spreads across 2channel's other boards and is profiled by news aggregators—parasite portals that curate lists of links to popular threads from the site, in hopes of reaping advertising revenue. Before long, it is discovered by publishers on the prowl for the next big thing. In October, the thread (by this point, close to thirty thousand posts long) is edited into a novel, preserving its onscreen appearance—emoticons and web-speak and all: a translation from screen to printed page. Much of it is so arcane to outsiders that the publisher is forced to add a detailed glossary, inadvertently making *Train Man* a Rosetta stone for those unfamiliar with online society. It sells a quarter of a million copies in the first three weeks. In 2005, *Train Man* (italicized now, no longer a person but a product) is all Japan's entertainment industry seems to talk about. It becomes a manga, a film, and a television series. (The latter's theme song is an animated homage to the old Hideaki Anno–directed fan-festival film short—set, naturally, to the very same soundtrack of Electric Light Orchestra's "Twilight.")

Train Man's arrival coincides with increasingly dire reports about the Japanese economy and the nation's perilously low birth rate, utterly unimproved from the decade before, which has triggered society-wide discussions about employment, gender roles, masculinity—even the very survival of Japan itself. *Evangelion* rehabilitated the image of the otaku from outcast losers, making them unlikely trendsetters. The popularity of the *Train Man* franchise—

one lonely man, now a national franchise!—reframes these eternal loners as potential marriage material. Suddenly otaku is no longer a four-letter word, no longer a euphemism for child-murderer. Otaku are simply misunderstood fans, who just need a little extra love and understanding. Society's message of redemption is simple: *You can have your anime girls (or boys), and real ones, too!*

If you think Train Man's story sounds a little too good to be true, you aren't alone. 2channel is an anonymous bulletin board system, where posts disappear as soon as more popular ones push them off the top screen. On forums as popular as the Single Men board, the average thread's life span can be measured in minutes; that Train Man's persisted for months and years was both a rare exception and a testament to its popularity. With no way to ascertain the identity of the original poster, the rights for the story fell to 2channel's creator, Hiroyuki Nishimura—or just Hiroyuki, as everyone on the site knew him. It was he who negotiated deals with the publishers and media companies on behalf of Train Man.

To preserve Train Man's identity, the book is credited to the pseudonym Nakano Hitori, a punning homonym for "one of many." To this very day, even after a great deal of digging on the part of newspapers, magazines, and websites, nobody knows who Train Man might be. Conspiracy theories swirl, of course. He was created by admen in an elaborate viral Hermès marketing scheme. He was created by the publisher to sell books. He was created by Hiroyuki himself in a bid to raise the profile of his popular but underground website—an accusation Hiroyuki has repeatedly denied. In a sense, it doesn't even matter whether Train Man truly exists or was a virtual construct, because the real question is why his story resonated with so many millions of Japanese.

"All of a sudden," writes otaku studies professor Hiroki Azuma of Train Man's moment in the public spotlight, "Japan became a nation composed wholly of otaku." Watching kids' shows and dressing up for cosplay are now accepted and even encouraged forms of leisure among grown-ups; video games, too, are a respected cultural export, with everyone from elementary-schoolers to the elderly searching for *Pokémon GO* in city parks. Super-kawaii idol singers, once consumed almost exclusively by teenybopper girls and horny otaku, now dominate the mainstream music industry. Politicians court the Akihabara vote by openly reading comic books and campaigning in anime costumes. Even staid organizations such as Japan Railways, the National Tax Agency, and the Japan Self-Defense Forces have created their own anime-girl mascots for citizen outreach efforts, because they know that the average young person is someone pretty much like Train Man—or at least shares his tastes.

TRAIN MAN'S APPEARANCE in Japan coincided with a delayed flourishing of otaku culture in America. There, cause and effect were reversed: Made-in-Japan video games, not anime or manga, paved the way. These were followed over the course of the nineties by a great number of English-language versions of Japanese multimedia franchises: the various incarnations of the *Power Rangers, Dragon Ball Z, Sailor Moon, Gundam Wing,* and, of course, *Pokémon.* A pair of unabashedly Japanophilic mainstream Hollywood hits bracketed the turn of the millennium: the Wachowski siblings' 1999 anime-inspired *The Matrix* and Tarantino's 2003 *Kill Bill: Volume 1.* Successful though they were, these movies still filtered anime culture through American sensibilities. (The Wachowskis reportedly hooked producer Joel Silver by sending him a copy of Mamoru Oshii's anime *Ghost in the Shell* with the note "We wanna do that for real.")

Now a new generation of millennials raised on the content quested for more, unmoderated by gatekeepers—authentic, and fresh from the source. They found it on the Internet, on a website called 4chan. It was launched in 2003 by a fifteen-year-old anime fan by the name of Christopher Poole, better known online by his handle: moot (always with a lowercase *m*). In its earliest days, 4chan was a sort of *Lord of the Flies* for anime-obsessed American teenagers. Thanks to the digital Darwinism of the Internet, it rapidly evolved into something much more. By the end of the aughts it had emerged as a key hub of Internet culture. In 2019, it was visited by forty to sixty million people from around the world every month.

4chan's most popular "not safe for work" boards were (and are) swirling maelstroms of adolescent hijinks, pornography, and political incorrectness, fueled by a constant hunger for something—anything—stimulating and new. Key to it all is ephemerality: Threads disappear forever as they are displaced by new ones. What happens on 4chan stays on 4chan—or so went the original idea. This seems like a recipe for sound and fury, signifying nothing. But 4chan's impact on American culture, both online and off, is quantifiably real—and occasionally scary. It became the world's wacky-meme factory, but so too did it devolve into a hothouse for sexism, misogyny, white supremacy, election tampering, even terror plots. In other words, 4chan embodied the dark side of the Internet—which is to say, in a way, modern life, as we know it.

And to understand it, we first have to go back to Japan, for that is where 4chan originated, both in terms of its software and its culture.

HIROYUKI NISHIMURA WAS once a lonely man, too—not much different from Train Man and the other participants on the Single Men board. He was a twenty-two-year-old foreign exchange student studying psychology at the University of Central Arkansas when, in the spring of 1999, he created 2channel.

He was lonely because classes had adjourned for the summer and the campus was all but empty. The name was a joke. 2channel was a "second channel" for users of a popular but unstable and frequently inaccessible Japanese website called Amezou, itself an outgrowth of a notorious underground website called Ayashii Warudo (Suspicious World). An added plus was that any Japanese otaku would instantly associate it with channel two: the "dead" channel used for connecting a Famicom to an analog television.

There was nothing particularly brag-worthy about 2channel's technology or its presentation. Even by the standards of the day it looked crude—downright ugly, in fact. Based on the same underlying software that Amezou used, it featured a similarly stripped-down user interface consisting purely of text. Even the imagery was text, constructed out of letters and punctuation in what was known as ASCII art, ASCII being the name of the standard for encoding text on computers. 2channel prized function over form, in a throwback to the old dial-up BBS (bulletin board system) popular a decade earlier. In their earliest eighties incarnation, BBSes existed on the fringes of society—the province of computer nerds and other early adopters with the specialized gear needed for access. (My friends and I were among them, using our dial-up modems to call in to local bulletin boards for a very early taste of now-ubiquitous systems such as email, threaded discussions, chat rooms, and filesharing.) In the nine years since the appearance of the first Internet browser and website in 1990, the World Wide Web's user base exploded from a handful of academics to an estimated 250 million, some 4 percent of the Earth's total population. Japan was particularly ahead of the curve; 1999 also marked the local launch of i-mode, the world's first widely adopted Internet service for mobile phones.

Unlike most online bulletin boards, there would be no need to register on 2channel: no passwords, no moderation or filtering of any kind. The software would let you input a temporary username, but if you didn't want to, you were free to use the default handle of *nanashi,* or nameless. And here was the best part. Hiroyuki made a point of hosting the site on an American Internet provider, so the Japanese authorities couldn't touch you, no matter what kind of weird stuff you chose to post. Other sites had promised privacy of varying degrees, but this here was real and true freedom right on your desktop, accessible simply by typing "2ch.net" into your browser. In rural Arkansas, a Japanese hacker created an online Wild West for the Far East. "Otaku of all types," evangelized one early chronicler, "have a space to talk about anime and manga without fear of being set upon by a mainstream public that actually hates their hobbies." In droves, they flocked to their new Babylon.

The first scandal hit just weeks after Hiroyuki launched his site. A user calling himself Akky posted the link to a website with a recording he'd made of a phone call to Toshiba's service center. In it a gruff, middle-aged company man shouted down a high-pitched, soft-talking electronics enthusiast who sounded, undoubtedly, a lot like the average 2channel user. Outraged posters flooded the company's website and phone lines with complaints. By July Akky's site had seven million page views, and Toshiba filed suit to have it taken down. But the tactic backfired. In a country as obsessed with presentation, image, and hospitality as Japan, news of a major corporation treating a customer in this way made headlines. No longer able to resolve the issue quietly, Toshiba capitulated. They even dispatched a senior vice president to bow in apology to Akky. Wielding 2channel like a digital megaphone, a bunch of nerds had compelled one of Japan's biggest companies to kowtow to them. Literally.

Shortly thereafter, 2channel's collective attention turned to a former juvenile delinquent turned pop star by the name of Masashi Tashiro. The R&B vocalist was having a very bad 2001. He was already dealing with charges for filming up a woman's skirt on the subway the year before. Then he was collared and literally dragged to the police station by a furious homeowner who'd spotted him peeping in the bathroom window. The nadir came in December of 2001, when he was simultaneously arrested for possession of methamphetamines and dropped by his talent agency.

The denizens of 2channel joined forces to make the pop star turned peeping tom into *Time* magazine's Person of the Year. Using a series of homebrewed automatic voting programs with names inspired by anime shows (one was called the Mega-particle Tashiro Cannon, a nod to a weapon from the *Gundam* series), 2channelers sieged the magazine's online ballot system. Within forty-eight hours, Tashiro beat out Osama bin Laden and George W. Bush for the top spot. Confused American editors quickly removed the singer from the running, but it was yet another win for the anonymous masses of 2channel. They didn't call the stunt a hack or a troll or a raid.

They called it *matsuri*—a festival, tellingly the very same word that Tomino had used to describe the Anime New Century Declaration.

The first festival to spill into the real world occurred the following year. The occasion was the 2002 World Cup. It was a contentious event from the very start. Tensions ran high between Japan, which had initially lobbied for the right to host, and South Korea, which argued that it was more qualified than its rival. (Unable to sever the Gordian knot of historical mistrust, weary FIFA officials finally split the duties between the two countries, to absolutely nobody's satisfaction.) Matches in which the South Korean team played proved particularly contentious. 2channelers were infuriated by Fuji Television's sportscasters, who (in their opinion) weren't doing enough to denounce questionable calls by the ref in favor of the South Korean soccer team. In this they weren't alone; fans in Spain and Italy were equally upset about the refereeing of their matches against the South Koreans. But Europeans were mad at the referees and with the organization itself. 2channelers didn't blow up at FIFA or the South Koreans—that would have demanded some kind of direct confrontation. Instead they resolved to humiliate Fuji Television, the station that broadcast the matches in Japan.

One poster half-jokingly suggested disrupting a Fuji TV–sponsored beach cleanup event. If enough 2channelers could get to the beach and clean it up first, the poster reasoned, they would deprive the station of the PR effect from sponsoring the event. Within hours, the joke was spun into a plan. Arranging times, meeting spots, and even a kawaii mascot character, participants advertised the sneak cleanup in boards across the site. On July 5, two days before the date of the official event, hundreds of 2channelers wearing pink armbands descended upon the beach and scoured it of litter. When the TV cameras finally arrived forty-eight hours later, there wasn't a speck of garbage on the beach to film. Fuji's producers scrambled to create a new narrative about how they'd inspired grassroots efforts—and studiously avoided any mention of 2channel at all. "Fake news?" sighed one participant on his blog—the first stirrings of a global culture war brewing between Internet users and the gatekeepers of mainstream media.

The beach cleanup had been a pleasant sort of protest, but the frustrations that sparked it continued to stew as relations deteriorated between Japan and neighboring China and South Korea. In the same year as the World Cup, it emerged that North Korean agents had kidnapped dozens of Japanese citizens in the seventies; then a series of territorial disputes over islands with South Korea and China inflamed tensions all the more. The seeming impotence of Japanese politicians in the face of shocking revelations and diplomatic slights helped fuel the rise of a new breed of 2channel user: *netto uyoku* (the "net right-wing"). Fueled by a corrosive mix of insecurity and pride, net-rightists dismissed mainstream media as tainted by political correctness, reveled in anti-Korean and anti-Chinese racism, furiously denied Japan's wartime atrocities, and plotted campaigns to humiliate anyone whom they perceived as critical of their country. In a way, they represented the weaponization of the otaku mindset. Adroit with fantasy, hungry for drama, obsessed with minutiae, evangelical about their interests, and accustomed to devoting most of their considerable free time to their hobbies, they positioned themselves as gatekeepers of online conversation in spite of representing a minority of a minority—around 1 percent of netizens, according to one study. "I was lonely and had nothing to do. That's why I was on the net all the time," explained a self-described former net righter in a 2015 blog post. "I felt great, because I thought I was getting information of the sort they didn't teach in school or show on TV."

Net-rightists' single-minded obsession with Japan's status in the world unwittingly revealed a stark reality. Their nation was entering the second of what was increasingly looking to be two Lost Decades. For many idle youth, stranded at home by a stagnant economy with an unemployment rate unprecedented for the postwar era, computer screens became their only connection to the outside world. "I thought of myself as a total dropout from society in every aspect," as a former self-described *hikikomori* (recluse) put it in a tweet. "The only thing that remained was that I was Japanese."

AS 2CHANNEL'S FAME and infamy grew, so too did the cost of running the site. The companies that hosted websites charged by bandwidth. That meant that the more people using 2channel, the more it cost Hiroyuki to run. Although he later introduced advertising to cover the fees (and turned a handsome profit), in those early years he paid for everything out of pocket. More than once the site went dark as Hiroyuki scrambled to pay the bills. In a measure of just how integral a presence 2channel had become in the lives of its participants, a group of frustrated users launched a "refuge" website in the late summer of 2001 to serve as a backup meeting spot on the occasions 2channel went down. Called Futaba Channel, it bore no official relationship to Hiroyuki's site, but the name (which means "two leaves" in Japanese) was a clear nod, as was its URL: 2chan.net.

Futaba Channel started life as little more than a clone of its predecessor. Shortly after its inception, however, administrators introduced a new function for users: the ability to upload images. This seemingly simple addition would have a profound impact on the atmosphere of the site. Even if you were a native speaker of Japanese, it was easy to get lost in 2channel's chaotic sea of text, what with the in-jokes, emoticons, and arcane net slang. You had to be highly literate to make sense of it all. Futaba's visuals-centric forums threw users a life preserver. On "imageboards," posts didn't need to be parsed; a reader could take the scene in simply by scrolling through the visuals: screenshots of anime, manga, fan art, pornography—whatever users felt like uploading at that particular moment. The effect was not unlike paging through an ever-changing, never-ending manga.

Though designed as a temporary haven, Futaba quickly developed an independent culture, emerging as more a creatively focused counterpart to 2channel's social satire and protests. Legions of amateur artists gathered there to post their fan art of famous characters from

Japanese comic books, cartoons, and video games. It was a swirling typhoon of scans and screen captures and homages and collages, ranging from the innocuous to hardcore pornography, blurring the line between creator and consumer in ways inspired by the nation's enduringly vibrant fan convention scene. Seriously vibrant: The annual summer Comic Market festival swelled to thirty-five thousand exhibitors in 2001 and was visited by nearly five hundred thousand fans—more than double its size at the dawn of the Lost Decades in 1991.

Futaba's visual focus provided foreign fans their first window into the twin worlds of Japanese fandom and anonymous online culture. Getting to Comic Market required a plane ticket. To get to Futaba all one needed to do was stumble across a link to the site. In America, the online establishment was already leaning away from anonymity, toward what was then the cutting-edge concept of social networking. The idea was that by compelling users to register names and passwords, they could establish online reputations—and, not coincidentally, be tracked for marketing purposes. But it turned out that a lot of people didn't want to use the Internet as an extension of their real-life identities. They were up to things they didn't want anyone in their real lives knowing about.

One of them was fifteen-year-old Christopher Poole. He discovered anime in the summer of 2003. In an earlier era, to find new content he would have had to peruse television listings, prowl video-rental shops, and join clubs or attend conventions. By this point, he didn't even need to leave his home. Like-minded fans were posting huge quantities of anime on semilegal file-sharing sites, and you didn't need to haul yourself out to a convention for the latest info; all you had to do was find the right online community. One of the most popular anime forums of the day was hosted on a website called Something Awful.

Launched in 1999, Something Awful started life as a repository for the writings of its founder, Rich "Lowtax" Kyanka, then quickly expanded into a vibrant online community for its many readers. In the years before sites like Twitter, Reddit, Facebook, and Instagram emerged as the hubs of online life, Kyanka's fascination with, as he put it, "crappy internet things"—weirdo websites, bizarre fetishes, parodies of Silicon Valley groupthink—made Something Awful one of the earliest hotspots for online culture. If you happened across something funny online at the turn of the twenty-first century, chances are it originated in one of the site's many user forums.

There, nobody knew Christopher as Christopher. They all called him by his handle: moot. What did it mean? Who cared! On the Internet, no one knew you were a teenage cartoon fiend, though your choice of bulletin board might telegraph it: ADTRW. It stood for Anime Death Tentacle Rape Whorehouse.

The name was, like so many things on the Internet, a joke. Kyanka disliked anime so intensely that, upon finally relenting to the demand to add an anime forum to his site, he made sure to assign it as embarrassing a name as possible. That he associated anime with sex was the legacy of huge quantities of direct-to-video anime pornography that had found its way to American video stores over the course of the 1990s. American fans didn't call it porn, though. They called it *hentai*, a word borrowed from the Japanese for "abnormal." (Japanese don't call pornography hentai; they tend to use the English loanword *ero*, from erotic.)

Carefully crafted to skirt strict obscenity laws in Japan, hentai productions (which is to say anime porn in general) eschewed intercourse for metaphor. One of the earliest and most popular to arrive in translation was the 1987 film *Urotsukidoji: Legend of the Overfiend*, which featured lengthy scenes of innocent schoolgirls being ravished by bizarre monsters with slimy prehensile tentacles. This novel approach to illustrating human sexuality was in fact a direct result of government antiobscenity laws. For while porn was nothing new, neither were attempts by authority figures to regulate it. Article 175 of the Japanese Penal Code, enacted in 1907, states that "A person who distributes or sells obscene writing, pictures, or other objects . . . shall be punished by imprisonment." It remains in force today, a relic of prewar law that has survived into modern times. Critics have long derided its vagueness as an affront to free expression. (Many have tried and failed to challenge its scope, such as the Japanese performance artist Rokudenashiko, who was arrested in 2014 for sharing the data for a series of objects based on 3-D scans of her own vulva, including a functional kayak.)

Fear of Article 175 compels Japanese publishers to use masking techniques such as pixelated "mosaics" to blur out genitalia, whether photographic or illustrated. Yet in one of those every-action-has-an-opposite-and-equal-reaction sort of situations, this attempt to regulate morality backfired. Making it more difficult to portray natural sex acts between two human beings didn't cut down on the amount of pornographic material being produced at all. It simply spurred artists to embrace increasingly stranger forms of fetishized sex that didn't involve the act of penetration. By censoring the nude body and turning a blind eye to almost everything else, Japanese authorities essentially promoted fetish sex over natural copulation.

I spoke to tentacle-porn maestro and *Urotsukidoji* creator Toshio Maeda for some insight into the situation. We met in a Tokyo bar; he arrived impeccably dressed in a suit and a necktie with an anime girl on it. Why tentacles, I asked? "I couldn't even so much as show two people lying on top of one another!" he explained. "Tentacles were simply a trick to get around the rules, to get some distance between the two parties."

Maeda's ingenious innovation left such a mark on Western erotic fantasies that tentacle porn remains a popular search term even today, long after it went out of style in the motherland. (Google the phrase if you dare, and you'll get forty-two million hits.) While mainstream productions like *Ghost in the Shell* and *Pokémon* made global headlines in the nineties, hentai quietly flourished in the shadows, adding a veneer of edginess to the image of anime, which was at the time still seen as an underground subculture. In America, where cartoons were at the time widely regarded to be kiddie fare, the appearance of animated porn was shocking stuff.

All the best material at Anime Death Tentacle Rape Whorehouse came directly from Futaba Channel—reposted by American fans who had stumbled across the Japanese site while searching for anime online. Impressed by the speed at which Futaba's forums replenished with new content, moot downloaded a copy of Futaba's opensource software and used the online translation application Babel Fish to render it into English. (His reliance on translation software led him to make one subtle linguistic mistake: He rendered nanashi—nameless—as "anonymous.") Next, he needed a domain. 3chan was already taken. 4 it would be. He announced his new creation via a triumphant ADTRW post October 1, 2003, entitled "4chan.net—English 2chan.net!" He nicknamed the site Yotsuba—"four leaves," a nod to Futaba's two, and an homage to his favorite manga at the time, Yotsuba&!—a feel-good series about an elementary school girl. At launch, the site had just one board: /b/, a random grab bag for whatever anyone chose to post.

Within twenty-four hours, so much hentai content overwhelmed the forum that moot was forced to spin it off onto its own board. A week later came one specializing in kawaii anime. Then yaoi, that Japanese term for illustrated boy-on-boy romances. From these anime roots, the site began branching into the adjacent interests of broader nerd culture such as technology and video games, much of it also made in Japan. In real life, Japan and the West were separated by continents and oceans. Online, they swirled and merged into one.

"I'M GONNA TEACH you a special word today," Shut says as he leans into his microphone. He looks less like a programmer than a hipster, clad in a seventies-style wide-collar button-down shirt. Shut's his handle; he doesn't offer his real name. He looks about twenty. Maybe. "It's German. It's pretty long but it's easy to pronounce. Schadenfreude. Can we all say that? Basically, that's enjoying someone else's displeasure. Like, getting off on trolling someone or annoying someone, just because you can. That's a pretty fucking important factor in any Internet message board, and that's pretty much what 4chan is about . . . getting off." The crowd claps and whistles appreciatively.

It is August of 2005, almost two years after 4chan opened for monkey business. From 4chan's very beginnings, moot has depended on the help of volunteer moderators, of which Shut is one. He's delivering this bit of online wisdom to a raucous crowd at Otakon, one of America's most popular anime conventions. This is the second year in a row that Otakon has welcomed more than twenty thousand participants to the Baltimore Convention Center, a sign of the role Japanese fantasies have begun to play in the lives of young Americans. So is 4chan's panel discussion, for that matter. The conference room is filled to capacity. The atmosphere is like a mix between an after-school hangout in your parents' basement and the final period before classes let out for the summer. The audience—mostly male, mostly white, mostly Shut's age, entirely hyperactive—shouts memes and in-jokes and jovial obscenities as Shut attempts to tell the story of how the site came to be. A PowerPoint slide flashes on the screen.

> 4chan is a free, English-language anonymous BBS and imageboard network modeled after the immensely popular Japanese sites 2ch and 2chan . . . The primary focus at 4chan is discussion related to Japanese anime, manga, dojinshi, culture, and language, however this is by no means the only topic under discussion at any given time.

The crowd roars as Shut deliberately mispronounces 2ch as "tootch," like a clueless grown-up might. This crowd knows the Japanese pronounce it "ni-channeru." Nobody asks what a *dojinshi* is. Nobody needs to. (It's Japanese for self-published illustrated fan fiction, much of it pornographic, the bread and butter of Japan's otaku community.)

Finally moot pipes up. He's small and thin, sitting behind a laptop screen and wearing a baseball cap pulled down over his eyes, as though he's trying to disappear onstage. "The one thing I really liked about 2chan was that you could refresh a page every few minutes and you'll get like twenty new images. I think that's really cool, the lack of retention. You always find something new, and hopefully interesting and fun."

"That's why we copied it," another moderator chimes in. "Japan can't do anything wrong, right?"

He's being ironic, but these kids are seriously obsessed. They've played video games virtually since birth, spent their formative years reading imported manga and watching anime on cable TV, and their teens cruising for cartoon porn online. 4chan was *their* Babylon. As the site grew from just a few hundred visitors a day in 2003 to more than fifty thousand daily in 2005, its user base emerged as the vector for a totally unexpected new wave of Japanese pop-cultural influence.

Until this point, Japanese fantasy-devices entered the Western world in the form of products whose appearance on the scene was mediated entirely by corporations. That was how it had gone for the Walkman boom, the karaoke fad, the console wars of the nineties, Sanrio's Gift Gates, the Toonami anime-block on the Cartoon Network, the "100 percent authentic" manga aisle at Borders bookstore, and Nintendo-sponsored Pokémon competitions in the mall. 4chan was something different: grassroots and chaotic, channeling the edgiest otaku content directly into Western subculture, in real time. It was only because so much groundwork had been laid in the eighties and nineties that turn-of-the-millennium Internet users in America and Europe were so uniquely primed to accept content from Japan, whether at face value or reinterpreted in unexpected ways.

Take, for example, "All your base are belong to us." The screenshot of a garbled mistranslation from a forgotten Sega game called *Zero Wing* emerged on the Something Awful forums circa 2000. Within a year it had become one of the Internet's first truly popular memes. That combinations of anime art and wacky catchphrases remain a staple of modern Internet culture exemplifies the power that this crossing of the pop-cultural streams had over the global zeitgeist.

And then there was the dark side.

As Japanese and American sensibilities mingled on 4chan, the site's users would unwittingly retrace the footsteps of the pioneers at 2channel. Just like its predecessor, after 4chan launched as a haven for otaku, it grew through headline-grabbing protests and pranks, and then slid into a morass of race baiting, conspiracy theories, and extremist identity politics. Like a mighty river inexorably winding its way to the ocean, both 2channel and 4chan's drive for constant stimulation led their users to an equally vast natural resource: humans' seemingly infinite capacity for outrage.

In an echo of 2channel's Masashi Tashiro incident, a star triggered 4chan's first real-world action. It involved a recruitment video featuring a gloriously unhinged Tom Cruise singing the praises of Scientology. Intended for internal consumption only, it was leaked to the Internet by parties unknown and went viral. When the Church of Scientology subsequently launched a legal campaign against websites hosting the video, 4chan snapped into action. Who was Scientology, or anybody, to tell them who they couldn't make fun of on the Internet?

Organizing under the cheeky nickname of Anonymous, 4chan users organized their efforts in chat rooms to deluge Scientology centers with prank calls, faxes, and pizza orders, while hackers launched denial-of-service attacks on their websites. The climax arrived on the morning of February 10, 2008, when seven thousand 4chan users descended upon Scientology facilities in cities around the world wearing Guy Fawkes masks (inspired by the Wachowski siblings' film *V for Vendetta*), carrying signs and chanting anti-Scientology slogans. That this was more of an elaborate prank than a righteous demonstration was made clear by the fact that they also blasted Rick Astley's "Never Gonna Give You Up" through boom boxes, in a real-life Rickroll, before quietly dispersing an hour later. Who was behind it all? Was *anyone* behind it all? There wasn't any easy way to tell whether any given user was a follower, a leader, or a rubbernecker.

2channel history repeated the following year, when 4chan users launched a carefully orchestrated campaign to rig a poll on *Time* magazine's website. "In a stunning result," announced the magazine in 2009, "the winner of the third annual *TIME* 100 poll and new owner of the title World's Most Influential Person is moot." A variety of technical tricks—to call them hacks would stretch the definition of the word, given the near-total lack of security on *Time*'s website at the time—allowed 4chan's anonymous hordes to cast 16,794,368 votes for moot. As a result he handily beat out the likes of Barack Obama, Vladimir Putin, and Oprah Winfrey. And 4channers hadn't simply gamed the system to place moot at the top. They gamed all the top twenty-one spots so that the first letters of the winners' names spelled out two in-jokes from the site: mARBLE-CAKE. ALSO, THE GAME. In perfect 4chan form, moot attended the award ceremony accompanied by his mother. The twenty-one-year-old didn't have a significant other to invite.

Online stunts spilling over into the real world really was something "new, interesting, and fun," to paraphrase moot's hopes for his fledgling website. Driven in turns by organic growth and press from the site's stunts, online and off, 4chan's traffic ballooned to seven million visitors a day by early 2010. Now an Internet celebrity thanks to the *Time* poll, moot transformed from a teenage purveyor of Japanese cartoons into an impassioned advocate for 4chan's "radical anonymity." In a conversation with *MIT Technology Review,* he positioned himself as the antithesis to Facebook's Mark Zuckerberg, who had famously declared that "having two identities for yourself is an example of a lack of integrity." (Hoo boy.) The way moot saw it, 4chan had become something more than an online cantina for people obsessed with anime, porn, video games, and anime-porn video games, of which there were many. It was a bastion of free speech in the face of rapidly eroding online privacy. Without anonymity, how would netizens speak truth to power or express unpopular opinions free from ostracism? Even if they said and did some pretty stupid things, moot felt, "People deserve a place to be wrong."

It wouldn't take long for his convictions to be put to the test. One trial came in the form of the online harassment campaign that came to be called Gamergate. The other, in a loosely affiliated collective of white-nationalist trolls calling themselves the alt-right. Both rose to prominence in the lead-up to the 2016 presidential campaign, and both shared a love for things Japanese: Gamergate in its embrace of video games, and the alt-right in a deluded misconception of Japan as an ethnostate. 4chan gave these extremist groups their place to be wrong.

GAMERGATE'S ROOTS TRACE back to the summer of 2014, when a twenty-four-year-old computer programmer broke up with his girlfriend and proceeded to take it very, very badly. His name was Eron Gjoni, and he worked in the robotics lab of a Boston hospital. Her name was Zoë Quinn, and she made video games for a living. They'd drifted apart, busy with their respective careers, less a burnout than a fadeaway. Their final night together was filled with arguments, accusations, and—Quinn claimed—physical abuse. Afterward, she ghosted him. Furious and humiliated, Gjoni took to his keyboard. But he was no Train Man. He wasn't looking for a shoulder to cry on. He wanted revenge.

On August 15, Gjoni posted a nine-thousand-word screed on Something Awful. One of its first readers there declared it a "psychopathic helldump"; a journalist would later call it a "semantic pipe bomb." Rambling, mopey, and packed with an excruciating degree of personal information, it was designed for the sole purpose of destroying Quinn's personal and professional reputation. Moderators at Something Awful deleted the post almost immediately. (You know you're in trouble when a place called Something Awful thinks you've gone too far.) But Gjoni had prepared for this possibility. He quickly reposted the material on a personally hosted website, where it couldn't be taken down. Then a link mysteriously appeared on several 4chan boards. It proved particularly popular on one called

/r9k/. Originally developed to test a piece of moderation software called Robot9000, it had evolved into a home for sharing painful anecdotes from socially awkward users who self-deprecatingly called themselves "robots"—an American rendition of 2channel's Poison Men forum.

Here the story took another swerve from Train Man's rosy narrative. The participants didn't rally behind Gjoni. Deriding him as a "beta," board slang for a submissive "beta male," they instead latched on to a dark insinuation that Quinn had slept with a video game journalist to land a positive review of her 2012 role-playing game *Depression Quest*. This wasn't true. Gjoni even amended his missive to clarify as such. By that point it didn't matter: The anonymous hordes were readying their digital torches and pitchforks.

Publicly, the lonely robots of /r9k/ rallied around the supposed cause of ethics in video game journalism, whatever that meant. In private chat rooms they made their true intentions clear, declaring, "WE'RE CRASHING HER CAREER WITH NO SURVIVORS." Over the days and weeks to come, anonymous trolls doxxed Quinn's contact information in an invitation to flood her with abuse, then repeated the act for any who dared stand up in her defense. As the vitriol went viral under the hashtag #Gamergate, death threats forced her and numerous other female voices in the game industry into hiding, some for months on end. The harassment campaign would roil the Internet for close to two years.

Gamergate was as decentralized as the original Anonymous escapades had been, making it maddeningly difficult to pin down exactly what it stood for or hoped to gain. Supporters quickly labeled any who attempted to push back against them online as "betas," "cucks" (cuckolds), or "social justice warriors," which in Gamergate's twisted vernacular meant a man who espoused progressive stances for the sole purpose of tricking women into sleeping with him. Fueling it all was the deep-seated belief that feminism was a zero-sum game. It was bad enough that women were hell-bent on stripping all the fun out of life for boys in the real world, with all the political correctness and sensitivity training and forced inclusiveness. Now they were coming for the video games!

The irony, of course, was that women had always been there. Close to 50 percent of gamers are female, as has been the case since the Game Boy era. Though American developers were only starting to consider this underrepresented demographic, Japanese producers had understood, virtually from the beginning, that diversity is good business. Way back in the Famicom era, Nintendo's 1986 hit *Metroid* shocked fans by revealing its armored hero to be a woman, and mainstream hit series such as *Dragon Quest, Final Fantasy,* and *Kingdom Hearts* had long attracted large shares of female gamers.

But none of that mattered, because the hysteria of Gamergate wasn't really about games at all. It was about the increasingly vocal presence of women in the formerly male-dominated sphere of nerddom. Take, for example, the 2014 San Diego Comic-Con, held just months before Gamergate broke out, which played host to a nearly equal number of male and female attendees. You'd think a bunch of nerdy guys would welcome an influx of nerdy girls. If you were the sort who framed your solitude as a rebuke from society, however, you might see women as competition. Or, worse, you might see women as usurpers of the last role in which a fragile male could truly feel dominant: as a superconsumer of pop culture, whether it be games or movies or cartoons or comics. Such was the role that fandom had come to play in the personal identities of so many self-described disenfranchised young Americans.

This time, moot put his foot down. He still retained total control over the site. Or, rather, he was the only one to whom the anonymous hordes might actually listen. Citing long-standing rules against harassment and the posting of personal information, he ordered Gamergate-related threads scrubbed from 4chan. The response was predictable. "moot sides with anti-Gamergate! 4chan is dead," wrote one anguished poster. So began a mass exodus to an even more lawless spin-off, with the predictable name 8chan. Tired of the constant controversies, and the site's most vocal users politicizing the site itself, in early 2015 moot announced that he would step down as 4chan's administrator. In September he sold it outright. But who on earth would pay money to associate themselves with the site? From virtually its very inception, the scandalous behavior unfolding on 4chan made the site radioactive to advertisers or investors.

The answer was none other than Hiroyuki. In a strange twist of events, Hiroyuki had been forced out of 2channel in 2014 in a coup d'état by the owner of 8chan, who hosted both sites on servers in the Philippines to keep them out of the hands of Japanese and American authorities. Now Hiroyuki jumped back into the game by taking over the website his own had indirectly inspired so many years before. "moot came to Tokyo and we [got] drunk," he told *Forbes*. "He said he wanted to quit. But he and I want 4chan [to] survive." Poole was more specific about his own thinking. "He is one of few individuals with a deep understanding of what it means to provide a digital home for tens of millions of people for more than a decade." Hiroyuki continues to administer 4chan as of this writing.

"THE LOST FRANCHISE: Why Digimon Deserves a Glorious Renaissance." When the headline appeared on Breitbart in 2014, the site was already known for its militant op-eds—but this one was, on its face, unusual. "Japanese culture enjoyed unique purchase on the imaginations of children and teens in the 1990s, creating beloved franchises such as *Dragon Ball* and *Yu-Gi-Oh!*" the author declared. "In addition to significant financial success, these brands left oversized cultural footprints, thanks to the spread of obsessive fandom behaviors sometimes collectively called otaku."

Digimon, short for Digital Monsters, was the 1999 follow-up to Tamagotchi. Created by the same team, it was a palm-sized digital toy containing a virtual pet that players could not only raise but battle with, by connecting to a friend's toy. By the turn of the millennium, when it was released in America, the toy, game, and anime series emerged as an underdog rival to the ongoing success of the

Pokémon franchise. Even many fans mistakenly assumed it was a simple copy of the Pokémon concept. But not this particular writer. Decrying Pokémon the game as "soulless," he aligned himself with "ideological purists in the video games community" who believed "Digimon fans are the Wagnerians of video game and anime culture . . . ravenous, determined and intellectually curious."

This was one serious Digimon fan. Posted in the midst of Gamergate, this ornate otaku screed would likely have faded into oblivion were it not for a singular fact. It was one of the first articles published by an up-and-coming writer named Milo Yiannopoulos. Nobody knew who the thirty-year-old with the shocking bleach-blond coif was yet, but that was about to change, and fast.

Yiannopoulos's boss was a man named Steve Bannon, who believed that Breitbart could be more than just another news site. He wasn't satisfied with being a website editor; he hungered to wield real political clout, to really change the dialogue—if only he could tap into the right network of people. "Rootless white males," he called them.

By rootless he basically meant otaku. Not precisely, of course. But close enough. A Pew study of data collected from 2014 demonstrated that, for the first time since 1940, more American men between the ages of eighteen and thirty-four were living at home with a parent than with a partner or spouse. The lower the educational level, the higher the chances an individual would be still living at home; no real wonder, given the bleak financial prospects for non-college-grads in the midst of the Great Recession. Blessed (or cursed) with large amounts of leisure time, these men spent the majority of their days immersed in the computer worlds of video games and online forums, far more so than socializing with friends "in real life." For them, real and virtual blended—in ways both stimulating and emasculating, both invigorating and isolating.

They were ripe for the picking. Bannon knew right where to find them: on 4chan. Even disguised by anonymity, 4chan's vernacular—wrought from the language of fragile adolescent masculinity—laid the site's homogeneity bare. "Fag" was an endlessly productive morpheme in 4chan's grammar: Beginners were "newfags," veteran users "oldfags," those who insisted on taking personal credit for posts "namefags," and the average users "faggots." (Actual gays were, predictably, "fagfags.") Add to this a fixation with using the most provocatively offensive forms of expression they could imagine. Constant references to supposed Jewish conspiracies, feminist cabals, and endless slurs referring to virtually any group *other* than white men: The general makeup of 4chan's demographic was perfectly clear by omission. Underlying it all was a Stockholm syndrome-esque belief system that anyone who didn't get it was the enemy. "Why u mad, bro? It's all about the lulz."

Bannon could use these people.

What he lacked, as a pudgy, gray-haired sixtysomething dude, was the cool factor to really break through. That's where Milo came in. Bannon knew he would connect right away. "You can activate that army," said Bannon. Yiannopoulos was young. He was opinionated, articulate, provocative, and an ideological purist . . . when it came to spouting off about Digimon, anyway. About anything else Bannon wasn't really sure; but then again, he didn't care. He needed a shit-stirrer. He just wanted results. He dreamed of turning Breitbart into what he called "a killing machine."

Under Bannon's tutelage, Yiannopoulos pivoted the focus of his venom from nerdventing about Pokémon to heaping scorn on progressive causes. Both Bannon and Yiannopoulos instantly grasped the potential of the Gamergate campaign; Yiannopoulos penned a spirited defense of Gamergaters "striking fear into the previously unchallenged bullies of the authoritarian Left." This proclamation that trolls weren't harassers but mighty crusaders for justice was music to the ears of lonely men who felt marginalized by mainstream society. Yiannopoulos became the effective spokesperson of the Gamergate crusade, drawing huge numbers of new readers to Breitbart. Then he co-authored a manifesto entitled "An Establishment Conservative's Guide to the Alt-Right." This hagiographic portrayal of a group that included outspoken Nazis earned a public rebuke from Hillary Clinton, singling out the movement as "emerging racist ideology." To her it was excoriation. To alt-rightists, it was nothing less than a coronation—and it instantly bought Milo, and Breitbart, a great deal of credibility among the far-right political fringe.

Nervous though the increasingly polarized rhetoric made them, Republican leaders knew a good thing when they saw it. Yiannopoulos and Bannon's troll tactics were channeling young people into the Republican Party like never before. "They come in through Gamergate or whatever and then get turned on to politics and Trump," explained Bannon. As his army of Gamergaters and alt-rightists flooded other websites with memes featuring kawaii anime girls in "Make America Great Again" hats, major news outlets were forced to rush out explainers with titles like "How Anime Avatars on Twitter Help Explain Politics Online in 2015." Not every conservative was on board: "The screamers and the crazy people on the alt-right, as they call it, who love Donald Trump, who have plenty of Hitler iconography in their Twitter icons . . . are childless single men who masturbate to anime," declared GOP strategist Rick Wilson on MSNBC in 2016. Richard Spencer, founder of the alt-right, riposted on Twitter that "Anime—indeed, even anime porn—has done more to advance European civilization than the Republican Party." The irony that this same style of illustrated entertainment had once nourished Japan's far left sailed right over the heads of proponents and critics both.

Things didn't play out so well for Yiannopoulos. Twitter, his favorite platform, suspended him and then banned him for life after he stirred up a hate mob to attack Leslie Jones, the African American co-star of the 2016 *Ghostbusters* remake. Then a series of compromising videos surfaced. One captured him belting out "America the Beautiful" in a Dallas karaoke bar while an audience that included Spencer hailed him with Nazi salutes. Another featured him declaring that pedophilia could be "perfectly consensual," a stance he doubled and then tripled down on when challenged by the mass media.

The Conservative Political Action Conference disinvited him from addressing the crowd; Simon & Schuster killed a quarter-million-dollar deal it had signed for his autobiography; and perhaps most distressingly for him, Breitbart let him go. He was finished as a commentator. Deeply in debt, he turned to the crowdfunding site Patreon for assistance. He was promptly banned from there, too. But Bannon's gambit actually worked. He was tapped to run Trump's election campaign in August of 2016, then rewarded with the title of chief strategist and senior counselor to the president. He'd been carried right into the White House by his legion of rootless anime fans.

Bannon's tenure ended shortly after it began, but the administration's connection to anime remained. There is even, somewhat improbably, a U.S. Department of State website celebrating "Anime's supersized U.S. audience." With pretzel logic, it paints *Astro Boy*'s creator, Osamu Tezuka, as a crypto-patriot, claiming "his father believed strongly that Japan's future prosperity lay in partnership with the United States and raised his son on American imagery"—as though Japan's God of Comics worked with a bald eagle sitting on his shoulder.

In October 2018, a man named Gavin McInnes addressed a crowd at the New York Metropolitan Republican Club on the Upper East Side. Cherubic, bearded, and bespectacled in thick horn-rim glasses, McInnes looked every part the hipster, which was fitting. He had cofounded the Vice media empire, then left in 2008 to re-envision himself as a conservative provocateur. It seemed to be working: That night he was addressing roughly a hundred members of the organization he had launched two years earlier. The Proud Boys, as he called them, were a surprisingly diverse crowd; only the plethora of MAKE AMERICA GREAT AGAIN hats really gave the vibe away. McInnes uses the term "Western chauvinism" to differentiate himself from white-power types, though in practice the differences are vanishingly slim. A Proud Boy gathering was like a 4chan political forum in the flesh, a celebration of racial slurs, anti-Semitism, misogyny, nationalism, and ultraconservative political views. (McInnes believes feminism to be a "myth" and once penned an essay titled "Transphobia Is Perfectly Natural.") Before taking the stage, McInnes donned glasses with slanted eyes drawn on the lenses and brandished a prop katana. Then he proceeded to reenact the murder of Inejiro Asanuma—the same televised assassination (described in chapter 1) that shocked the world in 1960. In front of the crowd, McInnes cast himself in the role of murderer Otoya Yamaguchi, pantomimed slashing an Asian Proud Boy masquerading as Asanuma, then cracked open a beer and declared, "Never let evil take root." Somehow, improbably, Yamaguchi had emerged as a darling of the online alt-right—reframed from an unstable young man into a defender of traditional conservative morals from the purported evils of socialism. (A widely shared meme circulating around this time captioned the famed moment of Asanuma's murder with "This is the reason you can masturbate to anime girls today.") Never mind that Japan has one of the world's most robust socialized medicine systems. Online and onstage, Japanese history and fantasy mingled in the minds of young Americans who saw themselves as victims of progress.

A similar form of magical thinking leads many modern white supremacists to embrace an adjacent fantasy about Japan: that it represents a role model for creating "a self-consciously European, majority white nation," in the words of Jared Taylor, editor of the white supremacist magazine *American Renaissance*. "It's an ethnostate and it's deeply nationalist," Taylor told the *Guardian*. "And they have resisted the pressure to admit refugees. I say: 'God bless them!'" While it is true Japan has a checkered history with refugees, political leaders are belatedly recognizing the need to admit migrant workers to pick up the slack from its super-aging population. In 2017 and 2018, the politically conservative Abe administration passed laws fast-tracking permanent residency for skilled immigrants and greatly expanding the number of blue-collar work visas that would be granted. In Tokyo alone, more than one in eight young people coming of age as adults in 2018 were not of Japanese descent.

The double irony of it all was that Caucasian men of the sort who inevitably espoused these beliefs were by no means the only fans of manga and anime in the United States. In fact some of the most devoted fans of imported Japanese fantasies were minorities who thrilled to the same underdog characters that had appealed to downtrodden Japanese otaku. The show *Dragon Ball Z*, broadcast in America on the Cartoon Network, is a perfect case in point. It's an absurd, over-the-top martial arts fantasy in which a young boy grows into the universe's strongest fighter through life-and-death battles against rivals, robots, aliens, and even a certain Mr. Satan. The show's "extra lives" (in the form of repeated resurrections of killed-off characters), gravity-defying action moves, and extended scenes of characters "powering up" were instantly recognizable to anyone who'd played a video game. The protagonist Son Goku's brute-forcing his way through every obstacle, even death, resonated deeply with young African Americans who felt they "needed to work twice as hard to get half as much," as one fan put it. *Dragon Ball Z* represented nothing less than "the journey of the black man in America," in the words of the rapper RZA.

So it was that, in the run-up to the 2016 presidential election, Americans found themselves in a socioeconomic landscape eerily reminiscent of post-bubble Japan. With the nation's youth adrift in much the same way their Japanese counterparts were during their Lost Decades, it seemed to some that America, too, was becoming "a nation composed wholly of otaku"—or people who thought like them: self-described outcasts and underdogs hyperfocused on their own personal spheres of interest, their favorite websites and You-Tube channels, heads down in their personal niches and plugged in to networks of like-minded folks who reinforced their beliefs, whatever they might be.

Japan's otaku were more than superfans; they were canaries in the coal mine for late-stage capitalism. The bursting of the bubble prophesized similar downturns in economies around the globe. That gave its citizens a nearly two-decade head start in developing cultural tools for living in an era of less, with fantasies playing an even more key role when hope was in increasingly short supply. Put another way, Japan represented something of a neatly packaged fantasy in and of itself: an easy-to-understand, miniaturized version of the world at large, a nation-sized virtual reality, which made the fantasy-delivery devices its citizens clung to as survival tools all the more relevant abroad. Which is why, if one were to draw a Venn diagram of shared interests—with circles for Japan's otaku and *netto uyoku* net-rightists, for the far-left Antifa and the alt-right, for Gamergaters and YouTubers and edgelords who define themselves by outraging others, for Black Lives Matter supporters and for LGBT activists—the overlap would center, improbably, on things Japanese: manga, anime, and the idea of Japan as a fantasyland in and of itself.

LOOKING BACK, IT'S easy to scoff at the utopian ethos that colored 4chan's earliest years, as seen in the Otakon presentation promising that total anonymity would discourage cliques and promote truly open discussion. It's true that things didn't quite work out that way. As might be expected from a website whose raison d'être was the celebration of anime porn, 4chan's population consisted almost entirely of adolescent men; it was a clique from the get-go. But so too was it a mark of the power that communities founded on Japanese fantasies had come to have in the English-speaking Western world.

A deep-rooted culture of gleeful disdain for the establishment in any form made 4chan a haven for all sorts of creative rebels, oddballs, and outcasts; total anonymity made it a sandbox for extreme forms of expression. The combination was rocket fuel for fandom and subculture. Yet so too did it nourish trolling, fanaticism, and hate. On one hand, 4chan was a forge of fun, the birthplace of LOL-cats and Rickrolling and doges, and countless other memes that have spread from its boards into mainstream Internet culture. Neither, though, can one discount its proven ability to radicalize marginal groups, ranging from the left-leaning social-justice activist collective Anonymous to the nihilist hacker group LulzSec to the alt-right white supremacy movement and all those "rootless white males" Bannon activated.

This is scary stuff, to be sure. But, amid all the wrong on 4chan, there was also much right. 4chan's anonymous lulz really did provide crucial tools for letting new generations of activists speak truth to power. Its decentralized online organization, behind-the-scenes hacking exploits, and Guy Fawkes masks went on to play key roles in both Occupy Wall Street and the Arab Spring uprisings of 2011. Anonymous Internet organization and the lack of any discernible leadership are also core features of the 2019 Hong Kong protest movement, sparked by a controversial law that would have made it easier to extradite Hong Kong citizens to mainland China. The movement's incorporation of cartoon imagery—borrowed from 4chan, and from anime such as *One Piece* and *Neon Genesis Evangelion*—echoes the way *Ashita no Jo* nourished the would-be revolutionaries of 1960s Japan. Meanwhile, over on the mainland, anime such as Makoto Shinkai's film *Your Name* and the long-delayed theatrical releases of classic Miyazaki films such as *My Neighbor Totoro* and *Spirited Away* continue to set box office records.

So it happened that a Japanese imageboard—quietly transplanted to America by fans of manga and anime newly connected by the Internet—concentrated, supercharged, and reinjected Japanese fantasies of all sorts into the global cultural sphere, which has increasingly come to resemble those dark years in so many ways: economically, politically, socially, and even on an individual level. We may lament the unease we feel in a divisive era of constant technological disruption, economic turmoil, political gridlock, and growing concern about our planet's and our own futures, but one thing is for certain: In our taste—our need—for fantasies from Japan, we remain undivided.

EPILOGUE

There's something to be learned from everything. From even the most ordinary, commonplace things, there's always something you can learn.
—HARUKI MURAKAMI, *PINBALL*, 1973

OUR PROTAGONIST IS a divorced thirty-four-year-old former salaryman who lives in downtown Tokyo. He is a writer who makes his living producing ad copy and magazine articles, work at which he excels but which brings him little pleasure. "Somebody's got to write these things," he tells us. "And the same thing can be said for collecting garbage and shoveling snow. It doesn't matter whether you like it or not—a job's a job." That he is never named, not once, at any point over the course of the book only heightens the sense of numbness and dislocation. He's a productive member of an affluent society. He should be thriving, but he's really only surviving.

But this man is no average disenchanted urbanite. He is the protagonist of a Haruki Murakami novel. In this case, *Dance Dance Dance*. Released at the height of the bubble in 1988, it was the sequel to his breakthrough 1982 bestseller, *A Wild Sheep Chase*. Between the two, Murakami somehow managed to capture the existential angst many modern Japanese felt amid what was supposed to be the triumph of their nation's economic miracle.

From the elevator in the hotel where our unnamed hero is staying, he finds a portal into another realm, an ink-black twilight zone right where the sixteenth floor should be. Of course, he steps inside. What does he have to lose? Down a chilly corridor he finds the Sheep Man, the person who helped him out of his predicament in the previous book. Actually, "person" might be stretching it. Clad in a fuzzy, filthy sheep costume and speaking with all his words running together *justlikethis,* the Sheep Man obviously exists on a plane removed from our own reality. He is a benevolent face dwelling behind the scenes of our humdrum existences, offering a helping hand (or is that hoof?) when life gets too complicated for mere humans to figure out on their own.

"I've lost and I'm lost and I'm confused. I'm not anchored to anything," our protagonist confides in the Sheep Man. "So what do I have to do?"

"Dance," says the Sheep Man. "Yougottadance. Aslongasthe musicplays. Yougottadance. Don'teventhinkwhy."

"Wait, one last thing," the protagonist says after a few more lines. "I guess you've been around all this time, except I haven't seen you. Just your shadow everywhere. You're just sort of always *there*."

Murakami goes on: "The Sheep Man traces a vague shape in the air with his finger. 'That'sright. We'rehalfshadow. We'reinbetween.'"

Even through the veil of translation, Murakami has an impeccable ability to make readers around the world feel as though he's addressing them personally. "He's an American writer who happens to write in Japanese," English translator Alfred Birnbaum says. Yet Polish translator Anna Zielińska-Elliott celebrates the "universal" nature of his writing, while Russian translator Ivan Sergeevich Logatchov says that local readers "discover their own identity" in Murakami. Even South Korea and the People's Republic of China, nations that historically regard things Japanese with a great deal of ambivalence, are consumed by Murakami fever. "People in South Korea feel an affinity for his works," reports translator Yang Eok-Kwan, because "there is a cultural basis for appreciating him."

We love Murakami not only because of the deftness with which he tells profoundly weird stories, but also because his stories make us feel better. They're custom-made for our times, hyperconnected but lonely, looped in to the news 24/7 but still clueless, fed up with all our junk but still shopping—what Philip Roth calls "Murakami's vision of our materialist, garishly illuminated age." By sharing his own encyclopedic and exquisitely idiosyncratic pop-cultural tastes on the page, he makes us feel witty and sophisticated. By throwing his unflappable everymen into touchingly weird love affairs and supernatural setups, he makes us believe in our potential for making it through any situation, no matter how bizarre. Existential angst suffuses his books, but never quite devolves into hopelessness. Often, he manages to creep out and comfort at the same time, as though we were bumping into David Lynch in a Sanrio Gift Gate.

We love him because, in our own ways, all of us are looking for Sheep Man, grasping for answers in the shadows of what we've built.

IN 1999, THE journalist Mary Roach journeyed to Tokyo to cover the exotic culture of kawaii that was suffusing Japanese life. After interviewing Sanrio's Shintaro Tsuji and Yuko Yamaguchi, she concluded: "The further you get from elementary school, the heavier the American resistance will be to cute in its purest incarnation. For that you must go to Japan." It took just six years for this idea of kawaii as some bizarre Japan-only trend to be proven wrong. In 2005, *Fortune* reported on a startling new phenomenon: female executives ostentatiously bringing Hello Kitty notepads into the boardroom. And in 2017, when close to a million protesters descended upon Washington, D.C., for a protest called the Women's March, they wore "pussyhats" knit from soft yarn, sending a sea of tiny pink ears bobbing across the National Mall in solidarity. "I was practically raised in Sanrio shops," the hat's co-creator Krista Suh later told me.

In 1972, the Hollywood trade magazine *Variety* dismissed animator Osamu Tezuka's pioneering X-rated anime *Cleopatra: Queen of Sex* by declaring that it was "difficult to imagine anyone being aroused by the naked breasts of a cartoon character." In 2019, the website Pornhub announced that "hentai" had been the second-most-used search term for three years running.

In 2001—the year, not the space odyssey—science-fiction writer William Gibson noticed something strange on a trip to Tokyo: "a schoolgirl busily, constantly messaging on her mobile phone (which she never uses for voice communication if she can avoid it). What is it that the Mobile Girls are so busily conveying to one another?" Six years later came the iPhone, and now we no longer need to ask. Good luck finding a smartphone-equipped teen anywhere on the planet who isn't busily, constantly messaging (and never using voice communication).

The story of Japan being a little ahead of the curve isn't really new. It is a story as old as the opening of Japanese ports to the West in the nineteenth century, when a flood of art from the likes of Hokusai and Utamaro upended generations of conventional artistic wisdom and inspired the Impressionist movement. Van Gogh was so taken by what he saw in their prints and scroll paintings that he abandoned his studio altogether, heading into the French country-side in search of what he called "Japanese light."

History repeated—as it always does—in 1950s America with the arrival of one D. T. Suzuki. Elderly, balding, and possessed of an impressive pair of eyebrows, the tiny-statured Buddhist scholar served as a real-life Yoda to a generation of postwar counterculture icons. Comfortable on camera and capable of writing in plain English, he "localized" the rigid doctrine of Zen Buddhism as practiced by Japanese elites into a nonsectarian, metaphysical tool for personal growth for everyone. It was under his tutelage—delivered in lectures and more than a hundred books—that Americans first grappled with the ideas that less might be more, that reality is transient and illusory, that journeying inward might result in spiritual transcendence. In the Zen quest for enlightenment, adherents saw an escape from the hamster wheel of modern consumer society.

Enthusiastically adopted by writers, poets, and musicians, Japanese Zen spread from the Beats into subsequent waves of American pop culture. Without Suzuki's exhortations to let go of our worldly attachments, how much longer would it have taken us to tune in, turn on, and drop out? Over the decades, the concept has been further polished into a shorthand for cool detachment, for mindfulness, for getting "in the zone" professionally—and perhaps most of all, in idiomatic usage, for minimalism of any stripe. Zen, in this colloquial form, is no less a fantasy than Oscar Wilde's "pure invention" of the Victorian age. To Americans today, Zen is the featureless black rectangle of the iPhone. Zen is found in Murakami's prose. Zen is the state to which Marie Kondo's magical art of tidying up transports us.

It may seem jarring to speak of Murakami, literary titan, in the same breath as Marie Kondo, tidying-up guru. Surely nobody reads Kondo for her prose; they turn to her for advice to escape the tsunami of material goods inundating their lives. Yet the way we refer to Murakami's and Kondo's outputs is telling: One writes in a style often described as "magical realism"; the other dispenses texts brimming with "life-changing magic."

And why shouldn't Japanese be the wizards of this strange new era? We live in an attention economy, its currency our eyeballs and thumb-clicks—drawn to content provided around the clock on that descendant of the Walkman and Game Boy: the smartphone. Many of the tools and techniques that the architects of the online world use to keep us coming back for more are based on technocultures' pioneered on the streets of Japan: emoji; swapping selfies; the video-gamification of daily activities, like exercise or even simple conversation. When we yearn for escape, we follow in the footsteps of the early otaku and embrace the pleasures that sustained us as children: comic-book heroes, video game sessions, even cosplaying as our fictional idols—or physically visiting them, as four million did when the producers of *Gundam* unveiled a life-sized statue of the titanic robot on the shores of Tokyo Bay in 2009. In the years since, cities across Japan have erected their own giant-robot memorials: a Gigantor in Kobe, a Scopedog in Tama, an Evangelion in Kyoto. They were joined by the appearance of a life-sized Godzilla head that appeared atop a hotel in Shinjuku, a stone's throw from where the New Anime Century was declared in 1981. And then came the inevitable evolution. As the world battled the COVID-19 pandemic in 2020, an updated full-scale Gundam roared to life and stepped out of a specially constructed gantry on the Yokohama waterfront, blurring the line between fantasy and reality all the more. Few if any of the media outlets that covered the event questioned the necessity for creating such a thing. These are trying times; everyone needs a hero.

IN 1942, *LIFE* magazine estimated fewer than a hundred Americans not of Japanese descent had any proficiency in the language. The U.S. military launched a series of crash language programs for servicemen and -women. The woman who would five decades later become my own teacher, Jean Morden, was one of them. When I enrolled in her Japanese language class in the fall of 1987 at my suburban Maryland high school, it seemed a very strange subject for an American kid to want to study. A *Washington Post* profile from a few years earlier marveled at students interested in learning "one of the world's more difficult and less useful languages."

Others supported what we were doing. One day, a series of large cardboard boxes arrived in our classroom. A man named Osamu Tezuka had sent them, and they were brimming with his entire oeuvre of manga. All his classics were inside: *Mighty Atom, Black Jack, Buddha, Phoenix*. He included a personally signed illustration and a letter promising to come visit us on his next trip to America.

The year before, Crown Prince Akihito and Princess Michiko had made a surprise visit—surprise to us; Morden-sensei had coordinated with the government of Japan for weeks, keeping it secret until the day of, for security reasons. But to me, the promise of meeting Tezuka outshone an encounter with actual royalty. I pored through his comics with the help of a pocket dictionary, putting more effort into deciphering those panels than into the tests for which I should have been studying. But our meeting was not to be. Tezuka had a secret of his own: He was battling stomach cancer. His death in February of 1989 came just weeks after that of Emperor Hirohito: a startling coda to the postwar era. The crown prince and princess were now emperor and empress. And I would never get a chance to meet my hero.

SO MANY THINGS have changed since Kosuge's first jeep rolled off a makeshift assembly line in a freezing cattle shed.

Japan is no longer the world's manufacturer of toys; that title belongs to the manufacturer of almost everything now: China.

Karaoke, still a household word around the world, is in steady decline in its home country. A 2018 survey revealed that it has shed more than ten million regular participants, from a peak of fifty million singers in 1995. "We see karaoke-going as more of a kitsch, even loser, activity," a thirtysomething female office worker told *Japan Today*. Of those who do sing on, 20 to 30 percent prefer to do so by themselves—less surprising when you realize that more than a third of all Japanese households now consist of just a single person.

Sony struggled mightily to remain relevant following the surprise retirement of Akio Morita in 1993, after he suffered a stroke during a game of tennis. Morita passed away in 1999 at the age of seventy-eight. In spite of having literally every piece of the puzzle it needed, from portable electronic expertise to owning its own record label, Sony missed out on the digital-audio and smartphone revolutions. In 2013, it emerged that the company made more money selling life insurance in Japan than it did electronics to the world. The one bright spot on its electronics balance sheet continues to be its gaming division, home of the PlayStation.

Shintaro Tsuji is still going strong; he finally stepped down as CEO of Sanrio in summer of 2020, at the age of ninety-two. Hello Kitty remains the foundation of his firm's fortunes, but the company has enjoyed a string of hits in recent years with new characters such as Gudetama, the depressive egg yolk, and Agretsuko, a red panda office-lady by day who vents her frustration by rage-singing death metal karaoke at night—often by herself, of course.

Japanese makers no longer dominate the global video game industry. Only three Japanese titles cracked the top ten of 2019; the world's most popular gaming platform is no longer the home console but the smartphone. The debut of Microsoft's Xbox in 2001 cracked the code for Western developers, whose military and crime simulations quickly overwhelmed Japan's gentler fantasy fare. On the other hand, the game industry is bigger than ever. The American marketplace alone hit $43.4 billion in 2018, four times Hollywood's take—larger, in fact, than the entire global film industry.

Anime studios in Japan are enjoying boom times thanks to more and better ways of delivering their content to consumers around the world, such as streaming services like Netflix. The industry's worth broke two trillion yen (around $19 billion) in 2017, a new record. But little of these fortunes trickles down to those actually making the art. The average monthly income for animators aged twenty to twenty-four is just 128,800 yen—around $1,100, well below the poverty line for a major city like Tokyo. Predictably, those who might once have found themselves working in anime studios have turned their talents toward better-compensated work in other fields, such as video games. "Perhaps the biggest problem in the Japanese animation industry," gravely reported the animator Keiichi Hara, "is that there are no more young animators." This status quo, often bemoaned but little addressed, casts a dark shadow on the medium's future.

Gekiga is no more. After the bubble collapsed, otaku turned increasingly from aspirational macho power fantasies to something closer to home: schoolgirls. Local fans call the style *moé*—a pun based on the homonym for "burning" and "bursting into bud," as in coming of age. In the seventies and eighties, boys generally consumed cartoons about boys and girls consumed cartoons about girls. In the late aughts, it emerged in surveys of self-identifying otaku that the favorite show of young men was *K-On!*, a series about high school girls forming a rock band. Numbers two and three were about high school girls, too. In fact, 80 percent of the list was. As for the female otaku of Japan? Number one went to *Gundam*, because some things never change.

4chan no longer holds the sway over the Internet that it once did, but trends launched there continue to resonate online and in real life. "QAnon" appeared on a 4chan forum in 2017. What began as a conspiracy theory evolved over the course of the Trump administration into a social movement bound by paranoia and imagined victimhood. Supercharged by the stresses of the COVID-19 pandemic, these dark fantasies became reality for many desperate citizens, culminating in the fatal siege of the U.S. Capitol in January 2020. Many of its perpetrators were in cosplay of one sort or another. And more than a few, it later turned out, were accompanied by their mothers or fathers—an eerie manifestation of another demographic trend inherited from Japan, where a majority of young American adults continued living with parents, unable to strike out on their own.

JAPAN HAS PROBLEMS. The ongoing cleanup from the Fukushima meltdowns of 2011. A suicide rate that, while on the decline as of 2019, still ranks as one of the highest among industrialized nations. A work culture that, despite much government lip-service to the contrary, remains infuriatingly hostile to career women and young mothers. Never-ending regional tensions with China and the Koreas. And the problems of a super-aged society manifest in ways both heartbreaking and bizarre. There are increasing numbers of citizens who die alone and aren't discovered for months or years; as the countryside hollows out from a migration of young people seeking their fortunes in cities, those left behind yearn for companionship. One seventy-year-old woman in Shikoku populated her desolate hometown with handmade, human-sized doll families. "We never see children here anymore," explained Tsukimi Ayano to *The New York Times*. "So I made them."

Yet there are bright spots. Young adults, freed of the shackles of the older generation's lockstep salaryman lifestyle, report surprising levels of contentment. Public facilities and infrastructure remain in tip-top shape, providing a great many venues for connecting with one another in the vibrant urban culture of Japan's major cities. Those cities are networked with trains that run on time, and faster, than nearly anywhere else. The schools and streets are among the cleanest and safest in the world, even in the heart of Tokyo, the largest metropolitan area on the planet. There are no guns on the streets. There is almost universal access to high-quality subsidized health care. And while there are still street protests—sometimes massive (an April 2017 demonstration drew thirty thousand critics of the Abe administration to the national legislature)—there is little in the way of the internecine strife and toxic partisanship that have so polarized America's public discourse.

It is hard to imagine anything like the conspiratorial meme of QAnon sweeping the citizenry of Japan as it has the West, or a major political leader stubbornly refusing to recognize the results of an election. Or is it? Japan has had no shortage of politicians willing to bend or break rules to exercise their agendas: recall from chapter 1 Nobusuke Kishi's forcibly removing opposition party members from parliament in order to get the Anpo treaty passed, a move that sparked nationwide protests and violence. And there is no forgetting the emergence of the Aum Supreme Truth cult, which launched a fatal nerve-gas attack on the Tokyo subway system in 1995. They gathered followers in part through pop media including tabloid magazines, comic books, and dial-up BBS systems. Looking back, the cult's apocalyptic mishmash of beliefs, cherry-picked from Far Eastern philosophy, anime, and video games, seems like an eerie precursor to the QAnon movement—which tellingly launched from the platform of 4chan.

Amid ongoing political, economic, demographic, and coronaviral uncertainty, so similar to the West, what keeps Japan from flying apart? One reason could be that Japan is more secular than America and many other Western nations; its domestic Shinto and imported Buddhist spiritual traditions only rarely enter the sphere of public debate. Another can be found in a broadcast fairness doctrine that precludes the rise of politically polarized talk shows or television channels. A mutual sense of reality, borne from a standardized school curriculum that ensures at least a basic level of shared educational experience also helps. So too a more egalitarian pay ethic, with far less income disparity between managers and workers (on average, a Japanese CEO earns just one-ninth of an American executive's compensation). Or might it be the soothing power of the fantasy-delivery device? It's tempting to think so: even (or perhaps especially) amid the fear and uncertainty of a global pandemic, Japanese citizens packed theaters for the anime movie *Demon Slayer: Infinity Train,* which set a new record for opening weekend box office.

On one hand, Japan doesn't make toys anymore, missed the boat on the smartphone, doesn't even sing. On the other, in a 2015 speech on the lawn of the White House, President Obama thanked Japan for inventing manga, anime, and emoji. Japan isn't ahead of the curve anymore—but neither is it behind. We in the rest of the developed world have finally caught up. Globally, the average age for a video gamer is early thirties; more American adults now live with their parents (rather than alone or with partners) than at any time in recent history; the Western toy industry sells increasing quantities of its products to adults every year; and grown-ups around the planet throng to multibillion-dollar superhero movie franchises based on comic books originally intended for kids. We cocoon ourselves indoors: Netflix-nesting, never bored, often lonely; unnamed protagonists in a magical-realist novel in progress. Yet we know we'd never go back; our futures depend on us mastering the technologies that connect, soothe, and bind us. If there is any one lesson to learn from the heroes of the stories that unfolded in these pages, it is that the way out of the strange post-capitalist techno-political hellscape we find ourselves in is to create.

This isn't some hollow platitude. The shimmering products in this book shine new light on the roadmap of how we got to today, but so too do they represent something more: a constellation for navigating the twenty-first century to come. None of the fantasy-delivery devices chronicled here represented quantum leaps of innovation in and of themselves, nor were their eventual uses clear even to their creators. Recall that the Walkman and first karaoke machines were built from off-the-shelf components, and that the emoji were originally envisioned as simple design flourishes to help websites load faster. It wasn't creators but *consumers* who made the cognitive leaps that unexpectedly transformed simple products into tools for a new era. The tools for the era ahead undoubtedly already exist in some form today. It is up to us to figure out what they are, and how they can help us survive—and thrive—in the unpredictable turbulence of modern life.

The 2020 COVID-19 epidemic offers a case in point. As orders to shelter in place and socially distance turned people around the world into involuntary *hikikomori* shut-ins, legions unwittingly turned to the old tools of the otaku to assuage their loneliness: games, videos, and playthings. A surge in demand at streaming services such as Netflix and PlayStation Network forced the companies to throttle back server speeds as the sheer volume of entertainment data began to overwhelm European telecom networks. And then there is the curious case of the Nintendo Switch title *Animal Crossing: New Horizons*. It was released on March 20, seemingly terrible timing amid a global pandemic. It sold 11.7 million copies in just twelve days, and a total of 31 million copies by the end of the year. In this soothing simulation of outdoor life, populated by bobbleheaded kawaii animal characters, millions escaped the tedium of lockdowns by taking online trips to virtual islands built by their friends.

The new role of gaming as a balm for isolation was so widely recognized that when Pfizer announced a promising COVID-19 vaccine candidate in November 2020, the stocks of Nintendo and other major game companies tumbled. "Once the pandemic is over, more consumers will be willing to engage in physical outdoor activities as leisure," the UBS Securities analyst Kenji Fukuyama told *Nikkei Asia*. "That would be a horror story for Nintendo."

I don't think the future will be made in Japan. It will be made everywhere else, with values borrowed from Japan. I can't take full credit for this insight; it, too, dates back to the nineteenth century, when the term *wakon-yosai*—"Japanese spirit, Western know-how"— guided the long-isolated nation in its relentless drive to catch up with America and Europe. The phrase is antique, but the concept lives on in a new form. This is evident in ways big and small. It is no coincidence that millions of young Americans made their first forays into online political activism on 4chan, an anime imageboard repurposed by U.S. netizens. But perhaps the most obvious examples can be seen in the proliferation of codeveloped products. Sony's PlayStation 5 debuted in November of 2020 to great fanfare. It was designed in Silicon Valley to Japan's specifications for gamers all over the world. And then there is *Pokémon GO*, the first globally popular application of "augmented reality," which involves overlaying computer graphics on views of the world. AR represents a potentially transformative technology that lingered on the fringes of tech subculture until *Pokémon GO*'s creators got the idea of populating their platform with kawaii monsters.

One hundred thirty million fans downloaded the application in just thirty days after its release in 2016, thrilling to the experience of holding up their smartphones to seek out and capture imaginary Pokémon digitally superimposed on the world around them—real life, but even better. Today, the app has been downloaded more than one billion times worldwide.

Instead of mediating our realities with fantasy, we're increasingly eliminating the difference. A thousand otaku waving glow-sticks at an anime-girl hologram singing idol songs onstage sounds like something out of sci-fi, only it's already old hat: The "virtualoid" Hatsune Miku performs regularly in Japan. She went on the American talk show circuit in 2014, and we have our own holographic doppelgängers of departed stars like Tupac, Freddie Mercury, and Roy Orbison. Talk about Japanese light.

In a way, we've never stopped searching for those sparks of joy— but we no longer have to. Japanese light is delivered to us directly now, through the intraocular drips of countless display screens of countless fantasy-delivery devices; little Japans in the palms of our hands, wherever we may be. Oscar Wilde was half right. The Western world's concept of Japan may have been pure invention, but he couldn't possibly have predicted how the nation would reinvent all of us. A planet of dreamers, made in Japan.

ACKNOWLEDGMENTS

A BIG HUG to my wife and partner in so many projects, Hiroko Yoda, for understanding and supporting me throughout this long journey. So too Dado Derviskadic, agent extraordinaire, for taking a chance— then going above and beyond afterward. I could not have done it without you. And a third for my editor Meghan Houser, without whose insight this would have been a much different, and I strongly suspect much lesser, book. Group hug!

I'd also like to recognize some of my earliest readers. Andrew Szymanski suffered through many early drafts, shared his insights about the game industry, and soothed the stress with many an expertly mixed cocktail. David Marx was there for brainstorming early on in the process and advice throughout. Matthew Penney offered keen advice on early chapters.

Thank you to the many organizations that helped me along the way, in particular Emi Hotoda of Sunrise; Eiji Kaminaga of Marusan; Shiro Kataoka and the staff of the All-Japan Karaoke Industrialist Association; Masaru Kitsu of the Otsu City Museum of History; Takanobu Kishi of the Sony Archives; Ado Mizumori's Mirai Gekijo; Etsuko Nakamura and the staff of the Ritsumeikan University Center for Game Studies; Hiromi Shiga of Tezuka Productions; and Yuko Tokoro of Rune Co., Ltd.

I owe a great debt to the people who agreed to be interviewed for the book, including Alfred Birnbaum, Andy Hertzfeld, Senri Hasegawa, Rebecca Heineman, Shuhei Hosokawa, Mimi Ito, Saburo

Ishizuki, Susan Kare, Gene Pelc, Krista Suh, Toshio Maeda, Masayuki Uemura, Shu Ueyama, Larry Vine, and Yuichi Yasutomo. I owe a very special thanks to the retired Sony engineer Shingo Tamura, who arranged many interviews with former colleagues and his own sister, the talented illustrator Setsuko Tamura, who hosted me at her studio for an afternoon of memories from the front lines of kawaii culture.

Many others helped me along the way, including Ana Arriola, Brian Ashcraft, Dale Beran, Mark Bergin, Ben Boas, Konami Chiba, Joshua Dale, Catherine DeSpira, Thomas F. French, Adam Fulford, Patrick Galbraith, Matt Gillan, Ryoichi Hasegawa, Michael Herman, Ryusuke Hikawa, Dan Kanemitsu, James Karashima, Atsuko Kashiwagi, Shinya Kikuchi, Chris Kohler, Yutaka Kondo, Shigetaka Kurita, Philippe de Lespinay, Patrick Macias, Jeremy Parish, Nozomi Naoi, Frederik Schodt, Don Smith, Noah Smith, Shinkichi, Eisuke Takahashi, Jim Ulak, Andrew Vestal, and Will Wolfslau.

A tip of the hat to old friends who've been there for endless jam sessions, brainstorms, and various other requests, including Robert Duban, Joshua Fraser, Roger Harkavy, Ryan Shepard, Alexander O. Smith, Greg Starr, and Alen Yen. And of course to family—Fred, Carol, and Allyson; Tsuyoshi, Noriko, Kikaku, and Honoka; Lois and Ben, Eileen and G.G., and everyone else who supported me along the way.

NOTES

ix **"In fact the whole of Japan is pure invention"**: Harold Bloom, *Oscar Wilde* (New York: Bloom's Literary Criticism, 2008), ix.

INTRODUCTION

4 **Sony's marketing team poured $30 million**: Matt Leone, *"Final Fantasy VII: An Oral History,"* Polygon, January 9, 2019, https://www.polygon.com/a/final -fantasy-7. (Statistic quoted from then president and CEO of Square, Tomo-yuki Takechi.)

5 **"They said it couldn't be done in a major motion picture"**: David L. Crad-dock, "How *Final Fantasy 7* Revolutionized Videogame Marketing and Helped Sony Tackle Nintendo," *Paste*, May 8, 2017, https://www.pastemagazine.com /articles/2017/05/how-final-fantasy-7-revolutionized-videogame-marke.html.

5 **The previous bestselling PlayStation title, the British-made** *Tomb Raider:* Jer Horwitz, "Saturn's Distant Orbit," videogames.com, May 15, 1997, https:// web.archive.org/web/20000312083957/http://headline.gamespot.com /news/97_05/15_belt/index.html.

5 **Japan was "a great and glorious country"**: William S. Gilbert, *The Story of the Mikado* (London: Daniel O'Connor, 1921), IB.

5 **A decade later, notoriously gruff secretary of state**: John P. Glennon, ed., *Foreign Relations of the United States, 1952–1954: China and Japan*, vol. 14, part 2 (Washington, D.C.: United States Government Printing Office, 1985), 1725. See https://history.state.gov/historicaldocuments/frus1952-54v14p2.

6 **"suicide is not an illogical step"**: Keith A. Nitta, "Paradigms," in Steven Vogel, *U.S.-Japan Relations in a Changing World* (Washington, D.C.: Brookings Institution Press, 2002), 74.

6 **My own childhood was punctuated by images**: Matt Novak, "That Time Republicans Smashed a Boombox with Sledgehammers on Capitol Hill," Giz-modo, May 9, 2016, https://paleofuture.gizmodo.com/that-time-republicans -smashed-a-boombox-with-sledgehamm-1775418875.

10 **Japanese call the years after the burst of the bubble**: See, for just one of many examples, Yoichi Funabashi, ed., *Examining Japan's Lost Decades* (New York: Routledge, 2015).

10 **When an earthquake leveled huge sections of Kobe**: James Sterngold,

"Gang in Kobe Organizes Aid for People in Quake," *The New York Times*, January 22, 1995, 6.

12 **One of the first was the British diplomat:** Sir Rutherford Alcock, *The Capital of the Tycoon, a Narrative of Three Years' Residence in Japan* (New York: Harper & Brothers, 1863), 416.

12 **"We frequently see full-grown men and able-bodied natives":** William Elliot Griffis, *The Mikado's Empire*, book 2 (New York: Harper & Brothers, 1876), 453.

FALL 1945

15 **"PEACE! IT'S OVER":** *The Charlotte Observer*, August 15, 1945, 1.

15 **"forty-three and a half square miles":** "Superforts Keep Tokyo Fires Hot," *The Tuscaloosa News* (Associated Press), April 16, 1945.

15 **"JAPAN A HOLLOW SHELL":** "Japan Hollow Shell," *The Lawrence Journal-World*, October 13, 1945, 1.

15 **"Work harder, longer with *Philopon*™":** "Hiropon Tanjo" ("The Birth of Philopon"), Tanken.com, August 23, 2009, https://tanken.com/kakusei.html.

15 **"HEY, KIDS!":** Masayuki Tsusui, "Donguri no eiyo to itadakikata: donguri wo sakande tabemashou" ("Nutrition and Cooking Methods of Acorns: Let's Fill Our Stomachs with Acorns"), *Fujin Kurabu (Women's Club Magazine)*, August 1945, https://livedoor.blogimg.jp/mukashi_no/imgs/e/2/e2b589a0.jpg.

15 **"WASHINGTON—The return of toys and games":** "SBP Issues Order for Surplus Aid," *The New York Times*, May 8, 1945.

15 **"Ueno station reports":** Nobumasa Tanaka, *Dokyumento Showatenno (A Documentary of the Showa Emperor)* (Tokyo: Ryokufu Shuppan, 1984), 234.

15 **"Japan has fallen to a fourth-rate nation":** Jonathan Bailey, *Great Power Strategy in Asia: Empire, Culture and Trade, 1905–2005* (New York: Routledge, 2007), 149.

1: TIN MEN

17 **"In the toy-shops of Japan":** Griffis, *The Mikado's Empire*, 452.

17 **"Toys are not really as innocent":** Marlow Hoffman, "Five Things Charles & Ray Eames Teach Us about Play," Eames official website, blog entry, December 1, 2015, http://www.eamesoffice.com/blog/five-things-charles-ray-eames -teach-us-about-play/.

17 **"Skeletons of railway cars and locomotives":** Mark Gayn, *Japan Diary* (North Clarendon, Vt.: Tuttle, 1981), 1.

17 **The "U.S. Army Truck, ¼-ton, 4×4, Command Reconnaissance":** *SNL G-503 Standard Nomenclature List Willys MB Ford GPW*, War Department, 1944. See https://archive.org/details/SnlG-503StandardNomenclatureListWillys MbFordGpw/page/n15.

18 **General Eisenhower went so far as to credit the jeep:** Roger E. Bilstein, *Airlift and Airborne Operations in World War II*, Air Force History and Museums

Program, 1998, 17, https://media.defense.gov/2010/Sep/22/2001330050/-1/-1/0/AFD-100922-024.pdf.

18 **And they did radiate a sort of charm:** Phil Patton, "Design by Committee: The Case of the Jeep," Phil Patton blog, April 23, 2012, https://philpatton.typepad.com/my_weblog/2012/04/design-by-committee-the-case-of-the-jeep.html.

18 **The sailorman's sidekick Eugene the Jeep:** John Norris, *Vehicle Art of World War Two* (South Yorkshire, U.K.: Pen & Sword Books, 2016), 46.

19 **Police were required to salute:** National Diet Library, Modern Japanese Political History Materials Room, eds., "Supreme Commander for the Allied Powers Directives to the Japanese Government (SCAPINs) (Record Group 331)," April 2007, 38. ·

19 **The first English words:** John W. Dower, *Embracing Defeat* (New York: W. W. Norton, 1999), 110.

19 **obsessed with material *things*:** Susan B. Hanley, *Everyday Things in Premodern Japan: The Hidden Legacy of Material Culture* (Berkeley: University of California Press, 1997), 24–25.

20 **With a million residents, Edo, as Tokyo was known:** Sumie Jones and Kenji Watanabe, eds., *An Edo Anthology: Literature from Japan's Mega-City, 1750–1850* (Honolulu: University of Hawaii Press, 2013), 4.

20 **For many generations, department stores:** Penelope Francks and Janet Hunter, eds., *The Historical Consumer: Consumption and Everyday Life in Japan, 1850–2000* (New York: Palgrave Macmillan, 2012), 268.

21 **Charles Tiffany harnessed Japanese flourishes:** Hannah Sigur, *The Influence of Japanese Art on Design* (Layton, Utah: Gibbs Smith, 2008), 154.

21 **"We do not know of any country in the world":** Griffis, *The Mikado's Empire*, 453.

22 **Germany, the United Kingdom, and France jostled:** Janet Holmes, "Economic Choices and Popular Toys in the Nineteenth Century," *Material Culture Review* 21 (1985). Retrieved from https://journals.lib.unb.ca/index.php/MCR/article/view/17244.

22 **At the 1915 Panama–Pacific International Exposition:** David D. Hamlin, *Work and Play: The Production and Consumption of Toys in Germany, 1870–1914* (Ann Arbor: University of Michigan Press, 2007), 1; *Japan and Her Exhibits at the Panama-Pacific International Exhibition 1915*, Société des Expositions, 1915.

22 **A skilled Japanese craftsman might earn in a day:** The daily wage for a Japanese toy maker in the mid-1910s was reported as thirty-seven cents by *The New York Times* in an article entitled "Japan's Toy Trade" (June 24, 1917). Around the same time frame, American workers in the metal trades earned between fifty-five cents and a dollar per hour, depending on location and specific work being performed. See, for example, this data compiled by the United States Bureau of Labor Statistics: https://fraser.stlouisfed.org/title/3912/item/476870?start_page=74.

22 **proved so adept at their task:** "Japanese Toys," *Gazette and Bulletin*, April 7, 1934.

22 **Matsuzo Kosuge was born in 1899:** Masaru Kitsu, *Buriki no Omocha to Otsu: Sengo Daiichigo no Kosuge no Jiipu* (*Tin Toys and Otsu: Kosuge's Jeep, a Postwar First*) (Otsu, Japan: Otsu City Museum of History, August 1, 2000), 10.

23 **Life on Etorofu was hard:** Kanako Takahara, "Nemuro Raid Survivor Longs for Homeland," *The Japan Times*, September 22, 2007.

23 **Exports of playthings from Japan to the United States alone quadrupled:** "Japan's Toy Trade," *The New York Times Magazine*, June 24, 1917, 3.

23 **the molds were the beating hearts:** Masayuki Tanimoto, "The Development of Dispersed Production Organization in the Interwar Period: The Case of the Japanese Toy Industry," in *Production Organizations in Japanese Economic Development*, ed. Tetsuji Okazaki (New York: Routledge, 2007), 183.

23 **In 1922, Kosuge launched:** Tokyo City Governor's Office Research Division,"Tokyo-fu Kojo Tokei" [City of Tokyo 1930 Factory Census] (Tokyo: City of Tokyo, April 25, 1932), 19.

24 **We don't know exactly how he managed:** YouTube user toygaragechannel, *Buriki no Tatsujin*, vol. 5: *Marusan Kyadirakku Kaihatsu Chiimu* (*Masters of Tin*, vol. 5: *Marusan Cadillac Development Team*), November 22, 2011, https://www .youtube.com/watch?v=Y6eGMRmHYu8&feature=emb_logo.

24 **It was a think tank for toys:** *Chuuko Kogyousha no Jitsujou* (*The Situation Facing Small and Midsized Businesses*), Tokyo Shiyakusho (Tokyo City Hall, October 1935), 17.

24 **"We're in business to make our own designs":** YouTube user toygarage-channel, *Masters of Tin*, vol. 5.

25 **Sometime in the thirties he created the world's first mass-produced toy robot:** Anonymous, "Nihon ga Taukutta Sekaihatsu no Buriki Robotto Riripatto" ("The Japanese-Made First Tin Robot: Lilliput"), *Mandarake Zenbu* 54 (March 25, 2012): 1–4.

25 **In the early thirties, there were only 1,600:** Masatoshi Okui, "Taisho/Showa Senzenki ni Okeru Jidosha no Fukyuu Katei" ("The Extent of Motorization in Taisho and Early Showa"), *Shinchiri* 36, no. 3 (December 1988): 32.

25 **Before long, everyone:** Masaru Kitsu, "Buriki Gangu to Otsu" ("Tin Toys and Otsu"), *Otsu-shi Rekishi Hakubutsukan Kenkyu Kiyo* (*Otsu City Historical Museum Research Bulletin*) 8 (Otsu City Historical Museum, 2001), 34.

25 **By 1935, his little workshop:** Ibid., 38.

25 **Their efforts contributed:** "Japanese Trade Studies: Special Industry Analysis No. 8: Toys" (memo prepared for the Foreign Economic Administration by the United States Tariff Commission, March 1945), 1.

25 **As the prime minister declared ambitions:** Erich Pauer, ed., *Japan's War Economy* (New York: Routledge, 1999), 14; 45.

26 **"From now on, Japanese boys":** Toy Journal Editorial Department, *Omocha no Meekaa to Tonya no Rekishi to Ima ga Wakaru Hon* (*Understanding the History of Toy Makers and Wholesalers, Then and Now*) (Tokyo: Tokyo Toy & Doll Wholesaler Cooperative Association, 2003), 34.

26 **The authorities ordered Kosuge:** Kitsu, "Tin Toys and Otsu," 40.

26 **They even stripped school classrooms:** Chiba Prefectural Educators Coun-

cil, eds., *Ega Shiryo wo Yomu Nihonshi no Jugyo* (*An Illustrated Primer to Japanese History*) (Tokyo: Kokudousha, 1993), 178–79.

27 **"It made a lot of sense":** Thomas R. Searle, " 'It Made a Lot of Sense to Kill Skilled Workers': The Firebombing of Tokyo in March 1945," *The Journal of Military History* 66, no. 1 (January 2002): 103.

28 **The stench of charred flesh:** Barrett Tillman, *Whirlwind: The Air War against Japan, 1942–1945* (New York: Simon & Schuster, 2010), 147–52.

28 **The structure was rustic:** Kitsu, "Tin Toys and Otsu," 41.

28 **"American jeeps were everywhere":** Shoichi Fukatani, ed., *Nihon Kinzoku Gangu-shi* (*A History of Japanese Metal Toys*) (Tokyo: Kuyamasha, 1997), 442.

29 **So Kosuge used the only tool:** Kitsu, "Tin Toys and Otsu," 40.

29 **He had no molds:** YouTube user toygaragechannel, *Masters of Tin*, vol. 5.

29 **Back at the workshop:** Kitsu, "Tin Toys and Otsu," 41.

31 **It had been five years since a 1940 government edict:** National Archives of Japan, Japan Center for Asian Historical Records, "Senjichu ni Depato wa Eigyo Shitetano?" ("Were Department Stores in Business during the War?"), undated, https://www.jacar.go.jp/english/glossary_en/tochikiko-henten/qa /qa03.html.

31 **They were priced at ten yen:** Ryosuke Saito, *Omocha no Hanashi* (*Toy Talk*) (Tokyo: Asahi Shimbunsha, 1971), 284.

31 **the cost of a quick meal:** Akira Yamamoto, *Sengo Fuzokushi* (*Postwar Popular History*) (Osaka: Osaka Shoseki, 1986), 68.

31 **Kosuge's entire first run of jeeps:** Hideo Takayama, ed., *20 Seiki Omocha Hakubutsukan* (*Twentieth Century Toy Museum*) (Tokyo: Dobun Shoin, 2000), 60.

31 **He immediately scaled up his operation:** Kitsu, "Tin Toys and Otsu," 41–42.

32 **Every time a new batch arrived:** Saito, *Toy Talk*, 284–85.

32 **By the end of the month:** Toy Journal Editorial Department, *Understanding the History of Toy Makers and Wholesalers*, 38.

33 **Even children fortunate enough:** Dower, *Embracing Defeat*, 110–12.

33 **"We can keep them fed":** Saito, *Toy Talk*, 280.

33 **"Everyone in the industry said to each other":** Fukatani, *A History of Japanese Metal Toys*, 442.

33 **Inspired by Kosuge's success:** "Jeeps from Tin Cans," *Stars and Stripes* (Pacific edition), May 26, 1946.

33 **In a 1946 pictorial:** *20 Seiki Omocha Hakubutsuka-ten* (*Twentieth Century Toy Museum Exhibition*), pamphlet packaged with replica jeep toy (Japan Toy Culture Foundation: 2000).

33 **"Japanese grown-ups hated toys":** Nobuo Kumagai, *50's Japanese Mechanical Tin Toys* (Osaka: Yubunsha, 1980), 171.

34 **"all efforts be made to ramp up":** Saito, *Toy Talk*, 288.

34 **Christmas of 1947 was fast approaching:** William H. Young and Nancy K. Young, *World War II and the Postwar Years in America: A Historical and Cultural Encyclopedia* (Santa Barbara, Calif.: ABC-CLIO), 709.

34 **When the toy's distributor:** Takara Tomy, "Kiseki: Yume wo Katachi ni: Daisanwa" ("Tracks: Making Dreams Reality, vol. 3"), undated, https://www.takaratomy.co.jp/company/csr/history3.html (retrieved February 3, 2020).

34 **Yonezawa eventually sold:** Akiko Furuno, "File 146: Buriki no Omocha" ("Tin Toys"), *NHK Bi no Tsubo*, undated, https://www.nhk.or.jp/tsubo/program/file146.html.

34 **Products like the B-29:** Anne Allison, *Millennial Monsters: Japanese Toys and the Global Imagination* (Berkeley: University of California Press, 2006), 40.

35 **Japan idolized American culture:** YouTube user toygaragechannel, *Masters of Tin*, vol. 5.

35 **In 1947, Haruyasu Ishida:** Takashi Kuraji, *Marusan Burumaaku wo Ikita Otoko* (*The Man Who Lived Marusan and Bullmark*) (Tokyo: Tozai Planning, 1999), 14–15.

35 **As a teen in Singapore:** Eiji Kaminaga to author via email, May 30, 2018.

36 **"We really turned heads":** Saburo Ishizuki, personal interview, June 14, 2018.

36 **A toy car like no other:** Kuraji, *The Man Who Lived Marusan and Bullmark,* 45.

36 **by 1958, that number:** Information comes from the Office of Highway Information Management, Federal Highway Administration, "State Motor Vehicle Registrations by Years, 1900–1995," *Highway Statistics Summary to 1995,* stock no. 050-001-00323-6, https://www.fhwa.dot.gov/ohim/summary95/mv200.pdf (retrieved April 8, 2019).

37 **"one huge supply depot":** Michael Schaller, "The Korean War: The Economic and Strategic Impact on Japan 1950–1953," in William Stueck, ed., *The Korean War in World History* (University Press of Kentucky: 2004), 148.

38 **The no-compromise approach:** Kuraji, *The Man Who Lived Marusan and Bullmark,* 46.

38 **In fact, the price was so high:** Ibid.

38 **Virtually from the moment foreign buyers first saw:** Joe Earle, *Buriki,* 14.

39 **Lined up at long tables:** Ibid., 13.

39 **The package for the Japanese edition:** Ibid., 15.

39 **Even that all-American idol:** "Barbie's Journey in Japan," *The New York Times,* December 12, 1996.

39 **In 1959, furious British toy companies:** Ray B. Browne and Pat Browne, eds., *The Guide to United States Popular Culture* (Madison: University of Wisconsin Press, 2001), 850.

40 **Kishi was an unlikely United States ally:** Dower, *Embracing Defeat,* 454.

41 **secret financial backing from the CIA:** "C.I.A. Spent Millions to Support Japanese Right in 50's and 60's," *The New York Times,* October 9, 1994.

41 **Fifteen months of political deadlock and demonstrations:** Nathan Hopson, review of Nick Kapur's *Japan at the Crossroads: Conflict and Compromise after Anpo,* New Books Network, September 21, 2018, https://newbooksnetwork.com/nick-kapur-japan-at-the-crossroads-conflict-and-compromise-after-anpo-harvard-up-2018/.

42 **"Not exactly an advertisement for democracy"**: "Parliament's a Riot (1960)," YouTube video uploaded by British Pathé, https://www.youtube.com /watch?v=mpY_CO2Zdhk.

42 **Broadcast widely in Japan and abroad**: Takemasa Ando, *Japan's New Left Movements: Legacies for Civil Society* (New York: Routledge, 2014), p. 30, and Michael Liu, Kim Geron, and Tracy A. M. Lai, *The Snake Dance of Asian American Activism: Community, Vision, and Power* (Lanham, Md.: Lexington Books, 2008), 66.

42 **In what must be the first example**: The National Mobilization Committee to End the War in Vietnam, aka "The Mobe," actually employed an emoji-like image of a snake as a visual code for protesters gathering during the 1967 March on the Pentagon, as revealed in a later congressional hearing on the topic. The Columbia SDS anti-war protest group also threatened to lead a "snake dance . . . through the streets of Washington." See U.S. Congress, House of Representatives, Committee on Un-American Activities, "Hearings before the Committee on Un-American Activities, House of Representatives, Ninetieth Congress, April 30, May 2 and 22, 1968," 90th Cong., Second Session, 2769, and Tom Wells, *The War Within: America's Battle over Vietnam* (Lincoln: iUniverse, 2005), 185.

2: THE REVOLUTION WILL BE TELEVISED

44 **"It seems almost inevitable"**: Margaret Talbot, "The Auteur of Anime," *The New Yorker*, January 9, 2005.

45 *Mighty Atom* **was a bootstrap affair**: Hiromichi Masuda, *The Digital Transformation of the Anime Business* (Tokyo: NTT Shuppan, 2016), 173.

45 **The resulting imagery was so stilted**: Hiromichi Masuda, *Anime Bijinesu ga Wakaru* (*Understanding the Anime Business*) (Tokyo: NTT Shuppan, 2010), 152.

46 **It also introduced the world to a new word**: Masuda, *Digital Transformation*, 173.

48 **His fascination bordered on obsession**: Osamu Tezuka, *Tezuka Osamu Mirai e no Kotoba* (*Osamu Tezuka's Words for the Future*) (Tokyo: Ko Shobo, 2007), 113.

48 **In 1941, the imperial military screened a copy of** *Fantasia*: Soji Ushio, *Tezuka Osamu to Boku* (*Me and Osamu Tezuka*) (Tokyo: Soshisha, 2007), 193.

48 **He was disciplined**: Natsu Onoda Power, *God of Comics: Osamu Tezuka and the Creation of Post–World War II Manga* (Jackson: University Press of Mississippi, 2009), 61–62.

49 **"They would barely even read the work"**: Gary Groth, "Yoshihiro Tatsumi Interview," *The Comics Journal*, http://www.tcj.com/yoshihiro-tatsumi-inter view/ (accessed October 15, 2019).

49 **Newspapers of the day railed against vulgar comics**: Ryan Holmberg, "The Bottom of a Bottomless Barrel: Introducing Akahon Manga," *The Comics Journal*, January 5, 2012, http://www.tcj.com/the-bottom-of-a-bottomless -barrel-introducing-akahon-manga.

49 **Tezuka made his long-form debut at the age of eighteen**: Ryan Holmberg,

"Tezuka Osamu Outwits the Phantom Blot: The Case of *New Treasure Island* cont'd," *The Comics Journal*, February 22, 2013, http://www.tcj.com/tezuka -osamu-outwits-the-phantom-blot-the-case-of-new-treasure-island-contd.

50 **In an era when publishing a thousand copies:** "About Tezuka Osamu," page from Osamu's official website, undated, https://tezukaosamu.net/en /about/1940.html (accessed February 3, 2020).

52 **Their first act was to mail out a postcard manifesto:** Osamu Tezuka, *Boku ha Mangaka* (*I, Manga Artist*) (Tokyo: Rittorsha, 2016), 248.

53 **At the end of World War II:** The Institute of Population Problems, Ministry of Health and Welfare, Japan, Supplement to *Population Problems in Japan* (United Nations World Population Conference, June 1974), 1.

54 **Shirato had grown up during the war years:** Tetsuo Sakurai, *Haikyo no Zankyo: Sengo Manga no Genzo* (*Reverberations of Ruin: Postwar Manga Origins*) (Tokyo: NTT Shuppan, 2015), 115.

54 **The vast majority of these newcomers were young men:** Akira Yamada, *Uenohatsu no Yakoressha Meiressha* (*Departing Ueno: Night Trains and Famous Trains*) (Tokyo: JTB Publishing, 2015), 64.

55 **Insecure by nature:** Power, *God of Comics*, 97.

55 **he tumbled down a flight of stairs:** Tezuka, *I, Manga Artist*, 251.

56 **Founded three years prior with the explicit aim:** Toei Doga, eds., *Toei Doga Henshu Anime Daizenshu* (*A Total Collection of Anime Edited by Toei Doga*) (Tokyo: Tokuma Shote, 1978), 4–5.

56 **He had toyed with becoming an animator:** Power, *God of Comics*, 131.

57 **But Tezuka was no longer a wide-eyed student:** Tezuka, *I, Manga Artist*, 271.

57 **One of its fans was a seven-year-old named Shigeru Miyamoto:** "I like Toei Animation's work from around the time of *Alakazam the Great*, and the ox that appears in that," Miyamoto said. See Shigeru Iwata, "Iwata Asks: Vol. 8, Yoichi Kotabe, 4. My First Project: Draw a Rug," Nintendo.com, un- dated, http://iwataasks.nintendo.com/interviews/#/ds/dsi/7/3.

57 **Heavily rewritten and sanitized:** Harry Medved, with Randy Dreyfuss and Michael Medved, *The Fifty Worst Films of All Time (And How They Got That Way)*, (New York: Warner Books, 1978), 21–23.

57 **troubles brewing within Toei Doga's eternally overworked:** Jonathan Clements, *Anime: A History* (London: Palgrave Macmillan, 2013), 104.

57 **The studio offered to discuss the suggestions:** Yuka Minagawa, *Shosetsu Tezuka Gakko 1 Terebi Anime Tanjo* (*The Tezuka School Dramatized: The Birth of Television Anime*) (Tokyo: Kodansha, 2009), 127.

59 **In early 1948, after a long series of failed negotiations:** Clements, *Anime*, 80.

59 **"human relationships far outweighed the art":** Tezuka, 272.

60 **In numerous interviews with the press:** Minagawa, *The Tezuka School Dra- matized*, 136.

60 **Tezuka funded everything out of his own pocket:** Ibid., 163.

61 **The film's syrupy sentimentality so disgusted him:** Hayao Miyazaki, *Starting Point 1976–1996* (San Francisco: Viz Media, 1996), 195.

61 **"Drawing a salary from a company":** Minagawa, *The Tezuka School Dramatized*, 163.

61 **Tezuka estimated that production costs would run:** Tezuka, *I, Manga Artist*, 280.

62 **"There's no way they'll invest three or even two times that":** Ibid.

62 **"By modern standards":** Ibid., 281–82.

63 **Among its fans was the director Stanley Kubrick:** Schodt, *The Astro Boy Essays*, 92.

64 **"The God of Comics":** Takeshi Kaiko, "Manga no Kamisama Tezuka Osamu" ("The God of Manga, Osamu Tezuka"), *Shukan Asahi*, February 21, 1964.

65 **"Those cute characters are dying! They're having sex!"** In this, Tezuka unwittingly anticipated the concept of Western "furry" fandom. In 2014, his daughter Rumiko announced the discovery of a sheaf of sketches of mice-women in sensual poses found in a locked drawer of her late father's desk. The quote about the characters is from Tamaki Saito, *Otaku Shinkei Sanatoriumu* (*Otaku Mental Sanatorium*) (Tokyo: Futami, 2015), 154. Rafael Antonio Pineda, "Osamu Tezuka's Previously Unreleased Erotic Illustrations Unveiled," Anime News Network, October 7, 2016, https://www.animenews network.com/news/2016-11-07/osamu-tezuka-previously-unreleased-erotic -illustrations-unveiled/.

65 **it grew so popular that when Joe's archrival, Riki-ishi, died:** Frederik Schodt, *Manga! Manga! The World of Japanese Comics* (Tokyo: Kodansha, 1983), 85.

66 **A 1968 survey asking young men how they spent their free time:** Oguma Eiji and Nick Kapur, "Japan's 1968: A Collective Reaction to Rapid Economic Growth in an Age of Turmoil," *The Asia-Pacific Journal* 13:12, no. 1 (March 23, 2015), 7.

66 **The passage of the Anpo in 1960 dealt a serious blow:** Ibid., 2.

67 **"We all had high hopes when we entered university":** Akiyama Katsuyuki, *Zengakuren ha Nani wo Kanageru ka* (*What Is Zengakuren Thinking*) (Tokyo: Jiyu Kokuminsha, 1969), 121–26; 137–39.

68 **Images of the violence, broadcast on the nightly news in vivid color:** Ibid., 3.

68 **On October 21 of that same year:** William Andrews, *Dissenting Japan: A History of Japanese Radicalism and Counterculture from 1945 to Fukushima* (London: Oxford University Press, 2016), 112–15.

69 **"The youth of Zengakuren developed their revolutionary movement from the gekiga of Shirato Sanpei":** Minami Shinbo, *Nihon No Meizuihitu Bekkan 62 Manga* (*Famous Japanese Writings,* vol. 62: *Manga*) (Tokyo: Sakuhinsha, 1996), 110.

69 **"Because the widely held notion was that manga were for children":** Oguma and Kapur, "Japan's 1968," 16.

70 **Taking direct inspiration from the animated:** Michinori Kato, *Rengo Sekigun Shonen A* (*A United Red Army Boy*) (Tokyo: Shinchosha, 2003), 42–43.

70 **"We only worried about justifications":** Oguma and Kapur, "Japan's 1968," 14.

70 **"We didn't care about Marxist philosophy"**: Mamoru Oshii and Kiyoshi Kasai, *Sozo Gannen 1968* (*Year One of Creation 1968*) (Tokyo: Sakuhinsha, 2016), 24.

70 **In January of 1969, more than eight thousand riot police**: Alex Martin, "The Todai Riots: 1968–69," *The Japan Times*, https://features.japantimes.co.jp /student-riots/.

70 **Now lawmakers hastily passed**: Oguma and Kapur, "Japan's 1968," 5.

71 **Early one morning in March of 1970, a group of eight young men and one woman**: Jonathan Watts, "Japanese Hijackers Go Home after 32 Years on the Run," *The Guardian*, September 8, 2002, https://www.theguardian .com/world/2002/sep/09/japan.jonathanwatts1.

71 **It ended with the cryptic declaration "Never forget: We are *Tomorrow's Joe"***: Masahiro Tachikawa, "Tokushu Yodo-go Jokyaku 100nin no Shogen," ("Special: Testimonials from 100 Yodo-go Passengers"), *Bungei Shunju*, April 6, 1970, 220.

71 **"We certainly read a lot of manga"**: Takaya Shiomi, *Sekigunha Shimatuki* (*A Record of the Extermination of the Red Army*) (Tokyo: Sairyuusha, 2009), 57.

73 **"in terms of animation"**: Miyazaki, *Starting Point*, 197.

3: EVERYBODY IS A STAR

75 **"Hell is full of musical amateurs"**: George Bernard Shaw, *Selected Plays* (New York: Gramercy Books, 1996), 300.

75 **a group of musicians gather**: Hiromichi Ugaya, *Karaoke Hishi* (*Karaoke: The Secret History*) (Tokyo: Shinsho, 2008), 43.

76 **"You tryin' to put us out of business"**: Ibid.

76 **Once, he even helped fend off a backstage assault**: Eiji Oshita, *Karaoke wo Hatsumei Shita Otoko* (*The Man Who Invented Karaoke*) (Tokyo: Kawade Shobo), 69.

77 **"We're musicians!"**: Ugaya, *Karaoke*, 43.

77 **"Yeah. Forget the machine"**: For Japanese speakers curious about this phrasing, it is a contextualized translation of 「おう、こんな機械に負けるかい」, as quoted in ibid.

78 **Karaoke machines were independently invented**: In addition to Daisuke Inoue and Shigeichi Negishi, Toshiharu Yamashita and Iwao Hamasaki are also recognized as early karaoke pioneers by the All-Japan Karaoke Industrialist Association.

79 **"Ideas of freedom and democracy"**: Akio Morita, *Made in Japan* (New York: E. P. Dutton, 1986), 51.

79 **the first postwar singing contest**: Ugaya, *Karaoke*, 69.

81 **an equal or perhaps greater number of the student radicals**: Oguma and Kapur, "Japan's 1968," 9.

81 **asking schoolboys what they wanted to be**: "Gendaikko no Natitai Shokugyyo ha . . ." ("Today's Kids Want to Be . . ."), *Asahi Shimbun*, November 2, 1970, 19.

82 **A 1969 newsreel for Japanese audiences:** *Sarariman Shokun* (*I, Salaryman*), newsreel no. 796, Chunichi News, April 2, 1969.

85 **Over the course of the fifties and sixties:** Ugaya, *Karaoke*, 49.

87 **He called his baby the Sparko Box:** This and all Negishi quotes that follow are from a personal interview conducted at his home in Tokyo on November 28, 2018.

90 **the 8 Juke was a wooden cube:** Oshita, *The Man Who Invented Karaoke*, 90.

90 **Inoue had another trick up his sleeve:** This account of 8 Juke's origins is from: Ugaya, *Karaoke*, 39–42.

92 **"I didn't build the thing from scratch":** Robert Scott, "Voice Hero: The Inventor of Karaoke Speaks," *The Appendix* 1, no. 4 (October 2013).

93 **The first to get its own machine:** Shiro Kataoka, ed., *JKA Setsuritu 20 Shunen Kinenshi* (*JKA Founding: The 20th Anniversary Book*) (Tokyo: All-Japan Karaoke Industrialist Association, 2015), 35.

93 **In the early hours of December 26, 1977:** "Shiwasu no Kurabu Maiku Sodatsu" ("Mic Fight at End of Year Club Party"), *Asahi Shimbun*, December 26, 1977.

93 **"We're losing the art of bar conversation":** Itsumade Tsuzuku, "Itsumade Tsuzuku Karaoke Buumu" ("The Ongoing Karaoke Boom"), *Asahi Shimbun*, January 25, 1978.

94 **A 1979 Japanese newspaper op-ed:** Unsigned, "Tensei Jingo" ("Vox Populi, Vox Dei"), *Asahi Shimbun*, December 29, 1979, 1.

94 **And in 1984 the music critic:** Tadashi Fujita, "Karaoke Buumu" ("The Karaoke Boom"), *Kikan Kuraishisu* (*Seasonal Crisis*), no. 18 (Winter 1984): 158–61.

94 *enka*, **a schmaltzy genre:** Christine R. Yano, *Tears of Longing* (Cambridge, Mass.: Harvard University Press, 2002), 31–40.

95 **"The youth have their guitars":** "Popuraa Shin Fuzoku: Karaoke" ("Popular New Trends: Karaoke"), *Asahi Shimbun*, April 5, 1977, 7.

95 **it changed quickly, thanks to another Boss:** "Born in the U.S.A. Becomes Karaoke," *Asahi Shimbun*, November 19, 1985, 9.

95 **more than a hundred** *nagashi* **serviced Tokyo's downtown:** Hisatake Yamashita, "Onna Nagashi no Ikiru Michi" ("The Life of the Female Nagashi,"), *Okamura Wave+*, May 2, 2016, http://www.okamura.co.jp/magazine/wave /archive/1605chieA.html.

96 **some 170,000 rooms:** Kataoka, *JKA Founding*, 80.

96 **fifty million:** Xun Zhou and Francesca Tarocco, *Karaoke: The Global Phenomenon* (London: Reakton Books, 2013), 32.

97 **"After a long day at the office":** Ronald L. Rhodes, "What's New in Japanese Consumer Electronics; in New Products, Small Is Beautiful," *The New York Times*, May 8, 1983, section 3, 15.

97 **"We're running against the karaoke kids":** *Public Papers of the Presidents of the United States: George H. W. Bush, 1992–1993* (Washington, D.C.: U.S. Government Printing Office, 1993), 1371.

97 **Blige launched her career with a tape:** Mary J. Blige, "Music Interviews:

Mary J. Blige, Making 'The Breakthrough,'" *All Things Considered*, NPR, January 21, 2006.

98 **Negishi managed, in spite of all the resistance:** Personal interview, November 18, 2018.

98 **Inoue, on the other hand, made out like a bandit:** Scott, "Voice Hero."

98 **Singaporean karaoke channel:** Ugaya, *Karaoke*, 46.

99 **"Eastern Walter Mitty":** Pico Iyer, "Daisuke Inoue," *Time*, August 23, 1999, http://content.time.com/time/world/article/0,8599,2054546,00.html.

99 **Five years later in 2004, the Ig Nobel:** "The Man Who Taught the World to Sing," *The Independent*, May 24, 2006, https://www.independent.co.uk/news /world/asia/the-man-who-taught-the-world-to-sing-479469.html.

4: CULT OF CUTE

101 **A tiny translucent vinyl pouch:** Yasuo Ozaki, ed., *MY KITTY* (Tokyo: Asuka Shinsha, 1997), 12.

102 **She is the cornerstone of a massive multimedia franchise:** Sanrio has never released data for just Hello Kitty sales alone, but estimates are that her products account for as much as 80 percent of the firm's total revenues. Sanrio's annual earnings in 2018 were roughly sixty billion yen, off from a peak of more than ninety billion in 2008. See also Naoko Fujimura and Emi Urabe, "Sanrio to Cut Reliance on Hello Kitty," *The Japan Times*, July 14, 2011, https:// www.japantimes.co.jp/news/2011/07/14/business/sanrio-to-cut-reliance-on -hello-kitty/; License Global, "Top 100 Global Licensors," Licenseglobal.com, April 6, 2018, https://www.licenseglobal.com/stub/top-100-global-licensors; and Shared Research, "Sanrio / 8136," Sharedresearch.jp, May 11, 2018, https://sharedresearch.jp/system/report_updates/pdfs/000/019/191/origi nal/8136_EN_20180511.pdf.

102 **When Islamic Front commander Zahran Alloush:** Lizzie Dearden, "Syrian Rebel Leader Gives Speech to Islamist Militants with Hello Kitty Notebook," *The Independent*, July 4, 2014, https://www.independent.co.uk/news/world /middle-east/syrian-rebel-leader-gives-speech-to-islamist-militants-with -hello-kitty-notebook-9583629.html.

102 **The word "cute" derives from "acute":** Joshua Paul Dale, Joyce Goggin, Julia Leyda, Anthony P. McIntyre, and Diane Negra, eds., *The Aesthetics and Affects of Cuteness* (New York: Routledge, 2016), 37.

103 **The first known modern use of kawaii dates to 1914:** Masanobu Hosono, *Takehisa Yumeji* (*Yumeji Takehisa*) (Tokyo: Hoikusha, 1972), 123.

103 **His art proved so popular in Japan's roaring twenties:** Nozomi Naoi, "Beauties and Beyond: Situating Takehisa Yumeji and the Yumeji-shiki," *Andon* 98 (December 2014): 29.

103 **"the most widely used, widely loved, habitual word":** Osamu Kogure, "Kawaii no Judan Katsuyo" ("The Ten Uses of Kawaii"), *Crea* (November 1992): 58–59.

105 **Long before Kitty, long before Sanrio:** Junichiro Uemae, *Sanrio no Kiseki* (*Sanrio's Miracle*) (Tokyo: PHP Kenkyujo, 1979), 19.

105 **"The birthday parties":** Tomoko Otake, "Shintaro Tsuji: 'Mr. Cute' Shares His Wisdoms and Wit," *The Japan Times*, March 2, 2008, https://www.japan times.co.jp/life/2008/03/02/people/shintaro-tsuji-mr-cute-shares-his -wisdoms-and-wit.

105 **"They rode me constantly":** Shintaro Tsuji, *Kore ga Sanrio no Himitsu Desu* (*These Are Sanrio's Secrets*) (Tokyo: Fusosha, 2000), 113.

105 **One of the final issues of the popular boy's comic:** Frederik Schodt, *Manga! Manga! The World of Japanese Comics* (Tokyo: Kodansha, 2001), 51.

106 **As Tsuji and his classmates glumly filed back:** Otake, "Shintaro Tsuji: 'Mr. Cute.'"

106 **"The relief is wonderful":** Ruth Benedict, *The Chrysanthemum and the Sword* (New York: Mariner Books, 2005), 169.

106 **The listlessness proved so pervasive:** Dower, *Embracing Defeat*, 89.

106 **He snuck into the school's lab to secretly synthesize:** Tsuji, *These Are Sanrio's Secrets*, 114.

106 **"the second adversity, after my boyhood":** Ibid., 119.

107 **It distributed regional products:** Uemae, *Sanrio's Miracle*, 58.

107 **"Back then, around 1960":** Otake, "Shintaro Tsuji: 'Mr. Cute.'"

108 **The answer came to him:** It's key to note that Tsuji has never specifically indicated that Naito's work inspired him, but given the time frame and the choice of fruit, that it was one of Naito's products he saw is a virtual certainty. See Uemae, *Sanrio's Miracle*, 41.

109 **"Oh, it's so *cute*":** Ibid.

109 **Tiffany's, that bastion of sophistication:** Sigur, *Influence of Japanese Art on Design*, 154.

110 **A Japanese fancy good, on the other hand:** Sharon Kinsella, "Cuties in Japan," in Lise Skov and Brian Moeran, *Women, Media, and Consumption in Japan* (New York: Routledge, 2013), 226.

110 **"I wasn't disappointed, exactly":** Uemae, *Sanrio's Miracle*, 43.

110 **"He was almost like a little girl":** Ibid., 45.

112 **"the art of nudity, with a burning ambition":** Jonathan Bollen, "Nichigeki Music Hall," Research on Performance and Desire, March 20, 2011, http://jonathanbollen.net/2011/03/20/nichigeki-music-hall/.

112 **Mizumori's bohemian father took her:** Ado Mizumori, *Mizumori Ado* (*Ado Mizumori*) (Tokyo: Kawade Shobo, 2010), 96–97.

113 **"Backstage, the dancers were totally nude":** Takeda Kyoko, "Ikiru no ga raku ni naru, Mizumori Ado-san no Ochikomi Kaishoho" ("Ado Mizumori's Cure for the Blues"), *MYLOHAS*, March 15, 2013, https://www.mylohas.net /2013/03/028247post_1627.html.

113 **A ceramic figurine of Mii-tan:** Masafumi Nishizawa, *Sanrio Monogatari: Koshite Hitotsu no Kigyo ga Umareta* (*Sanrio Story: How an Industry Was Born*) (Tokyo: Sanrio, 1990), 43.

113 **He tried collaborating:** Tsuji, *These are Sanrio's Secrets*, 92–93.

114 **His name was Konrad Lorenz, and he was a Nazi:** Joshua Paul Dale, Joyce Goggin, Julia Leyda, Anthony P. McIntyre, and Diane Negra, eds., *The Aesthetics and Affects of Cuteness* (New York: Routledge, 2016), 44.

114 **Years later, the evolutionary biologist:** Stephen Jay Gould, "A Biological Homage to Mickey Mouse," *Ecotone* 4, no. 1–2 (Winter 2008): 333–40.

115 **"good mean little bastards":** Charles Schulz, *The Complete Peanuts*, vol. 1: *1950–1952* (Seattle: Fantagraphics, 2014), 294.

115 **"excited by the casual cruelty":** Matt Groening, "Oh Boy, Charlie Brown," *The Guardian*, October 11, 2008, https://www.theguardian.com/books/2008 /oct/11/peanuts-matt-groening-jonathan-franzen.

115 **"vibrated with fifties alienation":** Schulz, *The Complete Peanuts*, 1:293.

115 **In an exploration of the history of the character:** Sarah Boxer, "The Exemplary Narcissism of Snoopy," *The Atlantic*, November 2015.

115 **Tsuji knew it was only a matter of time:** Tsuji, *These Are Sanrio's Secrets*, 96–97.

116 **"Draw cats and bears. If a dog hit this big, one of those two is sure to follow":** Uemae, *Sanrio's Miracle*, 132.

116 **Tsuji called it a Gift Gate:** Nishizawa, *Sanrio Story*, 122–25.

117 **"'Sanrio' is a contraction of the Spanish 'san rio'":** Tsuji, *These Are Sanrio's Secrets*, 105.

117 **"Companies need their inside jokes":** Uemae, *Sanrio's Miracle*, 42.

117 **"Ultimate beauty. Life eternal":** Moto Hagio, *The Poe Clan*, vol. 1 (Seattle: Fantagraphics Books, 2019), 40.

117 **As an artist she was entirely self-taught:** Moto Hagio, "The Moto Hagio Interview conducted by Matt Thorn," *The Comics Journal*, March 9, 2010, https://web.archive.org/web/20100510033709/http://www.tcj.com/history /the-moto-hagio-interview-conducted-by-matt-thorn-part-one-of-four/.

118 **Upon seeing the first pages of *The Heart of Thomas*:** Frenchy Lunning, "Moto Hagio," in *She Changed Comics* (Portland, Ore.: Image Comics, 2016), 102.

119 **Comic Market was dreamed up:** Takanaka Shimonotsuki, *Komikku Maaketo Soseiki* (*A Record of Comic Market's Creation*) (Tokyo: Asahi Shinsho, 2008), 95–96.

119 **They were shocked when their event was besieged:** Comic Market Committee, eds., *Comiket 30's File* (Tokyo: Comiket Publishing, 2005), 31–35.

120 **Working for Sanrio was Maeda's first job:** Uemae, *Sanrio's Miracle*, 118–19.

120 **"Honestly, I told everyone I thought it was no good":** Ibid.

121 **a 1977 article in the *Asahi Shimbun*:** "Pati to Jimi no Sanrio: Aidia de Shobu Uriagedaka Rieki Toshi Goto Bai ni" ("Patty & Jimmy's Sanrio: Competing with Ideas: Sales, Profits Double Every Year"), *Asahi Shimbun*, July 16, 1977, 8.

121 **"What I was thinking was, *Wouldn't it be really fun*":** As quoted in Michiko Shimizu, "Ichigo Shimbun ni Miru Haro Kiti Zo no Hensen" ("Transitions in the Portrayal of Hello Kitty in the *Strawberry News*"), *Kansai Kokusai Daigaku Kenkyu Kiyo* (*Research Bulletin of Kansai International University*) 10 (March 31, 2009): 103.

121 **"I only thought it was okay":** Tsuji, *These Are Sanrio's Secrets,* 100.

122 **"It was selling way more than expected":** Shimizu, "Transitions," 103.

122 **"image as a purveyor of dreams and happiness":** "Patty & Jimmy's Sanrio."

122 **A minor backlash ensued:** Ibid.

123 **She introduced incremental innovations:** Yuko Yamaguchi, *Kiti no Namida (Tears of Kitty)* (Tokyo: Shueisha, 2009), 19–20.

124 **Shigeru Miyamoto was naked when the idea hit him:** Akinori Sao, "Nintendo Kurashikku Mini Famiri Konpyuta Kaihatsu Kinen Intabyu Daiikai Donki Kongu Hen" ("First Interview Commemorating the Development of the Family Computer Mini: Donkey Kong Chapter"), Nintendo.co.jp, October 14, 2016, https://topics.nintendo.co.jp/c/article/cb4c1aca-88fb-11e6-9b38-06 3b7ac45a6d.html.

124 **Miyamoto didn't have a lick of programming experience:** Chris Kohler, *Power-Up: How Japanese Video Games Gave the World an Extra Life* (New York: Dover, 2016), 33.

125 **For example, his game's hero would need to fit:** Satoru Iwata, "2: Obaoru wo Kiteu Riyu" (2: The Reason He Wears Overalls), "Shacho ga Kiku: New Supa Mario Burazazu Wii" ("The President Asks: New Super Mario Brothers Wii"), November 13, 2009, https://www.nintendo.co.jp/wii/interview/smnj /vol1/index2.html#list.

125 **"He was the first to bring that kawaii perspective to game characters":** Masayuki Uemura, personal interview, March 18, 2019.

126 **Gamers in the West dubbed *Donkey Kong* and other kawaii-style fare:** See, for example, the cover of the May 1983 issue of the magazine *Electronic Games* (Reese Publishing), which billed itself as "The PLAYERS GUIDE to THOSE 'CUTE' GAMES."

126 **"Their games don't cut it here":** Steve Bloom, *Video Invaders,* (New York: Arco, 1982), 42–43.

127 **"She's a symbol of friendship":** Ibid., 20, 101.

127 **"Even after they told me, 'Kitty's yours now'":** Ibid., 102.

127 **The word entered the lexicon in 1979:** Kazuma Yamane, *Gyaru no Kozo (The Structure of the Gal)* (Tokyo: Kodansha, 1993), 25.

128 **"If a 'gal' were an animal, she'd be a cat":** Ibid., 29.

128 **"gals embodied everything a proper young lady did not":** Koji Namba, "Concerning Youth Subcultures in the Postwar Era, vol. 5: 'Ko-gal' and 'Urahara-kei,'" Kwansei Gakuin University Sociology Department #100, March 2006.

129 **a concerted effort:** Shintaro Tsuji, *Sanrio Omoshiro Zukan: Daisuki! Haro Kiti (Sanrio Fun Visual Guide: We Love Hello Kitty!)*, Sanrio Video, November 1993, 30:00.

129 **Then, a miracle:** Apperosa Fukuoka, "Haro Kiti Ato Ten in Fukuoka" ("Hello Kitty Exhibit in Fukuoka"), Apperosa Fukuoka blog, October 7, 2011, http:// apefukuoka.blog55.fc2.com/blog-entry-24.html.

129 **It remains the only 1975-vintage Petit Purse:** Aaron Marcus, Masaaki Ku-

rosu, Xiaojuan Ma, and Ayako Hashizume, *Cuteness Engineering: Designing Adorable Products and Services* (Switzerland: Springer, 2017), 134.

129 **By 1979, 70 percent of Sanrio's new hires were female:** Uemae, *Sanrio's Miracle*, 113.

130 **Tsuji's Tokyo home in the late seventies:** Ibid., 87.

5: PLUGGING IN AND DROPPING OUT

131 **"The Sony Walkman has done more":** William Gibson, *Time Out*, October 6, 1993, 49.

131 **Steve Jobs was on his worst behavior:** Walter Isaacson, *Steve Jobs* (New York: Simon & Schuster, 2011), 146.

131 **Jobs was, to put it mildly, a Sony fanboy:** Alan Deutschman, *The Second Coming of Steve Jobs* (New York: Broadway Books, 2000), 29.

132 **He took it apart piece by piece:** George Beahm, *Steve Jobs's Life by Design: Lessons to Be Learned from His Last Lecture* (New York: St. Martin's Press, 2014), 29.

132 **"He didn't want to be IBM":** Ibid., 29.

133 **"4,000 Tiny Radios Stolen":** "4,000 Tiny Radios Stolen in Queens," *The New York Times*, January 24, 1958, 17.

133 **You'd naturally expect the victims to be outraged:** "How to Succeed by Being Robbed," Sony.net (page on company website), https://www.sony.net /SonyInfo/CorporateInfo/History/SonyHistory/1-07.html#block5 (accessed October 9, 2019).

134 **"Everybody in America wants big radios!":** Akio Morita, *Made in Japan* (New York: E. P. Dutton, 1986), 83.

134 **Morita met Masaru Ibuka, the man who would found Sony:** Ibid., 4, 30–32.

137 **Morita and Ibuka invented the word:** John Nathan, *Sony: The Private Life* (New York: Houghton Mifflin, 1999), 52.

137 **Through years of trial and error:** Martin Fransman, *Innovation Ecosystems: Increasing Competitiveness* (Cambridge: Cambridge University Press: 2018), 126–27.

137 **Sony wasn't first to get a transistor radio to market:** Michael B. Schiffer, *The Portable Radio in American Life* (Tucson: University of Arizona Press, 1992), 225.

138 **In Japan, Morita had special dress shirts:** Nathan, *Sony*, 35.

138 **At the peak of the phenomenon in 1969:** Schiffer, *The Portable Radio*, 223.

139 **The semiconductor industry analyst Jim Handy estimates:** David Laws, "13 Sextillion & Counting: The Long & Winding Road to the Most Frequently Manufactured Human Artifact in History," CHM Blog, April 2, 2018, https:// computerhistory.org/blog/13-sextillion-counting-the-long-winding-road-to -the-most-frequently-manufactured-human-artifact-in-history/.

139 **Morita was far from the only Japanese:** Morita, *Made in Japan*, 86.

139 **Better to eat in fancy restauraunts:** Ibid., 89.

139 **When thirty thousand of the latest transistor radios:** Ibid., 91.

140 **In spite of it all:** Ibid., 88.

141 **Opening day on Fifth Avenue was pandemonium:** "Chapter 13: Up through Trinitron—The Find at the IRE Show," Sony.net, undated, https://www.sony.net/SonyInfo/CorporateInfo/History/SonyHistory/1-13.html #block6 (accessed October 9, 2019).

141 **Behind the scenes, Morita ensured:** Ibid.

141 **Forging friendships with movers and shakers:** Nathan, *Sony*, 71.

141 **He shot footage of the glorious signage:** "Chapter 7 is 'Pocketable' Japanese-English? / The Neon Lights of Sukiyabashi," Sony.net, undated, https://www.sony.net/SonyInfo/CorporateInfo/History/SonyHistory/1-07 .html#block3.

141 **after catching one of Doyle Dane Bernbach's:** Nathan, *Sony*, 71.

142 **"The idea took shape":** Morita, *Made in Japan*, 79.

143 **"Back then, the black man wasn't being heard in society":** Lyle Owerko, *The Boombox Project: The Machines, the Music, and the Urban Underground* (New York: Harry N. Abrams, 2010), 26.

143 **In fact, the story is more nuanced:** The engineer Kozo Ohsone, who is generally credited as the head of the Walkman development effort, spoke about this at length to Seiji Munakata, "Kanrishitsu no Bakko de Sonii Kara Hitto ga Kieta" ("Too Many Managers Are Why Sony's Hits Dried Up"), *Nikkei Business*, May 30, 2016, https://business.nikkei.com/atcl/interview/16 /031800001/052700007/. See also Yasuo Kuroki, *Uookuman Kakutatakaeri* (*Walkman Struggles*) (Tokyo: Chikuma Shobo, 1990), 46.

143 **Apollo astronauts:** David Kamp, "Music on the Moon: Meet Mickey Kapp, Master of Apollo 11's Astro-Mixtapes," *Vanity Fair*, December 14, 2018, https://www.vanityfair.com/hollywood/2018/12/mickey-kapp-apollo-11 -astro-mixtapes.

143 **This caused a great deal of consternation:** Morita, *Made in Japan*, 79–80.

144 **anything you put in your ears to hear with:** Nathan, *Sony*, 154.

144 **Perhaps this was true abroad, too:** *Life*, October 24, 1960, 43.

144 **Today, headphones represent a ten-billion-dollar-a-year industry:** Grand View Research, "Earphones & Headphones Market Size, Share & Trends Analysis Report by Product," June 2019, https://www.grandviewresearch .com/industry-analysis/earphone-and-headphone-market.

144 **iPod sales have dwindled:** Mark Gurman, "Apple to Stop Reporting Unit Sales of iPhones, iPads and Macs," Bloomberg, November 1, 2018, https:// www.bloomberg.com/news/articles/2018-11-01/apple-to-stop-reporting -unit-sales-of-iphones-ipads-and-macs.

145 **purchased the headphone company Beats by Dre:** Heidi Moore, "Apple Buys Dr Dre's Beats for $3bn as Company Returns to Music Industry," *The Guardian*, May 28, 2014, https://www.theguardian.com/technology/2014 /may/28/apple-buys-beats-dr-dre-music-streaming.

145 **another Sony division already had a pair of lightweight headphones:**

Personal interview with the retired Sony engineer Shingo Tamura, conducted in Tokyo on January 29, 2019. Tamura played the role of matchmaker between Ohsone's tape recorder division and the hi-fi audio division, which developed headphones. "Mr. Ohsone was, how to put it, not a people person," Tamura told me. "He was someone who worked on his own timetable. Now, the man in charge of design and marketing for the Walkman, Yasuo Kuroki, knew he had to get the teams talking. So he called me." Tamura made the introduction and was in the room when the pair agreed to collaborate.

145 **"I was shocked the first time I heard it":** Kuroki, *Walkman Struggles,* 46.

146 **In an effort to offset the isolating nature:** Morita, *Made in Japan,* 81.

146 **"The public does not know what is possible":** Ibid.

146 **Five prototypes were loaded up:** Kuroki, *Walkman Struggles,* 61.

147 **"That's a function, not a product name":** This and subsequent quotes are from a personal interview with Tohru Kohno, conducted in Tokyo on March 12, 2019.

147 **Walkman it would be:** In fact, Morita briefly allowed Sony branches abroad to bestow their own names on the device. In a sign of the times the Americans suggested "Disco Jogger," then "Soundabout"; the British, "Stowaway"; and the Australians, "Freestyle." Morita finally put his foot down and standardized the name after getting numerous phone calls from foreign acquaintances asking for a "Walkman" instead of the other brand names. (Nathan, *Sony,* 154.)

148 **Citizens enjoyed an enviable combination of rapid economic growth, low inflation:** Tim McMahon, "Japanese Inflation Higher than U.S.—First Time Since 1978," Inflation Data Blog, June 28, 2014, https://inflationdata .com/articles/2014/06/28/japanese-inflation-higer-time-1978/.

149 **The first hit arcade game, *Pong*:** Steven L. Kent, *The Ultimate History of Video Games* (New York: Three Rivers Press, 2010), chapters 4–6.

150 **In a story now enshrined in Silicon Valley lore:** Owen W. Linzmayer, *Apple Confidential 2.0: The Definitive History of the World's Most Colorful Company* (San Francisco: No Starch Press, 2004), 3–4.

150 **"I knew that Jobs and Woz were fast friends":** Nolan Bushnell, "I'm Apple Co-founder Steve Wozniak, Ask Me Anything!" Reddit, undated, https://www .reddit.com/r/IAmA/comments/2e7z17/i_am_nolan_bushnell_founder_of _atari_chuck_e/ (accessed January 23, 2020).

150 **Pachinko, which was invented in Japan in the thirties:** Wolfram Manzenreiter, "Time, Space, and Money: The Cultural Dimensions of the 'Pachinko' Game," in *The Culture of Japan as Seen through Its Leisure,* ed. Sepp Linhart and Sabine Fruhstruck (Albany: State University of New York Press, 1998), 363.

151 **According to one estimate, so many Japanese adults play:** "Even without Casinos, Pachinko-Related Gambling Accounts for 4% of Japan's GDP," *The Japan Times,* February 7, 2017, https://www.japantimes.co.jp/news/2017 /02/07/national/even-without-casinos-pachinko-related-gambling-accounts -4-japans-gdp/.

151 **Nakamura was quick to realize the value:** Steven L. Kent, *The Ultimate His-*

tory of Video Games, vol. 2: *From Pong to Pokémon and Beyond* (New York: Three Rivers Press, 2010), chapter 6.

153 **The machines sucked in so much money:** Isao Yamazaki, *Nintendo Konpurito Gaido Gangu Hen* (*Nintendo Complete Guide: Toy Edition*) (Tokyo: Shufunotomo-sha, 2014), 135.

153 **"Critics say noisy space invaders":** Shiro Kunimitsu, "Inbeda Sakusen" ("Invader Invasion"), Rupotaju Nippon (Japanese Reportage), NHK, aired June 23, 1979.

154 **abroad they began to proliferate:** Mark J. P. Wolf, *The Medium of the Video Game* (Austin: University of Texas Press, 2010), 44.

154 **"We just got back from Paris":** Tom Zito, "Stepping to the Stereo Strut," *The Washington Post*, May 12, 1981, https://www.washingtonpost.com/archive/lifestyle/1981/05/12/stepping-to-the-stereo-strut.

155 **Now Sony did something similar:** Ibid.

155 **"One day, nobody in Tokyo had a Walkman":** Peter Barakan in personal discussion with the author, April 2018.

155 **Vitas Gerulaitis and Björn Borg picked them up on the tennis circuit:** Zito, "Stepping."

155 **"the disease of the eighties":** Ibid.

156 **"the middle- and upper-class answer to the [boom] box":** Matthew Lasar, *Radio 2.0: Uploading the First Broadcast Medium* (Santa Barbara, Calif.: Praeger, 2016), 23.

156 **"It gave Vancouver a kind of weird totalitarian grandeur":** Bruce Headlam, "Origins; Walkman Sounded Bell for Cyberspace," *The New York Times*, July 29, 1999, https://www.nytimes.com/1999/07/29/technology/origins-walkman-sounded-bell-for-cyberspace.html.

156 **"It's nice to hear Pavarotti":** Zito, "Stepping."

156 **A Japanese musicologist named Shuhei Hosokawa:** Personal interview conducted by the author with Shuhei Hosokawa in Kyoto, March 28, 2019.

158 **"Imagine a few years from now":** Randall Rothenberg, "Ads That Bash the Japanese: Just Jokes or Veiled Racism?" *The New York Times*, July 11, 1990.

159 **Part of this was because the Walkman represented such a breakthrough:** In fact a German-born, Brazil-raised inventor by the name of Andreas Pavel created what he called a "Stereobelt" in 1972 and patented it in Italy in 1977, a year before the Walkman's debut. Pavel shopped the idea around to several manufacturers but had yet to produce a product based on the idea when the Walkman came out, and there is no indication that anyone at Sony was aware of his work. Pavel sued Sony in 1990 and after many years of legal twists and turns, the company agreed to pay him an undisclosed amount of royalties in 2004. See Rebecca Tuhus-Dubrow, *Personal Stereo* (New York: Bloomsbury, 2017), 24, 34.

159 **The Walkman's marketing whiz, Kuroki, lamented:** Yasushi Watanabe and David L. McConnell, eds., *Soft Power Superpowers: Cultural and National Assets of Japan and the United States* (New York: Routledge, 2015), 104.

159 **In 1989, for a festive celebration of its fortieth anniversary:** Matt Alt,

"Japan's Forgotten First Astronaut," Néojaponisme, June 7, 2011, https://neojaponisme.com/2011/06/07/japans-forgotten-first-astronaut/.

THE NINETIES

161 **"GOODBYE, JAPAN INC.":** Unsigned editorial, "GOODBYE, JAPAN INC.," *The Washington Post*, November 25, 1997, https://www.washingtonpost.com/archive/opinions/1997/11/25/goodbye-japan-inc/.

161 **"It is the United States, not Japan, that is the master":** Sylvia Nasar, "The American Economy, Back on Top," *The New York Times*, February 27, 1994, https://www.nytimes.com/1994/02/27/business/the-american-economy-back-on-top.html.

161 **"There's a lot of interest in Japanese pop culture in America":** J. C. Herz, "GAME THEORY; The Japanese Embrace Hip-Hop, and Parappa Is Born," *The New York Times*, March 12, 1998, https://www.nytimes.com/1998/03/12/technology/game-theory-the-japanese-embrace-hip-hop-and-parappa-is-born.html.

161 **"Virtual Idol is just the right kind of magazine":** Andrew Pollack, "Japan's Newest Young Heartthrobs Are Sexy, Talented and Virtual," *The New York Times*, November 25, 1996, https://www.nytimes.com/1996/11/25/business/japan-s-newest-young-heartthrobs-are-sexy-talented-and-virtual.html.

161 **"She is twenty-six years old, beautiful, drives a BMW":** Kathryn Tolbert, "Japan's New Material Girls 'Parasite Singles' Put Off Marriage for Good Life," *The Washington Post*, February 10, 2000, https://www.washingtonpost.com/wp-srv/WPcap/2000-02/10/101r-021000-idx.html.

161 **"Japanese animation unleashes the mind":** Roger Ebert, "Japanese Animation Unleashes the Mind," Roger Ebert's Journal, October 7, 1999, https://www.rogerebert.com/rogers-journal/japanese-animation-unleashes-the-mind.

161 **"Maybe Japan's socially withdrawn kids":** Ryu Murakami, "Japan's Lost Generation," *AsiaNow*, May 1, 2000, https://edition.cnn.com/ASIANOW/time/magazine/2000/0501/japan.essaymurakami.html.

6: EMPIRE OF THE SCHOOLGIRLS

163 **"You learn much more about a country":** Joshua Green, "Inside Man," *The Atlantic*, April 2010. https://www.theatlantic.com/magazine/archive/2010/04/inside-man/307992/

164 **The author of *The Hunger Games* swears:** Akiko Fujita, "'The Hunger Games,' a Japanese Original?," ABC News, March 22, 2012, https://abcnews.go.com/blogs/headlines/2012/03/the-hunger-games-a-japanese-original.

164 **Kuriyama went on to play a similarly shocking role:** Lewis Wallace, "Tarantino Names Top 20 Movies Since *Reservoir Dogs*," *Wired*, August 17, 2009, https://www.wired.com/2009/08/tarantino-names-top-20-movies-since-reservoir-dogs/.

165 **Paper baron Ryoei Saito:** Doug Struck, "Van Gogh's Portrait in Intrigue," *The Washington Post*, July 29, 1999, https://www.washingtonpost.com/archive/lifestyle/1999/07/29/van-goghs-portrait-in-intrigue.

165 **$500 cups of coffee:** Eric Johnston, "Lessons from When the Bubble Burst," *The Japan Times*, January 6, 2009, https://www.japantimes.co.jp/news/2009/01/06/reference/lessons-from-when-the-bubble-burst.

165 **all of the land in Japan to $18 trillion:** Martin Fackler, "Take It from Japan: Bubbles Hurt," *The New York Times*, December 25, 2005, https://www.nytimes.com/2005/12/25/business/yourmoney/take-it-from-japan-bubbles-hurt.html.

166 **"Stock-Crazed Rogue CEO":** "Kabukurui Wanman Keiei de Sanrio ga Daiakaji ni Tenraku" ("Stock-Crazed Rogue CEO Drives Sanrio Deep into Red"), *Shukan Tiimisu*, November 7, 1990, 159.

166 **"I couldn't sleep without sleeping pills":** Tsuji, *These Are Sanrio's Secrets*, 13.

168 **she marched into a managing director's office:** Yamaguchi, *Tears of Kitty*, 148.

168 **Her destination was:** Ozaki, *MY KITTY*, 56.

168 **one of Sanrio's Gift Gates:** Ibid., 106.

168 **Thanks to these events:** Yamaguchi, *Tears of Kitty*, 161.

170 **The word was all anyone was talking about that year:** Katsushi Kuronuma later compiled his reporting into a book entitled *Enjo Kosai Joshi Kokosei no Kiken na Hokago* (*Compensated Dating: High School Girls in Danger after School*) (Tokyo: Bungeishunju, 1996).

171 **"Why do you sell yourself to men?":** Yamaguchi, *Tears of Kitty*, 162.

172 **So many of Yamaguchi's grown-up Kitty accessories sold:** Mark I. West, ed., *The Japanification of Children's Popular Culture: From Godzilla to Miyazaki* (Lanham, Md.: Scarecrow Press, 2009), 33.

172 **"communication cosmetics":** Yamane, *Structure*, 151.

172 **the king and queen of Japanese pop are on a date:** ASAYAN, "Komuro Gyaruson Tokushu Tomomi Kahara" ("Komuro Gal Song Special: Tomomi Kahara"), *TV Tokyo*, June 2, 1996, https://www.youtube.com/watch?v=EO3hDXsWl2s.

173 **"an expensive box":** Ken Belson and Brian Bremner, *Hello Kitty: The Remarkable Story of Sanrio and the Billion Dollar Feline Phenomenon* (Singapore: Wiley, 2004), 47.

173 **"If the dancers aren't sexy, fathers won't come":** Ibid., 49.

176 **"I never, ever sing":** Yuichi Yasutomo, personal interview conducted by the author, December 7, 2018.

177 **pornography spurred the development:** Jonathan Coopersmith, "Pornography, Technology, and Progress," *Icon* 4 (1998): 94–95.

177 **Sony's executives, reluctant to commit:** "In fact, the only reason I got involved was because I wanted to do home karaoke," said the retired Sony executive Shigeo Maruyama in 2016. "We didn't have streaming karaoke at the time." See Shigeo Murayama and Nobuo Kawakami, "Kutaragi ga omoshirokatta kara yatteita dake: Pureisuteshon no tateyakusha ni kiku sono hiwa" (" 'I Only Did It Because Kutaragi Thought It Was Interesting': Secrets from a

Driving Force of the PlayStation"), Denfaminicogamer, October 25, 2016, 2, https://news.denfaminicogamer.jp/interview/ps_history/.

180 **So it happened that Yasutomo accidentally invented:** Personal email correspondence, December 10, 2018.

180 **They used it to guide them in everything:** Hiromichi Ugaya, *J-poppu to ha Nanika? (What Is J-pop?)* (Tokyo: Iwanami Shinsho, 2005), 191.

181 **The government so thoroughly dithered its response:** James Sterngold, "Gang in Kobe Organizes Aid for People in Quake," *The New York Times*, January 22, 1995, 9.

182 **College grads, both male and female, desperately cast about for jobs:** Genda Yuji, "The Lingering Effects of Japan's 'Employment Ice Age,'" Nippon.com, May 23, 2018, https://www.nippon.com/en/currents/d00406/the-lingering-effects-of-japan's-employment-ice-age.html.

183 **But entrepreneur Akihiro Yokoi:** Akihiro Yokoi, *Tamagocchi Tanjoki (A Record of the Birth of Tamagotchi)* (Tokyo: KK Bestsellers, 1997), 36.

184 **Aki Maita:** Ibid., 109.

184 **Flipping through girls' fashion magazines:** Ibid., 48.

185 **Then twenty-five, she was only a little older:** Ibid., 51.

185 **For this, Maita and her co-workers:** Ibid., 185.

189 **By the peak of the phenomenon, in 1996, ten million beepers:** Jyoji Meguro, "0840, 724106, 14106: pokeberu ga 39nen no rekishi ni maku" ("0840, 724106, 14106: Curtain Falls on 39 Years of Pager History"), *Cnet Japan*, March 13, 2007, https://japan.cnet.com/article/20345133/.

190 **Emma Miyazawa:** This scene was assembled from recollections on several blogs, including:

Tsukiyono, "SP Tsurete Tamagocchi wo Kudasai (warai)" ("Special: One Tamagotchi Please LOL"), Tsukiyono no Burogu, April 21, 2016, https://ameblo.jp/tsukiyono-kd/entry-12152623726.html.

Unsigned, "Miyazawa Keiichi no Mago ga Kataru: Ojisan no Sugosugi Hiwa" ("Keiichi Miyazawa's Granddaughter Speaks: Incredible Behind the Scenes Talk about Her Grandfather") Josei Jishin, February 2, 2015, https://jisin.jp/domestic/1622622/.

Merenge, "Miyazawa Keiichi no Magomusume Merenge no Kimochi Rafura Miyazawa Ema 8gatsu 22nichi" ("Merenge's Thoughts on Keiichi Miyazawa's Granddaughter Emma Miyazawa La Fleur, 8/22"), Merenge no Kimochi Hatsu: Geino Joho, August 22, 2015, https://meringue4c.blog.ss-blog.jp/2015-08-22-2.

192 **When Apple launched the iPhone in 2007:** Yukari Iwatani Kane, "Apple's Latest iPhone Sees Slow Japan Sales," *The Wall Street Journal*, September 15, 2009, https://www.wsj.com/articles/SB122143317323034023.

7: A NEW ANIME CENTURY

194 **"The vast majority of Japanese animation is made":** Mami Sunada, dir., *The Kingdom of Dreams and Madness*, Toho Company, 2013.

194 **On July 18, 1997, a strange advertisement:** *Asahi Shimbun,* July 18, 1997, archived from https://evacollector.com/matome-newspaper/.

195 *The End of Evangelion* **would go on:** Motion Picture Producers Association of Japan, Inc., "Kako Haikyu Shunyu Joi Sakuhin 1997 1gatsu—12gatsu" ("Past Works Ranked by Earnings: 1997 January–December"), Eiren.org, undated, http://www.eiren.org/toukei/1997.html.

195 **Later,** *The End of Evangelion* **would win:** "Eva ga Goruden Gurosu Wadai Sho wo Jusho" ("Eva Wins Golden Gross Most Talked about Award"), Evangelion.co.jp, December 6, 2007, https://www.evangelion.co.jp/1_0/news/det _10641.html.

195 **As** *Evangelion***'s dark fantasy gripped the nation:** *Asahi Shimbun,* "Bumu ga Utsusu Yanda Sedai" ("Boom Reflects Sick Generaion"), July 19, 1997.

196 *Evangelion* **was the latest creation of an animation studio:** Yasuhiro Takeda, *The Notenki Memoirs: Studio Gainax and the Men Who Created "Evangelion"* (Houston: ADVManga, 2005), 167–71.

197 **It looked startlingly professional:** Ibid., 50–54.

197 **The staff was so perpetually behind schedule:** Dani Cavallaro, *The Art of Studio Gainax: Experimentation, Style and Innovation at the Leading Edge of Anime* (Jefferson, N.C.: McFarland, 2009), 59.

198 *Evangelion***'s creator and director:** Aaron Stewart-Ahn, "Neverending *Evangelion*: How Hideaki Anno Turned Obsessions and Depression into an Anime Phenomenon," Polygon, June 19, 2019, https://www.polygon.com/2019/6/19 /18683634/neon-genesis-evangelion-hideaki-anno-depression-shinji-anime -characters-movies.

198 **When the first rays of the sun crept over Tokyo's business district:** The descriptions, statistics, and quotes in this section were compiled and sourced from:

Masanobu Komaki, *Kido Senshi Gandamu no Jidai 1981.2.22 Anime Shin Seiki Senngen* (*The Era of "Mobile Suit Gundam": 2.22.1981 Anime New Century Declaration*) (Tokyo: Takeda Random House Japan, 2009), 23–37.

"Ano Toki Anime ga Kawatta: 1981 nen Anime Shin Seiki Sengen" ("The Moment Anime Changed: The 1981 Anime New Century Declaration"), *Asahi Shimbun,* October 17, 2009, 29.

"Dokyumento Anime Shin Seiki Sengen" ("A Documentary of the Anime New Century Declaration"), NHK, aired July 27, 2009.

199 **The show was designed:** "Gandamu Tanjo Hiwa" ("Secrets of Gundam's Creation"), NHK BS1, aired December 6, 2018.

200 **This wasn't uncommon; unable to find "normal" jobs:** Eiji Otsuka, "Otaku Culture as 'Conversion Literature,'" in *Debating Otaku in Contemporary Japan,* ed. Patrick Galbraith, Thiam Huat Kam, and Björn-Ole Kamm (New York: Bloomsbury, 2015), xiv.

201 **"The true theme of** *Gundam* **is a renaissance for humanity!":** Osamu Isawa, *"Gandamu* no Tema ha Saisei da" ("The True Theme of Gundam Is a Renaissance for Humanity"), *Asahi Shimbun,* March 25, 1981, 16.

203 **"Everyone, take it easy!":** Komaki, *The Era of "Mobile Suit Gundam,"* 32.

203 **"This is more than an event. It's a *matsuri*":** Ibid.

204 **In the sixties the psychoanalyst:** Takeo Doi and John Bester, trans., *The Anatomy of Dependence* (New York: Kodansha America, 2014).

204 **"Society embraces an increasing number of people":** Lise Skov and Brian Moeran, eds., *Women, Media, and Consumption in Japan* (New York: Routledge, 1995), 250.

205 **The very first known Japanese cosplayer:** Mari Kotani, "Mari Kotani, Pioneer of Japanese Cosplay—Origins," FutureLearn, undated, https://www .futurelearn.com/courses/intro-to-japanese-subculture/0/steps/23609 (accessed January 20, 2020).

206 **"I want to see the movie":** "Yangu Datte Shinbo Tsuyoiyo: Anime Eiga ni 600nin Gyoretsu" ("Youth Sure Are Patient: 600 Line Up for Anime Film"), *Asahi Shimbun,* March 14, 1981, 23.

206 **The movie went on to gross:** "Gandamu de Eigaka Sareta Sakuhin wo Furukaeru" ("Looking Back at the Making of the *Gundam* Movies"), Datagundam .com, October 11, 2018, https://datagundam.com/memo/gundam-movies/.

206 **sell an astounding thirty million:** Ibid.

206 **Supply ran so low and demand so high:** "Ijo Ninki no Puramoderu" ("Insanely Popular Plastic Models"), *Asahi Shimbun,* March 1, 1982, 3.

207 **One of them was a young Hayao Miyazaki:** Yoshiyuki Tomino, "Jidai wo Kakeru Tomino Yoshiyuki 4 Miyazaki Hayao Kantoku ni Chikazukitai" ("Driving the Era: Tomino Yoshiyuki 4: I Wanted to Get Close to Director Hayao Miyazaki"), *Mainichi Shimbun,* November 10, 2009, https://web.archive .org/web/20091124041900/http://mainichi.jp/select/opinion/kakeru/news /20091110ddm004070227000c.html.

207 **Most fans referred to themselves:** Matt Alt, "What Kind of Otaku Are You?" *Néojaponisme,* April 2, 2008, https://neojaponisme.com/2008/04/02 /what-kind-of-otaku-are-you/.

207 **The bestselling fantasy novelist Sumiyo Imaoka:** Parissa Haghirian, *Japanese Consumer Dynamics* (New York: Palgrave Macmillan, 2011), 147.

208 **It was 1983 when a young journalist:** Personal interview with Akio Nakamori, conducted May 28, 2014, Tokyo, Japan.

210 **"Tomino did not realize the impact":** Patrick W. Galbraith, *The Moé Manifesto: An Insider's Look at the Worlds of Manga, Anime, and Gaming* (Singapore: Tuttle Publishing, 2014), 181.

211 **"It was like, finally, we had a word for them":** Personal interview, Tomohiro Machiyama, conducted April 5, 2014, via Skype.

211 **In 1989, a young man by the name of Tsutomu Miyazaki:** Ibid.

212 **There was pre-Otomo and post-Otomo:** Nobunaga Minami, *Gendai Manga no Bokentachi: Otomo Katsuhiro Kara Ono Natsume Made* (*Adventurers of Modern Comics: From Otomo Katsuhiro to Natsume Ono*) (Tokyo: NTT Shuppan, 2008), 32–38.

212 **Upon meeting Otomo around this time:** Kei Ishizaka, *Suntory Saturday Waiting Bar Avanti,* "Vol. 132," Tokyo FM Podcast, October 4, 2008, https:// podcasts.tfm.co.jp/podcasts/tokyo/avanti/avanti_vol132.mp3.

213 **Tellingly, some film critics invoked comparisons:** Dave Kehr, "Japanese Cartoon 'Akira' Isn't One for the Kids," *Chicago Tribune*, March 30, 1990.

215 **In 1982, President Reagan's staunchly anti-regulation:** James B. Twitchell, *Adcult USA* (New York: Columbia University Press, 1997), 103–4.

216 **"We knew they would appeal to kids in America, just as they did in Japan":** Gary Cross and Gregory Smits, "Japan, the U.S. and the Globalization of Children's Consumer Culture," *Journal of Social History* 38, no. 4 (2005): 873.

216 **the "media mix":** Marc Steinberg, *Anime's Media Mix: Franchising Toys and Characters in Japan* (Minneapolis: University of Minnesota Press, 2012).

217 **1996 Anime Expo in Anaheim:** As reported on Animecons.com, "Anime Expo 1996 Information," https://animecons.com/events/info/150/anime-expo-1996 (accessed January 20, 2020).

217 **A respectable showing:** Comic Market Preparations Committee, "What Is the Comic Market?," Comiket.co.jp, February 6, 2008, https://www.comiket.co.jp/info-a/WhatIsEng080225.pdf.

218 **Reveling in the attention, Anno gleefully teased:** Lawrence Eng, "In the Eyes of Hideaki Anno, Writer and Director of *Evangelion*," Evaotaku.com, undated, http://www.evaotaku.com/omake/anno.html (accessed January 20, 2020).

218 **"Anno wanted his characters":** Personal communication with Michael House, January 27, 2020.

218 **There is anime for the very young:** Hiroko Tabuchi, "In Search of Adorable, as Hello Kitty Gets Closer to Goodbye," *The New York Times*, May 14, 2010, https://www.nytimes.com/2010/05/15/business/global/15kitty.html.

219 **In Japan, anime is so widely accepted:** CINEMA Rankingu Tsushin, "Rekidai Rankingu: Rekidai Koshu Besto 100" ("Historic Rankings: Top 100 Earners"), Kogyotsushin.com, January 19, 2020, http://www.kogyotsushin.com/archives/alltime/.

219 **The Academy only reluctantly:** Robert Osbourne, *85 Years of the Oscar: The Official History of the Academy Awards* (New York: Abbeville Press, 2013), 357.

219 **This was a seriously strange turn of events:** "Miyazaki Mum on Oscar, Citing War," *The Japan Times*, March 25, 2003, https://www.japantimes.co.jp/news/2003/03/25/national/miyazaki-mum-on-oscar-citing-war.

220 **"It is regrettable that I cannot rejoice":** Ibid.

220 **in the wake of the meltdowns:** Egan Loo, "Ghibli Hangs Anti-Nuclear Power Banner on Rooftop," Anime News Network, June 17, 2011, https://www.animenewsnetwork.com/interest/2011-06-17/ghibli-hangs-anti-nuclear-power-banner-on-rooftop.

220 **"When I first saw *Totoro*,"** Roger Ebert, "My Neighbor Totoro," RogerEbert.com, December 23, 2001, https://www.rogerebert.com/reviews/great-movie-my-neighbor-totoro-1993.

220 **For his part, Miyazaki claims to be baffled:** Bill Higgins, "Hollywood Flashback: 13 Years Ago, 'Spirited Away' Was an Anime Smash," *The Hollywood Reporter*, December 15, 2016, https://www.hollywoodreporter.com

/news/hollywood-flashback-13-years-spirited-away-was-an-anime-smash
-955244.

221 **Tellingly, Studio Ghibli chose to shutter:** Brian Ashcraft, "Studio Ghibli Is
Not Dead Yet," Kotaku, August 4, 2014, https://kotaku.com/studio-ghibli-is
-not-dead-yet-1615520289.

222 **James Franco's character:** W. David Marx, "'30 Rock' Features the Japanese
Body Pillow Meme," CNN Travel, January 19, 2010, http://travel.cnn.com
/tokyo/none/30-rock-plays-japanese-body-pillow-meme-989189/.

222 **American anime fans remain defensive enough:** Gita Jackson, "It's Time
to Stop Acting Like Nobody Watches Anime," Kotaku, March 12, 2015,
https://kotaku.com/it-s-time-to-stop-acting-like-nobody-watches-anime
-1823713450.

8: GAMING THE WORLD

224 **I think video games are evil:** Christian Nutt and Yoshi Sato, "CEDEC 09:
Keynote—Gundam Creator: 'Video Games Are Evil'," *Gamasutra,* September
7, 2009. https://www.gamasutra.com/view/news/116062/CEDEC_09_Key
note__Gundam_Creator_Video_Games_Are_Evil.php

224 **Video games are bad for you?:** David Sheff, *Game Over: How Nintendo Conquered the World* (Wilton, Conn.: GamePress, 1999), 208.

224 **It is July of 1999 at the Mall of America:** This scene is a composite compiled from several sources:
Justin Berube, "Poke Memories," Nintendo World Report, February 27, 2016,
http://www.nintendoworldreport.com/feature/41952/poke-memories
-justin-berube-features-editor.
John Lippmann, "Creating the Craze for Pokémon: Licensing Agent Bet on
U.S. Kids," *The Wall Street Journal,* August 16, 1999, https://www.wsj.com
/articles/SB934753154504300864.
Mary Roach, "Cute Inc.," *Wired,* December 1, 1999, https://www.wired.com
/1999/12/cute/.
Andrew Vestal, "Pokémon League Summer Training Tour 1999," The Gaming
Intelligence Agency, undated, http://archive.thegia.com/features/f990814
.html (accessed December 10, 2019).
Andrew Vestal, email interview, October 2019.

225 **Truth be told, Nintendo didn't have particularly high expectations:**
Howard Chua-Eoan and Tim Larimer, "Beware of the Pokemania," *Time,*
November 14, 1999, https://content.time.com/time/magazine/article/0,9171
,34342-3,00.html.

225 **Its creator, the veteran engineer Gunpei Yokoi:** Gunpei Yokoi and Take-
fumi Makino, *Yokoi Gunpei Game Kan* (*Yokoi Gunpei's House of Games*) (Tokyo:
Chikuma Bunko, 2015), 151.

226 **"I was told":** Kohler, *Power-Up,* 225.

226 **Just twelve months later, at the end of 1999, Nintendo announced:**

"Pokemon Red Version History," IGN Entertainment, April 3, 2012, https://www.ign.com/wikis/pokemon-red-blue-yellow-version/History.

226 **"Pokemania," *Time* declared it:** "Pokemania! Crazy for Pokemon," *Time*, November 22, 1999, http://content.time.com/time/world/article/0,8599,205 4246,00.html.

227 *Time*'s **breathless coverage:** Ibid.

227 **The monsters that paraded through its virtual world:** Ibid.

227 **It proved so popular in America that when Warner Bros.:** Fred Ladd and Harvey Deneroff, *Astro Boy and Anime Come to the Americas* (Jefferson, N.C.: McFarland, 2009), 120. See also David Plotz, "Pokémon: Little. Yellow. Different. Better," *Slate,* November 12, 1999, https://slate.com/news-and-politics /1999/11/pokemon.html.

227 **"Tajiri is the kind of person the Japanese call *otaku*":** Chua-Eoan and Larimer, "Beware of the Pokemania."

228 **Tajiri's first exposure to video games:** Kohler, *Power-Up,* 225.

229 **What seemed a narrative device:** "Urutoraman ga henshin suru toki ni" ("When Ultraman Transforms") M-78shop, undated, https://www.m-78shop .jp/ultra/ (accessed January 20, 2020).

229 **An early Marusan hire with a keen eye for new trends:** Personal interview with Saburo Ishizuki, June 14, 2018.

230 **A decade before George Lucas realized of *Star Wars*:** Kevin Jagernauth, "'All the Money Is in the Action Figures': George Lucas Slams Empty Hollywood Blockbusters," IndieWire, January 30, 2015, https://www.indiewire .com/2015/01/all-the-money-is-in-the-action-figures-george-lucas-slams -empty-hollywood-blockbusters-267636/.

231 **Reporters shadowing the imperial family:** "Master Hiromiya's Shopping Trip," Chunichi Newsreel n.o. 696-1, May 1967, https://www.youtube.com /watch?v=x41SCa-1ydU.

231 **The postwar fiction writer Yukio Mishima penned:** Yukio Mishima, *Ketteiban Mishimi Yukio Zenshu* (*The Collected Works of Yukio Mishima,* vol. 35), (Tokyo: Shinchosha, 2003), 288.

231 **In 1990, when Satoshi Tajiri drafted the proposal for *Capsule Monsters*:** "A History of Pokémon through the Internal List—Lost Pokémon," Helix chamber.com, August 24, 2018, https://helixchamber.com/2018/08/24/lost pokemon/. The same website has archived the proposal document in its entirety at https://helixchamber.com/media/capsule-monsters/.

232 **derived from the Japanese word *paku-paku*:** Kohler, *Power-Up,* 22.

232 **Namco only changed the title:** Ibid., 200.

234 *Donkey . . . what? Donkey Hong? Konkey Hong?:* Sheff, *Game Over,* 49.

235 *Donkey Kong*'s **origins could actually be traced back to a cartoon:** Ibid., 47. While Yokoi never specified the cartoon in question, it seems to be the Fleischer Brothers' 1934 short "A Dream Walking."

235 **Introduced to Yamauchi by a family friend:** Ibid., 46.

235 **Miyamoto's manager, Gunpei Yokoi, came up with the core idea:** Yokoi

and Makino, *Yokoi Gunpei Game Kan* (*Yokoi Gunpei's House of Games*) (Tokyo: Chikuma Shobo, 2015), 119–21.

235 **This classic trope, incidentally, also inspired:** Toru Iwatani, *Pakku Man no Gemu Nyumon* (*An Introduction to Pac-Man's Methodology*) (Tokyo: Kadokawa, 2009), 45.

236 **Miyamoto originally wanted to call him Mister Video:** Satoru Iwata, "2: Obaoru wo Kiteu Riyu" ("2: The Reason He Wears Overalls"), Shacho ga Kiku: New Supa Mario Burazazu Wii (The President Asks: New Super Mario Brothers Wii), November 13, 2009.

236 **"It's a good game" was Yamauchi's curt response:** Sheff, *Game Over*, 49.

236 **For years to come, Nintendo of America employees:** Jake Rossen, "How Nintendo Conquered Manhattan in 1985," Mental Floss, March 20, 2015, retrieved from https://www.mentalfloss.com/article/62232/how-nintendo -conquered-manhattan-1985.

237 **After a catastrophically oversized investment:** Richard Hooper, "The Man Who Made 'The Worst Video Game in History,'" BBC News, February 22, 2016, https://www.bbc.com/news/magazine-35560458.

237 **Masayuki Uemura is the architect of Nintendo's "Family Computer":** The discussion that follows, and the quotes within, are from a personal interview conducted with Uemura at Ritsumeikan University on March 18, 2019.

241 **It arrived seven months after the enactment of a new law:** Kenjiro Ishikawa, *Randomaku Shohin no Kenkyu* 3 (*Landmark Product Research* 3) (Tokyo: Dobunkan, 2008), 219.

241 **twenty-six thousand video game arcades:** Yasunori Nakafuji, "Supesu In-beda Daibakuhatsu, Soshite Reja Kakumei e" ("Space Invaders Blows Up, Revolutionizes Leisure"), CESA, June 6, 2013, http://www.cesa.or.jp/efforts /keifu/nakafuji/nakafuji03.html.

241 **greatly alarmed authorities:** Masayuki Uemura, Koichi Hosoi, and Akinori Nakamura, *Famicom to Sono Jidai* (*The Famicom and Its Era*) (Tokyo: NTT Shup-pan, 2013), 197–99.

241 **Critics of arcades had pushed for similar ordinances in the United States:** Carly A. Kocurek, *Coin-Operated Americans: Rebooting Boyhood at the Video Game Arcade* (Minneapolis: University of Minnesota Press, 2015), 67.

241 **The pull of this newfound pastime of home gaming:** Luke Plunkett, "When Mario Had a Best-Selling . . . Book?" Kotaku, May 18, 2011, https:// kotaku.com/when-mario-had-a-best-selling-book-5802916.

241 **That video games might have the potential to transcend:** The mania surrounding *Dragon Quest III*, including scenes of huge queues and reports of children skipping school, was widely covered by newspapers and mainstream television news programs such as *FNN Date Line* in early February of 1988.

243 **By 1993, Nintendo was making more money than all of Hollywood's:** Sheff, *Game Over*, 9; 439.

243 **In the States, for example, more children were playing Nintendo:** Ibid., 8.

244 **Echoing Nintendo of America's initial reaction:** Michael Katz, "Interview: Michael Katz (2006-04-28) by Sega-16," Segaretro.com, April 4, 2006, https://segaretro.org/Interview:_Michael_Katz_(2006-04-28)_by_Sega-16.

244 **Sega did everything they could:** Sheff, *Game Over,* 445.

245 **Never a company at the forefront of technological innovation:** Gunpei Yokoi, *Monotsukuri no Inobeshon Kareta Gijutsu no Suihei Shiko to ha Nanika? (Creation and Innovation: What Is "Lateral Thinking with Withered Technology"?)* (Tokyo: P-Vine Books, 2012).

246 **"We called it the Lameboy":** Personal interview with Rebecca Heineman, April 3, 2019.

246 **One specimen, carried into Kuwait:** Cameron Sherrill, "This Game Boy Survived a Bombing in the Gulf War," *Esquire,* April 21, 2019, https://www.esquire.com/lifestyle/a27183316/nintendo-game-boy-survived-gulf-war/.

247 **It also proved incredibly popular among girls:** Keith Stuart, "Nintendo Game Boy—25 Facts for Its 25th Anniversary," *The Guardian,* April 21, 2014, https://www.theguardian.com/technology/2014/apr/21/nintendo-game-boy-25-facts-for-its-25th-anniversary.

247 **"I have become quite a fan," admitted Hillary Clinton:** Phil Edwards, "The Sad Story of How Hillary Clinton Got Addicted to Game Boy," Vox, April 20, 2015, https://www.vox.com/2015/4/20/8459219/hillary-clinton-gameboy.

248 **"The combination of portability and kawaii design sensibilities":** Keith Stuart, "Why Only Nintendo Understands Handheld Gaming," *The Guardian,* September 29, 2015, https://www.theguardian.com/technology/2015/sep/29/nintendo-handheld-gaming-sony-playstation-vita.

248 *A Childhood in Solitude:* Fumio Nakamura, *Kodomo-beya no Kodoku Terebi Geemu Daicichi Sedai no Yuke (A Childhood in Solitude: The Fate of the First Generation of Home Gamers)* (Tokyo: Gakuyo Shobo, 1989).

249 **"There was still so much nature then":** Satoshi Tajiri and Tsunekazu Ishihara, "Pokemon Supesharu Taidan Tajiri Satoshi vs. Ishihara Tsunekazu" ("Pokémon: A Special Talk between Satoshi Tajiri and Tsunekazu Ishihara"), Nintendo.co.jp, undated, https://www.nintendo.co.jp/nom/0007/taidan1/index.html (accessed January 20, 2020).

249 **"I couldn't catch bugs anymore":** Ibid.

250 **"Ever since I was a teenager":** "The Ultimate Game Freak," *Time,* November 22, 1999, http://content.time.com/time/magazine/article/0,9171,2040095,00.html.

250 **"It *is* my childhood":** Tajiri and Ishihara, "Pokémon: A Special Talk."

250 **The Game Boy wasn't the first handheld:** The Lynx beat the Game Boy to market as the first cartridge-based networkable game system, but Yokoi actually created the first commercially available networkable gaming device: Nintendo's 1983 Yakuman, a mah-jongg machine that could be connected to opponents' Yakumans with a cable for multiplayer matches.

251 **"That cable really got me interested":** "The Ultimate Game Freak."

9: THE ANTISOCIAL NETWORK

253 **Train Man is your stereotypical otaku:** The descriptions here are gathered from a variety of sources, including an archive of the original thread on the topic.

Densha Otoko, "Sure Keitai 2channeru" ("Train Man Thread, 2channel Mobile"), Densyaotoko.3.tool.ms, November 7, 2007, http://densyaotoko.3 .tool.ms.

Brian Ashcraft, "Train Man's Love Train," *Wired*, January 12, 2007, https:// www.wired.com/2007/01/train-mans-love/.

Alisa Freedman, "Train Man and the Gender Politics of Japanese 'Otaku' Culture: The Rise of New Media, Nerd Heroes and Consumer Communities," *Intersections: Gender and Sexuality in Asia and the Pacific* 20 (April 2009), http:// intersections.anu.edu.au/issue20/freedman.htm.

254 **"Young People, Don't Hate Sex":** Paul Wiseman, "No Sex Please—We're Japanese," *USA Today*, June 2, 2004, http://www.usatoday.com/news/world /2004-06-02-japan-women-usat_x.htm.

255 **It sells a quarter of a million copies:** Ashcraft, "Train Man."

256 **To this very day, even after a great deal of digging:** See, for example, Atsushi Suzuki, *Densha Otoko ha Darenanoka Netaka Suru Komyunikeshon (Who Is Train Man? The Meme-ification of Communication)* (Tokyo: Chuo Koronsha, 2005).

256 **"All of a sudden":** Hiroki Azuma, *Otaku: Japan's Database Animals* (Minneapolis: University of Minnesota Press, 2009), 117.

257 **Politicians court the Akihabara vote:** Jean Snow, "Akihabara Nerds Rally Behind Likely Japan PM," *Wired*, September 15, 2000, https://www.wired .com/2008/09/japan-pm-candid/000.

257 **Even staid organizations:** See, for example:

Matt Alt, "MBA? CPA? LOL!," AltJapan.typepad.com, October 6, 2012, https://altjapan.typepad.com/my_weblog/2012/10/accounting-moé.html.

Matt Alt, "Yokohama Police Mascots More Cute Than Cop," CNN Travel, September 7, 2010, http://travel.cnn.com/tokyo/life/yokohamas-cop-charac ter-caper-724032/.

Matt Alt, "Japan's Cute Army," *The New Yorker*, November 30, 2015, https:// www.newyorker.com/culture/culture-desk/japans-cute-army.

257 **"We wanna do that for real":** Steve Rose, "Hollywood Is Haunted by *Ghost in the Shell*," *The Guardian*, October 19, 2009, https://www.theguardian.com /film/2009/oct/19/hollywood-ghost-in-the-shell.

257 **website called 4chan:** The basic details of 4chan's launch, structure, and early years are gleaned from a variety of sources, including:

Nick Bilton, "One on One: Christopher Poole, Founder of 4chan," *The New York Times*, March 19, 2010.

Caitlin Dewey, "Absolutely Everything You Need to Know to Understand 4chan, the Internet's Own Bogeyman," *The Washington Post*, September 26, 2014.

Christopher Poole, "IAM Christopher Poole, aka 'moot,' founder of 4chan & Canvas. AMA!" Reddit, March 29, 2011, https://www.reddit.com/r/IAmA/comments/gdzfi/iam_christopher_poole_aka_moot_founder_of_4chan/.

258   **In 2019, it was visited by forty to sixty million:** "4chan.org: Web Analysis and Traffic History for 11 Years," Traffic and Alexa Rank History, https://www.rank2traffic.com/4chan.org (accessed January 3, 2020).

258   **Hiroyuki Nishimura was once a lonely man, too:** This section was based on reporting from a number of sources, including:

Dale Beran, *It Came from Something Awful: How a Toxic Troll Army Memed Donald Trump into Office* (New York: St Martin's Press, 2019).

Norimitsu Onishi, "Japanese Find a Forum to Vent Most-Secret Feelings," *The New York Times*, May 9, 2004, https://www.nytimes.com/2004/05/09/world/japanese-find-a-forum-to-vent-most-secret-feelings.html.

Shii, "2channel," *Everything Shii Knows*, August 2004, http://shii.bibanon.org/shii.org/knows/2channel.html.

259   **"Otaku of all types," evangelized one early chronicler:** "The Second Channel: 2channel—Part I," Yotsuba Society, July 5, 2011, http://yotsubasociety.org/the2ndchannel_pti/.

260   **A user calling himself Akky:** Mutsuko Murakami, "Playing to the Cowed: A Japanese Consumer Incites a Web Revolt," Asiaweek, 2001, http://web.archive.org/web/20010713214149/http://www.asiaweek.com/asiaweek/technology/990806/web_revolt.html (accessed January 20, 2020).

260   **The R&B vocalist was having a very bad 2001:** "TV Comedian Indicted over Drug Use," *The Japan Times*, December 29, 2001, https://www.japantimes.co.jp/news/2001/12/29/national/tv-comedian-indicted-over-drug-use/. See also Mark D. West, *Secrets, Sex and Spectacle: The Rules of Scandal in Japan and the United States* (Chicago: University of Chicago Press, 2006), 189; 203.

260   **Mega-particle Tashiro Cannon:** Dojin Yogo no Kiso Chishiki (A Primer of Fanzine Slang), "Tashiroho / Chotashiroho" ("Tashiro Cannon / Super Tashiro Cannon"), Paradise Army, May 26, 2002, http://www.paradisearmy.com/doujin/pasok7s.htm.

261   **They called it *matsuri*:** Tsunehira Furuya, *Intanetto ha Eien ni Riaru Shakai wo Koerarenai* (*The Internet Will Never Conquer Real Society*) (Tokyo: Discover 21, 2015).

261   **It was a contentious event:** Jeremy Yi, "The Controversy of South Korea: 2002 World Cup," *Soccer Politics*, April 29, 2019, https://sites.duke.edu/wcwp/2019/04/29/the-controversy-of-south-korea-2002-world-cup/.

261   **One poster half-jokingly suggested disrupting:** Mizuko Ito, Daisuke Okabe, and Izumi Tsuji, eds., *Fandom Unbound: Otaku Culture in a Connected World* (New Haven, Conn.: Yale University Press, 2012), 76.

262   **"Fake news?":** Seiji Takeda, "Natsu ga koreba omoidasu: 2channeru no natsukashii matsuri: Shonan gomi hiroi ofu" ("Summer Reminds Me of 2chan-nel's Nostalgic Festival: Shonan Garbage Pick-Up Event"), July 20, 2016, Hitotsubashi Sotsu Hosuto Takeda Seiji no Burogu Ppoi (Hitotsubashi Grad

Seiji Takeda's Blog or Something), https://ameblo.jp/stakedadada/entry-1218 1991273.html.

262 **"I was lonely and had nothing to do":** Izumi Mihashi, "Confessions of Former Japanese 'Netto-Uyoku' Internet Racists," Global Voices, March 23, 2015, https://globalvoices.org/2015/03/23/confessions-of-former-japanese-netto -uyo-internet-racists/.

262 **an unemployment rate unprecedented:** Ibid.

263 **"I thought of myself as a total dropout from society":** Ibid.

263 **Although he later introduced advertising:** Lisa Katayama, "Meet Hiroyuki Nishimura, the Bad Boy of the Japanese Internet," *Wired,* May 19, 2008, https://www.wired.com/2008/05/mf-hiroyuki/.

263 **Futaba Channel started life as little more than a clone of its predecessor:** It was commonly described as a refuge for 2channel users when that site's servers went down. See, for example, Ndee "Jkid" Okeh, "A Briefing on Futaba Channel," Yotsuba Society, August 18, 2011, http://yotsubasociety .org/Futaba_Channel_briefing/.

264 **Comic Market festival swelled:** "What Is the Comic Market? A Presentation by the Comic Market Preparations Committee," Comiket, February 2008, https://www.comiket.co.jp/info-a/WhatIsEng080225.pdf.

264 **He discovered anime in the summer of 2003:** koutaku003, "moot and Hiroyuki," July 11, 2012, 1:23:05, https://www.youtube.com/watch?v=0vf5lh PkfYo.

265 **In the years before sites like Twitter, Reddit, Facebook:** Taylor Wofford, "Fuck You and Die: An Oral History of Something Awful," Vice, April 6, 2017, https://www.vice.com/en_us/article/nzg4yw/fuck-you-and-die-an-oral -history-of-something-awful.

265 **Kyanka disliked anime so intensely:** Beran, *It Came from Something Awful,* 49.

265 **Article 175 of the Japanese Penal code:** Anne Allison, "Cutting the Fringes: Pubic Hair at the Margins of Japanese Obscenity Laws," in *Hair in Asian Cultures: Context and Change,* ed. Alf Hiltebeitel and Barbara D. Miller (Albany: State University of New York Press, 1997), 198.

266 **Many have tried and failed to challenge its scope:** Suzannah Weiss, "Meet Rokudenashiko, the Artist Arrested for Making a Boat Out of Her Vagina," *Glamour,* June 19, 2017, https://www.glamour.com/story/rokudenashiko -japanese-artist-arrested-for-vagina-art.

266 **"I couldn't even so much as show two people":** Personal interview with Toshio Maeda, June 25, 2019.

267 **3chan was already taken:** Nishimura, 2012.

267 **Within twenty-four hours, so much hentai content:** The "/h/ hentai" board appeared on October 2, the second day of the site's existence; "/c/ Anime/ Cute" appeared on day five. And on the seventh day launched "/l/ lolicon." See vestrideus (username), "4chan History Timeline," GitHub, March 23, 2017, https://github.com/bibanon/bibanon/wiki/4chan-History-Timeline.

267 **"I'm gonna teach you a special word today":** 4chan, "4chan: The Otakon 2005 Panel," September 24, 2013, 51:45, https://www.youtube.com/watch ?v=2mRp3QNkhrc.

269 **Take, for example, "All your base are belong to us":** There is some debate as to whether Something Awful users actually created the meme, but there is consensus that the site was instrumental in spreading and popularizing it. See, for example, Matt (username), "Something Awful," Know Your Meme, 2011, https://knowyourmeme.com/memes/sites/something-awful (accessed December 19, 2019).

270 **4chan's first real-world action:** Julian Dibbell, "The Assclown Offensive: How to Enrage the Church of Scientology," *Wired*, September 21, 2009, https://www.wired.com/2009/09/mf-chanology/.

271 **"In a stunning result," announced the magazine:** Time Staff, "The World's Most Influential Person Is . . . ," *Time*, April 27, 2009, http://content.time .com/time/arts/article/0,8599,1894028,00.html.

271 **"People deserve a place to be wrong":** Julian Dibbell, "Radical Opacity," *MIT Technology Review*, August 23, 2010, https://www.technologyreview.com /s/420323/radical-opacity/.

272 **Gamergate's roots:**
"Timeline of Gamergate," RationalWiki, October 24, 2019, https://rational wiki.org/wiki/Timeline_of_Gamergate.
Eron Gjoni, "Act 0: Whereof One Cannot Speak, Thereof One Must Be Silent," *thezoepost* (blog), August 8, 2014, https://thezoepost.wordpress.com /2014/08/16/act-0-whereof-one-cannot-speak-thereof-one-must-be-silent/ (last accessed January 3, 2020.)
Zachary Jason, "Game of Fear," *Boston Magazine*, April 28, 2015, https://www .bostonmagazine.com/news/2015/04/28/gamergate/2/.

272 **"psychopathic helldump":** James Giuran, "How Message-Board Culture Remade the Left," *Jacobite*, August 12, 2017, https://jacobitemag.com/2017/08 /12/how-message-board-culture-remade-the-left/.

272 **"semantic pipe bomb":** Jason, "Game of Fear."

273 **Gjoni even amended his missive:** Eron Gjoni, "TL;DR," *thezoepost* (blog), August 16, 2014, https://thezoepost.wordpress.com/2014/08/16/tldr-2/ (accessed January 3, 2020).

273 **"WE'RE CRASHING HER CAREER":** A log of the August 2014 chat room discussion can be found at http://puu.sh/boAEC/f072f259b6.txt.

274 **Close to 50 percent of gamers are female:** Tom Risen, "Study: Adult Women Gamers Outnumber Teenage Boys," *US News & World Report*, August 25, 2014.

274 **Take, for example, the 2014 San Diego Comic-Con:** Rob Salkowitz, "New Eventbrite Survey Reveals Convention Demographics, Spending Patterns," ICv2, June 28, 2015, https://icv2.com/articles/columns/view/31899/new -eventbrite-survey-reveals-convention-demographics-spending-patterns.

274 **Citing long-standing rules against harassment:** moot, "Regarding Recent

Events," 4chan, September 18, 2014. An image of the post is archived at https://imgur.com/snmdgRT.

275 **In September he sold it outright:** Klint Finley, "4chan Just Sold to the Founder of the Original 'Chan,'" *Wired*, September 21, 2015, https://www .wired.com/2015/09/4chan-sold/.

275 **Hiroyuki had been forced out of 2channel:** Akky Akimoto, "Who Holds the Deeds to Gossip Bulletin Board 2channel?," *The Japan Times*, March 20, 2014, https://www.japantimes.co.jp/life/2014/03/20/digital/who-holds-the -deeds-to-gossip-bulletin-board-2channel/.

275 **"moot came to Tokyo and we [got] drunk":** Lauren Orsini, "'Welcome to 4chan, B***h': Site's Users Greet Their New Overlord," *Forbes*, September 23, 2015, https://www.forbes.com/sites/laurenorsini/2015/09/23 /4chan-sold-hiroyuki-nishimura-qa-christoper-poole-moot-new-owner/.

275 **"He is one of few":** Finley, "4chan Just Sold."

275 **"Japanese culture enjoyed unique purchase":** Milo Yiannopoulos, "The Lost Franchise: Why *Digimon* Deserves a Glorious Renaissance," Breitbart, November 20, 2014, https://www.breitbart.com/europe/2014/11/20/the-lost -franchise-why-digimon-deserves-a-glorious-renaissance/.

276 **"Rootless white males":** Joshua Green, *Devil's Bargain: Steve Bannon, Donald Trump, and the Nationalist Uprising* (New York: Penguin, 2017), 145.

276 **A Pew study:** Richard Fry, "For First Time in Modern Era, Living with Parents Edges Out Other Living Arrangements for 18- to 34-Year-Olds," Pew Research Center, May 24, 2016, https://www.pewsocialtrends.org/2016/05 /24/for-first-time-in-modern-era-living-with-parents-edges-out-other-living -arrangements-for-18-to-34-year-olds/.

277 **"Fag" was an endlessly productive morpheme:** Eric (username), "-fag (Suffix)," Know Your Meme, January 18, 2010, https://knowyourmeme.com /memes/fag-suffix.

277 **"You can activate that army,"** Green, *Devil's Bargain*, 147.

277 **He dreamed of turning Breitbart into what he called "a killing machine":** James Oliphant, "After Firing, Bannon Returns to His 'Killing Machine'," Reuters, August 19, 2017, https://www.reuters.com/article/us-usa -trump-bannon-right/after-firing-bannon-returns-to-his-killing-machine.

277 **penned a spirited defense of Gamergaters "striking fear":** Milo Yiannopoulos, "Sneaky Little Hobbitses: How Gamers Transformed the Culture Wars," Breitbart, September 1, 2015, https://www.breitbart.com/politics /2015/09/01/sneaky-little-hobbitses-how-gamers-transformed-the-culture -wars/.

278 **"emerging racist ideology":** Abby Ohlheiser and Caitlin Dewey, "Hillary Clinton's Alt-Right Speech, Annotated," *The Washington Post*, August 26, 2016, https://www.washingtonpost.com/news/the-fix/wp/2016/08/25/hillary -clintons-alt-right-speech-annotated/.

278 **"They come in through Gamergate or whatever":** Green, *Devil's Bargain*, 147.

278 **"How Anime Avatars"**: Max Read, "How Anime Avatars on Twitter Help Explain Politics Online in 2015," *New York*, November 5, 2015, http://nymag .com/intelligencer/2015/11/dreaded-anime-avatar-explained.html.

278 **"The screamers and the crazy people"**: Cameron Joseph, "Racist Trump Supporters 'Masturbate to Anime,' Says GOP Strategist," Mashable, January 20, 2016, https://mashable.com/2016/01/19/trump-supporters-anime-gop -strategist/.

278 **"Anime—indeed, even anime porn"**: Richard Spencer (@TheRickWilson), "Anime—indeed, even anime porn—has done more to advance European civilization than the Republican Party," January 19, 2016, 10:13 P.M., https:// twitter.com/richardbspencer/status/689692099009097729?lang=en.

278 **Things didn't play out so well for Yiannopoulos**: Dorian Lynskey, "The Rise and Fall of Milo Yiannopoulos—How a Shallow Actor Played the Bad Guy for Money," *The Guardian*, February 21, 2017, https://www.theguardian .com/world/2017/feb/21/milo-yiannopoulos-rise-and-fall-shallow-actor -bad-guy-hate-speech.

278 **One captured him belting out**: Joseph Bernstein, "Here's How Breitbart and Milo Smuggled White Nationalism into the Mainstream," BuzzFeed, October 5, 2017, https://www.buzzfeednews.com/article/josephbernstein/heres -how-breitbart-and-milo-smuggled-white-nationalism.

278 **pedophilia could be "perfectly consensual"**: EJ Dickson, "Furries Got an Alt-Right Troll Banned from Their Convention," *Rolling Stone*, September 16, 2019, https://www.rollingstone.com/culture/culture-news/milo-yiannopolous -furry-convention-884960/.

279 **Simon & Schuster killed**: Lynskey, "The Rise and Fall of Milo Yiannopoulos."

279 **Deeply in debt**: David Uberti, "Milo Yiannopoulos Says He's Broke," *Vice*, September 10, 2019, https://www.vice.com/en_us/article/59n99q/milo -yiannopoulos-says-hes-broke.

279 **"Anime's supersized U.S. audience"**: Mark Trainer, "Anime's supersized U.S. audience," ShareAmerica (U.S. Department of State), June 28, 2017, https://share.america.gov/animes-supersized-u-s-audience/.

280 **"a self-consciously European, majority white nation"**: Sanjiv Bhattacharya, "'Call Me a Racist, but Don't Say I'm a Buddhist': Meet America's Alt Right," *Guardian*, October 9, 2016, https://www.theguardian.com/world/2016 /oct/09/call-me-a-racist-but-dont-say-im-a-buddhist-meet-the-alt-right.

280 **"It's an ethnostate"**: Ibid.

280 **In 2017 and 2018, the politically conservative Abe administration**: Noah Smith, "Japan Begins Experiment of Opening to Immigration," Bloomberg, May 23, 2019, https://www.bloomberg.com/opinion/articles/2019-05-22 /japan-begins-experiment-of-opening-to-immigration.

281 **"needed to work twice as hard to get half as much"**: Gita Jackson, "Why Black Men Love *Dragon Ball Z*," Kotaku, July 5, 2018, https://kotaku.com /why-black-men-love-dragon-ball-z-1820481429.

281 **"the journey of the black man in America"**: Emma Finamore, "From

Kanye to Frank: Why Hip-Hop Loves Anime," i-D, *Vice*, February 21, 2018, https://www.vice.com/en_asia/article/zmwqy5/from-kanye-to-frank-why -hip-hop-loves-anime.

283 **Occupy Wall Street and the Arab Spring uprisings:** Quinn Norton, "2011: The Year Anonymous Took on Cops, Dictators and Existential Dread," *Wired*, January 11, 2012, https://www.wired.com/2012/01/anonymous-dicators -existential-dread/.

283 **Meanwhile, over on the mainland:** Elaine Yau, "Studio Ghibli Film *Spirited Away* sets China Box Office Record," *South China Morning Post*, June 25, 2019, https://www.scmp.com/lifestyle/entertainment/article/3016033/studio -ghibli-film-spirited-away-sets-china-box-office.

THE 2010S

285 **"Sony halted the manufacture":** Lauren Indvik, "Sony Retires the Cassette Walkman after 30 Years," Mashable, October 24, 2010, https://mashable .com/2010/10/24/sony-walkman-rip/.

285 **"These are for abnormal people, for perverts":** Hiroko Tabuchi, "In Tokyo, a Crackdown on Sexual Images of Minors," *The New York Times*, February 9, 2011, https://www.nytimes.com/2011/02/10/business/global/10manga.html.

285 **"The movement's called #CosplayIsNotConsent":** Andrew McKirdy, "Cosplay Conquers the World," *The Japan Times*, undated, https://features.japan times.co.jp/cosplay/ (accessed January 3, 2020).

285 **"things we love from Japan,":** Jose A. DelReal, "President Obama Thanks Japanese Leader for Karaoke, Emoji," *The Washington Post*, April 28, 2015, https://www.washingtonpost.com/news/post-politics/wp/2015/04/28 /president-obama-thanks-japanese-leader-for-karaoke-emojis/.

285 **"Pokémon GO caused hundreds of deaths":** Simon Sharwood, "Pokémon GO Caused Hundreds of Deaths, Increased Crashes," *The Register*, November 27, 2017, https://www.theregister.co.uk/2017/11/27/pokemon_go_caused _car_accidents_and_deaths/.

285 **"She refused an invitation to her only son's wedding":** Gary Boyle, "Japanese Man Marries Hologram," *Bangkok Post*, November 12, 2018, https:// www.bangkokpost.com/learning/advanced/1574554/japanese-man-marries -hologram.

285 **"In May, the World Health Organization":** Ferris Jabr, "Can You Really Be Addicted to Video Games?," *The New York Times Magazine*, October 22, 2019, https://www.nytimes.com/2019/10/22/magazine/can-you-really-be-addicted -to-video-games.html.

EPILOGUE

287 **"Somebody's got to write these things":** This and subsequent quotes were taken from Haruki Murakami, *Dance Dance Dance* (New York: Vintage, 1994), 85–87.

288 **Even through the veil of translation:**
Alfred Birnbaum, personal communication, October 2019.
Anna Zielińska-Elliott: Jingnan Peng, "Meet the Woman Who Brings Haruki Murakami Works to an Enthusiastic Poland," *The Christian Science Monitor*, August 2, 2017.
Ivan Sergeevich Logatchov, "What Russians See in Murakami," in *A Wild Haruki Chase*, comp. Japan Foundation (Berkeley, Calif.: Stone Bridge Press, 2008), 74.
Yang Eok-Kwan, "Haruki Murakami's Popularity in S. Korea," NHK World, December 9, 2015, https://www3.nhk.or.jp/nhkworld/en/news/editors/1/20151209/index.html.

289 **In 1999, the journalist Mary Roach journeyed to Tokyo:** Mary Roach, Cute, Inc., *Wired*, December 1, 1999, https://www.wired.com/1999/12/cute/.

289 **In 2005 *Fortune* reported:** Christine Yano, "Monstering the Japanese Cute: Pink Globalization and Its Critics Abroad," in *In Godzilla's Footsteps: Japanese Pop Culture Icons on the Global Stage*, ed. William M. Tsutsui and Michiko Ito, (New York: Palgrave Macmillan, 2006), 156.

289 **"I was practically raised in Sanrio shops":** Skype interview with Krista Suh, April 30, 2018.

289 ***Variety* dismissed animator Osamu Tezuka's:** "Cleopatra, Queen of Sex," *Variety*, Wednesday, May 10, 1972.

289 **Pornhub announced that "hentai":** Pornhub Insights, "2018 Year in Review," Pornhub, December 11, 2018, https://www.pornhub.com/insights/2018-year-in-review.

290 **"a schoolgirl busily, constantly messaging on her mobile phone":** William Gibson, "Modern Boys and Mobile Girls," in *Distrust That Particular Flavor* (New York: Berkley, 2012).

290 **"Japanese light":** Simon Schama, quoted by Graham Brown in *Eventscapes: Transforming Place, Space and Experiences* (New York: Routledge, 2020), 185.

290 **D. T. Suzuki:** Michael Oldenberg, *A Zen Life, D. T. Suzuki*, Dharma Documentaries, 2008.

292 **In 1942, *Life* magazine estimated:** James C. McNaughton, *Nisei Linguists: Japanese Americans in the Military Intelligence Service during World War II* (Washington, D.C.: Department of the Army, 2007), 63.

292 **"one of the world's more difficult and less useful languages":** Kathryn Tolbert, "'Hai,' Japanese Enjoys New Popularity," *The Washington Post*, December 11, 1980.

293 **A 2018 survey revealed that it has shed more than ten million:** All-Japan Karaoke Industrialist Association, "Karaoke Gyokai no Gaiyo to Shijo Kibo Karaoke Hakusho 2019 Ichibu" ("Overview and Market Size of Karaoke Industry, Excerpted from Karaoke Whitepaper 2019"), undated, http://www.karaoke.or.jp/05hakusyo/2019/p1.php (accessed January 3, 2020).

293 **"We see karaoke-going as more of a kitsch, even loser, activity":** "What Killed the Karaoke Stars?," editorial letter, *Japan Today*, January 31, 2013,

https://japantoday.com/category/features/opinions/what-killed-the-karaoke
-stars.

293 **more than a third of all Japanese households now consist of just a single person:** Justin McCurry, "Karaoke for One: Japan's Surging Singles Give Rise to Solo Business Boom," *The Guardian*, December 25, 2018, https://www.the guardian.com/world/2018/dec/25/going-solo-japanese-businesses-target -customers-who-want-to-be-alone.

293 **surprise retirement of Akio Morita:** Kenichi Ohmae, "Akio Morita: Guru of Gadgets," *Time*, December 7, 1998.

293 **made more money selling life insurance:** Hiroko Tabuchi, "Sony's Bread and Butter? It's Not Electronics," *The New York Times*, May 27, 2013.

293 **Shintaro Tsuji is still going strong; he finally stepped down as CEO:** BBC, "Hello Kitty founder Shintaro Tsuji steps down as CEO aged 92," June 12, 2020, https://www.bbc.com/news/world-asia-53029110

293 **Only three Japanese titles:** Grubb, Jeff, "NPD: The 20 best-selling games of 2019 in the U.S." *VentureBeat*, January 16, 2020, https://venturebeat.com /2020/01/16/20-best-selling-games-of-2019/.

294 **The American marketplace alone hit $43.4 billion:** Jeff Grubb, "NPD 2018: The 20 Bestselling Games of the Year," Venturebeat.com, January 22, 2019, https://venturebeat.com/2019/01/22/npd-2018-the-20-best-selling-games -of-the-year/.

294 **The average monthly income for animators aged twenty to twenty-four:** Matt Schley, "Younger Animators Still Struggling Amid Anime Boom," *The Japan Times*, May 8, 2019, https://www.japantimes.co.jp/culture/2019/05/08 /general/younger-animators-still-struggling-amid-anime-boom/.

294 **"Perhaps the biggest problem":** Sophie Laubie and Fiachra Gibbons, "Japan's Anime Industry in Crisis despite Its Popularity," *The Japan Times*, June 23, 2019, https://www.japantimes.co.jp/culture/2019/06/23/films/japans-anime -industry-crisis-despite-popularity/.

294 **In the late aughts it emerged in surveys:** Matt Alt, "Girls Who Like Boys (Who Drive Giant Robots)," AltJapan, November 6, 2009, https://altjapan .typepad.com/my_weblog/2009/11/girls-who-like-boys-who-drive-giant -robots.html.

295 **remains infuriatingly hostile to career women and young mothers:** Motoko Rich and Hisako Ueno, "Shinzo Abe Vowed Japan Would Help Women 'Shine.' They're Still Waiting," *The New York Times*, September 13, 2020, https://www.nytimes.com/2020/09/13/world/asia/japan-women-abe .html?smid=tw-share.

295 **"We never see children here anymore":** Motoko Rich, "There Are No Children Here. Just Life-Sized Dolls," *The New York Times*, December 18, 2019, A4.

295 **surprising levels of contentment:** "Young Japanese Are Surprisingly Content," *The Economist*, February 17, 2018, https://www.economist.com/asia /2018/02/17/young-japanese-are-surprisingly-content.

297 **So too a more egalitarian pay ethic:** Koki Kubota, "Top Bosses in Japan Draw Record Pay but Gap with US Widens," *Nikkei Asian Review*, August 2,

2019, https://asia.nikkei.com/Business/Business-trends/Top-bosses-in-Japan-draw-record-pay-but-gap-with-US-widens.

297 **Western toy industry sells increasing quantities of its products to adults:** Harry Pettit, "The Rise of the Kidults: Growth in the Toy Market Is Being Driven by Millennials Playing with Children's Games," *Daily Mail*, April 11, 2017, https://www.dailymail.co.uk/sciencetech/article-4400708/1-11-toys-sold-bought-adult-themselves.html.

298 **A surge in demand at streaming services:** Jacob Kastrenakes, "Sony will slow down PlayStation downloads in Europe, but says multiplayer will remain 'robust,'" *The Verge*, March 24, 2020, https://www.theverge.com/2020/3/24/21192370/playstation-coronavirus-download-speeds-slowed-europe-multiplayer.

298 **31 million copies:** Kyle Orland, "Why Animal Crossing: New Horizons' 31 million sales are so incredible," *Ars Technica*, February 2, 2021, https://arstechnica.com/gaming/2021/02/putting-31-millionanimal-crossing-new-horizons-sales-incontext/.

298 **"That would be a horror story for Nintendo":** Jada Nagumo, "Hit the Switch," *Nikkei Asia*, Nov 16-22 2020 edition.

299 **One hundred thirty million fans downloaded the application in just thirty days:** "'Pokemon Go' Sets 5 Guinness World Records," *Nikkei Asian Review*, August 17, 2016, https://asia.nikkei.com/Business/Pokemon-Go-sets-5-Guinness-World-Records.

ILLUSTRATION CREDITS

All of the images in this book appear with permission of the
    following:
© Ado Mizumori: 113
Asahi Shimbun: 69, 152, 169, 188
Author: iv (bottom and middle left), 26, 87, 101, 176, 233
Getty Images: 157, 184
Joshua Fraser: iv (bottom)
Kodansha/© Asao Takamori, Tetsuya Chiba: 66
Kodansha/Aflo: 111
Kyodo News: 189
The Mainichi Newspapers Co.: 30, 45, 64, 78, 83, 232
Marusan: 38, 40, 230
National Diet Library of Japan/© Yoshihiro Tatsumi: 53
Otsu City Museum of History: v, 18, 32
© R.S.H/RUNE: 108
Sony Archives: iv (top), 132, 138, 145
Sunrise ©: 202
Dan Szpara: iv (right)
© Tezuka Productions: 48
© Tezuka Productions • Shichima Sakai: 50
© TSRFcars.com: 25
William J. Clinton Presidential Library: 248
Walkman is a registered trademark of the Sony Corporation.

INDEX

1. The book's title comes from a famous quote by the playwright Oscar Wilde at the peak of the Japan craze of the late nineteenth-century: "In fact the whole of Japan is a pure invention. There is no such country, there are no such people. . . . The Japanese people are, as I have said, simply a mode of style, a fancy of art." What does this say about the way foreigners view Japan? Why do you think Matt Alt chose this title for his book?

2. *Pure Invention* uses products as the lens to examine the relationship between Japan and the world. Why might consumer products give us insight?

3. Traditional *shokunin*—Japanese craftspeople—believe that the creative process begins with studying and carefully copying masters, and they attempt innovation only after long years of apprenticeship. How does this differ from the Western approach to craftsmanship?

4. Alt profiles a great many creators in his portrayal of Japan's rise from the ashes of war and its reinvention as a purveyor of fantasies, both physical and virtual, including the image of the nation itself. Which of their stories stuck with you the most?

5. Did or do you use or own any of the products discussed in the book? What was your experience with them?

6. Some critics feel that Hello Kitty, with her passive demeanor and lack of a mouth, is a repressive symbol of anti-feminism. Others have hailed her as a symbol of getting in touch with one's

feminine side, regardless of gender or orientation. How do you feel about Hello Kitty? Do illustrations really have the power to repress or empower?

7. Critics accused many of the products in this book of creating new forms of bad behavior, from the Walkman's self-isolating tendencies to the supposed link between video games and juvenile delinquency. Yet now portable listening via earbuds, portable electronic entertainment devices, and video gaming are part of the fabric of daily life. What does that say about how people come to terms with new technologies?

8. Japan was portrayed as America's economic archrival in the eighties. Today we in the West have a much gentler image of Japan, shaped by products like Hello Kitty and Pokémon, the books of Haruki Murakami and Marie Kondo, and the films of Hayao Miyazaki. How much of this change in viewpoint is due to Japan, and how much is due to us? What does this say about the images we build up in our minds about foreign countries?

9. The histories of the anonymous online bulletin boards 2channel in Japan and 4chan in America played out along very similar paths in their respective countries, from online activism to real-life protests to fostering all sorts of extreme behavior online and off. What is revealed about human behavior when we are given the ability to express ourselves anonymously and without consequences?

10. In the conclusion, Alt says that the future won't be made in Japan, but rather made everywhere else with Japanese sensibilities. Do you agree with this statement? Can you think of any examples? (Hint: One is the app *Pokémon GO*, made in Silicon Valley with Japanese characters.)

ABOUT THE AUTHOR

MATT ALT is a Tokyo-based writer, translator, localizer, and reporter. He is a contributor to TheNewYorker.com, CNN, *Wired, Slate, The Economist's 1843, Newsweek Japan, The Japan Times,* and *Asahi Shimbun,* and is the co-author of six illustrated books about Japan.

mattalt.com
altjapan.com